Contents

✑ Acknowledgments

This book could not have been written without the support of many friends, colleagues, and institutions. First and foremost I'd like to thank those who read various drafts of the book and gave generously of their time in helping to make it better: David Bevington, Michael Bristol, Mark Thornton Burnett, Philippe Cheng, Harold Fisch, Coppélia Kahn, David Scott Kastan, M. Lindsay Kaplan, Theodore Leinwand, F. R. Levy, Claire McEachern, John McGavin, Arthur F. Marotti, James V. Mirollo, William F. Monroe, Martin Orkin, Mark Petrini, Phyllis Rackin, Robert Stacey, Herbert and Lorraine Shapiro, Michael T. Shapiro, William Sherman, Debora Shuger, Michael Seidel, Edward Tayler, Michael Warren, Linda Woodbridge, James Young, and Froma Zeitlin. Maurice Charney, Annabel Patterson, and an anonymous third reader for Columbia University Press provided incisive criticism. Robert Griffin, Richard McCoy, and Alvin Snider deserve a special note of thanks for their many suggestions. The students in my graduate seminars on "Englishness and Jewishness" offered many insights, and three outstanding graduate research assistants—Michael Mack, Aviva Taubenfeld, and Chloe Wheatley—helped out immeasurably.

Support for this project was provided by three endowed lectures—the James Parkes Lecture at the University of Southampton and the Nadav Vardi Memorial Lecture and the Shimshon Carmel Lecture at Tel Aviv University. A yearlong grant from the National Endowment for the Humanities provided the time and support needed to complete the research and writing, as did a short-term grant from the Henry E. Huntington Library. A Fulbright award, sponsored by Bar Ilan and Tel Aviv Universities, facilitated early stages of research.

This book profited enormously from the responses of audiences at a number of colleges and universities, including Tel Aviv University, the University of Southampton, Columbia University, Queen Mary and Westfield College, the University of Pennsylvania, the University of Illinois at Urbana, Trinity College, the University of Massachusetts at Amherst, the University of Houston, Wayne State University, the City University of New York, the University of Alberta, Brown University, Princeton University, Dartmouth College, and the University of California at Los Angeles. I am also grateful for the suggestions made by those who heard portions of this book delivered at meetings of the Modern Language Association, the Shakespeare Association of America, the Renaissance Society of America, the International Shakespeare Conference in Stratford-Upon-Avon, the Society for the Study of Women in the Renaissance at the Graduate Center, City University of New York, and at the Shakespeare Festival at the University of California at Santa Cruz.

The account that follows would not have been possible if considerable ground had not been cleared by scholars working in a range of disciplines. The study of the place of the Jews in English culture and history has undergone a renaissance of late, and I owe a large debt to the work of Robert Stacey, Miri Rubin, Tony Kushner, David Cesarani, Nabil I. Matar, Arthur H. Williamson, Todd M. Endelman, David Feldman, Bryan Cheyette, Michael Ragussis, Richard H. Popkin, and, above all, David S. Katz. My understanding of the consequences of the English Reformation has been informed by the magisterial work of Patrick Collinson and Christopher Hill as well as by the revisionist history offered by Eamon Duffy and Christopher Haigh. Sander Gilman's influential work on Jewishness, race, and gender has also shaped my thinking, as has Howard Eilberg-Schwartz's anthropological approach to Jewish identity. And I am deeply indebted to the understanding of Shakespeare's place within our culture mapped out by Michael Bristol, Annabel Patterson, and Stephen Greenblatt. Though I find myself differing at various points with many of these scholars, I am nonetheless grateful for the theoretical clarity and historical specificity they have made available.

A number of outstanding archival collections—and archivists—made this research possible: the Henry E. Huntington Library (whose superb photographic and reader services staff deserve special thanks), the Folger Shakespeare Library, the British Library, the Cambridge University Library, the Bodleian Library, the Israel Solomons Collection at the Library of the Jewish Theological Seminary (especially Sharon Liberman Mintz), the Macotta Library at the University of London, the James Parkes Library at the University of Southampton, the William Andrews Clark Memorial Library, the Yale University Library, the McAlpin Collection at the Union Theological Seminary Library, and the Columbia University Library.

Part of chapter 7 first appeared in *Shakespeare Survey* as "Shakspur and the Jewbill"; I would like to thank Cambridge University Press for permission to reprint this material here.

I am deeply grateful to my outstanding manuscript editor, Susan Pensak, and to Teresa Bonner, the book's talented designer. Jennifer Crewe, my editor at Columbia University Press, has been wonderfully supportive from first to last. So too has my family, including my late uncle, Stanley Snyder, whose early enthusiasm for the project was warmly appreciated. My greatest debt is to Mary Cregan. She first encouraged me to write this book, patiently read and improved successive drafts of it, and provided intellectual companionship, and much more, through the years that it took to complete it.

In the interest of making early modern texts more accessible, I have silently modernized the spelling and punctuation of quotations throughout (except for titles, where I have regularized capitalization but kept the original spelling, so that sources can be tracked down more easily). Quotations from *The Merchant of Venice* are cited from William Shakespeare, *The Merchant of Venice*, ed. Jay L. Halio (Oxford: Oxford University Press, 1994).

Shakespeare
AND THE Jews

This book is concerned with what Shakespeare and his contemporaries thought about Jews. While there were not many Jews in early modern England, it was nonetheless a society surprisingly preoccupied with Jewish questions. Some of the more frequently addressed questions include: In what ways were Jews racially and physically different? Did those who converted lose all trace of their Jewishness? Was it true that Jews habitually took the knife to Christians, circumcising and murdering their victims? Should Jews be formally readmitted into an England that had long ago banished them, or were Englishness and Jewishness mutually exclusive identities? Were the Jews in their diaspora still a nation, and, if so, should they be restored to their homeland? It needs to be said at the outset that the English turned to Jewish questions in order to answer English ones. From our own perspective their interest in Jews provides unusual insight into the cultural anxieties felt by English men and women at a time when their nation was experiencing extraordinary social, religious, and political turbulence.[1]

The seven chapters that follow are linked and interdependent. The first two try to clear away some myths and misconceptions about who and what was a Jew and how many Jews there were in Shakespeare's England. The next two chapters also form a pair, exploring Elizabethan notions of Jewish criminality, especially the alleged "Jewish crime" in which Jews reputedly abducted, circumcised, then ritually murdered Christians. *The Merchant of Venice* figures largely in chapters 3 and 4, as well as in chapter 5, which focuses on conversion.

The discussion of conversion and of the potential instability of religious identity leads to the central concerns of chapter 6: how post-Reformation theology shaped attitudes toward Jewish national, racial, and political status. The final chapter brings the narrative to a close with the "Jew Bill" controversy of 1753. This debate over what constituted a natural-born subject reveals how ideas about Jews that emerged in Shakespeare's lifetime continued to influence notions of English identity; it also provides insight into the extent to which *The Merchant of Venice* had come to embody English conceptions of Jewish racial and national difference.

A point of departure for the approach undertaken here can be found in the reading notes Samuel Coleridge made while browsing through John Donne's sermons. Coleridge was surprised to discover Donne describing a "barbarous and inhumane custom of the Jews," who "always keep in readiness the blood of some Christian, with which they anoint the body of any that dies amongst them, with these words, 'If Jesus Christ were the Messiah, then may the blood of this Christian avail thee to salvation.'"[2] Donne's sermon neatly yokes the fantasy that deep down the Jews secretly acknowledge Jesus as their Saviour to the myth that Jews ritually murdered Christians. Coleridge wonders, "Is it *possible* that Donne could have given credit to that absurd legend!" Coleridge also recognizes that such beliefs were an unfortunate but intrinsic feature of Donne's culture: "It was, I am aware, not an age of critical account: grit, bran, and flour were swallowed in the unsifted mass of their erudition. Still, that a man like Donne should have imposed on himself such a set of idle tales for facts of history is scarcely credible; that he should have attempted to impose them on others, most melancholy."[3] For most of the nearly two centuries since Coleridge wrote these words, historians and literary critics have sifted through the cultural record of early modern England, carefully separating out the grit from the bran and flour. One of the aims of this book is to recover some of the grittier and, for many, less palatable aspects of this age.

There have been many moments in the course of writing this book when I have shared Coleridge's sense of incredulity that someone of Donne's intelligence could have perpetuated such "absurd" myths about secret Jewish practices, including that most sinister one of all, ritual murder. After reading a good many plays, pamphlets, histories, commentaries, and sermons published in early modern England, I can extend the list of "idle tales" to include accounts of how Jews stank and Jewish men menstruated; how Jews abducted Christian children; how Jews sought to emasculate Christian men; and how Jews after their expulsion from England had migrated to Scotland, which was thought to explain why the Scots were so cheap and hated pork. I began to wonder why these and other Jewish questions (such as proposals to settle foreign Jews in Ireland) almost never appear in modern histories of Shakespeare's England, though virtually every major writer, theologian, and political figure of that period had at some point dealt with one or more of them. Was the study of the place of the Jews in early modern English culture in some way felt to be taboo, or simply not worthy of serious attention?[4]

One explanation is simply disciplinary: the great majority of those who currently write about early modern England tend to see Jewish questions as footnotes to theological ones; for them, stories about Jews offer little insight into Elizabethan society. This holds true for both revisionist and traditional scholars. The former have shown little interest in religion as a category of analysis, preferring instead the modern trinity of class, race, and gender; the latter not only resent the intrusion of Jewish questions into English studies, but also balk at the idea that social identity is contingent upon the kinds of stories a culture tells itself. In arguing that Elizabethans considered Jews to be unlike themselves in terms of religion, race, nationality, and even sexuality, and in showing how ideas about difference emerged out of post-Reformation thinking in England, I am thus also interested in challenging some of the systems of belief that currently dominate early modern studies. Reformation theology, and the political and social theories it generated, had a profound impact on how cultural identity was imagined; it also marked a significant departure from medieval English conceptions of Jews. A closer look at some of the Jewish questions that were a by-product of the English Reformation will also show that to write about nation and race in the sixteenth century independent of each other (and of theological paradigms) is to underestimate how racialized nationalism was, and how nationalized racial thinking was, at this time.

Even as mainstream scholars have been content to deflect Jewish questions, those on the fringe of the academic world have been eager to take them up. In the past few decades a book and a number of articles have appeared arguing that Shakespeare himself was Jewish.[5] Another book even proposes that Queen Elizabeth herself was a secret Jew—which explains why she never found a suitable husband.[6] Still others have struggled to exonerate her physician, "Lopez the Jew," from the charge of conspiring to poison the Queen, for which he was drawn and quartered in 1594. Though never made explicit, the purpose of these studies is undoubtedly to insist on the positive contribution of Jews, albeit secret ones, at this formative moment in the emergence of England's imperial greatness.

Arrayed against these writers are those who are convinced that England was great precisely because in those halcyon days it wisely excluded all but the "true-born Englishman." Theirs is a nostalgic fantasy whose roots can be traced back at least as far as the eighteenth century, when poets celebrated a time when "good Queen Elizabeth sat on the throne," Jews "were unknown," and each "Briton might then call his birthright his own."[7] One of the most recent writers in this camp has even warned of an international conspiracy now underway in which revisionist Jewish scholars are taking over the Shakespeare business and trampling upon the very "banks of the Avon."[8]

It is crucial to resist the temptation simply to dismiss such outlandish claims, because they reveal what is at stake but never quite acknowledged in more guarded scholarly discussions. It becomes clearer why unresolvable questions such as how many Jews there were in Shakespeare's England, or whether Shakespeare was an antisemite, or Lopez innocent, never go away. Such questions cannot be so easily disposed of because they are poor but necessary substitutes for what is really being fought over: the nature of Englishness itself and who has the right to stake a claim in it. And insofar as Shakespeare has come to personify Englishness—he is aptly described in Jane Austen's *Mansfield Park* as "part of an Englishman's constitution"[9]—much of this battle has been waged over the pages of *The Merchant of Venice*.

It is important to make clear that while I believe that there are people who are English and people who are Jewish, I do not believe that these people are either English or Jewish because they are endowed with certain innate qualities. Rather, I think of these as layered identities, shaped by a multitude of conditions that are themselves contingent upon both time and place. I also believe that there is something called Englishness and something called Jewishness, though their meanings too have changed under the pressure of competing historical narratives. Finally, I believe that Englishness would not be the same as it is without the existence of Jewishness, even as it would not be the same without the existence of Irishness, Scottishness, Welshness, Frenchness, or Spanishness. This is especially so because the first and only story of mass deportation of people from England—what has come to be known as "the Expulsion of the Jews in 1290"—has meant that Englishness has in part defined itself by the wholesale rejection of that which is Jewish (even long *after* Jewish communities were openly reestablished in England in the seventeenth century).

For individuals, of course, experiencing a sense of being English could not have meant the same thing in the year 1300 as it would in 1600 or 1900, given the effects of religious reformations, a civil war, a union with Scotland, an industrial revolution, and an empire. Nor can we identify with any precision the moment when the great majority of people inhabiting the territory now known as England began to think of themselves first and foremost as English (supplanting other collective identities that had once been more powerful, including guild, religious, class, regional, and local affiliations). Moreover, while the physical boundaries of England had remained more or less constant, the legal definition of what constituted an English subject had not; it underwent repeated challenges and revision from early modern times until the present century. Problems continued to surface: was someone born abroad to

English parents still English? What if one was born on English soil to non-English parents? What if one's father was French and one's mother English? What conditions did an alien seeking to become a denizen or naturalized English subject have to meet? And, given the fact that after the Reformation the English monarch was also the head of the Church, to what extent was English identity necessarily Christian as well?

It proved much easier to identify those who were English by pointing to those who were assuredly not—e.g., the Irish or the Jews. Invariably, however, this required a tacit agreement that these others epitomized the very antithesis of Englishness. Not surprisingly, in order to enforce this point, differences were greatly exaggerated and at times simply invented: other people were deemed un-English in the way that they looked, prayed, ate, smelled, dressed, walked, and talked. One of the things that most distinguishes medieval from early modern conceptions of Jews is that Jewish identity had been unquestioned in medieval Europe—on biological, social, and religious grounds—by both Jews and Christians. The early modern Jew, in contrast, confounded those who sought more precise definitions in terms suited to emerging notions of nationhood and race.

Before turning in the next chapter to the question of who early modern English men and women would have considered Jewish, I think it useful at this point to set out the three basic ways in which Jewish identity has been historically understood.[10] The first category has consisted of those who believe themselves to be Jews (for not everyone who is Jewish by descent necessarily assents to being considered Jewish). The second category has included those whom other Jews accept as Jews, either by descent or through conversion. The third and final category is comprised of those whom non-Jews have thought of as Jews. Some individuals have fit easily within all three categories; others have not. There are those who have thought of themselves as Jews—say, those born of a Jewish father and a non-Jewish mother—who are accepted by some Jewish authorities (e.g., the Israeli government's Law of Return) while rejected by others (e.g., the Israeli rabbinate). Others, like the "Jews for Jesus," while believing themselves to be Jews, are not considered Jews by most fellow Jews (except in the legal sense that even apostates are still technically Jews). Then there are those who, while they do not consider themselves to be Jewish, are Jewish by descent, and are perceived by non-Jews to be Jews; no doubt thousands of those who died in Nazi concentration camps fell into this category. Jewishness has thus been understood not only in terms of religious practices and beliefs but also in the context of racial and national identifications.

In the sixteenth and seventeenth centuries Jews who had converted or whose ancestors had converted to Catholicism under inquisitorial pressure (they are known variously as New Christians, Conversos, or Marranos[11]) played havoc with conventional ways of thinking about religious identity. We do not know how many of them thought of themselves as Jews. Some Jewish authorities accepted them as Jews more readily than others, while many Christians were unsure whether these converts were truly coreligionists. The conversion of these Jews to Christianity, some by choice and some under threat of death, laid bare the bedrock of the problem of determining religion by means of assent. In the company of Christians many Conversos vigorously assented to being Christians. In the company of Jews many reconnected with their Jewishness. Left to their own thoughts, who knows what they considered themselves to be? Some English writers struggled to invent new terms—such as *Christian Jew, false Jew,* and *counterfeit Christian*—to deal with these disturbing ambiguities, which they found themselves confronting abroad and occasionally at home as well. Others, like William Prynne, likened the performance of Marranos—individuals skilled at "playing the Jew in private"—to that of professional actors, expert at putting on and taking off disguises.[12] Small wonder that Prynne, best remembered today for his vitriolic attacks on the public theater, was also a staunch opponent of the readmission of the Jews to England.

For European Jews, no less than for the English, the late sixteenth century was a time of unprecedented changes in how collective identity was constituted. As Jonathan Israel puts it, this was a period in which "Jewish society, indeed Jewish nationhood"—as "something distinct from Jewish religion"— were emerging "as much more definite realities than before."[13] The early part of the sixteenth century had been a grim one for Europe's Jews, who by 1570 had been expelled not only from Spain and Portugal but from much of western and central Europe as well. Paradoxically, this forced migration from west to east "was a form of economic emancipation," for it "shifted an entire people from a rigid, narrowly confined, economic framework to a much broader-based economy, encompassing a wide spectrum of crafts, trade, and management." When this migratory trend was reversed in the closing decades of the sixteenth century, and Jews once again reestablished communities in western Europe, "the whole hitherto fixed pattern of restricted interaction between western Christendom and the Jews was transformed."[14] The resulting changes were not only economic: European Jewry in the late sixteenth century experienced a new political and historical self-consciousness as well as an increased interest in mysticism, messianism, the arts, and anti-Christian polemic.[15] Despite what European Christians may have believed, the nature of Jewish identity at this time was far from static.

Although both Jewish and English people were increasingly identified in terms of nationality, race, and religion, their relationship to these categories was hardly commensurate. From the perspective of Shakespeare's contemporaries, while the Jews had once been a nation, and might be one again, they were now landless vagabonds. And though the Jews were a race, they were an exceptional one insofar as they reputedly could never commingle with others (after all, if they intermarried and mixed with other peoples, how could Paul's prediction in Romans about the future calling of the Jews ever be realized?). Some writers pointed to the Jews' dark or "black" skin color as a marker of their racial difference. In addition, as members of a religious community from which the founders of the Church had emerged, Jews were at once the opposite of Christians and at the same time potential Christians. From a Christian perspective, the only thing that stood in the way of their conversion to the true faith was the Jews' stubborn refusal to acknowledge that Jesus was indeed the Messiah predicted by their own prophets, especially Daniel. Nonetheless, while Jews who were admitted into the Church of England might share the same religion as the English, they did not necessarily belong to the same race or nation.

Even as England could be defined in part by its having purged itself of Jews, English character could be defined by its need to exclude "Jewishness." In the decades following the Reformation, the English began to think of the Jews not only as a people who almost three centuries earlier had been banished from English territory but also as a potential threat to the increasingly permeable boundaries of their own social and religious identities. The challenge of preserving these boundaries was intensified by the difficulty of pointing to physical characteristics that unmistakably distinguished English Christians from Jews (setting aside the obvious sign of circumcision). Indeed, some of Shakespeare's contemporaries, like the traveler John Sanderson, were the first Englishmen to confront the heretofore unthinkable possibility of being mistaken for Jews. "Turning" Jew was also an unnerving possibility, one that even manifested itself in the subconscious life of a seventeenth-century Englishman: Ralph Josselin records a dream he had in 1655 in which he was told that Thurloe, the Secretary of State under Oliver Cromwell, "was turned Jew." Josselin found himself arguing in the dream that "perhaps it was a mistake," that Thurloe "might declare he was a Jew born, the Jews having lived here, and he pretend by old writings his pedigree from them, to ingratiate" himself "with the Jews."[16]

The possibility that a leading Englishman could suddenly and inexplicably turn Jew was a nightmare indeed. Josselin's anxious hope—that Thurloe was merely declaring himself "a Jew born, the Jews having lived here"—hardly helped matters, because it raised the equally unattractive alternative that the banishment of English Jewry in 1290 might not have been absolute, and, even if it had been, those Jews who had converted and remained rather than accepted exile might have mingled racially with English stock. This belief would not only surface in dreams: John Toland mentions this possibility in the early eighteenth century and Richard Burton roughly a hundred years ago confidently observed that those "familiar with the annals of old families in England are aware of the extent to which they have been mixed with Jewish blood. . . . Here and there an old country house produces a scion which to all appearance is more Jewish than the Jews themselves."[17] The Jews represented the threat of both cultural and personal miscegenation, a threat that—to one eighteenth-century parliamentarian—was even more pernicious than intermarriage with England's colonial black slaves.[18]

English anxiety that Jewishness was on the verge of reasserting itself from within intensified in the decades following the Reformation, a period in which Catholics and Protestants repeatedly accused each other of Judaizing tendencies. The seventeenth century also witnessed a new and unprecedented phenomenon: Christians deliberately masquerading as Jews. A Scot named Thomas Ramsay even underwent circumcision in order to convince proselytizing English Baptists that he was Jewish. Some radical Puritans, especially members of the group that surrounded John Traske, identified so strongly with Judaism (to the extent of keeping kosher and circumcising children) that they were punished for and forced to repudiate their Jewish opinions.

The idea of an Englishman's potential Jewishness was also deeply embedded within the English language. Consider, for example, the proverbial phrase repeated so often on the Elizabethan stage: "I am a Jew . . . else." Examples come easily to hand: "I am a Jew if I know what to say"; "I were a Jew . . . "; "I were worse than a Jew . . . "[19] Shakespeare's plays offer the greatest number of instances of this formula: Benedick says of Beatrice that "if I do not love her, I am a Jew";[20] Lancelot declares that "I am a Jew if I serve the Jew any longer";[21] and Falstaff swears "or I am a Jew else, an Ebrew Jew."[22] By explaining that one is a Jew if one does not do something—love Beatrice, leave Shylock, or in Falstaff's case, insist that the lie he tells is the truth—the door is left open that one might very well be that which is the opposite of what one thinks oneself to be. I suspect that some of the force of Shylock's famous speech—the one that begins with the words "I am a Jew . . . "—depends in part on the formulaic nature of the phrase. Crucially, however, his lines take us in a strikingly different direction, for Shylock's insistence on the similarity of Jews and Christians is mirrored in the proverb's double message, one that can be traced back to Paul's epistles: a Christian is the antithesis of a Jew and yet, in certain circumstances, is potentially indistinguishable from one.

The challenge to insulate oneself and one's nation from the threat of Jewishness was intensified by the fact that that which was Jewish was not so easily discerned. The fear that Jews might taint English character did not diminish following the resettlement of Jews in England. It culminates in accounts like

Richard Burton's late nineteenth-century argument that the Jew is like a cuckoo that once let into the nest displaces or destroys the native offspring:

> He—the ordinary Englishman—may be dimly conscious that the Jew is the great exception to the general curse upon the sons of Adam, and that he alone eats bread, not in the sweat of his own face, but in the sweat of his neighbour's face—like the German cuckoo, who does not colonize, but establishes himself in the colonies of other natives.[23]

In England, Jewish crime—like Jewishness itself—was invariably hidden and insidious, a secret waiting to be unearthed. In this respect early modern English conceptions and representations of Jewish criminality differ markedly from what one finds on the continent, where Jewish communities still existed and Jews continued to engage openly in usury. While concern over Jewish financial exploitation increased after the resettlement of Jews in England in the late seventeenth century, one of the arguments of this book is that the current scholarly focus on usury (no doubt because of its presence in *The Merchant of Venice*) has occluded more widespread and disturbing conceptions of Jewish criminality. The central chapters of this book set out the various kinds of criminal activity attributed by English writers to the Jews, especially that most disturbing and secret Jewish practice, ritual murder. This "absurd legend" had a long and special history in England—it remained in circulation even when there were hardly any Jews in the land and no manifestations of this crime in England—and its popularity (even into the present century) reveals much about entrenched English anxieties about the Jews.

According to one of the better known Victorian promulgators of this charge, Richard Burton, the source of the Jewish practice of ritual murder was to be found in the Jews' habituated condition as persecuted outcasts and the "darker shades which the religious teachings of the later centuries has diffused over the Jewish mind." The Lamarckian Burton asks his English readers:

> Is it surprising that amongst an ignorant and superstitious race of outcasts such random acts and outbreaks of vengeance, pure and simple, should by human perversity pass, after the course of ages, into a semi-religious rite, and be justified by men whose persecution has frenzied them as a protest and a memorial before the throne of the Most High against the insults and injuries meted out by the Gentile to the children of Abraham?

According to Burton, for proof of this "spirit of vengeance" the English reader "need look no further than *The Merchant of Venice*":

Shakespeare may not have drawn Shylock from a real character, but his genius has embodied in the most lifelike form the Jew's vengefulness and the causes that nourished it. How many cities of the world are there where he might hear these words: "Hath not a Jew eyes? hath not a Jew hands, organs, dimensions, senses, affections, passions? fed with the same food, hurt with the same weapons, subject to the same diseases, healed by the same means, warmed and cooled by the same winter and summer, as a Christian is? If you prick us, do we not bleed? If you tickle us, do we not laugh? if you poison us, do we not die? and if you wrong us, shall we not revenge?"

Burton silently omits Shylock's conclusion: "If we are like you in the rest, we will resemble you in that." Quoting these lines would have brought his argument to a halt. For where others have seen Shylock's famous speech as an futile though eloquent plea for the fundamental likeness of Jews and Christians, Burton chooses instead to find in it confirmation of the Jews' insatiable lust for revenge. For him, these lines offer irrefutable evidence that Shakespeare's genius enabled him to see beyond the surface and recognize "the existence of cruel murders and similar horrors" perpetrated by the "Hebrew race."[24] While I repudiate Burton's racist interpretation of Jewish character (for he confuses national character with that of a dramatic character and then misreads that character's speech), I'm nonetheless interested in the ways in which the plot of ritual murder, with its threat of a Jew taking a knife to a Christian, informs Shakespeare's play. In considering Shylock's threat to cut a pound of Antonio's "fair flesh" within the larger discourse of ritual murder, I draw upon a range of sources, sermons, and biblical commentaries, and focus especially on what kind of religious and physical threat Shylock's action poses to Antonio's identity.

At the center of this book, then, are Shakespeare and the cultural moment in which *The Merchant of Venice* was first staged. I work outward from this moment, going back fifty years or so to the early years of the English Reformation and then moving forward to the 1650s and the debates over the readmission of the Jews in England. Shakespeare's play is central not only because so many of the arguments about Jewish identity circulate through *The Merchant of Venice* but also because the play has emerged as a touchstone of cultural identification. Larger circles of interest move backward to 1290 and the narratives recounting Edward I's decision to expel England's Jews, and look forward to 1753 and beyond.

Readers expecting to find in the following pages a systematic account of how Jews were represented in sixteenth- and seventeenth-century English drama and poetry will be disappointed; there are many fine books already published on this topic, and it is not my intention to provide yet another survey.[25]

Nor can I hope to satisfy those in search of clear-cut definitions of national and racial identity. While I frequently allude to race, I want to make clear at the outset that ideas about race, much like those about nation, have no basis in any kind of essential or biological reality, and are therefore often muddled or contradictory.[26] My interest in race is narrowly concerned with what led early modern English men and women to think of themselves and of other people, especially Jews, in terms of what they imagined to be racial difference. As the pages that follow confirm, race may not be a reality, but racial thinking is, and, as such, warrants closer examination. Finally, those expecting a definitive answer to the question of whether Shakespeare was anti- or philosemitic will not find that answer here. I try to show instead that these anachronistic terms, inventions of nineteenth-century racial theory (and, since they are premised upon an imaginary racial category, uncapitalized here), are fundamentally ill-suited for gauging what transpired three hundred years earlier, especially since the objectives of early modern English "philosemites" and "antisemites" were not all that far apart. The philosemite sought to overcome the problem of difference either by inviting Jews to England in order to convert them, or alternatively, reestablishing them in a distant homeland in order to hasten the Day of Judgment. The antisemite preferred to maintain cultural difference by keeping the dangerous Jews out. In seventeenth-century England tolerance and equal, permanent status for Jews were not yet possibilities, not even, as we shall see, for John Locke, the greatest proponent of toleration.

It also needs to be stressed that, while Jews were not fully tolerated or granted citizenship in early modern England, they were never subject to violent attacks, forced to convert, penned up in ghettos, or burned in inquisitorial fires, as they were elsewhere in Europe. Nor can one call to mind an English political or religious writer in this period whose anti-Jewish polemic came anywhere near the virulence of Martin Luther's late diatribes, which called for the burning of synagogues, prayer books, and Jewish homes (indeed, no early modern English writer even thought these diatribes worth translating).[27] The fate of the Jews in England proved to be quite different than it was, and would be, in other European nations, both Protestant and Catholic. My intention therefore is neither to celebrate nor condemn early modern English men and women (or their descendants) but rather to explore what their conception and representation of Jews reveals about their own nation.

In recovering how Jewish questions were understood in early modern England I have drawn for the most part on what many may regard as nonliterary sources. While I do refer to a number of contemporary literary works besides *The Merchant of Venice*, the bulk of my evidence is drawn from other kinds of contemporary writing: travel diaries, chronicles, sermons, political tracts, confessions of faith, legal textbooks, parliamentary debates, and New Testament commentary. Some of these materials—such as Roger Edwards's "Conversion and Restitution of Israel" (1581) and Thomas Scales's "The Original or Moderne Estate, Profession, Practise and Condition of the Nation of the Jews" (c. 1630)—remain in manuscript and are known to very few scholars. Other texts, though published, have not received the attention they deserve and are scattered in various archival collections in the United States and Great Britain. I have also collected and included printed illustrations of "Jews" available to English readers at this time to give some sense of what Jews were thought to look like.[28] My idea of what constitutes an imaginative work has also been expanded in the course of this research, for virtually everything written about the Jews at this time has a good deal of fantasy and inventiveness associated with it. Much of the evidence comes from texts published in the mid-seventeenth century, and I use this very cautiously when reflecting back on what was going on seventy or a hundred years earlier. Nonetheless, I argue for strong continuities in thinking about the Jews from the 1570s well into the 1650s. In some cases—such as conversion tracts—continuity well into the eighteenth century is striking; in others—such as ideas about millenarian aspirations—twenty years make a significant difference. I have tried throughout to be alert to the dangers and limitations of reading later material back into Shakespeare's age.

If the chapters that follow have anything to offer, it is the lesson Coleridge learned reading Donne: we need to think twice before reflexively accepting and promulgating "a set of idle tales for facts of history."

I

False Jews and Counterfeit Christians in Early Modern England

Marrano. A nickname for Spaniards, that is, one descended of Jews or infidels, and whose parents were never christened, but for to save their goods will say they are Christians. Also as Marrana.
—*John Florio, 1611*

If extraordinary care be not taken herein . . . under pretext of Jews, we shall have many hundreds of Jesuits, Popish priests, and friars come over freely into England from Portugal, Spain, Rome, Italy, and other places, under the title, habit, and disguise of Jews.
—*William Prynne, 1656*

Marrano. A Jew counterfeitly turned Christian.
—*James Howell, 1660*

 Any discussion of the presence of Jews in Shakespeare's England depends upon what one means by *Jew*. The answer to that question is as difficult and complex today as it was two thousand years ago when Paul tried to articulate the difference between Jew and Gentile in Romans and Corinthians. The question of who and what was a Jew was no less complicated in Shakespeare's day; indeed, it was arguably more so, with the rapid proliferation of categories like "false Jew" and "counterfeit Christian."

Until the sixteenth century the question of who was a Jew had rarely (if ever) come up in England. There was little reason that it should have. Sermons, paintings, Chaucer's *Prioress's Tale*, Corpus Christi plays, and a host of other sources confirmed that Jews, who had been subject to persecution and then exiled from England's shores in 1290, were the accursed descendants of those who had killed Christ and who continued in their devilish ways. Such people could hardly be mistaken for fellow Christians. Although chroniclers reported that after 1218 Jews had been required to wear distinctive badges so that they would not be confused with Christians, no one in medieval England ever commented on the seeming inconsistency between this decree and the widespread belief that Jews were recognizably different.[1]

By the early seventeenth century, however, in the wake of the Spanish and

Portuguese Inquisitions, the Protestant Reformation, and the expansion of English overseas travel and trade, the question of who was a Jew began to be asked with greater frequency and, on occasion, urgency. Thousands of Iberian Marranos throughout Europe, including a few who had emigrated to England, were now masquerading as Christians, even as a handful of Englishmen were passing themselves off as Jews. The study of Hebrew, Cabala, and rabbinical sources was on the rise. English Protestant sects were emulating Jewish Sabbath observance and dietary laws. Claims that the ten lost tribes of Israel had been discovered in the New World were finding their way into print. The resulting desire to know who was a Jew led to the no less puzzling question of what was a Jew, as early modern English writers tried to define what distinguished the Jews from themselves. One of the effects of this sustained interest in the nature of the Jews was the pressure it put on what had been assumed to be, in comparison, a stable English and Christian identity.

I. Who is a Jew?

No event in the early modern world complicated the issue of Jewish identity more than the Spanish Inquisition.[2] Its shock waves were felt as far away as the shores of Turkey, England, and the New World. Like Ferdinand and Isabella's decision to expel the remaining Jews from Spain in 1492, the Inquisition, first introduced in Castile in 1478, was an acknowledgment of a serious failure. Hundreds of thousands of Spanish Jews, including much of the social and intellectual elite, had undergone conversion to Christianity in the late fourteenth through mid-fifteenth centuries, some voluntarily, some by force. By 1492 over three-quarters of Spanish Jewry had converted. The decision to banish those who had refused to convert was thus a belated effort to mark a clearcut distinction between Christian and Jew. The hope was that with their former coreligionists in exile, New Christians would be less tempted to return to the faith they had abandoned.[3] Contrary to what many now believe, the purpose of the Inquisition was not to persecute Jews—in theory there were none left in Spain, and, after the required conversion of all Jews by Manuel I, none in Portugal either—but to discover the few apostates among the many Jews who had undergone baptism. Indeed, as early as 1449, Conversos had been the object of attack and of legislative curbs.[4] Despite its efforts to extract confessions and its public autos-da-fé, which offered theatrical displays of faith and brutal punishment of heretics, the Inquisition also failed in its mission insofar as the prospect of a camouflaged Jewish presence continued to haunt the Spanish and Portuguese. The subsequent institution of *limpieza de sangre*, blood laws that distinguished between those of Jewish lineage and Old Christians, signaled yet another failure, since adopting them meant abandoning the fundamental tenet of Christianity as a religion based on brotherhood, substituting for it a model (like that of Judaism) based on lineage.[5] Nonetheless, neither persecution nor racial laws could resolve the threat to Iberian Christian hegemony and identity posed by the counterfeit Christian.

The resulting destabilization of cultural identity has triggered considerable debate among historians of the Inquisition about whether, as one writer puts it, "the majority of the Conversos were real Jews"[6]—whatever "real" means— or whether this notion of secret Jewish heresy is merely a "fiction," since the New Christians after several generations of separation from Judaism were so "detached from Judaism" as to be basically Christian.[7] One of the stranger twists in the history of this debate is that Jewish historians have eagerly supported the inquisitors' claim that apostasy was widespread among the Conversos. Thus, while the tortured victims of the Inquisition insisted upon their fidelity to Catholicism (to save their lives, family, or property, or simply because it was true), the inquisitors and a good many Jewish historians since then have preferred to believe otherwise. This has certainly been the case in scholarship written not long after the Holocaust, when Jewish historians read back into sixteenth-century history the cruel lesson of the twentieth: anti-semites make no distinction between observant and apostate Jews. Thus, for Yizhak Baer, Conversos "and Jews were one people, united by bonds of religion, destiny and messianic hope which in Spain took on unique coloration typical of the people and country."[8] Baer's equally influential disciple, Haim Beinart, similarly elides the distinction between Jew and Converso, and sees in the Inquisition a paradigm of Jewish survival:

> Out of the deeds done to Jews and Conversos alike shines the internal strength of a Jewry rich in spirit and deed, a Jewry that was able to hold its stand against great waves that tried to engulf her. The deeds of those tried by the Inquisition, those who as martyrs sanctified the Name of God, their vicissitudes and sufferings, may serve as beacons of light for Jewry wherever they are.[9]

While the traumatic history of European Jewry in the 1930s and 1940s goes a long way toward excusing the distortions of such claims, the approach taken by Baer, Beinart, and their followers nonetheless occludes one of the most unsettling issues generated by the Inquisition: who was a Jew, and how could you know for sure? What the Inquisition thought to be Jewish was in large part based on fantasy. Reviewing Inquisition testimony, Jerome Friedman has argued that most "records indicate that New Christians were convicted of being secret Jews because they often abstained from pork, used olive oil rather than lard, changed sheets every Friday, called their children by Old Testament names, prayed standing rather than kneeling, or turned to face a wall when hearing of a death," which, he adds, is like accusing people of being Jewish today because they have been observed "reading *The New York Times*, eating bagels, or supporting the American Civil Liberties Union."[10] This list of offenses gives some sense of how rapidly Jewish cultural memory had faded in over a century without instruction in Jewish law and customs. To what extent were these crypto-Jews—who for the most part were raised as Catholics, only to learn of their Jewish heritage at the age of twelve, or even twenty—to be considered Jewish?

Not surprisingly, sixteenth-century Jewish authorities found themselves at a loss in dealing with the complexities created by the Inquisition, for the situation required a fundamental reconsideration of whether Conversos were Jews or not. As might be expected, rabbinical opinion differed considerably over time and place (distant Ashkenazic Jewish authorities being on the whole less tolerant in their judgment than the Sephardic ones who had a clearer sense of the strain that Iberian Jews were under). For the most liberal interpreters, the Conversos were Jews; for others, they were only to be treated as Jews "in matters relating to family law" (e.g., divorce cases); still others concluded that the Conversos were non-Jews in every respect (and, for some, "worse than non-Jews").[11] Even as Christian Spain adopted the term *Marrano* to describe lapsed New Christians, rabbis struggled with their own new categories, distinguishing, for example, between *anusim*, those whose conversion was forced, and *meshumadim*, those who embraced Christianity voluntarily. Jewish communities that accepted the Iberian Conversos usually required the men to undergo circumcision before further reeducation or integration into the new community in order to demarcate all too fluid religious boundaries.[12] This particular requirement sometimes met with resistance from those unwilling to commit to total affiliation with the Jewish community. For example, recent scholarship has shown that a good number of Jews living in England in the period from 1650 through 1720 fell into this category; these uncircumcised individuals were described by London's Jewish authorities in the 1680s as "those who have withdrawn in order to enjoy their liberty."[13] Yosef Kaplan has argued that the "members of this marginal group sharpened the 'boundary crisis'" within London's small Jewish community "by virtue of the de facto recognition of their right to live a Jewish life according to their own rights."[14] Marking cultural boundaries proved difficult for both Jewish and Christian authorities.

It is likely that what individual Conversos actually believed ranged from devout Catholicism to equally devout Judaism, with all kinds of permutations in between, including ambivalence and confusion about their cultural identity.[15] Yirmiyahu Yovel has persuasively argued that the ensuing mixture of Jewish and Christian beliefs also "led to various cases of skepticism, secularism, neopaganism, rationalist deism, or (in most of these cases) to a rather inarticulate confusion of symbols and traditions." Some surely experienced forms of a religious duality unprecendented in the West, which would have profound implications for the development of the history of ideas in Europe. According to Yovel, this

17

> duality penetrated the consciousness (and the subconsciousness) of the most ardent Judaizers. Even the Marrano martyrs and heroes were rarely Jews in the conventional sense. The clandestine character of worship, the Catholic education, the lack of Jewish instruction, and the isolation from Jewish communities outside Iberia created a special phenomenon in the history and sociology of religion: a form of faith that is neither Christian nor Jewish.[16]

Rather than stamping out crypto-Judaism, the Inquisition unexpectedly created and exported a new problem: the fear that some Christians were not really Christians. As such, Converso apostasy was pernicious, and was made even more troubling by the fact that, with the widespread dispersion of Iberian Conversos (especially after the institution of the Portuguese Inquisition), these counterfeit Christians could be found anywhere. The Inquisition ultimately revealed that, torture notwithstanding, it was next to impossible to root out marranism or to know what faith people really professed. Faith was disguisable, religious identity a role one could assume or discard if one had sufficient improvisational skill.

II. The English perspective on marranism

English interest in these events in Spain and Portugal peaked in the late sixteenth and early seventeenth centuries, at a time when England was at war with Spain and anti-Catholic sentiment ran highest. While in Tudor and Stuart accounts of the events in Spain there is almost no interest in how the Spanish mistreated their Jewish population, there is considerable attention paid to the threat Marranos posed to the Spaniards, and the Inquisition itself to Spain's social fabric. John Foxe's observation in his *Actes and Monuments* is representative in its insistence that the Inquisition strayed from its initial premise of rooting out apostate Jews, in the end trapping all kinds of others in its net. This failure to discriminate meant that those who were not even Jews were subject to the greed and self-interest of the inquisitors. For Foxe, the "cruel and barbarous Inquisition of Spain, first began by King Ferdinandus and Elizabeth his wife," was "instituted against the Jews" who, "after their baptism maintained again their own ceremonies." Yet "now it is practiced against them that be never so little suspected to favor the verity of the Lord."[17]

The confusion generated in Spain and Portugal over the status of secret Jews also led other early modern English writers to warn of the proliferation of marranism. James Howell writes that "the tribe of Judah . . . is settled in

Portugal," where "they give out to have thousands of their race, whom they dispense withal to make a semblance of Christianity, even to church degrees." Howell adds that this "makes them breed up their children in the Lusitanian language; which makes the Spaniard have an odd saying, that *El Portugueze se crío del pedo de un Judío*," that is, a "Portuguese was engendered of a Jew's fart."[18] Henry Blount writes in a similar vein of the Jews' "boast" in Portugal and Spain "to have millions of their race to whom they give complete dispensation to counterfeit Christianity, even to the degree of priesthood, and that none are discovered but some hot spirits, whose zeal cannot temporize."[19]

A Londoner in early Stuart England, curious about what the word *Marrano* meant, might have turned for help to John Florio's Italian-English dictionary (Florio was himself of New Christian descent), where the term is defined as "a nickname for Spaniards, that is, one descended of Jews or infidels, and whose parents were never christened, but for to save their goods will say they are Christians. Also as Marrana."[20] This marked only a slight improvement over the 1598 edition of the dictionary, where the definition had read "a Jew, an infidel, a renegado, a nickname for a Spaniard."[21] Florio's attempts at defining the term seem to raise more questions than they resolve: is *Marrano* a nickname for all Spaniards? Did the Marranos hold any religious beliefs at all? Did they consider themselves to be Jews, infidels, renegades, or Christians? Should they be thought of as lapsed Jews or fake Christians? How could one know for sure, after all, since to save their goods they "will say they are Christians" anyway? Furthermore, by identifying Marranos with *renegades* (the term used to describe Christians who had "turned Turk") Florio links two kinds of circumcised apostasy.[22]

Other English accounts of what transpired in Spain also dwell on the confusion of religious and national identity that was a by-product of the Inquisition. Edward Grimeston, in his 1612 translation of Mayerne Turquet's *Historie of Spaine* (1583), writes that one result of the Spanish Jews' "profession, either true or fained, of Christian religion, such as they could learn and comprehend in so short a time," was that in the "process of time the noble families of Spain, allying themselves by marriage to that race, did wholly contaminate and pollute themselves both in blood and belief," while the forced conversion of the Jews in Portugal "did beget infinite apostasies, sects, and heresies in Portugal, as it could not fall out otherwise."[23] And Thomas Browne, noting that the Jews left Spain and "dispersed into Africa, Italy, Constantinople, and the dominions of the Turk, where they remain as yet in very great numbers," cites rumors of their secretly passing themselves off as Christians elsewhere in Europe, including England itself: "according to good relations, where they may freely speak it, they forbear not to boast that there are at present many thousand Jews in Spain, France, and England, and some dispensed withall, even to the degree of priesthood."[24] Others, including John Donne, suggested that even when Jews believed that they had remained faithful to the laws of their forefathers, their close proximity to Catholicism over time had contaminated Judaism with papist practices. Donne takes as his evidence late sixteenth-century Jewish mourning rites, of which he can find no mention in the Old Testament, leading him to conclude that the Jews had absorbed these practices from the Catholics: "After the Jews had been a long time conversant amongst the Gentiles, and that as fresh water approaching the sea, contracts a saltish, a brackish taste, so the Jews received impressions of the customs of the Gentiles, who were ever naturally inclined to this misdevotion, and left-handed piety, of praying for the dead." Donne had apparently been an eye-witness to the Jewish prayer for the dead, the kaddish, a rite that to him smacked of Catholic ways: it "is true which I have seen, that the Jews at this day continue it in practice, for when one dies, for some certain time after, appointed by them, his son or some other near in blood or alliance, comes to the altar, and there saith and doeth some thing in the behalf of his dead father, or grandfather respectively."[25]

By the mid-seventeenth century there was an increasing sense among English writers that Jewish conversion to Christianity had never been sincere and that baptized Jews would ultimately prove counterfeit Christians. According to William Prynne,

> most of the Jews, who since their dispersion have been baptized and turned Christians in any age or place, have done it either out of fear, to save their lives, or estates, when endangered by popular tumults, or judgments of death denounced against them for the crimes, or for fear of banishment, or by coercion of penal laws, not cordially and sincerely, they still playing the Jews in private upon every occasion, and renouncing their baptism and Christianity at last, either before or at their deaths.[26]

His judgment was confirmed by travelers on the continent, including a visitor to Elizabethan England, Thomas Platter. After observing Jews in 1596 in Avignon, France who were "compelled under severe penalty to attend" the conversion sermons of Jesuit preachers, Platter wondered, "Has it ever been known, in the memory of man, that a Jew hath been converted?"[27]

Some were even reluctant to call Jewish converts Christians. Samuel Purchas notes that among "unChristian Christians, who Jewishly hate the name of a Jew," that name cannot "be washed from it with the sacred tincture of baptism." The "vulgar scoff and point at them, saying, 'There goes a baptized Jew' (a term best fitting themselves)." Purchas is also quick to note that this leaves baptized Jews in limbo, since "on the other side their own countrymen hate and abhor them as apostates, renegados, and fugitives," here projecting Christian categories of heresy upon Jewish communities.[28] This increasing sense of the impossibility of sincere Jewish conversion in the late sixteenth and early seventeenth centuries occurs at precisely the same time that apocalyptic belief in the imminent conversion of the Jews was on the rise, creating a sharp and disturbing division between the two positions.

William Prynne's allusion to "playing the Jews in private" calls to mind those who had literally played the Jews in public: the professional actors who enacted the roles of Shylock, Barabas, and a host of Jewish characters from the cycle, miracle, and conversion plays of the early English theater through the more complex representations of the Tudor and Stuart drama. That this hint comes from Prynne, who had earlier railed against the theater in his *Histriomastix*, is not surprising: Jews, like actors, were skilled at exploiting representation itself. The Marranos, then, were consummate actors for whom Jewishness, no less than Christianity, was a role to be assumed or shed, sometimes with a change of costume, as the situation demanded. The English were constantly impressed—and disturbed—by this ability to "temporize," a word that, according to the *Oxford English Dictionary*, found its way into the language at just this time. Lancelot Addison writes in the 1670s of "a very late instance of two Jews who in Spain having for several years professed the religion of St. Dominique, coming to Leghorn in their friar habits they instantly changed their cowl for a *ganaphe* [the gown worn by Jews], and of idle friars became progging [i.e., begging] Jews." He also writes of another Jew with whom he was acquainted "who for about five years had studied physic at Saragoza in Spain, being asked how he could comply with the religion, he merrily made this reply, 'That his compliance was only the work of his nerves and muscles, and that his anatomy told him nothing of the heart was therein concerned.'" Costumes, muscles, and nerves are the indispensible tools of both actors and Jews. Addison, who obtained his knowledge of the Jews of Barbary firsthand, confirms that "there are many such temporizing Jews, especially in Spain and Portugal, I have been assured from their own mouths." He adds that some "affirm that there want not Jews among the very judges of the Inquisition; which may be one reason why of late so few are convicted of Judaism by that dreadful tribunal."[29]

III. Judaizing in England

Any satisfaction that English Protestant observers might have taken in the troubles their Spanish and Portuguese enemies faced in trying to suppress marranism was tempered by the rise of Judaizing in England, a problem that had begun to take on serious enough dimensions by the early seventeenth century to warrant the imprisonment of a handful of Christians emulating Jewish ways. Catholic propagandists were quick to seize upon the Judaizing propensities of the English Reformation as early as the 1550s, with the accession to the English throne of the avowedly Protestant King Edward VI. Diplomatic papers recount that in 1551 Sir Richard Morison, the English ambassador to the court of Charles V, protested that a Catholic preacher in Augsburg was spreading the word that "the King of England, his council and kingdom had all become Jews and were waiting for the coming of the Messiah." While Charles V's ambassador in London said that his King "had known nothing about it," he said in defense of the Catholic preacher that he himself "had heard that there were many renegados and Jews at this time in England, but did not know whether they were Englishmen, rather believing them to be foreigners, as every one now took refuge here."[30]

At just this time the Portuguese Inquisition had imprisoned one of Scotland's most prominent intellectuals (and future tutor to King James), George Buchanan, on suspicion of Judaizing. Buchanan was imprisoned in August 1550 and by January 1551 had been subjected to nine inquisitorial examinations. He was released only after he agreed to abjure his alleged heretical opinions. When accused of having engaged in the Jewish practice of eating the paschal lamb during Lent as part of a Passover observance, Buchanan replied to his inquisitors that this was simply a misunderstanding. He explained that a friend of his was seriously ill "and though in peril of his life, would not venture to touch meat on Fridays and Saturdays. I not only exhorted him to eat meat, but also that he might do so more willingly ate along with him. . . . Hence, I suppose, originated that fable of the paschal lamb." The inquisitors pursued the topic of Buchanan's alleged Judaizing in a second examination, based on the information provided by witnesses who had heard that Buchanan "had fled from Scotland because he was a heretic and a Jew." Asked if he recalled "ever having performed any Jewish ceremony," Buchanan said no, and added that there were "no Jews in Scotland." In a carefully written defense submitted to his inquisitors, Buchanan also insisted that he had "never thought" of "Judaism."[31] Despite his denials and his subsequent release by the Inquisition, the story of Buchanan's alleged Judaizing continued to attract the interest of various writers in the course of the next century, and gives a sense not only of how vulnerable unsuspecting Christians were to such accusations but also of how convenient it became to label opponents, especially those who favored republicanism, as Judaizers.[32]

Protestants were no less inclined to accuse their Catholics foes of exhibiting Jewish tendencies, and there was a steady stream of polemic in Reformation Europe to this effect, typified by comments like the marginal gloss to Luther's commentary on Galatians, that the "Papists are our Jews which molest us no less than the Jews did Paul."[33] Andrew Willet, in an influential survey of Catholic practices, offers an extended account of how the "Papists borrow of the Jews," and concludes that "they do not content themselves with an apish imagination of Jewish ceremonies, but they also borrow from the corrupt practice of the Jews and the erronious glosses of their blind rabbis certain points of their . . . Catholic doctrine." According to Willet, "the weakness of [the] popish religion and feebleness of their cause" is revealed by the fact that Catholics "through very beggary are constrained to patch up their tattered garments with Jews' rags."[34] Other Protestants writers like Robert Parker insinuated that the Catholics were cozy with the Jews: "In Rome the Jews are counted better than Protestants, so that the Jews have toleration when true Christians are put to the fire."[35] Protestant reformers also accused each other of Jewish tendencies. Thomas Calvert recounts an instance when Martin Luther even charged John Calvin with Judaizing for denying that the virgin birth of Jesus was prophesied in Jeremiah 31, an interpretation "which made that Lutheran beadle provide so terrible a whip for Calvin, and lashed him with '*Calvinus Judaiʒans*, Calvin turned Jew.'"[36] With the outbreak of civil war, some royalists began to call their opponents Jews. John Warner, for example, attacked those who murdered Charles I as "accursed Jews." Like their Christ-killing forebears, these "Jewish-heathen . . . put a crown of thorns upon his head and a reed in his hand for a scepter." Moreover, they stripped him, then dressed "him in player's robes, and thus they mocked Charles their King." Warner concludes his attack upon his enemies by promising to set out the "true causes . . . which moved these accursed Jews to so horrid an act as to kill Charles the King," and then castigates them as "Jews who pretended" that they knew "so much Scripture" for failing to recall the example of David and Saul.[37]

The Elizabethan religious settlement, trying to strike an acceptable balance between reform and tradition, preempted the tendency to grant too much authority to Old Testament laws by including in its thirty-nine articles an affirmation that "the law given from God by Moses, as touching ceremonies and rites, do not bind Christian men, nor the civil precepts thereof ought of necessity to be received in any commonwealth."[38] Nonetheless, the pressure at the radical extremes of Protestant thought to value Old Testament teachings continued to produce believers whose ideas, in the eyes of contemporaries, bordered on Judaism. An early example occurs in 1561, when Richard Bruern, a freethinker and a Professor of Hebrew at Cambridge, was accused of having engaged in "Jewish ceremonies," a charge that was repeatedly leveled against him in the course of his career.[39] And by 1572 Englishmen had begun accusing one another of playing the Jew. Thomas Cartwright, who had argued that "we had the same laws to direct us in the service of God that the Jews had," was rebuked at the time by Archbishop Whitgift with the words "you Judaizer, play the Jew."[40]

Reflecting back upon this volatile period in 1636, Peter Heylyn recalls the publication of Nicholas Bownd's *Doctrine of the Sabbath* in 1595 as the great catalyst of English Sabbatarianism and of other forms of Judaizing.[41] More "like a Jewish rabbi, than a Christian doctor," Bownd had advocated the strictest kind of Sabbath observance, stipulating that there should be no buying, carrying, feasting, marrying, dancing, working, studying, shooting, fencing or bowling, or even talking "of pleasures . . . or any other worldly matter." Despite the fact that Bownd's "doctrine" was "Jewish and rabbinical," Heylyn writes, "it carried a fair face and show of piety, at the least in the opinion of the common people and such, who stood not to examine the true grounds thereof, but took it up." Heylyn also observes that it "is most strange to see how suddenly men were induced not only to give way unto it, but without more ado to abet the same, till in the end, and that in very little time, it grew the most bewitching error, the most popular deceit, that ever had been set on foot in the Church of England."[42]

According to Heylyn, Sabbath worship was not the only "fruit" of "such dangerous doctrines," and he describes how an Englishman named John Traske began to advocate the "Jewish doctrine about meats and drinks."[43] Traske was the most notorious Judaizer in England in the early seventeenth century.[44] Born about 1585, and ordained and preaching in London by his early thirties, Traske attracted a growing number of followers. By 1618 Traske and some of his sect were imprisoned. A sense of Traske's reputation can be gleaned from a contemporary letter that describes "one Trash or Thrash who was first a puritan, then a separatist, and now is become a Jewish Christian. . . . You will not think what a number of foolish followers he hath in this town and some other parts."[45]

Traske was accused of "having a fantastical opinion of himself with ambition to be the father of a Jewish faction." The Star Chamber also found him guilty of "teach[ing] that the law of Moses concerning the differences of meats forbidding the eating of hog's flesh, conies, etc., is to be observed and kept."[46] Traske was summarily expelled from the ministry, fined, and sent to prison in the Fleet for the rest of his life. The punishment did not stop there, however, for he was also sentenced "to be whipped from the prison of the Fleet to the Palace of Westminster with a paper on his head," and "then to be set on the pillory and to have one of his ears nailed to the pillory, and after he hath stood there some convenient time, to be burnt in the forehead with the letter 'J' in token that he broaches Jewish opinions."[47] Twelve days later Thomas Lorkin reported that "the sentence against the Jew hath been put in execution."[48] And if this were not enough, insult was added to injury; while in prison Traske was "only allowed [to eat] the . . . meats in his opinion supposed to be forbidden."[49]

One of the things that makes Traske's case so interesting is that contemporaries were stymied in their attempts to define whether Traske was in fact a "Jew." He simply defied existing categories. A number of writers reveal just how difficult situating Traske and his followers proved to be.[50] For one, the Traskites were Jews, "yea Jews, and worse than Jews, their congregations not true, but pretended Christian assemblies," a definition that slowly unravels as it proceeds.[51] Another throws the doubt back onto the Traskites themselves: "But yet in a doubting manner [they] think they may be Jews, for ought they know to the contrary; and therefore conclude, that seeing they do doubt, it is safest for them to keep Sabbaths and to live as do the Jews."[52] For still others, like Lancelot Andrewes, Traske's drift from Christianity toward Judaism turned him into a counterfeit Christian. Where John Chamberlain calls Traske a "Jewish Christian," Lancelot Andrewes terms him "a very christened Jew, a Maran, the worst sort of Jews that is."[53] One of the more ambiguous characterizations was offered by Alexander Harris, the warden of the Fleet during Traske's imprisonment, who was unsure whether to call Traske "a Jewdaser [Judaizer?] or half-Jew."[54] Part of the problem with such formulations was that the word *Jew* had entered into the English vocabulary in the thirteenth century as a catchall term of abuse, often directed at other Christians, "the symptoms thereof," Prynne writes, "yet continue amongst us in our proverbial speeches." Prynne cites as examples such stock epithets as "I hate thee as I do a Jew," "I would not have done so to a Jew," and "None but a Jew would have done so."[55] Even as these proverbial sayings define a sharp and seemingly unbridgeable gap between Christian and Jew, other proverbial expressions suggest a more slippery boundary between the two. Prynne recounts walking through the streets of London in late 1655, listening to the voices of the poor, including seven "or eight maimed soldiers on stilts" who complained that we "'must now all turn Jews, and there will be nothing left for the poor.'" Not far from them Prynne came across "another company of poor people" who "cried aloud to each other, 'They are all turned devils already, and now we must all turn Jews.'"[56] The Jew as irredeemable alien and the Jew as bogeyman into whom the Englishmen could be mysteriously "turned" coexisted at deep linguistic and psychological levels.

Traske subsequently renounced his Judaizing ways, won his freedom, and in 1620 published a recantation entitled *A Treatise of Libertie from Judaisme*. But what he and others had helped set in motion was not so easily arrested.[57] His own wife steadfastly maintained her Jewish beliefs, though long imprisoned. Another member of his sect, Hamlet Jackson, may have subsequently undergone formal conversion to Judaism in Amsterdam.[58] And another follower, "Mary Chester, Jewess," was sent to Bridewell prison in 1635; like Traske, she gained her freedom only after recanting "her errors on holding certain Judaical tenets touching the Sabbath and distinction of meats."[59]

Despite such acts of official suppression, individuals continued to practice aspects of Judaism. One of the most outrageous of these was the religious radical and millenarian Thomas Tany, notorious for having laid claim to the thrones of England, France, and Rome, and for having drawn his sword in Parliament in late December 1654, which landed him in prison.[60] His contemporary and fellow radical, Lodowicke Muggleton, reported that Tany had "declared himself to be the Lord's high priest, and that he was to act over the law of Moses again; therefore he circumcised himself according to the law." Muggleton also writes that Tany "declared that he was to gather the Jews out of all nations, and lead them to . . . Jerusalem."[61] According to Anthony Wood, Tany was "a blasphemous Jew,"[62] and indeed, Tany had himself declared, "I am a Jew of the tribe of Ruben begotten by the gospel."[63]

Anne Curtyn was yet another Judaizer, and was committed to the New Prison at Clerkenwell in 1649, because "she denied Jesus Christ to [be] a prophet," and for "being a professed Jew and causing children to be circumcised." Curtyn's case fell in the no-man's-land between the jurisdiction of English civil and ecclesiastical authority. Adoniram Byfield, who was scribe to the Assembly of Divines, certified to the court hearing her case "that, as they were an Assembly, they were only to consider and debate of such matters, as are referred to them from one or both Houses of Parliament." Juridical crisis was avoided when the assemblymen decided to pursue the case not as a body of clergymen but as individual Christians: "though not as an Assembly, yet [as] private Christians, they . . . had conference with . . . Anne Curtyn about her opinions and for what cause her opinion of Christ's being no prophet, etc." They were ultimately satisfied that "she only differed" from acceptable views "in terms but not [in] substance." Nevertheless, they still "found her obstinate" in "her profession and practice of a Jew." Since, however, this fell outside the jurisdiction of the court, it being "merely ecclesiastical," they ordered that she "be discharged from prison."[64] Here was a case where as long as the accused differed in terms rather than in substance on Christ's legitimacy as a prophet— even though she considered herself a Jew and engaged in circumcision and other Jewish rituals—the matter was deemed civil rather than ecclesiastical and therefore dismissed without prosecution. Judaizing here reveals the fault lines of the Christian commonwealth, the delicate boundary in the late 1640s between church and state. It also reveals a fundamental incompatibility between a strong impulse in English Protestant thought that centered on the conversion of the Jews, and a no less powerful sense of the dangers inherent in Judaizing and overfamiliarity with Jewish rites. For William Prynne, the risks of allowing Jews into England in large numbers far outweighed the potential spiritual good, for "thousands" of Christians would "in probability turn apostate Jews, instead of converting any of the Jews to Christianity."[65]

There are two ways to look at this curious and largely ignored episode in English cultural history. One is to argue that these Judaizers were a cultish extreme and that the preponderance of English men and women knew little of them and cared less. The other is to maintain that these examples provide a glimpse into the kinds of cultural fears that rarely find their ways into official histories (though they often found a place in popular sermons and plays). We have seen that contemporaries were surprised at how such beliefs caught on among the people and how many followers the Traskites were thought to have both within and outside of London. Certainly the Court of Star Chamber was sufficiently concerned about Traske to make his public punishment a particularly humiliating one. The overreaction to these Judaizers and the irrational fear that ordinary people could suddenly turn Jewish was surely symptomatic of deeper cultural anxieties about religious identity experienced by English men and women at the time.

The phenomenon of the counterfeit Christian also needs to be located within the context of the tumultuous Tudor religious history, which for most Elizabethans meant that their grandparents had turned from Rome to the Church of England under Henry VIII, while their parents might have reverted to Catholicism under Mary, before changing their faith again with the accession of Elizabeth. Moreover, by the late sixteenth century sharp distinctions between Anglican and Catholic, Christian and Jew, and Christian and Turk began to blur, even as religious dissimulation and equivocation were on the rise. Marranism thus took its place alongside a host of dissimulative strategies in the late sixteenth century, which ran the gamut from Nicodemism to Catholic recusancy to casuistry. Montaigne in his characteristically incisive way spoke of "dissimulation as the most notable quality of the age."[66]

IV. False Jews

The more intense the social and political changes experienced in England, the more severe the anxiety generated by counterfeit Christians and by those in a new and unprecedented category, false Jews (that is, Christians who purposely masqueraded as Jews). Outside of the theater the idea of Christians deliberately presenting themselves to the world as Jews was, until the seventeenth century, virtually unheard of. At first the appearance of false Jews was limited to works of fiction like *The Wandering-Jew, Telling Fortunes to English-men*, published in 1640 under the Jewish-sounding pseudonym Gad ben Arad.[67] We encounter what we are credibly informed is "the Jew" through the narrator, who on a dark night outside of London sees a light in a house and seeks shelter, only to discover that he has chanced upon the home of a famous fortune-telling Jew. We get some sense of what readers might have thought this Jew looked like from the striking woodcut illustration on the title page, which depicts a scene from the English countryside, with houses and steeples in the background. In the foreground the Jew reads the palm of one Englishman while another, palm extended, waits his turn. The Jew is barefoot, and wears a "Jewish gown" and "Jewish round cap" described in the text, along with a circular Jewish badge on his gown (see illustration 13).

As the story progresses, the nameless Jew welcomes the narrator into his house and invites him to observe the stream of visitors who come to him to have their fortunes told: courtiers, merchants, lawyers, lovers, citizens' wives—a cross section of English gulls and fools. After taking the narrator into his confidence, the Jew suddenly admits that he is not really a Jew but rather a native Englishman named Egremont. He further explains that he got the idea of impersonating a Jew in Venice when, during his travels there, it turned out that he exactly resembled a rich Jew named Orletto who invited him to pass as his double. Apparently, the idea of an Englishman who can be mistaken for the twin of an Italian Jew is not an issue here, suggesting that Jews were not necessarily or always seen as physically different.

A courtier seeking advice tells Egremont that while "we have in England" a "store of Jews," a "few in court, many in the city, more in the country, these I scorn; but come to you, a knowing Jew, a rabbi, a synagogue of learning." It is unclear whether he is speaking of real or metaphorical Jews here, and one wonders whether contemporaries would have taken these observations literally (as some modern critics have done).[68] The popularity of fictional Jews mirrors a rising interest in real ones, a feature that may account for the fact that in the original version of the story, published in 1609, the fortune-teller is no Jew but a reclusive Englishman named Fido.[69] What is most unexpected about the revised version of the story is the absence of surprise on the part of the narrator upon discovering that his host is no Jew but a freeborn Englishman whose improvisational skills enable him to capitalize on people's curiosity about Jews. Other, nonfictional, false Jews soon began appearing in England, though their motives proved to be more complex.

The phenomenon of the false Jew reached its peak during the politically unstable 1650s. Thomas Collier acknowledges that one of the arguments against readmission was that if the Jews "may be permitted to come in, yet the great doubt will be how we shall know them to be Jews, of the seed of Abraham. Papists and Jesuits may come over in pretence of being Jews, or proselytes, viz., Jews by profession, yet not of Abraham's seed by nature."[70] And William Prynne goes even further, maintaining that such individuals have already begun secretly infiltrating the country: "If extraordinary care be not taken herein . . . under pretext of Jews, we shall have many hundreds of Jesuits, Popish priests, and friars come over freely into England from Portugal, Spain, Rome, Italy, and other places, under the title, habit, and disguise of Jews." To substantiate his claim, Prynne reminds his readers of some of the more notorious cases already known to them. He writes that the Jesuits had recently sent over "under the notion and vizard of converted Jews" a number of individuals who were frauds, including "Ramsey the Scot, and Eleazar, and Joseph ben Israel, all jesuitical, wicked, cheating imposters, the two last whereof have cheated the honest people of the nation of many thousand[s of] pounds, being notorious villains."[71] Prynne repeatedly speaks of the danger in "this giddy apostatizing age" of a Jewish "plot" to "be received amongst us, to seduce us unto Judaism, to which many are now inclined." Predictably, these false Jews turn out to be practiced seducers. Prynne writes that one of them (it is unclear whether he is referring to "Joseph ben Israel" or to another imposter) was

> formerly a trooper and plunderer in Prince Rupert's army, as he confessed to his hostess at Dursley in Glocestershire in his drink, where he would have ravished the maid-servant of the house, locking the door upon her, while she was warming his bed in the night, and upon her crying for help, fled away presently in the night, to avoid apprehension.[72]

Paul Isaiah, who also wrote under the names Eleazar bar Isaiah Hacohen and Eleazar Bargishai, was probably not a false Jew (except to his fellow Jews) but rather a professional convert, born in Eastern Europe, baptized by Jesuits in Antwerp, who arrived with a fellow convert in England in 1651. Before his death five years later he published with the help of a translator a number of tracts which, among other things, purported to offer the untold secrets of the Jews.[73] He also introduced himself to Baptist circles eager to have the truth of their religious convictions validated, and in return took hundreds of pounds as well as a Christian wife he soon abandoned.[74] It is understandable why Prynne linked him to "Ramsey the Scot," a false Jew who had passed through the hands of the Jesuits before arriving in England. In fact, it may well be that Paul Isaiah was not originally Jewish at all but passed himself off as a Jewish convert knowing the attraction that would have for sects like the Baptists and Quakers who took a strong interest in the conversion of the Jews. Having read through Paul Isaiah's work a number of times, I admit to my own nagging sense of doubt. Was this a Jew who misremembered his Jewish learning and made up material that he thought his Christian readers would want to hear about the Jews, or, less probably, was he a Christian confidence man from abroad who learned enough Hebrew to pass himself off as a Jew and circumcised himself to convince skeptics?[75] Whatever the truth, the confusion is so great that Prynne, who was his contemporary and knew some of those with whom Paul Isaiah came into contact, chose to include him in his list of false Jews.

There can be no doubt, however, that unlike Paul Isaiah, "Ramsey the Scot" was unquestionably a false Jew, and as such confirmed one of England's worst fears. He was a Christian who could pass himself off as a Jew while in the service of Jesuit handlers abroad. He proved a nightmare as well for Thomas Tillam, the susceptible Baptist pastor whose reputation he discredited, and for the other members of Tillam's congregation who were similarly deceived.[76] Born Thomas Ramsey, he went by the Hebrew name Joseph ben Israel. He also called himself Thomas Horseley. His story survives in a number of contemporary pamphlets—variously titled *The False Jew*, *The Converted Jew*, and *The Counterfeit Jew*—that appeared in 1653.[77] From the perspective of Tillam and his fellow Baptists of Hexham, the story ran something like this: a young man by the name of Joseph ben Israel who had arrived by ship in Newcastle was directed to them by the Baptist deputy-governor of Newcastle, Paul Hobson. They welcomed him, and within a few days this Jew who had found Christ was baptized by Tillam in the "River Tyne" in "the presence of some hundreds."[78]

The confession of faith accompanying his conversion provides some sense of who the Hexham congregants believed he was. Joseph ben Israel told them that he was "a Jew, of the tribe of Judah, born in Mantua" and "trained up in the religion of my fathers." The intellectual journey that led to his conversion began with his exposure to platonism, a philosophy that first directed him away from the "sepher hattorah," that is, the Jewish scriptures. In his confession of faith Joseph ben Israel explained that the crucial discovery that "drew [his] meditations first toward the Christian Messiah" was the realization that while the verb for God's actions was singular, His name in Hebrew was plural, as in the garbled transcription in the text: "Nangas baaadams betrolmenus," "Let us perfect man with our image."[79] Joseph then told the congregants that while initially won over to Christ by these linguistic proofs, he nevertheless fell into "perplexities and distractions of spirit"; he "was almost swallowed up" by "despair," and "thought of returning to the way of my fathers."

Luckily, the hand of "Providence brought to [his] view the Syriac and Greek copies of Guido Fabricius Boderianus," which, when he compared these with "the law and the prophets," soon revealed "all prophecies fulfilled in Jesus Christ, without contradiction." After a brief sojourn in Germany, Joseph ben Israel describes how he then "came into England," where, having sought Christ "without," now "found him also within," presumably at Hexham. Under Tillam's guidance, and with thanks to God in broken Hebrew ("Baruch Adonay le golam vanged Amen be Amen") that he was "called upon to arise to be baptized," Joseph ben Israel brought his conversion narrative to a close.[80]

He was able to deceive the congregants at Hexham by offering them precisely what they would have expected from a converting Jew: a knowledge of the Bible (with a smattering of spoken Hebrew thrown in for good measure), an awareness of the limitations of the "rabbis," a wandering past, and crucially, what Tillam calls "that manifest token in his flesh, the distinguishing character of circumcision," which Tillam inspected "before [he] baptized him." But the "false Jew" quickly ran into trouble with the ministers of Newcastle who were not as gullible as Tillam. When challenged to explain why after so little time in the country his English was perfect, Joseph grew silent and let his supporters defend him. Tillam intervened and explained that in his own travels on the continent he learned that "many of the Jews could speak perfect English." In fact, the belief that Jews were naturally fluent in all languages had already circulated in England in versions of the story of the Wandering Jew, who, according to the Jacobean diarist Richard Shann, "whithersoever he went ... always spoke the vulgar tongue ... as if he had been born in the country."[81] Another of Joseph ben Israel's defenders ingeniously proffered that "because the Jews could pronounce Shibboleth, they could [also] speak English," here relying on the famous biblical precedent where the Israelites distinguished friend from foe by the capacity of each to pronounce the word *Shibboleth* correctly. Hard-pressed by his accusers and "with a feigned indignation," Joseph threatened apostasy and revenge: "Such hard usage would make him go back to his country and write to the confusion of all Christianity."[82]

Joseph's improvisational skills were described as extraordinary. In the words of the anonymous author of *The Counterfeit Jew*, it "would fill too much paper to describe all the lies, forgeries, hypocrisies, [and] slights of this miserable wretch, who writ himself Josephus ben Israel." Joseph was the consummate actor: he "was of an acute wit, an excellent linguist (spoke most languages, and Hebrew perfectly), a ready scholar, [and] a great traveler." He "could carry himself very smoothly, suit himself to any humor, company, discourse very accurately, by his ready subtle wit and tongue he could transform himself easily into what shapes he pleased, and act any part. He could command his eyes, his countenance, his tongue, and could speak orthodoxly, spiritually, learnedly, [and] practically." He was also quick-witted: "Ask him why he called himself Horseley? Why, he was a Jew, and feared to be known, in regard so many of their nation have suffered in England; and by their Talmud, in danger of life, any thing is allowed, but idolatry and murder. He was then in Judaism, but now a Christian." And when pressed why he came to England, he gave the answer that his impressionable and evangelizing interlocutors wanted to hear:

Why, he heard of the fame of the Christians of England above all others; he had seen Papists, Lutherans, Calvinists, they were all full of ceremonies and traditions. He had conversed with some Anabaptists in Germany (and they told him of the English Christians) but they held free will, and such points. And he desired to worship God in the purest way, without mixtures of men's inventions, therefore he came to the people of Hexham.[83]

His deception was ultimately revealed when a letter from his mother was intercepted. In it she chastized her son for having written to his father under a false name and pleaded with him to come home, "though never so poor." Exposed, he then offered a second confession. His real name was Thomas Ramsey, and he was born in London to parents of Scottish descent. He had studied at the University of Glasgow and at Edinburgh before traveling to the continent and arriving in Rome, where he enrolled at a Jesuit college. Under the guidance of his Jesuit teachers he was sent back to England "to use his best endeavors there to propagate their ends." If he is to be believed, Ramsey was to relay information to the Jesuits by means of letters written "in the Hebrew language."[84]

There is considerable irony—and confusion as well—in the Jesuits' infiltration of the English Baptists through a young man of Scottish descent impersonating an apostate Italian Jew. Their decision to disguise Ramsey as a Jew introduces an additional level of irony, surely unintended, for twenty-three years earlier, a Catholic polemic with the identical title—*The Converted Jew* (1630)—had ended with the convert revealing himself not to be a Jew after all, but a disguised Catholic priest.[85] When Catholics had bragged of just such a deception in a fictional account, was it any wonder that Protestants were fearful of such infiltration in real life? Identifying who was a Jew was no simple task.

Ramsey's story is also valuable for what it tells us about the criteria that the congregants in Hexham, and their leader Tillam, seized upon in identifying someone as Jewish. It was not Ramsey's physical appearance (other than the mark of circumcision) that compelled belief, but his knowledge of Hebrew and of the Scriptures, and his ability to provide what they expected a converting Jew might say. Even the fact that Ramsey spoke English perfectly was not enough to raise sufficient doubts; infused with the spirit of millenarianism that pervaded English religious culture in the mid-seventeenth century, the congregants at Hexham wanted to believe that Jews could and would renounce their mistaken ways. Oliver Cromwell's Council of State was not amused. During a period of such political instability the fear of infiltration ran deep: "A singular piece of their wickedness was this counterfeit Jew . . . sent from the Inquisition house to try his fidelity . . . by some notable attempt upon the state, army, by division, intelligence, poison . . . to propagate the Catholic ends." The danger that Ramsey posed was rooted in the fact that he was "empowered by the Pope's indulgence to do anything, swear anything, counterfeit anything," and "put off" or "put on any religion." [86] On July 13, 1653, the Council of State issued a warrant for his arrest. Jesuit infiltrators were not treated with great leniency at this time, and Ramsey was imprisoned for the next six years.[87]

It was proving increasingly difficult to define what distinguished Christian from Jew. This was certainly the experience of an Elizabethan merchant and traveler, John Sanderson, who found himself accused of being a Jew and a bit bewildered about how he could refute this charge. The incident occurred during Sanderson's travels in the Holy Land in 1601, on a visit to the sepulcher at "Anastasia."[88] Sanderson explains that he dutifully paid the Turkish guards his admission fee, when suddenly some Catholic "friars and others fell in an uproar, saying that I was a Jew." The Turks, who were in charge of the religious site, told Sanderson simply to ignore his Catholic accusers, "but the brabble was so terrible" that Sanderson "returned to the cadi [a civil judge] with the friars." Sanderson writes that the head friar "accused me to be a Jew, because I came in company of Jews." Part of the friar's accusation happened to be true—Sanderson was in fact traveling exclusively in the company of Jews in his tour of the Holy Land—but the friars were probably trying to revenge themselves on Sanderson, a Protestant, for having snubbed Catholic authorities nominally responsible for all Christian visitors to Jerusalem. By now quite a crowd had gathered to witness the cadi's judgment. While they were waiting, an "old Turk" who had "followed to hear the matter" made matters worse by urging Sanderson to convert to Islam. The situation was quickly getting out of hand. Sanderson protested that he had no desire to convert, and furthermore insisted that he was "a Christian, and no Jew." Not persuaded, the old Turk then "said in the hearing of all the Jews, Turks, and Christians, let him be searched." Before Sanderson was subjected to a bodily search, presumably to determine if he was circumcised, "the cadi appeared," and, "being a very discreet man," first "reprove[d] that Turk" and then the friars who had first accused Sanderson of being Jewish. At that point Sanderson himself was set free.[89] Sanderson not only had to endure the insult of being called Jewish, but the frustration of being unable—short, perhaps, of undressing—to prove that he was not. The question posed by Portia in the trial scene of *The Merchant of Venice*, staged just a few years before this episode—"Which is the merchant here, and which the Jew?"—had taken on new meaning.

Sanderson's diary of his travels in the Holy Land provides further evidence that it was no longer so easy to tell Christians and Jews apart based on their behavior or actions. During his three-month journey Sanderson found himself as the only Christian in the "company of Jews" who were his companions and protectors on the dangerous trip from Damascus to Jerusalem. The seasoned English merchant was particularly struck by the kindness of one of these Jews, Abraham Cohen, from whom Sanderson learned a good deal about Jews and their ways. Sanderson writes of Cohen that "my companion Jew . . . was so respective, kind and courteous that never in any Christian company, of what degree soever, I ever did receive better content. For moral carriage towards all, understanding, and honesty, this Jew was without company." Sanderson goes so far as to call Abraham Cohen a "Gentile-Jew," and describes him as superior to many Christians he had known: "a most devout, zealous, and softhearted man he was. I cannot speak too much good of him, in regard of his great humanity and extraordinary charity; his measure being more in those performances than is to be found in many of us Christians." Sanderson concludes that when they had to go their separate ways, it "was not without moist eyes between Jew and Christian."[90] Such unprecedented familiarity with actual Jews by growing numbers of English merchants and travelers called into question some of the preconceptions that had long shaped English ideas about what Jews were like.[91]

V. What is a Jew?

The erosion of recognizable difference paradoxically generated ever more strenuous efforts to distinguish Christian from Jew, and, with the increasing emergence of a sense of national identity, Englishman from Jew. One of the things that greatly complicated these efforts was that the answers depended on different ways of conceiving of difference—religious, national, racial, professional, physical, sexual—which often overlapped and just as often contradicted each other, though the contradictions were rarely acknowledged. Jews may well have struck European Christians as different, but what constituted that difference changed markedly over time and place; to collapse these distinctions is to obscure what these stereotypes can tell us about the different national and religious cultures that produced them. Thus, for example, by the late sixteenth century the widespread medieval identification of Jews and the devil had virtually disappeared in England,[92] as had charges of Jewish host desecration in a nation that had broken with its Catholic past. On the other hand, the kind of racial characteristics regularly attributed to Jews after the Enlightenment had not yet fully emerged in early modern England[93] and were only encountered in the odd aside, such as the observation by Robert Burton in *The Anatomy of Melancholy* that Jews have "goggle eyes"[94] and that their voice, pace, gesture [and] looks" are "likewise derived with all the rest of their conditions and infirmities" and passed along by "propagation."[95] Certainly, there are no allusions in early modern England connecting Jews to the spread of syphilis, or claiming that the Jews had weak feet or were prone to hysteria, characteristics increasingly attributed to European Jews by the late nineteenth century. Still other stereotypic notions, such as the belief that Jews had large hooked noses, had earlier appeared in medieval England (at least in the marginal drawings of monastic scribes), and would reappear in the eighteenth century, but were surprisingly rare in early modern English prints depicting Jews.[96] As such, the early modern period served as a crucial conduit, at some points sealing off the medieval from the modern, at other points appropriating older myths and recasting them as medically or scientifically sound evidence. In clarifying this process of cultural transmission, the rest of this chapter explores how English writers of the sixteenth and seventeenth centuries grappled with the theoretical challenge of defining what a Jew was. Issues of Jewish racial and national identity, only touched on briefly here, will be addressed at greater length in subsequent chapters.

As the history of the counterfeit Christians and false Jews outlined above shows, in theological terms the Jews were understood not only to be inveterate opponents of Christians but also imminent coreligionists whose conversion would confirm the rightness of the Christians' faith. One result was that Judaism was often imagined as a "mirror-image of Christianity,"[97] a "creed" religion, whose sacraments (such as circumcision) were comparable to Christian ones (such as baptism) that had superseded them. For Samuel Purchas, for example, the sad history "of the Jews may be a visible demonstration of the truth of Christian religion," because the Jews, who believe in the laws of Moses but obstinately refuse to see the fulfillment of the law in Christ, "hold out to us the light of Scripture, themselves walking in darkness, and reserved to darkness; like to a lamp, lantern, or candlestick, communicating light to others, whereof themselves are not capable, nor can make any use."[98]

The frontispiece to the 1632 English edition of Hugo Grotius's *True Religion Explained and Defended* visually conveys this sense of the Jews as both mirror image of Christians and at the same time blind to the light of Christ (see illustration 12). In this woodcut four male figures—Christian, Jew, Turk, and Pagan—appear in small frames on the title page, with Christian and Jew paired off above the lower pairing of Turk and Pagan. In the unusual explanatory note on the page facing the illustration, we learn that the "Christian kneels upon the cross, which he must take up . . . having a glory upon him to represent the brightness of the Gospel and true religion." The Jew faces the Christian and mirrors his posture, "kneel[ing]" before "the two tables of the law by which he hopes to be saved, not as yet believing in Christ, because his eyes are blinded." A number of other features are notable. Except for his blindness, and perhaps his cloak, there is little to distinguish the Jew from the Christian: both men kneel, hands clasped in prayer, young, bearded, devout. In contrast, the Turk and the Pagan are given distinct national identities and garb, with the militant Turk bearing a scimitar and wearing a turban, and the sun-worshipping Pagan barefoot, draped, with headdress, much like a New World inhabitant. Like the Christian, the Turk worships a prophet, though in his case a false one;

and, like the Jew, the sun-worshipping Pagan fixes his gaze upon a false image. Presumably, were the Jew to lift his eyes to heaven instead of fixing them on the laws of Moses, the last of the differences distinguishing him from his Christian opposite would disappear.

What made the opposition between Christian and Jew even more confusing in early modern Europe was that marranism itself (and the Jewish communities that Conversos helped establish in Amsterdam and elsewhere) often carried over a residual element of Christian thinking about Judaism. For example, some Conversos considered salvation to be a central tenet of their religion, though it was salvation through the law of Moses rather than the mercy of Christ.[99] It is easy to see how confusions could arise when Christians learned about Judaism from Jews whose knowledge of Judaism had at some point been influenced by Christian beliefs and misconceptions. Not until Leone Modena and Menasseh ben Israel wrote works translated into English in the seventeenth century did English readers have access to accounts of the Jewish faith written by those who were still practicing Jews.[100]

When Henry Blount published his *Voyage Into the Levant* he declared that the "chief sect whereof I desired to be informed was the Jews, whose modern condition is more condemned then understood by Christian writers."[101] Unwilling to take his knowledge of the Jews secondhand, either through preachers or through the increasing number of books about the Jews published in the late sixteenth and early seventeenth centuries, Blount adopts the role of the field anthopologist: he attends Sabbath services, sees how the Torah and Prophets are read, engages rabbis in debate, is curious about the Cabala, and deals with Jewish merchants on his travels through the Levant. This promisingly open-minded stance is offset, however, by the force of the preconceptions that Blount carried with him, such as the belief that physical degeneration had caused Jews to abandon the agricultural professions of their forefathers in favor of commerce. "Their primitive profession was shepherds," Blount writes, but "their frequent captivities, wherein the malice of their estate, and corruptions of the Gentiles, did extremely debauch their old innocence and . . . turned them to what they now are: merchants, brokers, and cheaters."[102] For Blount, character and profession went hand in hand: "the Jewish complexion is so prodigiously timid, as cannot be capable of arms. For this reason they are nowhere made soldiers nor slaves." The other collective defect "is their extreme corrupt love to private interest, which is notorious in the continual cheating and malice among themselves."[103] Yet in the very act of arguing that the Jews are essentially and racially different, Blount likens them to radical English Puritans, saying that Jews have "light, aerial, and fanatical brains, spirited much like our hot apocalypse men."[104] Besides effectively undermining his theory of Jewish degeneracy, Blount's argument suggests how difficult it was to separate anxieties generated by Jews from those produced within English Christianity.

The argument for a degenerative Jewish nature coexisted uneasily with the belief that the Jews inherited distinctive personality traits. Some early modern Spanish writers were especially fond of arguments that connected racial heritage with behavior, including Prudencio de Sandoval, who asked in 1604, "Who can deny that in the descendants of the Jews there persists and endures the evil inclination of their ancient ingratitude and lack of understanding, just as in Negroes [there persists] the inseparability of their blackness? For if the latter should unite them[selves], even a thousand times with white women, the children are born with the dark color of the father." For Sandoval, "it is not enough for the Jew to be three parts aristocrat or Old Christian, for one family-line [i.e., one Jewish ancestor] alone defiles and corrupts him."[105] Robert Burton's descriptions of the Jews' "infirmities" and Samuel Purchas's secondhand observation that Jews suffered from specific diseases— e.g., the "falling sickness is usual among the Jews"—offer additional evidence that the Jews were thought to be constitutionally different from Christians.[106] Similar claims were circulating in works like Henry Buttes's 1599 food guide, *Dyets Dry Dinner*, where Buttes notes that "Jews are great goose-eaters; therefore their complexion is passing melancholious, their colour swart, and their diseases very perilous." Buttes here draws upon popular English notions about the relationship between diet, disease, character, and skin color.[107]

Among English writers there was an unusually persistent belief that a hereditary feature transmitted by Jews was their stench, the so-called *foetor judaicus*.[108] James Howell, for example, writes that besides

> the abjection of their spirits and giddiness of their brains . . . it seems there is a kind of curse also fallen upon their bodies; witness the uncouth looks and odd cast of eye, whereby they are distinguished from other people. As likewise that rankish kind of scent no better indeed than a stink, which is observed to be inherent and inseparable from most of them above all other nations.[109]

Christopher Marlowe had earlier played upon the same belief when his character Barabas offers to stand downwind from his Christian interlocutors, explaining that "'tis a custom held with us, / That when we speak with Gentiles like to you, / We turn into the air to purge ourselves."[110] And Thomas Dekker draws on the same tradition in his play *The Whore of Babylon* (1607), which depicts "Ropus, a doctor of physic" plotting against "Titania, the Fairie Queene," in "whom is figured our late Queen Elizabeth." Ropus is clearly a stand-in for Roderigo Lopez, the physician of Jewish descent who was executed in 1594 for conspiring to poison Queen Elizabeth, an identification strengthened by Dekker's use of the name "Lupus" rather than Ropus in the first quarto of the play. Though Dekker does not say outright that Ropus is Jewish, the successive allusions to the *foetor judaicus* in act 4, scene 2, make this clear enough: Fideli declares that Ropus "smells" and orders that this "polecat" be taken away under guard. The others onstage add in one voice, "Away with him, foh."[111]

Thomas Browne wrestled at length with the racial and national implications of this alleged Jewish stench. What had been tacitly accepted by John Foxe and others—that Jewish converts were newly "aromatized by their conversion" having "lost their scent with their religion"—surely, Browne thought, could not be true. Moreover, he writes, that "Jews stink naturally, that is, that in their race and nation there is an evil savour, is a received opinion we know not how to admit." In trying to dispel one set of "vulgar opinions," Browne cannot help introducing others. He dismisses the idea of Jewish racial purity (and therefore a distinctive Jewish smell) by arguing that many "commixtures" have taken place between Christians and Jews, in part because Jewish women "desire copulation" with Christians "rather than [with men of] their own nation, and affect Christian carnality above circumcised venery." He concludes that given this racial cross-fertilization, "it will be hard" to maintain that Jews stink "unless we also transfer the same unto those whose generations are mixed, whose genealogies are Jewish, and naturally derived from them."[112]

Not everyone was so easily persuaded. Dean Wren wrote in the margin of Browne's text that Browne had erred in underestimating the effect of the Jews' diet. Wren notes that because the "Jews anxiously observ[e] the prohibited eating of blood," they keep meat "covered with onions and garlic till it putrify, and contract as bad a smell as that of rottenness from those strong sauces." He offers as further proof the experience of his friend, Mr. Fulham, who learned first-hand how bad this stench was "at a Jewish meeting" in "Italy," where the smell was so strong that he had to remove "into the fresh air."[113]

Often, arguments about the Jews' physical or sexual difference find confirmation in other myths. This appears to be the case with the idea that Jewish men menstruated. Menstruation would not only account for the *foetor judaicus* but also explain the Jews' desperate need for Christian blood to replace that which was lost through male menstrual discharge. Thomas Calvert cautiously suggests that there "is an excellent relation if it can be proved to bear its weight with truth, to show the original of child-crucifying among the Jews." This compulsive behavior, Calvert writes, stems from a mistaken belief on the part of Jews seeking to alleviate their "shameful punishment." This "punishment so shameful they say is that Jews, men as well as females, are punished *curso menstruo sanguinis*, with a very frequent blood flux."[114] Since Calvert believes that Jews had crucified children, it makes good sense that their need for blood has some biological rationale. Yet, still skeptical about this particular explanation, he leaves "it to the learned to judge and determine by writers or travelers, whether this be true or no, either that they have a monthly flux of blood, or a continual malodoriferous breath."[115] The roots of the belief that Jewish men lost blood and needed Christian blood to replace it can be traced at least as far back as the thirteenth-century account of Thomas de Cantimpré in his *Miraculorum et Exemplorum Memorabilium*, where Thomas describes how, mistaking the words of one of their prophets, the literal-minded Jews tried to cure themselves through Christian blood—"ut tali sanguine convalescent" (in order that by this blood they may be healed)—mistaking "sanguine Christiano" for the lifesaving "sanguine Christi" (that is, the blood of a Christian for Christ's blood).[116]

Versions of this theory continued to circulate throughout late sixteenth- and early seventeenth-century Europe, and can be found in Heinrich Kormann's *Opera Curiosa* (1614), in the convert Franco da Piacenza's influential catalogue of Jewish maladies, first published in 1630,[117] as well in the work of the Spanish physician Juan de Quinones, who "wrote a special treatise to prove the claim that male Jews have a tail and, like women, a monthly flow of blood."[118] Contemporaries apparently saw no contradiction between these effeminized portraits and those that depicted Jewish men as rapacious seducers. Indeed, when it came to the Jews, the boundaries between male and female were often seen as quite slippery. For example, writers about Jewish festivals were quick to point out that Jews practiced cross-dressing as part of their activities on the feast of Purim: the "men wear women's apparel and the women men's, against the law of God which they think at this time of mirth they may lawfully violate."[119] Further complicating racial and gender categories was the possibility that Jewish men were sometimes capable of breast-feeding. Samuel Purchas writes that "if you believe their *Gemara* (can you choose?), a poor Jew having buried his wife and not able to hire a nurse for his child, had his own breasts miraculously filled with milk, and became nurse himself." Purchas also cites a Midrashic tradition regarding the Book of Esther that the orphaned Esther had been breast-fed by Mordechai.[120] The fact that Jewish men were represented as endowed with male and female traits goes a long way toward explaining why representations of Jewish men almost entirely displaced those of Jewish women at this time. I have come across only two portraits of Jewish women in printed English books of the sixteenth century, both in T. Washington's translation of Nicholas de Nicolay's *The Navigations Into Turkie* (1585). One is of "A Maiden Jew of Andrinople," the other, "A Woman Jew of Andrinople." Aside from their garb, neither has any identifiably "Jewish" characteristics (see illustrations 5 and 6). Paradoxically, even as descriptions of Jews focused almost exclusively on men (except for some notable exceptions in plays), the Jews as a people were often thought of collectively as feminine, especially when juxtaposed to the masculine English (hence the ease with which analogies could be drawn between Jews and female prostitutes).

Consequently, there is far less that is written about the Jewish woman's body, other than the conviction that Jewish women reputedly desired uncircumcised men. There is more evidence of the danger that the bodies of Christian women posed for Jews, in particular, the danger that through breast-feeding Christian nursemaids could transmit their faith to Jewish infants. In 1738 D'Blossiers Tovey recounts how medieval English Jews had a "foolish custom" of forcing Christian nursemaids who were breast-feeding Jewish children "to milk themselves into a privy for three days after Easter," because they were afraid "that the body and blood of Jesus Christ [i.e., the Eucharist], which all Christians were obliged to receive upon that holy festival, should by incorporation be transfused into their children." This alleged practice, Tovey further notes, resulted in a proclamation by Pope Innocent III, as well as in legislation by King Henry III of England, forbidding Christian wet nurses to work for Jews.[121] Similar restrictions, generated by fear of pollution by those of Jewish stock, led to a law in Spain forbidding "a New Christian woman to serve as a wet-nurse for the royal children because her milk is polluted since she is of the despised and accursed race [of Jews]."[122] There is no evidence that similar legislation was ever proposed in England.

Virtually all early modern accounts of Jewish difference are hedged with reservations and qualifications. The cautious Thomas Browne, for example, is unsure whether to speak of the Jews as a "race or nation." While this was a time in which England was increasingly thinking of itself as a nation, there was still much confusion over the constitutive features of national identity: did it have to do with having a language, or laws, or simply territory? The Jews, who had once been a nation, and might one day be so again, fit uneasily into emerging categories of nationhood. In addition, the forced migrations of Jewish communities, subject to mass persecution first in England and France, then in Spain, Portugal, and elsewhere in medieval and early modern Europe, led some Christians to think of the Jews in the paradoxical terms of an international nation. Surely, the renewed interest in seventeenth-century England in the Wandering Jew is directly related to the historical situation of the early modern itinerant Jews. John Donne, for example, could preach in 1627 that ever "since the destruction of Jerusalem, the Jews" have been "a whole nation of Cains, fugitives, and vagabonds,"[123] a description that combines theological and criminal condemnation. Like Cain, the Jews were the archetypal murderers of the innocent, condemned to wander the earth.

Closely related to questions about the Jews as nation were those that concerned the Jews' racial purity. If the Jews were indeed a distinct race, and before (or even after) their Expulsion in 1290 had mingled with English blood, was it possible that English stock was contaminated with Jewish traits? One solution to this problem was simply to project these anxieties onto the Scots, and more than one seventeenth-century English writer suggested that the Scots had Jewish blood and characteristics, presumably because the Jews must have fled there, rather than remaining in England, following their banishment in 1290. Why else, James Howell wondered, were the Scots so tightfisted and what else could explain their distaste for blood pudding?[124] In 1691 readers of the popular *Athenian Mercury* were offered a similar answer to the question, "Why do Scotch-men hate swine's flesh?"[125]

Howell was a Royalist, and his polemic is shaped by his perception, shared by "a great many Englishmen, at some time probably a majority, [that] the Scots embodied an appalling synthesis of political revolution, apocalyptic expectations, and Judaizing identities."[126] In a series of recent articles Arthur H. Williamson has shown how Scottish political aspirations in the seventeenth century were shaped by the Scottish reformers' strong identification with the federated tribes of "covenanted Israel,"[127] especially in the Solemn League and Covenant of 1643.[128] For a great majority of the English, however, such a political reconfiguration would have been viewed with considerable alarm, since "a federated Britain would inherently mean a Judaized Britain."[129] Ethnographic and political anxieties about national identity, here projected onto the threatening (and Judaized) Scots, clearly nourished each other in seventeenth-century England and are not so easily untangled.

To suggest that Scottish blood was contaminated with that of Jews left open the possibility that some Jews might have remained behind in England too (we have already seen how this claim survived well into the late nineteenth century in the work of Robert Burton). In the early eighteenth century the tolerationist John Toland advanced a similar claim. A "considerable part of the British inhabitants," he announced, "are the undoubted offspring of the Jews." As for the Expulsion, many of the Jews on "this sad occasion chose rather to turn Christians than to leave their sweet native country to starve in a foreign land." Centuries later, according to Toland, these once Jewish families now misleadingly "derive their pedigrees" from the "Saxons," the "Danes," or "the Normans." Only "two or three families at most" are honest enough to admit they "are descended" from the more ancient "nation" of the Jews.[130] Toland here raises the troubling possibility that many of his fellow countrymen living happily in the assurance that they are of honorable and ancient British ancestry may in fact be of Jewish stock.

National arguments were no less dangerous than racial ones, and were clearly intertwined with them. They were further enmeshed with theological and economic issues when it was suggested by seventeenth-century English writers that the Jews had not merely lost their territory but had settled other lands, not only China and India but also perhaps the West and East Indies and the Americas, places ripe for colonizing and conversion. Books like Thomas Thorowgood's *Jews in America* (1650) exemplified the ways in which millenarian thought powerfully shaped—and was influenced in turn by—emerging theories of national identity.[131] One of the grounds for arguing that New World natives were Jewish was that the language they spoke sounded to European ears a lot like Hebrew, a compelling argument at a time when language was central to defining a nation. But the idea that a nation was defined by its language—which had worked well in a medieval world in which few Christians knew Hebrew—no longer worked in a post-Reformation Europe where increasing numbers of ordinary men, women (like Elizabeth Cary), and even children (like Rowland Cotton, who under Hugh Broughton's tutelage learned Hebrew by the age of seven or eight)[132] could read and sometimes even speak the language of the Jews.[133] In 1602 Simon Sturtevant published his *Dibre Adam, or Adams Hebrew Dictionarie*, composed when he was a Cambridge scholar a decade earlier, which he offers as a "rare and new invention for the speedy attaining and perfect retaining" of the language of the Bible; Sturtevant also notes that scholars had relied on an older learning device, a "Hebrew cube" designed by "Elias Hutterus."[134] By 1633 Thomas Ingmethorpe could even publish an authorized Anglican *Short Cathechisme* in facing columns of Hebrew and English whose pages were to be read from right to left, like a Hebrew book.[135] As early as 1524 Robert Wakefield argued that the "Jews do not have a particular language for common use, since their vernacular language, which had disappeared, belongs to us" (i.e., to Christian scholars).[136] Andrew Borde likewise maintained that Hebrew was no longer the common language of the Jews, and that the Hebrew spoken by modern-day Jews was as unlike the "true Hebrew tongue" as "barbarous" Latin was from true Latin.[137] The Hebrew language, then, was no longer a sufficient basis for defining Jewish identity; in fact, as British travelers were discovering, Jews were more likely to converse with other Jews in Spanish. According to the Scottish traveler William Lithgow, the only place where Jews still spoke Hebrew was in Salonica, where they "speak vulgarly and maternally . . . the Hebrew tongue, man, woman and child, and not elsewhere in all the world."[138] In this respect the early modern English example is markedly different from the one that developed in nineteenth-century Germany, where Jewish vocal and linguistic habits that came to be known as *mauscheln*, the special language of the Jews, were seen by Germans at the time as "a more or less indelible sign of Jewish identity."[139]

Though wide-ranging, the categories early modern English writers used to define Jewish difference—in terms of language, territory, law, religion, profession, race, gender, nationality, physiology—were never as conclusive as the writers who invoked them might have hoped. The unprecedented exposure to foreign Jews in the late sixteenth and early seventeenth centuries, rather than clarifying English perceptions of these people, muddied them, and in the process raised troubling questions for English writers about what it meant to be English and Christian. The desire on the part of the English to define themselves as different from, indeed free of, that which was Jewish, operated not only on an individual level but on a national level as well: that is, between 1290 and 1656 the English came to see their country defined in part by the fact that Jews had been banished from it. It is worth comparing this story to a similar narrative of a nation cleansed of a treacherous adversary, the myth of an Ireland cleared of poisonous snakes by St. Patrick.[140] While the presence of snakes in sixteenth-century Ireland remains undocumented, the same does not hold true of Jews in post-Reformation England. Nonetheless, the myth that there were no Jews in Shakespeare's England remains a powerful one, and is connected to two other events that have taken on mythic dimensions: that Edward banished a considerable Jewish population from England in 1290 and that Cromwell awarded the Jews the right to return in 1656. It is to these narratives about the presence of Jews in England that I now turn, not only to question the received histories of these landmark events but also to question the way in which Englishness has come to be defined in relationship to them.

II ⚘

Myths, Histories, Consequences

 Insofar as the Expulsion of the Jews from England in 1290 and their Readmission in 1656 have become symbols of opposing antisemitic and philosemitic (or alternatively, xenophobic and tolerationist) impulses in English culture, any account of Shakespeare and the Jews is necessarily framed by and contingent upon how these stories have been told. As a cultural historian, I am less interested in describing what exactly happened in 1290 and 1656 than I am in exploring how and why historians of various stripes have offered narratives of the Expulsion and Readmission so much at odds with each other and with what the available evidence suggests. The same holds true for historical accounts of that truth universally acknowledged—there were no Jews in England, or no more than a tiny handful, between 1290 and 1656—an exaggerated claim that continues to exercise a mysterious hold upon British historians. In reconsidering these received truths, a good many competing and long-buried versions of the past need to be unearthed and carefully reexamined.

Before turning to the various versions of the Expulsion, Readmission, and the intervening 366 years in which England was said to be essentially free of Jews, it is helpful first to situate these accounts within a larger myth, that of Englishness itself. Library shelves groan under the weight of books about the English (much as they do from books about the Jews); few peoples have had their stories repeated so often and in such detail. Necessarily, then, I cannot hope to provide more than a thumbnail sketch of the history of Englishness in the paragraphs that follow. I emphasize the idea of stories because it is through them that collective identities are imagined and refashioned. Historians credit Bede's *Ecclesiastical History of the English People*, written in 731, with giving a local habitation and a name to the various tribes, speaking a variety of dialects, who inhabited the territory that came to be called England. An even more impressive myth of national origins was provided by the Welshman Geoffrey of Monmouth in 1136 in his *History of the Kings of Britain*, in which he traces the roots of British history back to the survivors of Troy. Nationalist historiography tends to get written with some political purpose in mind, and Geoffrey's was no exception: by "portraying the British as a once great people with extensive dominions he could at once raise their status in the eyes of the new Norman overlords and suggest a precedent to the Norman kings in their imperialistic ambitions."[1] Geoffrey's king-centered myth of British origins (including the greatest ruler of all, King Arthur) held the field until the early modern period, when it was superseded by one in which English, rather than British identity, once again became central. Hugh MacDougall has persuasively shown that by the seventeenth century the "freedoms of Englishmen and past achievements in which they all might glory came more and more to be seen as proceeding along a path that led back not to Brutus, Troy, and the British kings, but rather to Saxon England and the forest of Germany."[2]

Shakespeare's age thus witnessed an important shift in the way that the English imagined their past and defined their present. This emergent myth of Anglo-Saxon origins, promulgated in works like William Camden's *Britannia* (1586) and Richard Verstegen's *Restitution of Decayed Intelligence* (1605)—which described "what a highly renowned and most honorable nation the Germans have always been, that thereby it may consequently appear how honourable it is for Englishmen to be from them descended"[3]—also introduced the idea of racially pure origins into the retelling of England's past. It was a version of the past that proved well suited to evolving English political, legal, and religious institutions; it had the added advantage of emphasizing how special the English people were. Indeed, by the late sixteenth century the Protestant English began to see themselves as having taken the place of God's first elect people, the Jews.[4] Outstanding theoretical issues—such as the relationship between Englishness and Britishness, or the problem of hybridization that the Celtic and the Danish peoples who had inhabited medieval England posed for those committed to an idealized vision of uncontaminated Anglo-Saxon roots—were quietly set aside.

This myth of Anglo-Saxon origins helped determine how early modern English writers reconceived of their nation in terms of Protestant Christianity, political liberty, linguistic superiority, and racial exclusivity. Put another way, by the late sixteenth century, Englishness had come to be defined in large measure in terms of racial, religious, and national affiliations, though conceptions of what exactly constituted these affiliations remained fuzzy at best, and would remain so for the next four centuries. In the late nineteenth century, with the rise of the disciplines of philology and anthropology, the idea of the English as an Aryan people, descended of "a race of outstanding character and possessed of an essentially democratic social organization," flowered most fully.[5] Even Shakespeare himself was analyzed in racialized terms; after examining the playwright's famous bust at Stratford, the Victorian anthropologist W. J. Jackson confidently concluded that "the bard of Avon was doubtless by descent of that well-mingled and thoroughly amalgamated Celto-Teutonic race, familiarly known as the Anglo-Saxon, but in reality consisting of elements from nearly every Caucasian stock in Europe, with possibly a remote tinge even of the Mongolic."[6] Racial thinking of this kind would die out in England by the mid-twentieth century: the myth of strong and pure Anglo-Saxon roots had finally outlived its political usefulness, though the accomplishments of the previous five hundred years of English imperial power, social stability, industrial advances, and artistic achievements, as well as the often violent oppression of a good many other peoples, could never have been possible without it.

Ironically, among the last to resurrect this myth were Nazi historians who traced the decline of their once great Anglo-Saxon enemy to the contamination of England's royal line with Jewish and Irish blood. Peter Aldag, in the introduction to his *Juden in England*, published in Berlin in 1941, tells a fanciful tale of how the remnants of the tribe of Dan, in their flight from Jerusalem, tried to reach England but ended up in Ireland instead, where a Jewish princess married an Irish chief. From "this association of the Jewish princess and the Irish chief, so it is said, the present English monarchy has proceeded" and "Judaism triumphs." Aldag, who tries to drive a wedge between the racially pure English "folk" and their Judaized rulers, also relates that there are many sects and associations in England founded to prove the theory that "the English and the Jews have had only one father," that "all men are brothers," and that "racial concepts are dead." Aldag's introduction ends with a nostalgic call for England to reassert its ancient, Jewless, heritage: "Here and there one can hear again the old wakening call: England awaken!"[7] As these racist fantasies make clear, the way in which Anglo-Jewish history has been recounted can reveal a good deal about how Englishness is imagined.

While Aldag's propagandistic motives are unmistakable, the investments of legitimate historians have not been quite so transparent. It is to their versions of the Anglo-Jewish past that I now turn, in order to understand how, through their efforts, Englishness has been in part defined by its relationship to Jewish-ness.

I. King Edward I expelled the Jews from England in 1290

The first country of Christendom, whence the Jews were expelled, without hope of return was our country of England, whence they were banished . . . by King Edward the First.
—*Edward Brerewood, 1614*[8]

Edward I . . . was the first European ruler to make his state permanently Judenrein.
—*Colin Richmond, 1992*[9]

It is one thing to say that Jews were expelled from England; it is quite another to answer the host of questions that follow hard upon such a statement. How many were expelled? Where did they go? Why were they expelled? Who was responsible for the decision? What were the consequences of the Expulsion, not just for those exiled, but for those who banished them? And, finally, how have historical accounts of the Expulsion changed over time, and how have these in turn transformed the meaning of the event? Satisfying answers to most of these questions are not easily found or widely available, either in the work of Anglo-Jewish or traditional British historians.[10]

The roots of these problems can be traced back to medieval chroniclers who wrote with disarming assurance and near unanimity about the raw num-ber of Jews deported. One of them puts the count at 15,060, another at 16,511, a third at 17,511.[11] Although these chroniclers never offer sources for their claims, their estimate of roughly 16,000 deportees appears in standard histo-ries to this day. Only quite recently when scholars looked at long-ignored evi-dence (such as detailed records of poll taxes paid by Jewish men and women over twelve years of age) has the figure shrunk to a total of 2,000 to 2,500 Jews still residing in England at the time of the large-scale deportation of 1290. Since the population of England at the time was somewhere between five and six million, only one out of every two or three thousand or so inhabitants was a Jew, an exceedingly small percentage, though regional perceptions must have differed since Jews living outside of London congregated in a handful of towns.[12]

The decline of England's medieval Jewish community was not a sudden event. The climax of Expulsion has eclipsed the harrowing events of the pre-vious century: the York Massacre, mass arrests, financial ruin, conversions, emigration, and over three hundred executions preceded this final blow.[13] The fate of individual exiles has also been subsumed within a larger story of how one group of people ridded itself of another. In painting a picture of England emptying itself of large numbers of Jews, a number of accounts that circulated in early modern England wildly inflated the scale of the Expulsion. Samuel Purchas, for example, offers the astounding number of "one hundred and sixty thousand, five hundred and eleven" Jews expelled.[14] While this is clearly a misreading of the count of 16,511 given in his source (and was corrected in the next edition of his popular work), for the many readers and writers who consulted Purchas's earlier edition the effect was to magnify the effect of depopulation. To cite but two instances of this, the anonymous author of the 1656 tract *The Case of the Jewes Stated* follows Purchas in recording the number of those banished as 160,511,[15] as does Thomas Scales in his unpublished history of the Jews, written around 1630.[16]

Medieval English chroniclers were apparently less interested in—and therefore prove less helpful about—where the exiled Jews went. Surviving documents indicate that 1,335 of the poorer ones paid fourpence for passage to France, and no doubt many of the wealthier ones went to France or other European countries as well.[17] A much repeated story, verified by court records and especially popular among sixteenth-century historians, describes how English sailors duped Jewish refugees into drowning in the Thames. Raphael Holinshed devotes most of his account of the Expulsion to this incident:

> A sort of the richest of them, being shipped with their treasure in a mighty tall ship which they had hired, when the same was under sail and got down the Thames towards the mouth of the river beyond Queenborough, the master mariner bethought him of a wile, and caused his men to cast anchor, and so rode at the same, till the ship by ebbing of the stream remained on the dry sands. The master herewith enticed the Jews to walk out with him on land for recreation. And at length, when he understood the tide to be coming in, he got him back to the ship, whither he was drawn up by a cord. The Jews made not so much haste as he did, because they were not aware of the danger. But when they perceived how the matter stood, they cried to him for help. Howbeit he told them, that they ought to cry rather unto Moses, by whose conduct their fathers passed through the Red Sea, and therefore, if they would call to him for help, he was able enough to help them out of those raging floods, which now came in upon them. They cried indeed, but no succour appeared, and so they were swallowed up in water.[18]

The familiar story of the Jews' safe passage to the Promised Land through the parted waters of the Red Sea is ironically reversed in a narrative that turns exiled Jews into drowning Egyptians. Presumably, the English have now supplanted the Jews as God's chosen people. Yet the moral of the story remains ambiguous. Holinshed notes that some chroniclers write that the "master returned to the ship, and told the King how he had used the matter, and had both thanks and reward," while "others affirm (and more truly as should seem) that diverse of those mariners, which dealt so wickedly against the Jews, were hanged for their wicked practice."[19] The unresolved conclusion—thumbing through his copy of Holinshed, Shakespeare might have wondered whether this was tragedy or comedy—points to the divided English view of their own role in the Expulsion. Are the prodigal English mariners to be admired for outwitting the rich Jews, and this a story of English sailors protecting their sceptered isle? Or are the mariners the "wicked" ones, and this a story celebrating English tolerance toward foreigners? Holinshed himself chose not to decide between the two endings. Perhaps both versions are needed to accommodate a sense of Englishness that embodies both tolerance and opportunism.

There has also been difference of opinion over the date of the Expulsion. Medieval English chroniclers are unanimous in placing the date in the year 1290. This date went unquestioned by English writers until the early seventeenth century, when the legal historian Edward Coke suggested that the chroniclers had gotten it wrong. Since no Expulsion order survived, Coke surmised that the Jews had gone into exile voluntarily in response to Edward I's harsh anti-Jewish statutes of 1275, passed in conjunction with Parliament, which among other things "established that no Jew shall take usury." Coke argues that before "this time Jews were diverse times banished this realm, but still they returned again. But this wise and worthy King by authority of Parliament banishing their usury, put the Jews into perpetual exile into foreign countries, where usury was tolerated."[20] If Coke was right, no legal obstacle stood in the way of Jews returning to England as long as they did not engage in usury.

A somewhat different account appears in the work of early modern Jewish historians on the continent, who record that the Expulsion took place in 1260 (one of them even dates it as early as 1242).[21] As for the actual day the Expulsion order was given, a tradition emerged in Jewish histories, revived in this century, that the decree fell on the ninth day of the month of Av, the anniversary of the destruction of the Temple in Jerusalem and a day of mourning in the Jewish calendar.[22] The implications of this claim are clear: the Expulsion fits neatly into what has been called the lachrymose model of Jewish history, a pattern of persecution, punctuated by brief periods of toleration, with millenial expectations of redemption and return. This vision is given full rein in Cecil Roth's standard history of the Jews in England:

> The final tragedy of 1290 was the first general expulsion of the Jews from any country in the medieval period. Local precedents only had been known before. But it was Edward I who set the example for the wholesale banishment of the Jews, which was followed with such deadly effect in France sixteen years after, by

Philip le Bel, and two centuries later by Ferdinand and Isabel of Spain, in the culminating tragedy of medieval Jewish history.[23]

Roth comes perilously close to insinuating that if Edward I had not established this precedent, the bloodier Iberian persecutions and expulsions that followed might never have occurred.

Without question, the greatest controversy circulates around the question of *why* the English expelled the Jews. Sifting through the mass of conflicting evidence in 1738, D'Blossiers Tovey was particularly struck by the fact that "whereas in all other records of their former punishments, the cause is particularly expressed, and sometimes aggravated, there is not the least mention of any cause assigned for this, though more than a hundred records are still remaining in the Tower which expressly mention and refer to the banishment itself." Even the medieval chroniclers were not much help: "though most of our ancient historians take notice of it, they say little more than that [the Jews] were generally disagreeable to the people," with some chroniclers "assigning no other cause than their usury, or misbelief." Finding such explanations wanting, Tovey reluctantly concludes that "the particular reasons for this banishment are as much a secret," though "it seems highly probable the King acted upon some other motive than was fit to be made public."[24]

Historical explanations for why the Expulsion took place have changed considerably over time. The earliest attempts by contemporary medieval chroniclers offer a dizzying array of reasons, helpfully summarized by Barnett Abrahams:

> In one chronicle the Expulsion is represented as a concession to the prayer of the Pope; in another, as a result of the efforts of Queen Eleanor; in a third, as a measure of summary punishment against the blasphemy of the Jews, taken to give satisfaction to the English clergy; in a fourth as an answer to the complaints made by the magnates of the continued prevalence of usury; in a fifth as an act of conformity to public opinion; in a sixth, as a reform suggested by the King's independent general enquiry onto the administration of the kingdom during his absence and his discovery, through the complaints of the Council, of the "deceits" of the Jews.[25]

Lost to subsequent historians of the Expulsion, at least until quite recently, was a sense of the extent to which these thirteenth-century narratives were themselves powerfully shaped by political attitudes of the chroniclers toward the barons, the Church, and the King, attitudes that hint at the complex political infighting that preceded the Expulsion order.

A radically different explanation for the Expulsion was offered by the sixteenth-century Jewish historian Samuel Usque. Usque, whose *Consolation for the Tribulations of Israel* was published in Italy in 1553, provides a wildly inventive account of the Expulsion. Although short on veracity—it is a fantastic narrative of seduction, apostasy, child abduction, mass conversion, and mass murder—Usque's version nonetheless provides insight into some of the darker impulses circulating around these events. Usque tells how in thirteenth-century England a friar fell "in love with a beautiful Jewish girl, contrary to the tenets of both their faiths. Though the friar wooed the girl for a long time, he found no way to win her; she spurned him and mocked his notes and promises. This only further inflamed his illicit love. He could no longer resist his rash desire, so he doffed the garb of his Christian faith and donned the garments of Judaism. He secretly became a Jew. And when he made this change, he was more successful in getting the beautiful Jewess to pay attention to his courting." Usque explains that this "Jewess was poor and fatherless, and under the influence of her mother, who was a woman of weak character, easily swayed by a chance for gain." And when "the mother saw the wealth of the erstwhile monk, she gave him her daughter in marriage on the condition that they leave the kingdom of England because of the great danger of their situation." Once made public, the transgressive marriage provoked considerable hostility: "The monks were greatly offended by what the friar had done; and the people taunted them. To repair the honor of their order, the monks endeavored to incite the King against the Jews. . . . Further, whenever the monks ascended the pulpit to preach, they directed their message against the Jews." The monks then "devised a new accusation," charging "that the Jews had converted a monk to Judaism in a Christian land, and that in return they had to be converted or die for the crime." To this end "all young Jewish children were taken from their parents and sent to the end of that island, a place called 'The North'" (perhaps meaning Scotland). There the abducted Jewish children were "taught the Christian doctrine and faith, so that, separated from their elders, they should not recall their ancient Law, and should completely lose the nourishment of the Jewish milk they had imbibed." The remaining Jews were banished. Relying more on fiction than on fact, Usque hits upon a number of fears—especially of being seduced by Jews and of turning Jewish—that continued to trouble the English well into the eighteenth-century and that were explored in plays and poems as well as polemic.

One of the more striking aspects of Usque's story is its emphasis on how the Jews were thought to threaten England and the English with contamination. Though their children were abducted and banished to the north, Usque writes that "converts were spread over the entire kingdom, and buildings of former synagogues that were converted into churches are still found, and a large number of the people have Jewish names."[26] Usque goes on to describe how these initial measures against the Jews proved unsuccessful, as the Jews soon returned to

1. "St. William Panel," Rood screen, Holy Trinity Church, Loddon, Norfolk (c. 1400-1450). Photograph courtesy of Ruth Batchelor. By kind permission of Loddon Church Council.

2. *Picture of a Jew in Andrew Borde,* The Fyrst Boke of the Introduction of Knowledge *(London, 1562), sig. N2v.*

Reproduced by kind permission of the Huntington Library.

3. *Picture of a Jew poisoning a well in Pierre Boaistuau,* Certaine Secrete Wonders of Nature, *trans. Edward Fenton, (London, 1569), p.26v.*

Reproduced by kind permission of the Huntington Library.

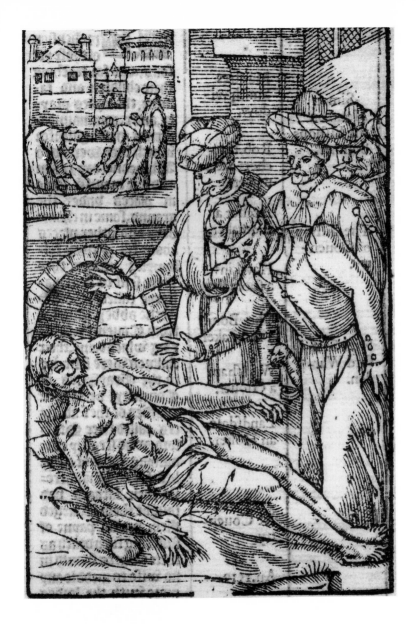

4. "The story of a Christian Jew in Constantinople Martyred by the Turks," in John Foxe, Actes and Monuments *(London, 1576), p.945.*

Reproduced by kind permission of the Huntington Library.

5. *"A Maiden Jew of Andrinople,"* in *Nicolas de Nicolay,* The Navigations Into Turkie, *trans. T. Washington (London, 1585), p.148.* Reproduced by kind permission of the Huntington Library.

6. *"A Woman Jew of Andrinople"* in *Nicolas de Nicolay,* The Navigations Into Turkie, *trans. T. Washington (London, 1585), p.147.* Reproduced by kind permission of the Huntington Library.

7. *"A Merchant Jew,"* in *Nicolas de
Nicolay,* The Navigations Into Turkie,
*trans. T. Washington (London, 1585),
p.132.* Reproduced by kind permission of the
Huntington Library.

8. *"A Physician Jew"* in *Nicolas de
Nicolay,* The Navigations Into
Turkie, *trans. T. Washington
(London, 1585), p.94.* Reproduced by
kind permission of the Huntington Library.

9. Detail "G" from title page of Thomas Coryate, Coryats Crudities
*(London, 1611)["fly from the Jews, lest they circumcise thee"
(as described in the dedicatory verse of Laurence Whitaker, sig. A3r)].*

Reproduced by kind permission of the Huntington Library.

10. *"Lopez Compounding to Poison the Queen," in, George Carleton,*
A Thankful Remembrance of Gods Mercy *(London, 1627), p. 164.*

Reproduced by kind permission of the Jewish Theological Seminary of America.

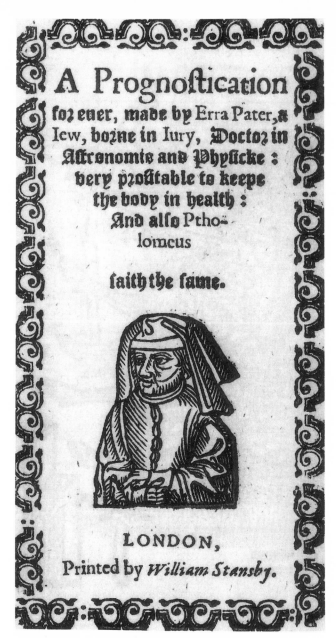

A Prognoſtication

fo2 euer, made by Erra Pater, a
Iew, bo2ne in Iury, Docto2 in
Aſtronomie and Phyſicke :
very p2ofitable to keepe
the body in health :
And alſo Ptho-
lomeus

faith the ſame.

LONDON,

Printed by *William Stansby*.

11. Title page of Erra Pater, pseud., A Prognostication for
Ever, Made by Erra Pater, a Jew, Borne in Jewry, Doctor in
Astronomie and Phisicke *(London, c.1630)*.

יְהֹוָה

Rom. 10.12
The Testa new ment

Gen. 17.7.
The Testa old ment

True Religion.

The Chriſtian
Math 16. 24.

The Iewe
Isa. 29. 20.

TRVE RELIGION EXPLAINED
And defended
againſt ẏ Archene;
mies therẏof in
theſe times,

In Six Bookes,

*Publiſhed by Authority
for the cõmon good.*

The Turke
Math. 24. 5. 24.

The Pagan
Psal. 72. 11.

Buy the trueth
Prov. 23. 23.

LONDON
*Printed for Ri.
Royſton in
Ivie-lane.*
1632, J. Cecill ſculp.

12. Title page of the English translation of Hugo Grotius's True Religion
Explained and Defended *(London, 1632).* Reproduced by kind permission
of the Huntington Library.

The WWandering-Jew,

Telling

FORTVNES

TO

Englifh-men,

LONDON;

Printed by *Iohn Raworth*, for *Nathaniel Butter*, 1640.

13. Title page of Gad ben Arad, pseud., The Wandering-Jew Telling
Fortunes to English-men *(London, 1640)*. Reproduced by kind permission
of the Huntington Library.

14. Print of "Erra Pater's Prophesy, or Frost Faire, 1685."

Reproduced by kind permission of the Huntington Library.

15. *Detail of a Jew hung in effigy, from an engraving by William Hogarth, "An Election Entertainment," The* Election *series (1755). The words on the effigy read "No Jews."*
Reproduced by kind permission of the Huntington Library.

England. The exasperated English finally decided to exterminate these Jews, but were afraid that this might pollute their land: "The Jewish people were numerous, and, if killed their bodies might contaminate the air. The King therefore ordered two pavilions to be set up by the seashore, one distant from the other. In one he placed the Law of Moses received from the Lord on Mount Sinai, and in the other the cross of Christianity. . . . He ordered brought before him all the Jews whom he had made Christian by force." Those who chose the law of Moses entered into a narrow passageway at the first pavilion, where each was "decapitated by a hidden English butcher and cast into the sea" for the fish to devour.[27] It is ironic that in drawing on Jewish ritual of purification (for that is what this kosher slaughter of unsuspecting Jews resembles) Usque invents a way for the English to kill off that which is Jewish without suffering the damage of contamination; their island is protected as the Jewish offal is cast into the waters outside the boundaries of the kingdom. Left unspoken is the troubling possibility that the Jews will once again pass into England when the English consume the fish that ate the Jews; sealing off England from Jewish contamination was no easy matter. Like English narratives of the Expulsion (though for markedly different reasons having to do with the imperatives of Jewish historiography at this time) Usque's places unusual stress on the Jews' ineradicable difference: not even conversion, banishment, or extermination could fully rid the English of Jewishness. While modern readers may find it surprising to encounter a Jewish historian emphasizing the fundamental incompatability of the Jews and their English hosts, it is important to remember that a major reason both English and Jewish historians have mutually accepted the broad contours of the Expulsion narrative is that this version of events suits the needs of both peoples. Like their English counterparts, early modern Jewish historians (and many of their heirs) needed to insist that Christians and Jews were autonomous peoples whose histories were ultimately distinct. There is one more strange twist: we know from a Portuguese Inquisitorial deposition of 1556 that shortly after its publication Usque's book was in the hands of Jews secretly living in England.[28]

It is important not to underplay points of real disagreement between English and Jewish versions of the Expulsion. Unlike their Jewish counterparts, for example, sixteenth-century English historians were particularly attracted to versions of the Expulsion that emphasized that the Jews were banished because they had committed economic and physical crimes against their Christian hosts. This interpretation was no doubt influenced by Elizabethan anxieties about an expanding alien population. While Tudor historians could not point to a single episode as decisive in leading to the Expulsion, their litanies of Jewish ritual murders, circumcisions, coin clippings, and other crimes committed by this alien community made Edward I's decision appear inevitable.

Despite the positive image with which Edward I was portrayed on the Elizabethan stage, many writers at the time did not flinch from stressing that the King had banished the Jews to line his own pockets. John Speed's description is representative: "King Edward . . . banished the Jews out of the realm, on account of their having eaten his people to the bones, not neglecting therein his particular gain."[29] Much the same line was taken by John Stow, who reminds his readers that Edward I exploited both the Jews and the commons: the "King made a mighty mass of money of their houses, which he sold, and yet the commons of England had granted and gave him [a tax of] a fifteenth of all their goods to banish them; and thus much for the Jews."[30] The playwright and historian Samuel Daniel also draws attention to Edward's profit motive: "Of no less grievance, the King the next year after eased his people by the banishment of the Jews. . . . And this King, having much to do for money (coming to an empty crown) was driven to all shifts possible to get it."[31]

By the time of the Interregnum and the ensuing debate over allowing Jews to resettle in England, the issue of the abuse of royal prerogative only hinted at by Tudor and Stuart historians had emerged as central to the meaning of the Expulsion. In addition, for those writing during the 1640s and 1650s, a good deal hinged on who had the authority to expel (or readmit) the Jews. After the execution of Charles I and the abolition of monarchy, did the edicts of kings like Edward I, if made without parliamentary approval, still have force? While William Prynne, for example, accepted as a matter of record that the "Jews had been formerly great clippers and forgers of money, and had crucified three or four children in England at least, which were the principal causes of their banishment,"[32] what really concerned him were the Expulsion's political lessons. Prynne, who was vehemently opposed to readmitting Jews but no less opposed to the arbitrary power of kings, found that his task of challenging Jewish readmission was complicated by the fact that "the particular Act and Parliament Roll for their banishment be utterly lost." Prynne nonetheless insisted that "their banishment was by the unanimous desire, judgment, edict, and decree both of the King and his Parliament, and not by the King alone. And this banishment" was "total . . . and likewise final: never to return into England."[33] D'Blossiers Tovey, who drew heavily on Prynne's work, departed from his predecessor in this important issue of parliamentary prerogative, arguing instead—as one would expect from someone writing after the Restoration of the monarchy in 1660 and Glorious Revolution of 1688—that the Expulsion offered a lesson in what happens when misguided policy destabilizes monarchical power. Tovey even speculates that if the Jews had not been expelled, the War of the Roses might have been avoided: "who can imagine, that if the Jews had continued in the kingdom, [King] Henry the Sixth would ever have been driven to supply his extravangancies by the beggarly shift of alchemy and sophistications of his coin!"[34] In an England rid of Jewish magic and coin clipping, kings who had once depended on Jews to fill their coffers now engaged in these Jewish practices themselves, with disastrous results for the nation.

The explanations offered by late nineteenth- and early twentieth-century historians, including for the first time Anglo-Jewish ones, give a sense of how England's social preoccupations had changed. The issues of Jewish criminality and royal prerogative recede as those of vulnerable Jewish legal status, the deteriorating economic position of the Jews, and deep-rooted antisemitism take their place as the primary causes of the Expulsion, explanations no doubt influenced by the large-scale immigration of poor Eastern European Jews into Victorian England, an influx that was finally curtailed with the institution of the Aliens Act in 1905.[35] William Prynne was surely turning in his grave when patriotic Anglo-Jewish historians of the early twentieth century explained that the Expulsion occurred because a generous monarch was forced to capitulate to the distasteful demands of a bigoted church and commons. Cecil Roth goes so far as to speak of Edward I's "pious resolve" in 1275 to end his reliance on Jewish usury (by forbidding the Jews to lend at interest) as a "well-meaning experiment" that "ended in failure."[36]

Only in the past few years has this account been seriously challenged, most scathingly by Colin Richmond, whose post-Holocaust perspective on the Expulsion leads him to depict Edward I as the consummate Jew-hater, a monarch who "deserves picking on" and who "knew exactly what he was doing on 18 July 1290." Richmond writes that Edward I "was a pioneering anti-Semite when he expelled the Jews," the "first European ruler to make his state permanently *Judenrein*."[37] For Richmond, the Expulsion was about a sense of Englishness grounded in anti-Jewishness:

> If by 1290 being Christian meant being anti-Jewish, did being anti-Jewish mean being English? The Expulsion is said to have been a "popular" measure. What may be meant by this is that it was done to please the parliamentary classes, who in summer 1290 granted the taxes Edward had asked them for. The only people in England in 1290 who may have regarded themselves as English were those parliamentary classes: the King, his bishops, his clerical bureaucrats, the judges, the barons, the knights, urban businessmen. These, I venture to suggest, were anti-Semites. It is, in other words, and entirely as one would expect, the governing elite who first equated Englishness with non-Jewishness.[38]

Richmond's work is strongly influenced by current scholarly interest in both English heritage[39] and nationalism, and is representative of the most recent revisionist wave of interpretations of the Expulsion, one that sees a reconfiguration of the English "political nation" as increasingly central to an adequate understanding of the Expulsion.[40] The historian most responsible for enabling this perspective is Robert Stacey, who has called into question many preconceived interpretations of the Expulsion and has come as close as anyone to piecing together what D'Blossiers Tovey deemed a "secret."[41] The first misconception Stacey corrects is that the Expulsion was an unprecedented act. He writes that expulsions "were not unusual in the high and late middle ages," and that in "England, foreign merchants, mainly Italians, were threatened with expulsions in the 1240s and again in the 1270s, although both threats were eventually bought off in return for cash payments to the crown."[42] Stacey thus shifts the question to 'Why in 1290?' since "in England, Jews could have been expelled at almost any date between 1066 and 1290." For him the "immediate answer lies . . . in a complex, four-month-long negotiation for taxation that took place between the King, his great men, and the representatives of the shires and boroughs in the Parliament of 1290." Edward I

> had returned in late 1289 from a three-year sojourn in Gascony that had left him deeply in debt, but without any obvious claim upon his subjects' purses. To pay his debts, he needed a tax; but to secure a tax, he was compelled to bargain with his subjects in parliament. The Expulsion of the Jews from England was the price the commons' representatives demanded for their consent to this voluntary grant of taxation.

Thus, the Expulsion "came about because the King concluded that he could not get the commons' consent to the tax he needed in any other way, and because anti-Jewish legislation had become by 1290 the essential precondition on which local society in England was prepared to vote voluntary taxation to the monarchy."[43]

This situation had also developed because in the century leading up to the Expulsion Jewish legal status had sunk. Like serfs, the "Jews were one of the groups in the kingdom which failed to make the transition" in the late twelfth century "from a basically Carolingian legal world of liberties to an essentially modern legal world which regarded liberty as a matter of civil rights guaranteed by a common law." Thus, not only in terms of their reduced legal status but in terms of their financial strength, the Jews were extremely vulnerable in 1290, ruinous taxation having reduced the community to a shadow of its former, vibrant self.

Stacey's conclusion—that the Jews were not expelled for any inevitable or ideological reason but because it was useful to Edward I "in negotiating with the much wider political nation which had emerged during the thirteenth century"[44]—has already led other scholars to reposition this explanation within the context of the origins of English nationalism.[45] In emphasizing the nationalist dimensions of the Expulsion order, Kenneth Stow concludes that "the Jews were expelled during what might be called a protracted constitutional crisis," a crisis that "occurred on ecclesiastical, baronial, and knightly fronts." Stow argues that as a result of this unusual confluence of political and economic objectives on the part of the clergy, the barons, the knights of the shires, the commons, and the crown, "it appears that for an instant, the expulsion truly did create 'one people'—at least the illusion of it."[46] The moment of stability in these relations did not last, of course, as we know from the barons' wars of the fourteenth century; indeed, as early as 1297 Edward I was forced once again to reconfirm the charters, having reneged on too many statutes. But what is becoming increasingly clear from the painstaking research of these medievalists is that in the struggle for prerogative between king, barons, knights, commons, and church, the Jews played a significant role, and the Expulsion proved to be less about English ill-will toward Jews (which, however, surely greased the various wheels of the decision) than about complex economic, legal, and political compromises, which helped forge and reconfirm the social and political configurations that, at this crucial juncture, were defining an emergent English nation. There can be no doubt that two thousand or so Jews, the remnants of what had been a larger and thriving community, were in fact expelled from England in 1290. There can also be no doubt that in the decades leading up to this banishment the Jews were brutally mistreated and the Jewish communities in England impoverished and eviscerated. But it is this final, sanitizing act of expulsion of the last two thousand or so Jews, rather than the gradual and often brutal disintegration of medieval English Jewry that preceded it, that has entered into history, and it has done so because of what it came to symbolize for the peoples who continued to inhabit England, and for their descendants in search of a satisfying narrative of their national past.

II. *The Jews were readmitted into England by Cromwell in 1656*

The Jews themselves pretend that Menasseh [ben Israel], before his departure procured for them such a firm and legal establishment as he desired. But upon the strictest inquiry I could never find any reason to believe it, there not being the least memorial of any such thing to be met with on our public registers.
—*D'Blossiers Tovey, 1738*[47]

We have no record of [the Readmission order] because the record has been destroyed. There does not seem to be any possibility of doubt on the matter.
—*Cecil Roth, 1961*[48]

Ralph Josselin, a minister in Essex, recorded in his diary on January 4, 1655, that he had dreamt the previous "night [that] one came to me and told me that Thurloe [Oliver Cromwell's Secretary of State] was turned Jew; I answered perhaps it was a mistake, he might declare he was a Jew born, the Jews having lived here, and he pretend by old writings his pedigree from them, to ingratiate with the Jews, or some compliance with them."[49] What are we to make of

Josselin's response in his dream that news of John Thurloe's conversion was "a mistake"? Not that this report was false, but that Thurloe was not really "turned Jew"; rather, he was simply pretending to be "a Jew born" for politic reasons. It is not entirely clear what it means here to "turn" Jew. Is this something one chooses to do, or is it somehow beyond one's control? Have religious or national identity become so unstable as to be vulnerable to such an unlikely transformation? Perhaps the most interesting feature of the dream is Josselin's notion that Thurloe would defend this claim by reinventing his "pedigree" through antiquarian records, "old writings" connecting his lineage back to the Jews who, centuries earlier, had lived in England. Here was the repressed returning with a vengeance: the buried past of medieval Anglo-Jewry was being unearthed at this time in unusual ways, some of them quite literal. The "common people," writes Tovey, "imagine that great treasures might be found by digging, which the Jews left behind them in hopes of a speedy return." In 1607, for example, "in Higham in Leicestershire" a large stone was dug up, "which lay in the great road," under which was found "a treasure of silver coin" judged "to have been Jewish."[50] The very walls built to protect Londoners from foreign threat revealed traces of England's Jewish past: John Stow records that when Ludgate was rebuilt in 1586 "there was found couched within the wall thereof a stone taken from one of the Jews' houses, wherein was graven in Hebrew characters" that "'this is the station or ward of Rabbi Moses, the son of the honourable Rabbi Isaac.'"[51] More significant for our purposes here was the unearthing of what Josselin calls "old writings," the recovery of archival material that was part of a broader attempt during the Interregnum to rewrite and reground English political and social history.

Josselin's dream may well have been based on a rumor circulating at the time that Cromwell and his circle were considering legally readmitting Jews to England, though almost a full year elapsed between Josselin's dream and the inception of the Whitehall Conference in December 1655, where Thurloe and a group of influential clergy, lawyers, and civic leaders chosen by Cromwell formally met to determine: "First, whether it be lawful, at all, to readmit the Jews?" and "Secondly, if it should be thought lawful, upon what terms to admit them?"[52]

The history of this so-called Readmission, like the Expulsion that preceded it, has generated a good deal of critical controversy.[53] Two issues in particular have been contested: Why did the English consider readmitting the Jews in 1656? And did the Jews legally resettle in this year? The alternative explanations for why the English considered readmitting Jews were concisely put by

William Prynne: either that "it may be a very probable hopeful means of the general calling and conversion of the Jewish nation to the Christian faith" or that the "allegation for bringing in the Jews is merely politic, that it will bring in much present and future gain and money to the state, and advance trad- ing."[54] Prynne's two categories—philosemitic millenarianism and economic self-interest—have held the field since 1656, and have been taken up on the one hand by David Katz, in his influential study *Philo-Semitism and the Readmission of the Jews to England*, and on the other by those who suggest instead that the "readmission of the Jews to England was part and parcel of the Commonwealth's mercantilist policy," though in "practice its results were far less dramatic and successful than its proponents might have hoped."[55]

To these two explanations I would add a third: the Readmission debate was not simply about the conversion or economic exploitation of the Jews but also, and perhaps more centrally, about redefining what it meant to be English during a period marked by social, religious, and political instability. The return to "old writings" signals the extent to which this was a debate grounded in the records of England's past about national identity and the validity of old laws still on the books, especially those that concerned heresy, conformity, and royal prerogative. In taking this approach, I would like to advance a related argument, one urged at the turn of this century but largely abandoned since then: contrary to popular belief, there was no formal or legal Readmission in 1656. Simply put, this historical "fact"—retailed today in scores of books about England in the seventeenth century—has strong elements of fiction, though a fiction that reveals much in turn about the construction of both English and Anglo-Jewish history.

To speak of a Readmission also presumes the Expulsion order that preceded it still had legal authority. As noted above, while medieval chroniclers recounting the events of 1290 made it clear that the Jews had indeed left England in that year, no parliamentary or even royal decree to this effect could be found to substantiate these accounts; all that survived were the writs Edward sent to his sheriffs informing them that the Jews were to leave England by November 1, 1290.[56] If these royal writs were the only surviving evidence, what authority did they carry in a monarchless England? Opponents of Readmission like Prynne were forced to argue the reason "the particular Act and Parliament Roll for their banishment be utterly lost" is that the Jews or their supporters had stolen or destroyed crucial documents.[57]

Compounding the problem of the Readmission was that, as with the Expulsion, no legislation survived to confirm that this was official policy. Tovey, reconsidering the issue in 1738, notes that while the "Jews themselves pretend that" they had obtained "a firm, and legal, establishment," he never could, even "upon the strictest inquiry," find "any reason to believe it, there not being the least memorial of any such thing to be met with on our public registers."[58] And in a mirror image of Prynne's claims that Jews had destroyed the Expulsion order, Cecil Roth briefly maintained that "we have no record of it because the record has been destroyed. There does not seem to be any possibility of doubt on the matter." According to Roth's conspiracy theory, "two pages were cut out of the Minute Book of the Council of State between the minutes of the meeting on Tuesday 24 June and that of Thursday 26 June 1656," the minutes having been "destroyed for political reasons."[59] Roth subsequently backed away from this claim, but his initial overzealousness may be partially excused, since even contemporaries were confused about the status of the Jews' petition for readmission.[60] Rumors about the return of the Jews had circulated as early as 1649, when Presbyterians warned of the design of Cromwell and his cohort to "plunder and disarm the City of London and all the country round about . . . and so sell it (the plunder) in bulk to the Jews, whom they have lately admitted to set up their banks and magazines of trade amongst us contrary to an Act of Parliament for their banishment."[61]

To complicate matters further, virtually all parties concerned in the debate were aware that there were Jews already living in England who practiced their faith in private, and that there had been a Jewish presence in England since at least the turn of the century, and perhaps earlier as well.[62] James Howell wrote from London in 1653 to a friend in Amsterdam regarding "Judaism," that "some corners of our city smell as rank of it as doth your's there."[63] Twenty leading Jewish households were well enough known. Cromwell had himself granted denizen status to a number of Jews, and had recently interceded in behalf of a prominent one, Manuel Dormido, whom he describes as a Jew in a letter to the King of Portugal.[64] I suspect that Thomas Browne's remark about numbers of secret Jews currently living in England, published in 1646, spoke to the fears of many of his countrymen: "according to good relations, where they may freely speak it," Browne writes, the Jews "forbear not to boast that there are at present many thousand Jews in Spain, France, and England, and some dispensed withall even to the degree of priesthood."[65] The author of *Anglo-Judaeus* writes in a similar vein in 1656 that since "they have been bolder to return hither, it's more then to be feared, they have made many proselytes; and that if they might with impunity show themselves, and had toleration of their religion, and an open way of their worship granted, hundreds, if not thousands, would then appear, who now are veiled under the name of Christians."[66] And the convert Paul Isaiah confirmed in 1655 that "though perhaps there may not be now in England, any great numbers of professed Jews (some to my own knowledge there are, who have their synagogues, and there exercise Judaism) yet, they who live here, as often as they are bound to use their office of prayer (which is twice a day) so often are they bound to blaspheme Christ."[67]

The Whitehall Conference of December 1655 was thus not about allowing Jews into England—some were already there, others continued to arrive—but rather about what rights should be granted them, and thus what their legal and social identity in England should be. A number of accounts of the conference survive. All, including the sympathetic view expressed by a participant, Henry Jessey, acknowledge that the conference ended inconclusively.[68] Tovey, who reprints the published record of this meeting, notes that nothing was resolved and that Cromwell concluded that instead of "clearing" the case, the debate "had made the matter more doubtful."[69] The *Parliamentary History* records that on December 4 the meeting ended with "nothing being concluded on"; the meeting three days later similarly came to a close with "nothing being resolved upon"; that of the 14th "broke up without coming to any resolution"; and finally the last one on December 18—opened by Cromwell to the public and highlighted by the Protector's own views on the matter—ended with "nothing . . . declared upon."[70] The rapidly published report of these proceedings was no doubt intended to squelch misleading rumors.[71] The deliberations and the interest they generated drew international attention. A Swedish diplomat in London, Peter Julius Coyet, reported back to King Charles X on December 28 that there was no "decision yet about the Jews." Cromwell "proceeds very cautiously; the theologians strongly oppose it, from every pulpit."[72] This last observation should make us think twice about how widespread philosemitism was among the clergy, and about how influential a force it was in promoting Readmission.

As the Swede's letter suggests, there was still much confusion after the Whitehall Conference ended. Though John Evelyn noted in his diary entry of December, 14, 1655, that "now were the Jews admitted,"[73] the foreign Jews who had arrived in London with great expectations were not as sanguine. Henry Jessey records that many

> Jewish merchants had come from beyond seas to London, and hoped they might have enjoyed as much privilege here, in respect of trading, and of their worshipping the God of Abraham, Isaac, and Jacob, here, in synagogues, publicly, as they enjoyed in Holland, and did enjoy in Poland, Prussia, and other places. But after the conference and debate at Whitehall was ended, they heard by some, that the greater part of the ministers were against this. Therefore they removed hence again to beyond the seas, with much grief of heart, that they were thus disappointed of their hopes.[74]

Envoys from Venice and Tuscany wrote home in December saying that after "long disputes and late at night the meeting dissolved without any conclusion, the discussion being postponed to another more convenient day."[75] Ralph Josselin writes in his diary on December 16 of "great rumours of the Jews being

admitted into England" and of "hopes thereby to convert them." He again
betrays his fear of the English turning Jewish, and this time it is not just Thurloe who is in danger of turning: "The Lord hasten their conversion, and keep

us from turning aside from Christ to Moses, of which I am very heartily
afraid."[76]

Anti-Jewish revisionism at the time went so far as to suggest, unfairly, that
Cromwell had actually been dead set against Jewish Readmission. Colonel
Whitley writes from Calais to Sir Edward Nicholas a month after the Whitehall Conference broke up "that Cromwell says it is an ungodly thing to intro-
duce the Jews."[77] Revisionism on the part of Anglo-Jewish historians has since
kept pace as well. So much so that the Jewish Historical Society of England at
the turn of this century decided—largely on the basis of a pair of contemporary allusions—that there was sufficient proof to establish an annual holiday,
"Resettlement Day," to be celebrated on February 4. While cautious voices
pointed to "the futility of attempting to create an anniversary for which there
is no historical justification," their advice was ignored.[78] David Cesarani
describes how Resettlement Day "assumed ritual status" in the decade after its
initial celebration in 1894, and was celebrated "in ever more expansive and lav-
ish fashion," reaching its "climax in February 1906 with the two hundred and
fiftieth anniversary celebration."[79] Cesarani underscores what for him are the
obvious historical pressures that produced this celebration:

> Surely it was less than a coincidence that at a time when there was a powerful
> movement to *prevent* Jewish immigration, English Jews were pointing to
> Cromwell who called them *back* into England. . . . The anniversary celebration in
> 1906 was held barely two months after the Aliens Act came into force. Again, was
> it just coincidental that the organizers of the banquet invited the former Conser-
> vative Prime Minister, Arthur Balfour, who had forced the Act through Parlia-
> ment in 1905?

For the record, Balfour declined the invitation, but sent a letter "emphatically
affirming that there was no 'Jewish Question' in England because 'the Jews
have themselves shown themselves entirely worthy of the rights and privileges
which they enjoy as citizens of this country.' "[80] The various Jewish and Gentile speakers who were in attendance at this commemorative event placed great
weight on what the event meant not only for the Jews but also for the English,
especially for their tradition of toleration. Lucien Wolf, for example, spoke of
how the Whitehall Conference "was epoch-making not only in Jewish, but
also in English, history. It widened the scope of the struggle for freedom; [and]
it postulated for the first time the true limitations of that struggle." Wolf por-
trays Cromwell and Menasseh ben Israel as Christian and Jew, "standing

together in the dawn of English liberty, twin champions of a wronged people, and heralds of a free state." Other speakers, such as Professor G. W. Prothero, praised the racial advantages of Readmission. For Prothero, what the English "are in politics, in commerce, in literature, we owe largely to the fervid temperament of the Celt, to the doggedness of the Saxon, to the political genius of the Norman, and to the daring of the Dane. That was the fourfold woof out of which our nation existed before the time of Oliver Cromwell," who "added a fifth thread, one more subtle, more capable, more competent than any other— that thread of Jewish origin."[81] One can only wonder if Jews in the audience were shifting uneasily in their seats as they listened to racial theorizing that admitted them into the fabric of English life while insisting on marking them as temperamentally different.

Fifty years later, a decade after the end of the Second World War and only a few years after quickly forgotten anti-Jewish riots in major British cities,[82] the tercentenary of the "Re-settlement of the Jews" was celebrated. The symbolic rituals of cultural acceptance that marked the celebrations are telling: an exhibit at the Victoria and Albert Museum, a banquet at Guildhall, a Garden Party at Lambeth Palace, and a commemorative volume.[83] We are left, then, with multiple and competing histories of the Readmission, histories that from an Anglo-Jewish perspective are about belonging to the dominant English community, and from an English perspective about myths celebrating their tolerance of outsiders.

In the 1650s, too, interest in readmitting the Jews turned on the question of their place within an English commonwealth. And the reasons offered for their exclusion from that commonwealth (since they were believed to endanger both the wealth and the common interests of the nation) give a good sense of English political instability at this time. The author of *Anglo-Judaeus* explains that "now there is the opportunity for perverters to stir matter," and that there "be certain times and seasons, which make that at one time dangerous, which might at another be admitted with more security.... This we must confess is the condition of our country at present; and I fear the Jews do well consider it. By so much the more therefore as they may desire to come in, doubtless in this respect the State hath as great to deny them."[84] For William Prynne, the "bringing of the Jews at this season, when the people are so generally divided" and "discontented . . . is the most probable means 'to disturb the peace of the nation.'"[85] Prynne justifies his claim by reminding readers of "the Jews themselves in all ages having been principle firebrands of sedition both in their own land, and all places where they have dispersed."[86] James Howell writes in a similar vein in 1653 that "'tis well known what runagates and landlopers they have been up and down the world."[87]

To claim that a formal, legal Readmission took place in 1656 is thus to assent to a set of unexamined assumptions about the legitimacy of the Expulsion, the absence of Jews before this date from England, and the nature of English toleration. Nonetheless, an important consequence of the inconclusive debate over legitimizing the right of Jews to live in England was that those who at this time tried to exclude the Jews on the basis of their ineradicable difference were forced to explain what the basis of the difference was. Ultimately, this challenge to define the Jews as somehow extrinsic to that which was English eventually demanded a more precise definition of the national, religious, and racial characteristics of Englishness itself. Despite the fact that Jews in increasing numbers began to enter England in the closing decades of the seventeenth century, and despite their success in securing royal protection, these Jews knew all too well that their status remained provisional and subject to challenge.

III. There were no Jews in Shakespeare's England

From the time of Edward to that of Cromwell no Jew touched English ground.
—J. R. Green, 1884[88]

Jews figured in the epoch-making controversies which raged round the divorce of Henry VIII, and Jews gave substantial assistance to Elizabeth when as the head of European Protestantism she waged a life and death struggle with Spain.
—Lucien Wolf, 1894[89]

In 1290 Edward I ordered about 16,000 of them to leave England. Until the days of Oliver Cromwell few Jewish feet touched English soil.
—Baldwin Smith, 1966[90]

Despite the blanket claims of Victorian historians (and their modern successors) that there were few or no Jews in Shakespeare's England, archival research over the past hundred years makes it clear that small numbers of Jews began drifting back into England almost immediately after the Expulsion, and began to arrive in larger numbers during the Tudor period. It has nonetheless proven difficult for this research to shake the myth of an England essentially free of Jews during these years. The period between 1880 and 1910 in particular witnessed a struggle between those who began to assert a Jewish presence in Shakespeare's England and those who rejected the merits of such claims. Looking back a century later, it is clear that the latter forces have been far more successful, and the current belief, overwhelmingly subscribed to by scholars in the field, is that there were few if any Jews in Elizabethan England. The debate itself is an exhausting and in many ways a foolish one. Its persistence can best be explained by looking past the circular arguments about how many Jews constitute a Jewish presence in Elizabethan England to what is more profoundly at stake in this controversy: whether Jews should be recognized as belonging to

England's past. For to trace Anglo-Jewry's past back to the sixteenth century is to stake a claim in the most celebrated age of English history, a period that encompassed the Reformation, the reign of England's most celebrated monarch, Elizabeth I, and its most celebrated playwright, Shakespeare. As Victorian Anglo-Jewish scholars understood, proving that one belongs to this particular part of the English past also made it easier to defend one's place in England's present.

When Sidney L. Lee (who had anglicized his given name, Solomon Lazarus) read his landmark paper on "Elizabethan England and the Jews" at the 131st meeting of the New Shakspere Society on February 10, 1888,[91] prevailing accounts of the place of the Jews in England's past were uncharitable, to say the least. Popular histories, like J. R. Green's *A Short History of the English People*, firmly reiterated the narrative that had remained in place since Prynne: "From the time of Edward to that of Cromwell no Jew touched English ground."[92] Green's account of the place of the Jews in relation to the English people before their Expulsion is even darker. He writes in the 1878 edition of his *History* that "the Jew had no right or citizenship in the land. The Jewry in which he lived was exempt from the common law. He was simply the King's chattel." Green utterly rejects the "picture which is commonly drawn of the Jew as timid, silent, crouching under oppression, however truly it may represent the general position of his race throughout medieval Europe," arguing that it was "far from being borne out by historical fact on this side of the Channel." For Green, a more accurate view was one that recognized how in "England the attitude of the Jew, almost to the very end, was an attitude of proud and even insolent defiance." Green also goes to considerable lengths to ghettoize the defiant and insolent Jewry. He writes of the Oxford Jewish community, for example, that here "as well as elsewhere the Jewry was a town within a town, with its own language, its own religion and law, its peculiar commerce, its peculiar dress. No city bailiff could penetrate into the square of little alleys which lay behind the present Town hall." In Green's fertile imagination, even Jewish buildings anthropomorphically took on this characteristic arrogance: "the Church itself was powerless to prevent a synagogue from rising in haughty rivalry over against the cloister of St. Frideswide."[93] Had Green examined the extensive extant records of the Plea Rolls of the Exchequer of the Jews, he would have seen how inaccurate his account of communal relations was. Eager to put the lie to such distorted versions of the past, the Jewish Historical Society decided shortly after it was founded that one of its first tasks was to publish material from the Plea Rolls showing how extensive dealings were between Jewish and Christian neighbors throughout medieval England.[94]

It was against this kind of popular history of "the English people" that Sidney Lee and his successors had to struggle and their excesses in combating these stereotypes can be understood (how does one respond to Green's habit of describing Jews collectively in the singular form, "the Jew"?). The influ-ence of Green's *History* is apparent from a lecture given by Arthur Quiller-Couch in 1916 while he was a Professor of English Literature at Cambridge University. Quiller-Couch told his audience that few "in this room are old enough to remember the shock of awed surprise which fell upon young minds presented in the late 'seventies and early 'eighties of the last century with Free-man's *Norman Conquest* or Green's *Short History of the English People*; in which as through parting clouds of darkness, we beheld our ancestry, literary as well as political, radiantly legitimised."[95] This radiance and the deep need for legit-imacy meant obscuring and delegitimizing others, including those "insolent" Jews of England's past.

It is important to stress that this view, while predominant among Victorian historians, was not universally accepted. It was sharply refuted by those like Luke Owen Pike, who maintained that the English themselves, and not the Jews, had been the criminals: if

> it could be said with strict precision of language that a nation can commit a crime, it would be true that one of the greatest national crimes ever committed, was committed in England when the Jews were expelled through the combined influ-ence of the clergy, the traders and the barons. . . . This remarkable episode in English history is specially worthy of note in a history of crime both because it is in itself an illustration of the bigotry, jealousy, and contracted partisanship through which barbarism had to pass in its progress towards civilization, and because there is good reason to suspect that it has a very close connection with one of the most audacious robberies ever perpetrated.[96]

The effort of Anglo-Jewish historians to offer an alternative version of the national past and the place of the Jews in it was spearheaded by Sidney Lee. Lee, who wrote the *Dictionary of National Biography* entries on Shakespeare as well as Roderigo Lopez, was also invited to provide an account of the "Jews in England" for the revised 1896 edition of the popular and frequently reprinted *Dictionary of English History*.[97] In this *Dictionary* entry Lee made clear that it "is frequently stated that after the banishment of 1290 no Jews came to Eng-land until the later years of Cromwell's Protectorate, but special investigation of the subject leaves little doubt that small numbers of them were present in the country from the fourteenth to the seventeenth century."[98] Nonetheless, Lee's entry had little impact on how traditional British historians dealt with early modern England's Jewish presence.[99]

The turn of century witnessed an institutionalized reinvention of an English past—what is now called the heritage industry—committed to rewriting the history of English society. The publication of various calendars of state papers gave a huge boost to this enterprise, as did the creation of university positions in the fields of history and English and the founding of organizations like the British Academy and the English Association. One by-product of this activity was the decision of the Jewish community of England to hold its first public exhibition celebrating the place of Jews in English history and culture. The successful Anglo-Jewish Historical Exhibition of 1887 in the Albert Hall was followed by the publication of an exhibition catalogue and the compilation of a major reference work, the *Bibliotheca Anglo-Judaica*. Six years later the Jewish Historical Society of England was founded and in its lectures and publications committed itself to reclaiming the rightful place of the Jews in England's heritage. This scholarly enterprise was also motivated by the challenge posed by the infusion of poor Eastern European Jews into England at this time, which threatened to undermine the political and social gains the three-centuries-old Anglo-Jewish community had quietly won for itself.[100]

Despite its impressive efforts, the Jewish Historical Society failed to penetrate the protective barriers set up by those authorized to write England's past. To get a sense of the degree of its failure, one need only turn to the standard volumes of the Oxford History of England, where, to pick but one example, the index to J. B. Black's *The Reign of Elizabeth*, published in 1959,[101] contains not a single entry on Jews. As for J. R. Green's legacy—and he is just a representative example—it continued to shape the way the place of the Jews in English society was recorded. As Baldwin Smith shows in his *A History of England*, published as recently as 1966, some myths die hard: "In 1290 Edward I ordered about 16,000 of them to leave England. Until the days of Oliver Cromwell few Jewish feet touched English soil."[102]

This situation has not gone unnoticed by modern historiographers. The story of why and how Jews have been written out of conventional medieval and early modern European national histories is the subject of Gavin Langmuir's searing critique, "Majority History and Postbiblical Jews."[103] Reviewing several centuries' worth of European (including English) histories published up through the 1960s, Langmuir, well-placed as an outsider in the debate, concludes that "majority historiography as it relates to Jews has been marked by lack of interest and by ignorance, when it has not also been marked by derogatory attitudes." Having inherited "a historiographic tradition hostile toward or ignorant of Jews, or both, and writing for a society little interested in Jewish history or more or less hostile to Jews, historians of the majority have been little attracted to Jewish history." Compounding this lack of interest has been "the tendency of historians, until recently, to stress actions rather than attitudes, to divide ideas under convenient categories rather than to search for their underlying bias, to avoid the shadowy area of social psychology," and, I would add, cultural and social history.[104]

It is in this context that Lucien Wolf's 1893 inaugural address to the newly formed Jewish Historical Society of England, "A Plea for Anglo-Jewish History," needs to be read. Wolf makes explicit why the sixteenth century was so crucial in defining the place of Jews in English history:

> One of the earliest tasks of this Society will be to ascertain the exact role enacted by Jews both in England and abroad on the passage of this country from Roman Catholicism to Protestantism. Enough is already known to show that this role was by no means inconsiderable. Jews figured in the epoch-making controversies which raged round the divorce of Henry VIII, and Jews gave substantial assistance to Elizabeth when as the head of European Protestantism she waged a life and death struggle with Spain.

For Wolf, this Jewish-influenced Reformation in Tudor England proved decisive to the reconfiguration of England's political and religious nature, and helped define England's particular greatness by having "inspired a great struggle for political freedom and a great constitutional revision." This revitalized and reformed England was also a more tolerant one, which, Wolf asserted, instituted a shift from a medieval, New Testament-based Catholicism that had banished the Jews to an Old Testament-inspired Protestant philosemitism: "This struggle . . . is not only the key to English social and political progress, but it also affords the explanation of the reversal by the English people in 1655 of the banishment which they had decreed against the Jews three and a half centuries before."[105] Subsequent research showed that the reality fell far short of Wolf's greatly inflated claims in this "Plea" for the direct role of the Jews in sixteenth- and seventeenth-century England, but we have here at the founding moment of the society some sense of how deeply the Anglo-Jewish community needed to ground itself in this most celebrated period of Protestant England's cultural and political past.

David Cesarani, reviewing the efforts of these early years of the Jewish Historical Society, has argued that the "construction of the Anglo-Jewish past, its heritage, was to stress the rootedness of Jews in English society and their positive contributions to politics, culture and the economy." Cesarani also points out what subjects were therefore taboo: the "discussion of anti-semitism was to be avoided because to raise it as an issue risked the appearance of ingratitude." Instead, the "readmission, the community of the resettlement and the emancipation period offered the perfect synthesis of Jewish and English heritage." They "melded together the story of the Jews with the notion of progress towards a liberal society, the glorious national institute of Parliament, and the careers of statesmen such as Cromwell, Disraeli and Gladstone, heroic and quintessentially English figures."[106]

While the Anglo-Jewish community has subsequently come to celebrate the resettlement of Jews in England in the period between the Expulsion and the Readmission, it is important to note that its initial reception to research into this past was surprisingly cool, in part because of fears that archival digging would unearth evidence of Jewish crimes. Reporting on Lucien Wolf's impressive findings, an editorial in the *Jewish Chronicle* of May 20, 1887, hints at these misgivings:

> It says much for the industry of Mr. Lucien Wolf that he was able in his paper at the Exhibition to add several facts to the exhaustive researches of Mr. S. L. Lee on the subject of the Jews in England between 1290 and 1656—a subject which the latter gentleman has made his own. . . . The character of the Jews who were here under those circumstances was not of the brightest, and the page thus added to Anglo-Jewish History is a rather tarnished one. Still it is something to add a page to history.[107]

The lead editorial in the same issue provides some context for this ambivalence: "There had recently been much talk about the influx of foreign Jews into this country, and absurdly exaggerated views have been expressed as to the extent of this addition to our numbers." Moreover, a

> new Jewry is arising rapidly in the East End with the views of which English Jews are for the most part entirely ignorant. Thus it is alleged that Socialism is rife among the Jews of the East End and the cry is raised that the influx of foreign Jews is importing the worser forms of Socialism into London. We believe this to be an entirely erroneous impression based upon the appearance of a few isolated cases of Socialistic views among East End Jews.[108]

The message is clear: to the extent that the lives of the Jews that Wolf reconstructs show them to be good English citizens and forerunners of the current Anglo-Jewish community, then that page added to history is a valued one. To the extent that they call to mind an "influx of foreign Jews" whose practices and political views are incompatible with those of the English (and of established Jews), such pages of history are "tarnished."

The archival evidence collected by Anglo-Jewish historians between 1880 and 1910 about Jews in Tudor England was substantial; additional material has been discovered since then as well. Given the fact that this evidence is scattered (as well as buried in journals that are not easily accessible or in books long out of print), it is useful, I think, to set out the scope of these investigations, weaving in, at various points, what has since been discovered.

The expulsion of Jews from Spain in 1492, followed by the forced conversion and then expulsion of Jews from Portugal, provided a strong impetus to the migration into England of individual Jews and gradually to the formation there of small Marrano communities. As early as 1492 the Spanish ambassador was complaining to English authorities about Spanish Jews living in London. Henry VII replied that he would "punish soundly any Jew or heretic to be found in his realms."[109] Nonetheless, King Henry and the Tudor monarchs that succeeded him did tolerate small numbers of Jews in England for the simple reason that they proved useful. Their numbers included merchants, a mining expert, teachers and translators of Hebrew, and physicians.

We know that in late 1530 and early 1531, King Henry VIII, concerned with the legal issues involved in divorcing Catherine of Aragon, sent for Jewish advisors. One who arrived in London at this time was Marco Raphael, a Venetian.[110] According to Charles V's ambassador in London, Eustace Chapuys, Raphael was a Jew "who pretends to have been baptized some time ago." Chapuys further reported that Raphael "has already seen the King twice, and been very well received, though not so well on the first as on the second audience." We also learn from Chapuys's correspondence that "the pith of the Jew's argument" was that rather than divorce Queen Catherine, Henry should simply take a second wife (something allowable under Ashkenazic Jewish law at this time under special circumstances). Marco Raphael soon outlived his usefulness, though he remained in London for three years.

Curiously, in the course of Henry's proceedings against her, Queen Catherine, along with her daughter Mary, stood as godmothers in 1532 to two foreign Jewesses, whose names are recorded as "Aysa Pudewya and Omell Faytt Isya." After their conversion the two were renamed Katherine Wheteley and Mary Cook, respectively.[111] These new Christians lived out the remainder of their lives in the Domus Conversorum, a house for converted Jews located on Chancery Lane first established by Henry III, in which converts were in residence for most of the sixteenth century.[112] What these two Jewish women were doing in England, and whether there were others who had the financial means to live outside of the Domus Conversorum (or Jews who chose not to convert), we will probably never know.

From 1290 until the mid-sixteenth century there is no evidence of organized communities of Jews in England. This changed after 1540, once Charles V had granted permission to New Christians to settle in the Netherlands, spurring Marrano migration, which was further accelerated by the establishment of the Inquisition in Portugal between 1537 and 1540.[113] The records of the Inquisitions in Spain, Portugal, and Italy provide the most detailed evidence of Jewish life in England at this time. Wolf's archival research turned up a total of sixty-nine Jewish men, women, and children who had been in England, had spent time there, or had relatives still there between 1539 and 1544.[114] We learn, for example, from the testimony of Gaspar Lopes before inquisitors on December 27, 1540, that he knew "Alves Lopes in London in whose house he . . . lived for four or five days." Lopes told the inquisitors that his host "holds a synagogue in his house and lives in the Hebrew manner, though in secret," and that

> in this synagogue they went on one day only, the Sabbath; and that on that day there came to Alves's house other false Christians to the number of about twenty, among whom he saw: Diego della Rogna and his wife, Enrico de Tovar and his wife, Jorge Diez, Goncales de Capra and his wife, Peter, their son, and his wife, Antonio della Rogna, Anna Pinta and Rodrigo Pinto, her brother, and others from London whose names he knows not at present; and that it is true that whenever any refugee false Christians come from Portugal to go to England and Flanders and thence to Turkey and elsewhere, in order to lead the lives of Hebrews, they come to the house of the said Alves, who helps them to go whither they want to go for this purpose.[115]

In addition, English sources indicate that in 1540 "a family of Spanish silk weavers were indicted" in London before the King's Bench for "holding firm to their 'Jewish and heretical faith,' for observing the Jewish sabbath and breaking the Christian one."[116] At roughly the same time, around 1541, Privy Council documents reveal that unnamed individuals, "suspected to be Jews," were arrested in London.[117] They might have been members of the community that centered around Alves Lopes. Alternatively, they might have been part of a different group of Jews, of Italian descent, who had been invited to England as court musicians, the Lupos, Bassanos, and Comys. Evidence to support this claim comes from the remark recorded by Eustace Chapuys, who describes the "New Christians who came from Portugal" that were imprisoned, and jokes about how they may sing well, but cannot fly away.[118]

More Inquisition testimony from the mid-1550s provides a glimpse into Jewish communities outside of London. In 1556 a "Portuguese sailor named Jurdao Vaz appeared before the Lisbon Inquisition and denounced Thomas Fernandes of Evora as a Marrano whom he had known some years before as an observant Jew in Bristol in England." They had quarreled over "a transaction in cloth," and Fernandes sued him; in revenge Vaz denounced Fernandes to the Lisbon Inquisition. From Thomas Fernandes's confession we know that Samuel Usque's history circulated among (and was copied by) members of the Jewish communities in England. In his deposition Fernandes gave the names of twenty-two Marranos living in Bristol and London in the decade between

1545 and 1555 (for the most part he omitted the names of wives and children). He also specified that the Bristol community held religious services in the house of Henrique Nuñez, and Yom Kippur was observed as well as the Sabbath and festivals. Nuñez's wife, Beatriz Fernandes, taught new Marranos prayers, baked unleavened bread for Passover, and in her trips to London "had trouble to find clean things to eat in the inns, and things which had not been cooked in pans used by Christians." The testimony notes that "she would not eat anything but what Jews are accustomed to eat acccording to their rites."[119] There were also connections between the Bristol and London communities. Thomas Fernandes told the inquisitors that he knew Hector Nuñez, a physician who lived in London and "sent word every year to his uncle [in Bristol] of the days on which Jewish festivals would fall." He also testified that "Simon Ruiz, New Christian, residing in London, used to write to tell his said uncle the date of the Passover of Unleavened Bread, and the Fast of [Yom] Kippur, and this confessant saw the letters in which he wrote this."[120]

Other Inquisition records—largely unexplored since Wolf's research at the turn of this century—offer further glimpses still. In March 1557, for example, "a slave of Gregorio Luiz, a New Christian, in the service of the Infante Dom Luiz, accused his master of going to England to visit his Marrano relatives. He lived there with one of them, named Ruy Nogueira. The informer accused Nogueira, his wife and Luiz of having tried to seduce him from the Christian faith."[121] Unfortunately, there has been no systematic attempt to collect casual allusions to anonymous Jews in this period, such as the record of a Jewish boy, caught "playing with false dice," who was brought to Christ's Hospital;[122] the Privy Council report of a "Doctor Arnande" who in 1562 was "esteemed to be a Jew and judged to ride through the streets in a cart";[123] or the memorandum from 1572 in Ipswich recording the payment of sixpence "for whipping of a Jewish man."[124]

That Jews continued to live in London without provocation is made clear from the *Confession of Faith* written by Nathaniel Menda, a Jew from Barbary, who had "been conversant among" the English for "five years" before his conversion, under the supervision of John Foxe, in 1577. Foxe published the Latin version of the conversion sermon along with Menda's confession in 1578, and the text was translated into English and republished that same year. After his conversion Menda moved into the Domus Conversorum and lived there until his death in 1608. For most of that time—from 1581 to 1598—he had for a companion a fellow convert, Cooba Massa, who took the name Fortunatus Massa. Elizabethans curious about Jewish practices would not have had far to seek in London to speak with those raised as Jews.

Perhaps the largest surviving body of evidence of the presence of Jews in Shakespeare's England concerns those Jews living in London in the last decade of the sixteenth century and the first of the seventeenth. In 1588 the prisoner of war Pedro de Santa Cruz was repatriated to Madrid after being detained in London for ten months. Once home he offered testimony against the Marranos he had encountered in England: it "is public and notorious in London," he told the inquisitors, "that by race they are all Jews, and it is notorious that in their own homes they live as such observing their Jewish rites; but publicly they attend Lutheran Churches, and listen to the sermons, and take the bread and wine in the manner and form as do the other heretics [i.e., Protestants]."[125] One of the accused was Dunstan Ames (or Añes). When Ames died in April 1594 and was buried under his pew at St. Olave's Church, London, his long-time fellow parishioners and his neighbors in Crutched Friars would probably have remembered him as a successful alien immigrant with a large family who had done quite well for himself in the business world: first freeman of the Grocer Company (though technically a "stranger"), then "purveyor and merchant for the Queen Majesty's Grocery," and finally, gentleman, having successfully applied for a coat of arms in 1568. While five of his fourteen children were christened with Old Testament names—Benjamin, Jacob, Hester, Rachel, and Sarah—there was probably little other outward indication that he might have secretly practiced Judaism. In fact, there is no evidence that the churchgoing Dunstan was an observant Jew at all. Yet we know that he was born into a Converso family in Valladolid, Spain, and was brought as an infant to England, via Portugal, around 1520. His elder brother Francisco also assimilated successfully into English society, entering the military, commanding the English garrison at Youghal, Ireland, and subsequently serving as burgomaster of that town. Dunstan's eldest son Benjamin was in Francis Walsingham's employ, gathering intelligence abroad, while his daughter Sarah had the ill luck of marrying the doomed Roderigo Lopez, who was executed shortly after his father-in-law passed away. The only other evidence that Jewish ties persisted in the Ames clan comes from Thomas Coryate, who in his travels to Constantinople in 1612 witnessed a circumcision at the "house of a certain English Jew, called Amis [sic], borne in Crutched Friars in London, who hath two sisters more of his own Jewish Religion . . . who were likewise born in the same place." The infant was probably Dunstan Ames's grandson. It is worth noting that Coryate expresses no surprise at encountering an "English Jew," one who "for the love he bore to our English nation, in the which he lived till he was thirty years of age . . . received us with very courteous entertainment."[126] Only in the tolerant world of Constantinople were Dunstan Ames's son and daughters able to live openly as Jews. The only other evidence suggesting that Dunstan Ames was a practicing Jew like his son and daughters comes from the Inquisition deposition of Pedro de Santa Cruz.

Other depositions from early on in James I's reign show that a Portuguese

Marrano community continued to thrive in London and that Jews continued to move between England and the continent. Vicente Furtado told the Inquisition in 1609 that four years earlier he had visited with Jews in London on his way to Amsterdam and Hamburg. He stayed in London at the home of two of them, Gabriel Fernandes and his younger brother Duarte Fernandes. Gabriel gave him an Old Testament in Spanish, and told him "that by keeping the Law of Moses he should observe the Sabbaths . . . that he should fast on the . . . day which they call *Kippur*, and that in July [during Tishah b'Av, commemorating the destruction of the Temple] he should also fast." Furtado added that he was also urged "not [to] eat pork or rabbit, nor believe in Christ . . . and that he should keep the Passover." Since Furtado happened to be in London during Passover, he was able to observe the holiday there, and on the first and last two days of the holiday and on the Sabbath in between "wore clean linen. . . . and ate unleavened bread." Furtado even listed those "resident in London" who celebrated the holiday with them, including Jeronimo Lopez, Lopo Rodrigues de Moura and his two brothers, as well as Gomes Davila who was "married to an Englishwoman."[127]

This Portuguese Marrano circle in London, whose leading citizens included physicians like Hector Nuñez and Roderigo Lopez and merchants like Alvaro de Lima, Jeronimo Lopez, Gabriel Fernandes, Fernando del Mercado, and Dustan Ames, numbered at least eighty or ninety.[128] This community was well enough established so that Salomon Cormano, the envoy of the Jewish Duke of Metilli, had no difficulties in finding fellow Jews to pray with during his embassy to England in 1592. Edward Barton, the English ambassador in Constantinople, complained to Lord Burghley in August 1592 that Cormano "and all his train used publicly the Jews' rites in praying, accompanied with diverse secret Jews resident in London."[129] But there appears to have been no official reaction to this kind of accusation, even when made in English courts. For example, in 1596 Mary May, widow of Richard May, brought charges at Chancery Court against two Portuguese Jews, Ferdinando Alvarez and Alvaro de Lima, and in the course of the testimony it was revealed that Jewish observances were held at the home of Portuguese Jews living in Duke's Place, London.[130] But there is no recorded expression of indignation, nor were charges of recusancy brought against the two.

When Jews were caught breaking the law in Tudor and Stuart England, their Jewishness could become a matter of public notice. Take, for example, the case of Ferdinando Lopus, "a Jew born, by report," who "should once have been burnt in Portingale." Lopus was a physician who lived as a "stranger" in St. Helen's Ward, London. He was arrested in a roundup in London in 1550 of those guilty of "bawdry" and "whoredom." Charles Wriothesley recorded at the time that Lopus was "cast for whoredom and condemned for the same," and though his punishment was temporarily stayed by the intervention of

Charles V's ambassador as well as members of the Privy Council, the majority of the council determined that "he should be banished the realm of England for ever, never to return upon pain of death." Though well connected to those at the highest levels of government, Lopus was not spared the public humiliation to which all offenders guilty of such crimes were subjected, and before his banishment he was paraded in a cart through the streets of London, wearing a "ray" or striped hood, in sign of his criminal behavior.[131]

The most notorious case of Jewish criminality in Elizabethan England is of course that of doctor Roderigo Lopez, mentioned briefly earlier, who had been resident in England since 1559 (and perhaps a relative of Ferdinando), and who was tried and executed in 1594 for an alleged plot to poison Queen Elizabeth. Well before the scandal broke, however, he was referred to as a Jew: Gabriel Harvey describes in his marginalia a "Doctor Lopez, the Queen's physician," who "is descended of Jews, but [is] himself a Christian, and [from] Portugal."[132] And in 1584 in the libelous *Leicester's Commonwealth* he is called "Lopez the Jew" and (proleptically) credited with skill in poisoning.[133] William Camden's account of the Lopez affair in his *History of the Reign of Elizabeth* places special weight on Lopez's Jewish sympathies, and suggests that these provoked laughter at his public execution: the "Spaniards, suspecting the fidelity of the English in a manner of so great weight, used the help of Roderigo Lopez, a Jew by religion, the Queen's domestic physician." Lopez went to his death strenuously "affirming that he loved the Queen as well as he loved Jesus Christ; which coming from a man of the Jewish profession moved no small laughter in the standers-by."[134] And Francis Bacon, who was involved in the prosecution of Lopez, describes him as "of nation a Portuguese, and suspected to be in sect secretly a Jew (though here he conformed himself to the rites of Christian religion)."[135] Decades after his execution, woodcuts depicting "Lopez Compounding to Poison the Queen" continued to appear in books recounting plots and treasonous acts (see illustration 10).[136]

For the past hundred years, ever since Sidney Lee published an article in *The Gentleman's Magazine* called "The Original of Shylock," Lopez has been seen by many as a "contemporary prototype" for Shylock.[137] While there is no real evidence in the play that Shakespeare modeled his character or plot upon these recent events, the fate of the unfortunate Marrano physician and the fictional Venetian usurer have nonetheless continued to be linked. As Arthur Dymock put it in 1894, "If Lopez did indeed supply Shakespeare with his greatest villain, he inflicted lasting injury upon his own unhappy race."[138] On the other hand, for many Anglo-Jewish writers (and non-Jewish ones as well) "it is almost an act of faith that Lopez's innocence be affirmed."[139] Were Lopez exonerated, a long shadow would be cast on interpretations that portrayed Shylock as one who truly conspired against the life of a Christian.[140]

The members of the Portuguese Marrano community, of which Lopez was a prominent member, were not the only Jews in the country, although they have received the most attention, being the easiest to trace through surviving sources. Evidence about other Jews, especially those of Eastern European descent, is more scarce. A particularly striking case is that of Joachim Gaunse, born in Prague, who apparently lived openly as a Jew in England in the late 1580s until his run-in with a Protestant minister named Richard Curteys in Bristol in 1589.[141] Until then Gaunse had served as a mining expert in Keswick and South Wales and had made a strong enough impression in this capacity to be invited to serve as the "mineral man" in Sir Walter Raleigh's Roanoke expedition. What Gaunse (a resident of Blackfriars in London) was doing in Bristol in 1589 we do not know. Reverend Curteys, eager to speak Hebrew with a Jew, turned the topic of conversation with Gaunse to Jesus Christ. When Curteys demanded to know whether he believed in Christ, Gaunse replied: "What needeth the almighty God to have a son, is He not almighty?" Curteys found Gaunse's reply "so odious" that he switched to "the English tongue" so that "others being . . . present might hear it and witness his speech."[142]

Gaunse was soon denounced by Curteys before the Mayor and Aldermen of Bristol. A second witness, Jeremy Pierce, confirmed Curteys's claim, and reported to the authorities that when he himself demanded of Gaunse whether "he did not believe in Jesus Christ the Son of God," Gaunse "answered that there was no such name, and that there was but one God, who had no wife nor child." Unsure what action to take, since Gaunse had not actually broken any laws (besides those concerning heresy), though believing that "his ungodly and most heathenish opinions" are "not meet to be suffered among Christians," the Mayor and Aldermen of Bristol chose to refer the entire matter to the Privy Council in London, with the following letter of explanation:

> Whereas one Joachim Gaunse being (as he saith) a Jew born in the city of Prague in Bohemia and now inhabiting in the Blackfriars in London was lately apprehended and brought before us, for that being in this city he used very blasphemous speeches against our Saviour Jesus Christ, denying Him to be the son of God, a matter ministering no small offence to her Majesty's people here.[143]

The likelihood is that Gaunse was told to leave the country; there is no further record of his presence in England.

Records from the late 1590s indicate that Jews continued to visit and live in England. There are some, like the unnamed "rude Jew" whose help was enlisted in deciphering a Hebrew letter sent to Hugh Broughton from Rabbi

Abraham Reuben in Constantinople in 1596, of whom we only have the briefest glimpse.[144] Others, like the anonymous Jew from "Barbary" who was taken from England by Sir James Lancaster to serve as his servant and as a negotiator in his East Indies voyage of 1601, leave slightly more revealing traces: "The General, before his going out of England, entertained a Jew, who spake that language [?] perfectly; which stood him in good stead at that time."[145] Another unnamed Jew, whose services were sought for cataloguing the university library at Oxford, is mentioned in 1607 in a letter written by Bodley to Thomas James, the first Keeper of the Library. Bodley urged James "to use the help of the Jew, if he may be won unto it . . . that the titles of all your Hebrew books may be aptly taken, and understood." A few days later, Bodley again reminds James to "get the help of the Jew, for the Hebrew catalogue. For it can not be done without him."[146] The arrest in 1614 at Plymouth of a "Jew Pirate"—the prominent foreign Jew, Samuel Palache, envoy to the King of Morocco—was newsworthy enough for John Chamberlain to comment upon it to his correspondent Dudley Carleton, in Venice. The Privy Council ultimately defended Palache as well as—in a separate incident—an unnamed Jewish merchant who had arrived in England with a shipment of sugar, from charges lodged against them by the Spanish ambassador.[147]

By the end of Elizabeth's reign the number of aliens in London had swelled to upwards of ten thousand, in a population that has been estimated at somewhere between one hundred and fifty and two hundred thousand. There were lists of "returns" of aliens, but these lists did not indicate whether an alien was Jewish. In some cases though, such as that of Jeronimo Lopez, it was clear: when Sir William Waad, clerk of the Privy Council, writes to Sir Robert Cecil in 1599, he refers to another Marrano (Pedro Rodriguez of Lyons) as a "Portugal by nation and a Jew by race" and goes on to describe Jeronimo Lopez as "one of *his* nation and sect, whom your honor doth well remember."[148] Foreign Jews, especially from Holland, were also known to visit London. Hugh Broughton writes that the Jews of Amsterdam reported to him in 1608 that many of them had been in England.[149] The ranks of Jews in England at the close of the sixteenth century included Alonso de Herrera, who had been taken hostage by Essex at Cadiz,[150] converts who entered the Domus for financial support (including Elizabeth Ferdinando, and Jacob Wolfgang, a German convert who taught at the universities),[151] and Philip Ferdinand, a Polish Jew born in 1556, who became a Catholic, then a Protestant, taught at a number of colleges and halls at Oxford beginning in 1596, and in 1597 published a Latin work about Jewish beliefs with a preface that contains some details of his Jewish past.[152]

As many of these examples indicate, Jews usually came to public attention and left traces of their existence either when converting or when breaking the law. Given their skill at dissimulating their religious beliefs and the incentive to keep their religious identities a secret, it is surprising that so much evidence attesting to their presence in England actually survives. This is not to suggest that their position was ever stable, and there is fairly strong evidence that in the course of the late sixteenth and early seventeenth centuries the size and stability of the Jewish population fluctuated considerably. But it was nonetheless able to overcome setbacks, such as the one that occurred in 1609, which may have resulted in something like a mini-expulsion. Privy Council records for this period do not survive, but the correspondence of various Catholic ambassadors is significant: the Venetian ambassador in London wrote home in August of that year that

> many Portuguese merchants in this city have been discovered to be living secretly as Jews. Some have already left and others have had a little grace to allow them to wind up their business, in spite of the laws which are very severe on this subject. These men are such scoundrels that, I am told, the better to hide themselves they have not only frequently attended Mass at some one or other of the embassies, but have actually received the Holy Eucharist.

The Tuscan ambassador sent home a similar report: "There are many Portuguese here who are trading, and have lately fallen out among themselves. Some of them have been accused of Judaism and have, therefore, been ordered to leave the kingdom and with much dispatch, for the law concerning this matter prescribes the death penalty." As for English sources, there is (possibly) a belated account of this incident by Sir Marmaduke Langdale in 1655, who notes that the Earl of Suffolk had been awarded a patent "for the discovery" of the Jews, "which made the ablest of them fly out of England."[153]

Even as some departed, others remained, and still others no doubt quietly arrived. There were Jews in Shakespeare's England, though probably never more than a couple of hundred at any given time in the whole country, a very small number in a population of roughly four million, and a small number even in relationship to the number of aliens residing in London. Their presence in England only seemed to disturb Catholic foreigners; in case after case the English show little surprise or concern at the discovery of Jews living in their midst. Indeed, even popular anecdotes in circulation at the time that describe how Englishmen tricked Jews convey no sense that the appearance of the Jews in England was unusual.[154] In identifying the anxieties produced by the idea of the Jew, then, we must look elsewhere.

IV. Shakespeare, Englishness, and the Jews

It is understandable that most of those who have written on the subject [of the Jews in Elizabethan literature] have had the modern "Jewish question" in mind; but this has had an unfortunate effect on scholarship, for it has tended to push modern reactions to modern anti-Semitism into a past where they do not apply.

—G. K. Hunter, 1964 [155]

The answer to Elizabeth's enigmatic life, ideas, and role [is] to be found in the fact that she was a secretly practicing Jewess.

—Alan Marlis, 1978 [156]

Was Shakespeare Jewish?

—Elliott Baker, 1992 [157]

While the vast majority of historians writing about the English people and the English past still ignore what for them seem pointless and annoying questions about the presence of Jews in early modern England, literary critics continue to address them. In some ways this has been unavoidable, since plays like *The Jew of Malta* and *The Merchant of Venice* are still taught and staged. John Gross's recent *Shylock: A Legend and Its Legacy* exhaustively surveys how since the eighteenth-century productions and criticism of Shakespeare's play have galvanized debate over a range of Jewish questions, many of them turning upon the key point of what familiarity Shakespeare and his contemporaries might have had with Jews and Jewish practices. I would go a step further than Gross in pursuing the implications of this sustained interest and argue that a central reason for the continuing fascination with Shakespeare and the Jews has to do with the increasing identification of Shakespeare with English culture. This identification has been compounded by a nostalgic view of the Elizabethan world—a time before the horrors of civil war, industrial revolution, and the waning of a once great empire—that fixes in Shakespeare's age a pristine, unsullied notion of Englishness. [158]

The creation of Shakespeare as the national poet, a topic that Michael Dobson, Jonathan Bate, Margreta de Grazia, and others have done so much to illuminate in the past few years, can be dated back to the early eighteenth century, the historical moment when *The Merchant of Venice* was so successfully revived and would hence become a mainstay of the repertory. [159] Since that time, to claim Shakespeare is to claim a stake in what is fundamentally English, and to assert a Shakespeare sympathetic to the Jews or critical of them has become as much a political as a literary judgment. As noted earlier, by the beginning of the nineteenth century a character in Jane Austen's *Mansfield Park* takes it as a matter of faith that "Shakespeare one gets acquainted with without knowing how. It is part of an Englishman's constitution." [160]

Michael Dobson concludes in *The Making of the National Poet* that the eighteenth century saw the emergence of a Shakespeare who "becomes the centre of a struggle for the right to speak for the core of the national culture."[161] Thus, for example, a month after the overturning of the notorious Jew Bill of 1753, in which Shakespeare's authority was invoked against Jewish naturalization, Arthur Murphy wrote in the pages of the *Gray's Inn Journal* that "with us islanders Shakespeare is a kind of established religion in poetry."[162] By 1769 David Garrick's "Stratford Jubilee" helped make this nationalized Shakespeare a permanent fixture in the cultural scene, and Garrick's popular play about the celebrations held in Stratford, *The Jubilee*, helped underscore the extent to which this was a Shakespeare carefully positioned against those at the periphery of English culture. Garrick's play not only includes a bumbling unnamed "Irishman," who travels from Dublin to witness the Jubilee only to sleep through it and return, as he says, to "go home and be nowhere," but also contains a comic exchange between the rustic folk of Warwickshire, who, when they hear the fireworks celebrating Shakespeare, fear that "'tis certainly a plot of the Jews and Papishes," a confusion no doubt exacerbated by the fact that to them, the word "ju—bil—ee" sounded a lot like "Jew Bill." Sukey, one of the better-educated locals, tells her only slightly less ignorant friend Nancy (who wonders "who is this Shakespur, that they make such a rout about 'en?'") that "had you lived at Birmingham or Coventry, or any other polite cities, as I have done, you would have known better than to talk so of Shakespur and the Jewbill."[163] By framing the Jubilee events within the skewed perspective of these outsiders, incapable of grasping the difference between a local hero and a Jewish threat, Garrick offers up a Shakespeare who cannot possibly belong to Stratford, let alone to the boorish Irish, but is the rightful property of a cultivated London culture that can properly know his worth. Sidney Lee subsequently observed in his biography of Shakespeare that the Jubilee "gave an impetus to the Shakespeare cult at Stratford which thenceforth steadily developed into a national vogue, and helped to quicken the popular enthusiasm."[164]

The recognition of the "promotion of Shakespeare as both symbol and exemplar of British national identity"[165] in the eighteenth century, then, goes a long way to explaining why a century later Sidney Lee would have chosen to present his early findings about the "Jews in Elizabethan England" in 1888 to the New Shakspere Society. Nor is it surprising to discover that the first Jewish professor of English literature in England, Israel Gollancz, was a celebrated Shakespearean.[166] In 1903 Gollancz was appointed Professor of English at King's College; that year he also helped found the British Academy. At the same time he worked for the causes of the Anglo-Jewish community and had been a founding council member of the Jewish Historical Society of England in 1893. Given how few Jewish Shakespeareans there were at the time (and it is worth noting that there would not be a tenured Jewish Shakespearean at a major university in the United States until considerably later), Gollancz's career warrants closer attention.

Gollancz's work in Shakespeare studies amply demonstrates the complex bind he experienced as a figure responsible for celebrating the dual heritage of Shakespeare and Anglo-Jewry. The two converged in 1916 when Gollancz served as honorary secretary of the Shakespeare Tercentenary Committee, in which capacity he published both the *Shakespeare Tercentenary Observance in the Schools and Other Institutions* and *A Book of Homage to Shakespeare* (an impressive international anthology that positions Shakespeare as a universal genius, as opposed to a more narrowly defined English one).[167] He also spoke on "Shylock" to the Jewish Historical Society on May 22, 1916, and published an edition of *The Merchant of Venice* the following year. In all these endeavors he went to considerable lengths to meld the two heritages. For example, in his essay entitled "Some Notes on Shakespeare the Patriot," included in *Shakespeare Tercentenary Observance in the Schools*, Gollancz tells his young readers that Shakespeare "taught how hatred" that divided "families, and castes, and nations, *and those of different religions*—too often causeless hatred—brings retribution as a divinely appointed law, the sacrifice, by way of atonement, of what is most cherished and beloved."[168] The passage he draws upon to support this broad claim—*Romeo and Juliet* (2.3.15–30)—suggests divided houses, but the issue of tolerating religious difference is nowhere to be found in that play. Gollancz obviously strains to find in Shakespeare a plea for religious and national toleration. This message comes shortly after a quotation from *The Merchant of Venice* which reads:

Such harmony is in immortal souls;
But whilst this muddy vesture of decay
Doth grossly close it in, we cannot hear it.[169]

Through his reading of these lines as moral allegory Gollancz effectively insulates himself from *The Merchant*'s potential antisemitism. For Gollancz, these lines reveal that the "hope of humanity rested on something above mere knowledge,"[170] and are thus central to his position on Shakespeare and the Jews. He later wrote that these lines suggest that "Shylock, too has an immortal soul; the muddy vesture of decay is made more muddy by the scorn and contempt of the Antonios of the time. There, too, is the music—if it could only be heard aright."[171] Apparently, it is the task of Gollancz, as Anglo-Jewish Shakespeare scholar, to make that music of toleration "heard aright." His Shakespeare is also the national poet, one who represents England's best self and the highest English ideals: "Shakespeare's boundless love of country is no mere poetic fervour; it is solidly based upon his belief that English ideals make for righteousness, for freedom, for the recognition of human rights and liberties."[172] It goes without saying that this is a very different sense of inclusiveness than Garrick had in mind a century and a half earlier.

Gollancz's *A Book of Homage to Shakespeare* includes among its many international contributions a Hebrew ode to Shakespeare written by his brother, the Hebrew professor Hermann Gollancz. The poem (partially translated), begins with a paraphrase of Shylock's words—"Hath not a Jew eyes? Hath not a Jew hands?"—before turning in the next stanza to a celebration of Shakespeare as national prophet: "When the days were dark, a Seer arose; lifting his voice in parable and song, he gave utterance to this plea." For Hermann Gollancz, too, Shakespeare's tolerance was inseparable from his patriotism, and the poem's last stanza speaks of Shakespeare's "prophetic spirit" that understood how "'England never did, nor never shall / Lie at the proud foot of a conqueror."[173] John Gross, commenting on this contribution, aptly notes that the "whole poem constitutes a tribute, not only to Shakespeare, but to the happy integration of practicing Jews into mainstream English culture."[174] Hermann Gollancz's efforts to attribute to Shakespeare a sensibility in tune with Jewish thought carried into the pulpit at London's Bayswater Synagogue, where on April 29, 1916, he delivered a Sabbath sermon on "Shakespeare and Rabbinic Thought," anticipating by a day "Shakespeare Sunday," in which Christian houses of worship paid tribute to the tercentenary of the national poet. The sermon was published shortly thereafter. As Gollancz reminds his congregation at the outset of the sermon, Jews should not be seen lagging behind their Christian counterparts: "Surely, dear friends, we as Jews cannot do less than allow the memory of Shakespeare to enter somewhat into our religious service on this Sabbath day, and thus to take some small part in the present commemoration." Gollancz's message is that "the human side of life, its observation and delineation, is a feature common both to the Rabbis of old and to the Shakespeare of Elizabethan England." At times his attempt to prove the connections are strained, as when he quotes from Portia's speech on the "quality of mercy," ignoring the fact that the speech is used in the play to vilify Shylock, and argues that these lines "carry us back" to a "Rabbinic interpretation" of a passage in Genesis.[175] Viewed in retrospect, the task confronting the Gollancz brothers—to claim Shakespeare as a patriotic poet whose work paradoxically transcends divisions between nations and religions—was an impossibly difficult one, especially at a time when a World War was being fought, and nationalism and xenophobia were rampant.

What John Gross describes as a "happy integration" would not go uncontested, not even in the world of Shakespeare studies. Several recent books and articles written by those at the periphery of the academic world have turned

their attention to Shakespeare and the Jews for polemical ends. These studies are eccentric and hardly representative of the best of Shakespeare scholarship. Still, they are worth a closer look, for their fantasies alert us to what is only faintly registered in the work of more responsible (or more restrained) schol-
ars. The most pernicious of these works is by Elliott Baker, the title of whose chapter—"Was Shakespeare Jewish?"—should prepare the reader for what is to come: a not-so-subtle diatribe on how Jewish academics have taken over the Shakespeare business. Baker locates the origins of this takeover in the 1880s, describing a feminized "Sidney Lee (née Solomon Lazarus)," as the "Pioneer" who "won himself a knighthood from Queen Victoria for his *A Life of William Shakespeare*," after which "the signal went out that the promised land could be along the banks of the Avon." In a double-edged dig, he adds that "at least [Lee] came out from behind his aryan name to confront Shylock, which is more than most of his American cousins have done so far." But he allows for the possibility that Jewish-American Shakespeareans will eventually confront the Jewish questions that until now they have successfully avoided—"Maybe in time." For Baker, "the big Shakespeare takeover had been comparatively recent."[176] What really gets under his skin is how the Jews presume to trespass upon "the banks of the Avon" that nurtured Shakespeare. Baker cites Peter Levi's admission—that "being British, as opposed to English," his "devotion to Shakespeare" may appear to be "that of an outsider seeking identification with the core of Englishness"—as confirmation of his own argument that Jewish Shakespeareans stand outside of Englishness and need to be prevented from forcing their way in. Baker also makes it clear that he would be happier if these Jewish academics simply went back to the professions of their ancestors; citing two prominent Shakespeareans, Baker laments that the names "Greenblatt and Levi [were] once a good masthead for a clothing store."

Baker is acutely sensitive to the presumed presence of Jews (or those he thinks are Jews on the basis of the "Jewish-sounding" names). He writes that if "Yeshiva University had a football team, the lineup could read pretty much the same [i.e., as the list of prominent American "Jewish" Shakespeareans]: [Janet] Adelman, [Joel] Fineman, [Jonathan] Goldberg, [Stephen J.] Greenblatt, [Coppélia] Kahn, [Murray] Schwartz, plus a few ringers from inter-marriages." The motives of these "Jewish" scholars are inscrutable to Baker, and in the spirit of the authors of the Protocols of the Elders of Zion, he hints at a Jewish conspiracy: "As for the signals currently being called in the minyan's huddle, one can only guess."[177]

Baker's chapter concludes with the inevitable question: "Was William Shakespeare Jewish? More outrageous suppositions have been advanced. . . . Experts have repeatedly cast him in their own image. . . . A Jewish American professor, treating him as a fellow 'lanzman' [i.e., another Jew] would only be

following suit. Why not?" Apparently, Baker was unfamiliar with a recent
essay in which Neil Hirschson makes this very claim.[178] Taking the diametri-
cally opposed position of a tolerant, philosemitic Shakespeare to an extreme,
Hirschson argues that such works as "The Phoenix and Turtle" and Shakespeare's contribution to the play of *Sir Thomas More* are explorations of the
sufferings of the Jews, particularly the York massacre of 1190. His reading of
The Merchant of Venice sees Shylock "provoked beyond endurance" by a "converted Jew, Antonio." The play, then, "dramatizes the suffering, confusion,
and discord of conversion." For Hirschson, it is not only Antonio who is a Jew
turned Christian, but Shakespeare himself: "the balance of probability tilts
towards a Shakespeare descended of forcibly converted Jews, and brought up
as a Christian resenting the condition" who "pondered . . . the massacres of
York, and called for a prayer of remembrance." Recently, David Basch has
taken Hirschson's argument a step further. The "central thesis" of his new
book is "that Shakespeare, the prototype of the universal man, speaking for all
men, was not only an intensely patriotic Englishman, but was in addition
grounded in the particularity of a proud and committed Jew."[179] Basch's desire
to imagine a universal Shakespeare who somehow straddles these two identities—patriotic Englishman and proud Jew—does not tell us much that we will
find persuasive about Shakespeare's religious orientation; it does help pinpoint, however, what is contested in the collision of identities embodied in
Englishness and Jewishness and how instrumental Shakespeare has been in
mediating between the two. No doubt stranger biographical claims have been
made for Shakespeare. What is so striking about this argument is that it epito-
mizes what others have more cautiously proposed: that Shakespeare is deeply
tolerant, must be tolerant of the Jews, and must repudiate what the English did
to the Jews.

In contrast to those like Hirschson and Basch, Elliott Baker is so insistent
that Shakespeare had no sympathy for the Jews that he reassigns authorship of
Shylock's celebrated speech beginning "I am a Jew," to someone other than
Shakespeare. His guess is that it was written by none other than Queen Elizabeth I: the "Queen was not only capable of writing Shylock's speech, but more
importantly, she had good reason to." So deep is Baker's own devotion to the
purity of Shakespeare, a devotion that conveniently dovetails with both his
antisemitism and his misogyny—a Shakespeare untarnished by a single line
expressing toleration of the Jews—that he is prepared to sully the honor of the
Queen. It is Shakespeare, even more than the monarch after whom the age is
named, that is at the center of Baker's "core of Englishness."[180]

Baker would hardly be amused to discover that his notion of a Jew-loving
Queen Elizabeth puts him firmly in the camp of his enemies. Alan Marlis, a
Jewish writer whose philosemitism, like Hirschson's, proves the perfect foil to

Baker's antisemitism, has in fact privately published a book—*Queen Elizabeth Tudor: A Secret Jewess*—arguing that Queen Elizabeth was deeply sympathetic to the Jews, a sympathy that can only be explained by the fact that she was Jewish herself. Like Baker, Marlis has combed the available evidence about Jews in early modern England; where this evidence leads Baker to conclude that "it's no wonder that Jews get little mention in the records of their time,"[181] Marlis sees the age as saturated in Jewish concerns. The title page bears the wonderful disclaimer—"Everything in this book is true, or based on the truth"—and there is an additional disclaimer in the opening paragraph, where we learn that this was all narrated by Elizabeth's "jester."[182] Marlis writes that "the answer to Elizabeth's enigmatic life, ideas, and role [is] to be found in the fact that she was a secretly practicing Jewess. She was called a Jewess's name, Deborah, throughout her reign, Old Testament rhetoric was the language of her age, her Welsh background had a Jewish legend in its origins, and her behaviour throughout her life can be interpreted in just such a Judaic manner." Even the absence of antisemitism in the drama of the age can be attributed to England's Queen: "As Queen Elizabeth destroyed all of the anti-Semitic religious plays in England and warred against anti-Semitic Spain," the suspicion of her "secret Judaism gains ground." By the end of the book the arguments begin to feel more than a bit strained, as Marlis's desire to place Jews at the center of the age becomes as single-minded as Baker's attempt to banish them. It reaches its nadir in the explanation of why Elizabeth remained unwed: "Another reason for Elizabeth's not marrying can be seen in her selectivity, for a Jewish Princess cannot marry just anyone. If she is to be exquisitely happy, and Elizabeth would not settle for less, she must be courted and wed by a Jewish man." Marlis concludes that although all "of the previous biographies of Elizabeth have seen her through the eyes of sentiment, glamour, and hand-me-down historical records," he has "seen Elizabeth through her own eyes—the eyes of a Jew."[183]

While it is easy to smile at the excesses of writers like Baker, Hirschson, Basch, and Marlis, their work needs to be read seriously for what it tells us about the cultural anxieties that continue to circulate in more responsible criticism around the twin poles of "Shakespeare" and the "Jews." The few professional Shakespeareans who have dealt with this topic have generally and often uncritically relied on the scholarship of earlier historians, sometimes with disturbing results. Perhaps the most significant example is the work of G. K. Hunter, one of the handful of Renaissance scholars who has tried to tackle the vexing questions of how Elizabethans viewed Jews and Blacks. Writing in 1964, the four-hundredth anniversary of Shakespeare's death, in two landmark essays—"Elizabethans and Foreigners" and "The Theology of Marlowe's *The Jew of Malta*"[184]—Hunter takes as his point of departure the fact that the

"many people who have written about the image of the Jew in Elizabethan literature have concentrated, on the whole, on social questions about real Jews, like
'what knowledge could the Elizabethans have had of genuine Jewish life?'"[185]
Hunter's "'Jewish question'" is not Karl Marx's but rather the post-Holocaust
Jewish Question that engendered Hitler's Final Solution and that, in turn, makes
this kind of wrongheaded but well-meaning critical interest "understandable."
Crucially, Hunter's argument depends upon "modern" reactions to "modern"
antisemitism rather than modern reactions to latent racism in an idealized Renaissance England.

In order to correct what he sees as the misguided impression that Elizabethan culture is racist, Hunter cites in support of his argument three prewar
studies: James Parkes's 1934 work on the theological assumptions guiding
Church fathers like Chrysostom; Jacob Cardozo's insistence in 1925 that representations of the Jew on the Elizabethan stage replicate medieval thinking—
in a book dedicated to proving that there "has been no continuity between pre-
expulsion Jewry and the Resettlement of (Spanish) Jews in the time of
Cromwell"[186]; and H. Michelson's 1926 argument that literary stereotypes of
Jews derive from the New Testament (and hence for Hunter are "theological
rather than . . . ethnographical").[187] But Hunter's main authority is an essay by
the German-Jewish refugee, Guido Kisch.[188] Citing Kisch's research on the
legal status of Jews in medieval Germany—that "considerations of a religious
nature alone are here at play," and that "of racial ideas not the slightest trace is
discoverable"—Hunter concludes that the "whole Elizabethan frame of reference discouraged racial thinking," and, as far as Marlowe's play is concerned,
the "structure of concepts in the play is theological and not racial."[189] What
Hunter fails to consider is that in late sixteenth-century England theology is
not juxtaposed with racial thinking; in fact, it helps produce and define it. It is
also unclear why Hunter expects his readers to accept as a matter of faith that
attitudes in early modern England should correspond exactly with those in
medieval Germany.

Hunter's reliance on Kisch's distinction between "race" and "faith" is also
apparent in his essay on "Elizabethans and Foreigners," where Hunter writes
that "modern scholars often labour to document the exact racial background of
Shylock (or Othello); and certainly we can say that Shakespeare *could* have
learned many true facts about these remote races [*sic*]. But the evidence of the
plays suggests that the old framework of assumptions about Jews, Turks, and
Moors—and this means theological assumptions—provided the controlling
image in his mind."[190] We can see how closely Hunter's thinking is aligned
with Kisch's, who writes earlier in the paragraph from which Hunter quotes
that "Nationalist-Socialist pseudo-science has claimed that the modern concept of race was already known to the Middle Ages, that the antithesis of races

was recognized then, and that besides religious and economic causes, one must look for the element of racial distinction as an important reason for the special legal treatment of the Jews and for their persecution, particularly at the close of the Middle Ages. No unambigous proof for this assertion has been brought forward from the wide domains of medieval legislation, legal doctrine, and judicial practice."[191] For Kisch, and through him for Hunter, religion and not race becomes the defining feature of premodern attitudes toward Jews.

Hunter's argument has proven remarkably resilient (which is why my critique of his work is so harsh), and, in addition to being reprinted in 1978, it is cited regularly and more or less definitively on the subject of Jews in Elizabethan England.[192] What Hunter fails to take into account, however, is the historical moment and bias that qualifies Kisch's historical claims. As Kisch himself acknowledges in the book published shortly after the brief article Hunter cites, his work is an act of defiance and intervention, having been "written in the midst of . . . the greatest distress ever suffered by the Jewish people."[193] Reading his text some fifty years later it is painful watching Kisch misread or ignore evidence that would mar his thesis. The reason is simple: the purpose of his work was to repudiate the racial thinking of the Nazis and to exonerate the medieval and early modern worlds. However well-intentioned and otherwise valuable his work is, its subsequent uncritical acceptance has had some pernicious side effects, in particular providing support for those who would deny that early modern people thought along racial lines.

Hunter's own efforts to protect Shakespeare and the Elizabethans from the taint of racism may unconsciously reflect a reaction on the part of a member of the academic establishment to protect Shakespeare scholarship from the "unfortunate effect" of those who have "had the modern 'Jewish question' in mind" eager to "push" their "modern reactions to modern anti-Semitism" into a "past where they do not apply."[194] His choice of language is in any case unfortunate. Reading Hunter thirty years after his articles were first published, watching him struggle with categories of race and otherness (denying that Jews are a racial construct in one sentence while in the next describing Jews and Blacks as "remote races") is not a comfortable experience. In this respect Hunter is saddled with the same burden as his Elizabethan predecessors when confronted with the categorical problems caused by the otherness of Jews.

Yet the cultural materialist and new historicist schools of criticism that for the past generation have challenged and largely superseded the kind of work done by scholars like Hunter have had their own, different problems with Jewish questions.[195] Generally, they have tended to simply ignore these issues. Their reluctance to deal with Jewish questions undoubtedly has much to do with problems that the cultural Left has had in reconciling itself to Zionism and Israeli policy, with the prevailing legacy of Marx's account of the "Jewish

Question," and with the fact that in their view Jews no longer constitute a disadvantaged or threatened social group. What is so strange about this is that the very categories of analysis which define a good deal of recent cultural criticism—race, nation, and gender—are precisely those that were invoked in the early modern period to address Jewish questions. But Jews, to whom so much early modern racial analysis was devoted, are no longer part of the "discourse of race" in the Anglo-American academic world. As Kisch's work shows, and as the title of Raphael and Jennifer Patai's book—*The Myth of the Jewish Race*—makes explicit, in a world that witnessed a genocide based on racial distinctions between Aryans and Jews, even Jewish scholars are more interested in disabusing others of the idea of a Jewish race than in exploring what racial thinking about Jews has to tell us about early modern cultures. Moreover, insofar as contemporary racial debates no longer concern the Jews, there is less political or intellectual passion (or, more to the point, urgency) that might motivate this kind of historical research. In discussions of the nation, too, the intense fascination of early modern authors with Jewish questions—including the troubling status of the international nation of early modern Jewry—has been replaced with a theoretical orientation that has simply ignored this rich and significant chapter in early modern English political thought. And, finally, the ideological imperatives of much feminist criticism of the 1970s and 1980s, insofar as it was based on binary and oppositional notions of gender, positioned Shylock as a restrictive patriarch (which he clearly is); this left little room for investigating how the often bizarre gendering of Jewish men in early modern culture radically complicated and undermined stable notions of sexual identity.[196] It is also peculiar that in the haste to place identity politics at the center of intellectual discourse the question of religious identity, one of the most pressing issues of identity in early modern England, has been almost completely ignored in recent, insistently secular, cultural criticism.[197]

One would especially have hoped that the new historicism, an approach dedicated in large measure to writing the history of the Other in the Renaissance, would have compensated for the relative silence of the traditional historians of early modern English culture when it came to the matter of the Jews. Unfortunately, this has not occurred. Though the new historicists have rediscovered virtually every marginalized Other that passed through early modern England—including witches, hermaphrodites, Moors, cross-dressers, Turks, sodomites, criminals, prophets, Eskimos, and vagabonds—they have steered carefully around the Other of Others in the Renaissance, the Jews. And this is all the more strange, perhaps, because so many of these scholars are themselves of Jewish descent.

Nonetheless, it would be a mistake simply to follow Elliott Baker and identify Stephen Greenblatt, probably the most influential cultural historian of early modern England writing today (and the progenitor of the new histori- cism), as someone who avoids Jewish questions. Although in his early work Greenblatt uncritically relies on the work of Hunter and others—in arguing that there "was no 'Jewish Question' in Marlowe's England; there were scarcely any Jews"—his interpretation of early modern English culture is unusually marked by Jewish questions, though from an angle that is at times so extraordinarily oblique these Jewish questions may well be missed.[198] Greenblatt most explicitly acknowledges the presence of Jewish questions in his most recent book on the conquest of the New World, *Marvelous Posses- sions*, where he writes: "I have tried in these chapters, not without pain, to register within the very texture of my scholarship a critique of the Zionism in which I was raised and to which I continue to feel, in the midst of deep moral and political reservations, a complex bond."[199] This acknowledgment brings into sharper relief earlier moments when these questions have pene- trated the surface of his work, such as the description in *Renaissance Self- Fashioning* of the brutal execution of Sir John Oldcastle, where Greenblatt writes that "it is only in a concentration camp that a monopoly of violence alone is sufficient to control a whole society," and that the early modern "Catholic Church had neither the will nor the technical means to create such a world."[200] Much the same kind of critique appears in his collection *Learn- ing to Curse*, where Greenblatt turns his attention to a 1943 Hakluyt Society edition of Edmund Scott's *Exact Discourse* (1606), a text that at one point recounts the cold-blooded torture and lingering execution of a Chinese gold- smith suspected of stealing from English merchant adventurers. In a telling phrase, Greenblatt condemns the twentieth-century editor for failing to con- demn Scott's brutality as a "crime against humanity," words that unmistak- ably echo the judgment at Nuremberg for crimes against humanity that were occurring at just the time the Hakluyt edition was published (1943 was also the year in which Greenblatt was born).[201] It is worth pondering the extent to which Greenblatt's influential new historicism is an extended meditation on his own Jewish questions, a point that is lent support by the most recent turn of his scholarship, in his work-in-progress, "The Mousetrap," to the Passover experiences of his childhood, and in his current exploration of "traumatic memory." I strongly suspect that recurrent attention in his work to cultural annihilation, state control, and the silence of victims owes less to Michel Foucault's theories about absolute state power than to the barely vis- ible but unmistakable pressure of the Holocaust. I have singled out Green- blatt's impressive scholarship because the honesty and openness he brings to these Jewish questions makes such analysis possible. But it is only the briefest of glimpses into the much larger problem—one that cannot be addressed at any length here—of how Shakespeare scholarship has been shaped in this century by the social and religious identifications of those whose profession it is to interpret and teach his works.

Certainly the greatest limitation of the approaches taken by historians and literary critics of all stripes is the manner in which most have steered around the questions of *how* and *why* the English were obsessed with Jews in the sixteenth and seventeenth centuries, and why this obsession continues to make its pressure felt in discussions of Shakespeare and the Jews. If Jews were just not that important to English culture, it is hard to make sense of their frequent appearance not only in Tudor and Stuart drama but also in English chronicles, travel narratives, and sermons, let alone in the various works on trade, millenarianism, usury, magic, race, gender, nationalism, and alien status. Even as the Elizabethans have something to tell us about the Jews, their obsession with Jews tells us even more about the Elizabethans (and again, I might add, those who write about them). Ultimately, it is not the raw number of Jews in early modern England that is of interest as much as the kind of cultural preoccupation they became, that is, the way that Jews came to complicate a great range of social, economic, legal, political, and religious discourses, and turned other questions into Jewish questions as well.

III

The Jewish Crime

One cruel and (to speak the properest phrase) Jewish crime was usual amongst them every year towards Easter, though it were not always known . . . to steal a young boy, circumcise him, and after a solemn judgment, making one of their own nation a Pilate, to crucify him out of their devilish malice to Christ and Christians.
—*Samuel Purchas, 1626*

Adding to the economic difficulties caused by the presence of this alien body [i.e., the Jews] was a series of most sinister crimes committed against Christian children, including murder (allegedly ritual) and forcible circumcision. Whatever we may think of the evidence in favour of "ritual murder" . . . a number of instances of mysterious child-murder undoubtedly did occur in twelfth- and thirteenth-century England, at least ten being well authenticated between 1144 and 1290.
—*John Hooper Harvey, 1948*

 In December 1775 a leading German intellectual from Gottingen University named Georg Christoph Lichtenberg wrote from London describing the production he had just seen of *The Merchant of Venice*, with Charles Macklin in the role of Shylock. "Picture to yourself," he writes, "a somewhat strong man, with a sallow, harsh face and a nose which is by no means lacking in any one of the three dimensions." Macklin's Shylock "is slow, calm in his impenetrable cunning, and when he has the law on his side he is unflinching, even to the extreme of malice." For Lichtenberg, "the sight of this Jew suffices to awaken at once, in the best regulated mind, all the prejudices of childhood against this people."[1] A half-century later, in one of those curious instances where art uncannily mirrors life, the novelist Maria Edgeworth, with no knowledge of Lichtenberg's letters, published *Harrington*, in which the eponymous hero finds himself at the identical performance of Shakespeare's play: "Shylock appeared—I forgot every thing but him—such a countenance!—such an expression of latent malice and revenge, of every thing detestable in human nature!"[2] For Harrington, too, watching Macklin's Shylock brought to the surface "childish prejudice." The novel proceeds to consider what effect this early exposure to myths of Jewish villainy has had upon the English psyche.

Reflecting back upon his formative years, Harrington fixes as the primal scene of his childhood the moment when his nursemaid Fowler, impatient to get him to off to bed, threatened to call upon "Simon the Jew," an "old man with a long white beard and a dark visage . . . holding a great bag slung over one shoulder" in which he carried secondhand clothes, who at that very moment was passing by in the street below. Fowler warned that Simon "shall come up and carry you away in his great bag" should Harrington refuse to obey her. Harrington explains that this "threat of 'Simon the Jew' was for some time afterwards used upon every occasion to reduce [him] to passive obedience." Pleased with her success, Fowler terrified him with "stories of Jews who had been known to steal poor children for the purposes of killing, crucifying, and sacrificing them at their secret feasts." At midnight she would recite a particularly chilling tale "about a Jew who lived in Paris in a dark alley, and who used to sell pork pies; but it was found out at last, that the pies were not pork—they were made of the flesh of little children." When young Harrington asked if there were "such things in London now, and were there ever such horrible Jews?" Fowler replied: "Oh yes! In dark narrow lanes there were Jews now living, and watching always for such little children." And Fowler ominously added that there "was no knowing what they might do." The effect on the young boy was overwhelming. "From that moment," Harrington says,

> I became her slave, and her victim. . . . Every night, the moment she and the candle left the room, I lay in an indescribable agony of terror; my head under the bed-clothes, my knees drawn up in a cold perspiration. I saw faces around me grinning, glaring, receding, advancing, all turning at last into one and the same face of the Jew with the long beard, and the terrible eyes, and that bag in which I fancied were mangled limbs of children. It opened to receive me, or fell upon my bed, and lay heavy on my breast.

The narrator reminds readers that in "our enlightened days" what Fowler did must seem "incredible," though "we may recollect, that many of these stories of the Jews, which we now hold too preposterous for the infant and the nursery maid to credit, were some centuries ago universally believed by the English nation, and had furnished more than one of our kings with pretexts for extortions and massacres."[3]

After Fowler took employment elsewhere—the boy was too frightened of Jews to go to sleep and Fowler grew weary of trying to calm him down—Harrington's mother bribed Simon the Jew not to pass by the door and cry out "'Old clothes.'" He agreed, but word leaked out about what had happened, and Harrington describes how the cry was heard again punctually under my window; and another and another Jew, each more hideous than the former, succeeded in the walk. Jews I should not call them; though such they appeared to be at the time. We afterwards discovered that they were good Christian beggars, dressed up and daubed, for the purpose of looking as frightful and as like the traditionary representations and vulgar notions of a malicious, revengeful, ominous-looking Shylock as ever whetted his knife. The figures were well got up; the tone, accent, and action, suited to the parts to be played.

The "stage effect" of these false Jews was "perfect."[4] Harrington began to see Jews everywhere, until his father at last interceded and the beggars were dispersed or punished. His father also decided to relieve Harrington's anxiety about Jews by removing his son from the world of women and introducing him into what he assumed to be the more rational society of men.

Yet even in the company of men stories abounded about the dangers of falling into the hands of the Jews. Harrington recalls his father's warning that it "is certain, that when a man once goes to the Jews, he soon goes to the devil. So Harrington, my boy, I charge you at your peril, wherever else you do, keep out of the hands of the Jews—never go near the Jews—If they once catch you, there's an end of you, my boy." But his father never thought to explain either "the reasons for the prudential part of this charge" or the dangers of "disgraceful transactions with the Hebrew nation." As a result, the advice only exacerbated Harrington's "fear and contempt," which soon turned "into the kindred feeling of hatred."[5] When Harrington was old enough to read, he began to pursue his obsession with the Jews in books, and "never saw the word Jew in any page of any book which [he] happened to open, without stopping to read the passage." He quickly discovered that there, too, "not only in the old storybooks, where the characters of the Jews are as well fixed to be wicked as the bad fairies . . . but in almost every work of fiction, [he] found the Jews represented as hateful beings." Thinking back upon the impression these books made upon him as a child, Harrington concludes that they "acted most powerfully and injuriously, strengthening the erroneous association of ideas I had accidentally formed, and confirming my childish prejudice by what I had then thought the indisputable authority of *printed books*."[6]

In describing how generations of English children were exposed to stories of how Jews abducted, mangled, and cannibalized Christian children, Edgeworth demanded that her readers confront one of English culture's darker secrets. Like Edgeworth, I believe that storytelling has important consequences for how a culture imagines itself in the act of imagining others. In this chapter, after exploring the broad range of economic, theological, and physical crimes ascribed to Jews by early modern English writers, I turn to the centrality of ritual murder, aptly described by Samuel Purchas in the early seventeenth century as the "Jewish crime."

I. "Their villainies here . . . in England"[7]

Perhaps the best place to start with is the Elizabethan theater, where audiences were entertained with catalogues of Jewish villainy. The most celebrated and influential litany appears in Christopher Marlowe's *The Jew of Malta* (1589), where the Machiavellian Jew Barabas brags:

> I walk abroad o'nights,
> And kill sick people groaning under walls;
> Sometimes I go about and poison wells;
> And now and then, to cherish Christian thieves,
> I am content to lose some of my crowns,
> That I may, walking in my gallery,
> See 'em go pinioned along by my door.
> Being young, I studied physic, and began
> To practise first upon the Italian;
> There I enriched the priests with burials,
> And always kept the sexton's arms in ure
> With digging graves and ringing dead men's knells.
> And after that I was an engineer,
> And in the wars 'twixt France and Germany,
> Under pretence of helping Charles the Fifth,
> Slew friend and enemy with my stratagems.
> Then after that was I an usurer,
> And with extorting, cozening, forfeiting,
> And tricks belonging unto brokery,
> I filled the jails with bankrupts in a year,
> And with young orphans planted hospitals,
> And every moon made some or other mad,
> And now and then one hang himself for grief,
> How I with interest tormented him.[8]

We have here the familiar categories of the Jew as murderer, poisoner, usurer, and political interloper. There is also a strong emphasis on the Jew's capacity to counterfeit effortlessly. Another example from the popular stage—Romelio's appearance dressed "in the habit of a Jew" in John Webster's *The Devil's Law Case* (1617)—gives some indication of how pervasive these associations were. In this speech Romelio, a Christian masquerading as a Jewish physician (who swears by his "Jewism"), imagines what kind of crimes and transformations a Jew is capable of:

> Why, methinks
> That I could play with mine own shadow now,
> And be a rare Italianated Jew;
> To have as many several change of faces,
> As I have seen carved upon one cherry stone,
> To wind about a man like rotten ivy,
> Eat into him like quicksilver, poison a friend
> With pulling but a loose hair from's beard, or give a drench
> He should linger of't nine years, and ne'er complain,
> But in the spring and fall, and so the cause
> Imputed to a disease natural; for sleight villainies,
> As to coin money, corrupt ladies' honours,
> Betray a town to th' Turk, or make a bonfire
> A th' Christian Navy, I could settle [to]'t
> As if I had eat a politician,
> And digested him to nothing but pure blood.[9]

Like Barabas, Romelio summons up the familiar images of the Jew as murderer, poisoner, military and political threat, and economic parasite. It is only his Jewish "habit" that sets Romelio apart—no exaggerated "Jewish" physical features and hence no easy way to tell Christian from counterfeiting Jew (in this case played by a counterfeiting Christian). Webster adds a few touches of his own: Jews seducing Christian women and cannibalizing Christian men. Each one of these reputed crimes had a long history. Under the pressure of various social, religious, and political changes in England in the course of the sixteenth century, some were fading from view, some were being revived,[10] and some, as *Harrington* reveals, maintained their power to terrify for centuries to come.

One legend that had virtually died out by the end of the sixteenth century describes how Jews would surreptitiously obtain the eucharistic host, and would "prick it, burn it, and very basely and scornfully abuse it, because they heard Christians call it the body of Christ." Inevitably, Christ's blood would pour forth from the host and the terrified Jews would either convert or be punished for their wickedness.[11] Stories of host desecration had first circulated on the continent in the late thirteenth century, around the time that Jews were banished from England.[12] Before long, these secondhand accounts passed from the fictional world of sermons and stories to the gritty world of the streets, where the accusations led to bloody attacks on continental Jewish communities.[13] For a time the myth of host desecration was popular in England as well, a popularity exemplified by the late fifteenth-century staging of *The Croxton Play of the Sacrament*, which literally reenacts the various scourgings to which the host is subjected before Christ himself appears, prompting the Jew to convert to Christianity. Sarah Beckwith has shown how the popularity of this myth owes much to the connection between the sacrament of Communion and Christian community: the celebration of this sacrament and the repudiation of skeptics who doubted the miracle of Christ's real presence in the eucharistic host were crucial to reconfirming communal identity in Catholic Europe.[14] In post-Reformation England, however, this identification would be replaced by other kinds of religious and communal identities, a process accelerated by the controversies over transubstantiation among English theologians.[15] As a result, by the end of the sixteenth century only vestiges remained in England of the charges that Jews tampered with the eucharistic host.

The ill-repute into which the veneration of the host had fallen in post-Reformation England is exemplified in an anecdote published in 1568 about a recent event in Catholic Spain. The story describes how during a Corpus Christi day celebration in Catalonia, as the procession prepared to "carry the mass bread about," the priest tried to "couch the blessed host in the golden pix." But "as the Devil would have it," the host "was too great a compass to be put in the box." Everyone was amazed, and "there was not a man in that great and notable assembly that knew what to do." At that moment an inquisitor named Molonio stepped forward and taking a "pair of scissors," he "pared his Maker where he was overgrown, and so by a little paring, put both him in the box, and the people out of doubt." The narrator concludes that while some will praise Molonio's wit, others will "bewail and lament the hard fortune of their God so to be pared and circumcised by the cursed hands of a cruel inquisitor." And, in a final aside, the narrator wonders how cruelly they would have "handled him" if this circumcisor had "had any Jew's blood in him?"[16] It is clear enough what price a Jew would have paid for symbolically desecrating and circumcising the host in such a fashion.[17]

About the closest thing to a tale of host desecration in seventeenth-century Protestant England was the story repeated by converts about how Christ's blood periodically streamed down upon the Jews (though no sacramental host had been pierced to produce this terrifying result). Citing Matthew 21.25, where the Jews cry out, "His blood be upon us and our children," the convert Paul Isaiah writes that this "blood hath since ensued and fallen both upon" the Jews "and their children in this manner" four times a year. Isaiah offers a remarkable first-person account of his own experience of this bloody shower while visiting his uncle, a rabbi in Russia. Together "with other . . . students"

Isaiah was sitting "round about the table for our learning or studies," when "a drop of blood" fell on the table. It "made a hole in the table, the which became wider and wider, and visibly bigger and bloodier, insomuch that the table was dyed with blood." His uncle quickly begged a Christian ("who was by nature of his faith invulnerable to this threat") to break up and burn the table and strew its ashes into a river. Isaiah then draws the obvious conclusion: "Beloved Christians, what do you think of this, or what can we suppose this to be, other than the innocent blood of our Saviour, that true Pascal Lamb, Jesus Christ the Righteous." Isaiah nervously hedges his claim by saying that the reason that Christians have never come across any reference to this event in Jewish books is that the information is "secretly kept" and known to only a "few of the Jews . . . besides their rabbis."[18] Isaiah's strange story was seconded by a later convert, John Meirs, who confirms that "the Jews themselves cannot deny, but that the blood of Christ falls upon them still" and "frightens them."[19] Insofar as the celebration of Christ's real presence in the eucharistic host was no longer the symbol of communal identity in Protestant England, Jewish attacks on it were no longer a meaningful threat, and stories of Christ's blood streaming down on the Jews passed out of currency.

Other myths also ran their course by the early seventeenth century, including ones that depicted the Jews as a military threat capable of invading and overthrowing Christendom. Mandeville's *Travels*, which first appeared in English in 1496 and was reprinted repeatedly for the next century and a half, provides a particularly chilling account of this Jewish threat. Seventeenth-century English readers could still learn how beyond Cathay are the hills that enclose the ten lost tribes of the Jews. Mandeville adds that while a handful of these Jews occasionally escape, the rest may "not pass there together, for the hills are so great and high." The situation is unstable, though, for

> men say in that country . . . that in the time of Antichrist they shall do much harm to Christian men, and therefore all the Jews that dwell in diverse parts of the world learn . . . to speak Hebrew, for they hope that these Jews that dwell among the hills aforesaid shall come out of the hills, and speak . . . Hebrew and nothing else, and then shall these Jews speak Hebrew to them and lead them into Christendom to destroy Christian men.

Furthermore, "these Jews say they know by their prophesies that those Jews that are among those hills . . . shall come out, and Christian men shall be in their subjection, as they be under Christian men now."[20]

The passage combines fantasies about the ten lost tribes, the secret language of the Jews, fears of an international Jewish conspiracy, and a frank acknowledgment that the Jews, who have long been kept in subjection by Christians, surely want to revenge this treatment. Perhaps this Jewish military threat was in the minds of Elizabethans when they read in 1585 how "the Marranos of late banished and driven out of Spain and Portugal" have "to the great detriment and damage of . . . Christianity" taught "the Turks diverse inventions, crafts, and engines of war, as to make artillery, harbusques, gunpowder, shot, and other munitions."[21] Stories about Jewish armies were often unclear about the object of the Jews' wrath: sometimes the Jews were said to join forces with the Turks against the Christians, sometimes with the Christians against the Turks, and sometimes they were described as fighting against both.[22] An example of how the story could still gain attention in the early seventeenth century appears in a 1606 pamphlet, *News from Rome*. Its author breathlessly describes how an army of Jews, with the navigational assistance of the Dutch, seeks to "recover the land of promise, towards the which the first army is already very near, to the great terror and dread of every man which hath either seen or heard of them." The author reports that "their first army is already arrived upon the limits of Turkey," putting all to fire and sword, and that they speak "bastard Hebrew."[23]

The force of such narratives clearly depended upon the extent to which Christian Europeans, including the English, felt vulnerable to attack from foreign invasion. An unusual and slightly hysterical account of this Jewish threat appeared as late as 1665 in a published "letter" from Aberdeen. The letter tells how three days earlier, because of "the foulness of the weather and storms," a ship "put into this place." Those who tried to speak with the foreigners aboard "could not understand them," but supposed that "they spoke broken Hebrew, and by a letter they had in High-Dutch, they found them bound for Amsterdam, and to have correspondence with their brethren (the Jews) there." The Jews' letter reveals that there are "sixteen hundred thousand of them together in Arabia, and that there came into Europe sixty thousand more." They have already "had encounters with the Turks and slain great numbers of them. None are able to stand against them. They give liberty of conscience to all, except the Turks, endeavouring the utter ruin and extirpation of them."[24] Even in this report, though, the Jews do not pose a threat to the local Christian population, only to the distant Turks. Despite the appearance of this late account, by the late seventeenth century the fantasy of massed Jewish armies was no longer believable.

In contrast, stories describing how Jews secretly threatened Christian society from within continued to flourish.[25] The favorite method of the Jews was usually poison, and by the sixteenth century the idea that Jews tried to poison Christians was proverbial: when a character in a play is asked, "Canst thou impoison?" he readily replies, "Excellently, no Jew, apothecary, or politician better."[26] While stories about Jews poisoning Englishmen in medieval England are rare, English chroniclers often reported instances of this crime on the continent. John Stow, for example, describes a conspiracy between three enemies of Christendom—lepers, Saracens, and Jews—in the year 1319. Lepers were blamed "through all Christendom" because "they had covenanted with the Saracens to poison the Christians in all places, which in diverse parts they brought to pass, putting poison into wells, fountains, pits, and other places." A number of them "in Provence and in other parts of France were burnt, and the Jews were detained in prison for consenting herein to them." Stow adds that in response, over twelve hundred Jews were put to death.[27]

Edward Fenton's 1569 translation of Pierre Boaistuau's *Certaine Secrete Wonders of Nature* repeated this story and illustrated it with a woodcut (see illustration 3). Fenton writes that the Jews "fully resolved amongst themselves, to extirp at one instant the name of Christians, destroying them all by poison." To accomplish this end "they allied themselves in consort with diverse lepers." The infamous Black Plague was blamed on this unholy alliance. It was caused by "an ointment with a confection of the blood of man's urine composed with certain venomous herbs, wrapped within a little lined cloth, tying a stone to the same to make it sink to the bottom." The Jews cast this potion "into all the fountains and wells of the Christians. Whereupon this corruption engendered such contagious diseases in all Europe, that there died well nigh the third person throughout the same."[28]

Perhaps the most unusual story recounting how Jews secretly poison Christians appears in the writings of the Elizabethan physician and occultist Robert Fludd. Fludd's posthumously published work contains a bizarre tale about a Jew in Barbary, who, seeking to create a poisonous "venom," seduced a red-headed English mariner, from whom he extracted this poison. Fludd relates that he heard the story from "a merchant that came newly from Fez," who told him that the English sailor initially went along with the plot, thinking he could outwit the rich Jew, "and feigning himself to be much taken with the love of him, wrought so with him, that for three hundred pounds, he agreed to sell himself unto him for his slave, thinking in time to come to give his Jewish master the slip, and run away." As it turned out, the Jew outsmarted the Englishman. When their ship was ready to sail, and the other English sailors went "to take their leave of their captive fellow, they resorted unto the Jew's house, who after they had demanded their fellow, led them into a back court, where they found the red-headed captive, his back being broke, and a gag in his mouth, and [his] chops and throat swollen." The tortured English sailor was still alive, and he explained to his friends that this swelling "was caused by the stinging of vipers, which were forced into his mouth." He added that he had been "hung up and exposed unto the hot sun, with a silver basin under his mouth to receive that which dropped from his mouth." Fludd records that the poison that dripped from the viper-filled mouth of the English sailor was "so deadly that it did surely kill where it touched."[29] One explanation for the association of Jews with poison is that Jews, celebrated as expert physicians, were suspected of abusing these healing powers, their knowledge used for sinister purposes. For example, William Biddulph writes that when Turkish Jews found it impossible to practice ritual murder openly, their physicians did so covertly: "They were wont amongst them to sacrifice children, but dare not now for fear of the Turks. Yet some of them have confessed that their physicians kill some Christian patient or other, whom they have under their hands at that time, instead of a sacrifice."[30]

The last broad category of Jewish criminality encompasses economic transgressions. There can be no doubt that Jews were commonly identified as usurers and financial brokers in early modern England, as indeed they were throughout Europe. The most casual allusions in the period underscore this point. The poet Edmund Spenser, for example, concludes a letter written to Gabriel Harvey with the words, "He that is fast bound unto thee in more obligations than any merchant in Italy to any Jew there."[31] These proverbial expressions were also borne out by the experience of English travelers. When Dudley Carleton had to return to his diplomatic post in Venice in 1613 and lacked household furnishings, he turned to the Jews, who exacted a high price: "I have been rescued by the assistance of the Jews here, whose courtesy," Carleton adds, "is no less ready than costly."[32] Other news from the continent, such as the information that the Jews were physically expelled from Frankfurt in 1614 because "their usurious exactions" had become "so odious" to the local population—offered further confirmation of this habitual Jewish practice.[33] With English travelers and merchants encountering significant numbers of Jewish traders, merchants, translators, and go-betweens in foreign ports, the conception of the Jew as mercenary broker had some basis in reality. English writers rarely bothered to distinguish between legitimate Jewish merchants and those they found or imagined to be unscrupulous or exploitative.

At the same time, it is important to emphasize that the concept of usury in Shakespeare's England underwent a radical transformation between the usury statutes of 1571 and 1624. In his illuminating discussion of the evolution of the practice of usury during this period, Norman Jones identifies several causes for this shift. One was the greater sophistication about finance in the late sixteenth century, a by-product of expanding overseas trade. Another was the landmark 1571 usury statute, which permitted individuals to obtain 10 percent interest on loans. Once Elizabethans became habituated to this rate of interest, the definition of usury gradually shifted from one that included any loan at interest to one that demanded an exorbitant rate. Moreover, the morality of usury was increasingly accepted as the responsibility of the individual rather than that of the state (leading the House of Commons in 1624 to strike out the declaration in the usury statute "that all usury was against the law of God, leaving it to be determined by divines").[34] By this time the transformation of attitudes toward usury was so complete that English moneylenders (and borrowers) could buy a copy of the handy *Money Monger; Or the Usurers Almanacke* (1626), which advertises that it sets out "the necessary tables of interest, the usurer's gain, and [the] borrower's loss." Still, even after the 1571 statute permitting usury, individuals who lent money at unacceptably excessive rates were prosecuted, including, interestingly enough, Shakespeare's father.[35]

By the end of the sixteenth century, then, Jews were increasingly identified not with usury per se, but with outrageous and exploitative lending for profit. Undoubtedly, English depictions of Jews as usurers during this period when the concept of lending money at interest was undergoing such rapid and startling revision strongly suggest that such representations were in part projections: Jews enabled the English to imagine a villainous moneylender whose fictional excesses overshadowed their own very real acts of exploitation. For example, when in 1594 the anonymous author of *The Death of Usury* attempts to distinguish between acceptable and exorbitant interest rates, the Jews exemplify the latter, thereby legitimizing the less injurious rates that Christian moneylenders in England were now permitted to exact. The accepted English rate of 10 percent pales in comparison with the rates reputedly demanded by medieval Jews and recorded in English histories like Grafton's *Chronicle*, which describes how cruel Jews had exacted "sixty, seventy, [and even] eighty" percent interest from Christian borrowers. Given these figures, if "our usury in money were all one with that of the Jews, the question" would be "soon answered" as to what constituted illegitimate exploitation.[36] It is also worth noting that laws pertaining to Jewish usury could still be found in Elizabethan law books. For example, William Rastall's 1594 collection of English legal statutes "now in force" retains a section that addresses "usury taken by Jews," as well as "debts to Jews and stolen goods in Jews' hands."[37]

Finally, Jewish usury was likened to the practice of female prostitution. Purchas writes that the "beastly trade of courtesans and cruel trade of Jews is suffered for gain" in Italy; both "suck from the meanest to be squeezed by the greatest. . . . So well is the rule of Paul observed. . . . not to be a lover of filthy lucre, from filthy stews, from filthy Jews."[38] Sucking on poorer citizens, being squeezed or sucked by those more powerful, the filthy Jews and prostitutes are only tolerated because they provided a necessary if distasteful service to the state. If early modern English writers came to recognize that illicit and unproductive usury, like illicit and nonreproductive sex, could not be eliminated from society, they also understood that the blame could nonetheless be projected onto those who provided the service rather than those who sought it out.

The identification of Jews with prostitution may have subtly shaped other kinds of social judgments; for example, when Sir William Brereton visited the Jewish community in Amsterdam in 1635 he met "an Englishman and his wife,

lately turned Jew, as is said, merely to enrich themselves. . . . 'Tis said his wife, being an handsome woman, was a courtesan in London."[39]

The chronicles, too, provide evidence of how medieval Jews had debased the coin of the realm, a lively issue in late sixteenth-century England, when the debasing of the currency was a major economic concern. Stow curtly notes that close to three hundred "Jews were put to execution" in 1278 for "clipping of the King's coin,"[40] while Holinshed's account of the same events also underscores his belief that medieval Jews were not really English but members of a distinct social category. Holinshed writes that "there was inquiry made in London for such as had clipped, washed, and counterfeited the King's coin, whereupon the Jews of the city and diverse goldsmiths that kept the exchange were indicted." Two hundred and ninety-seven people "were condemned and in diverse places put to execution," though Holinshed notes that there "were but three Englishmen among them, all the residue were Jews."[41] Well into the seventeenth century Jews continued to be identified with crimes that threatened the economic health of the nation. At a time when English men and women were increasingly engaged in lending at interest, sometimes demanding excessive rates of return, it was reassuring to learn that they were not as bad as Jews. Yet Jewish usury (perhaps because there was less and less difference between it and English financial practice) was insufficiently unnerving in and of itself to stimulate the kind of irrational prejudices still produced by the charge of ritual murder. Only when harnessed to the darker threat of taking the knife to Christians, as in *The Merchant of Venice*, did depictions of Jewish usurers prove so deeply unsettling.

II. The survival of a myth

Long after stories of Jews poisoning wells, desecrating hosts, and marching against Christendom had passed into the world of fanciful legends, the belief that Jews abducted children and killed them, using their blood for ritual purposes, continued to be told by various British writers. Among those who maintained this well into the twentieth century was Arnold Leese, a fascist propagandist of the 1930s who claimed that there were actually two kinds of ritual murders: those undertaken at Passover (in which a young Christian child would be killed and the blood used in baking the unleavened bread called matzoth) and those committed during the festival of Purim (in which adults would be killed, and their blood either saved for the upcoming Passover or used in the triangular pastry called hamentaschen). Leese believed that the racial background of the Jews—"which produced 'a physical manifestation of a desire

for bloody sacrifices'"—compelled them to commit these crimes.[42] While
Leese, as a leading member of a lunatic and fascist fringe, may be dismissed
from consideration, more mainstream figures, such as the much admired Victorian writer and ethnographer Richard Burton, cannot. Burton enthusiasts are
less than keen on exploring the implications of Burton's posthumously published *The Jew, the Gypsy, and El Islam*, in which Burton states that Sephardic
Jews still practiced ritual murder and cites specific instances that he knew about
in Damascus, Rhodes, and Corfu. Suppressed from publication in this volume,
as Burton's editor W. H. Wilkins tactfully notes, was an "Appendix on the
Alleged Rite of Human Sacrifice among the Sephardim."[43]

Literary scholars will be familiar with the name of another intellectual—
Montague Summers—who argued earlier in this century that Jews had indeed
practiced ritual murder in England and elsewhere. Summers is perhaps better
known for his editions of Aphra Behn, John Dryden, and adaptations of
Shakespeare. He also had a deep interest in witchcraft, and published *The History of Witchcraft and Demonology*, a scholarly work that was reprinted as
recently as 1973. In that book Summers, turning his attention to Jewish ritual
murder, states that in "many places the evidence is quite conclusive that the
body, and especially the blood of the victim, was used for magical purposes. . . .
A deed of particular horror was discovered at Szydlow in 1597 when the victim was put to death in exquisite tortures, the blood and several members of the
body being partaken of by the murderers. In almost every case the blood was
carefully collected, there can be no doubt for magical purposes, the underlying
idea being the precept of Mosaic law . . . 'For the life of all flesh is in the blood
thereof.'"[44]

Not even the Holocaust put to rest such allegations in England. A notable
example is John Hooper Harvey's popular postwar textbook, *The Plantagenets*, quoted at the outset of this chapter, in which Harvey writes that the
Jews engaged in a "series of most sinister crimes committed against Christian
children, including murder (allegedly ritual) and forcible circumcision." Harvey's eclectic racism is apparent in his assertion that whatever "we may think
of the evidence in favour of 'ritual murder' (its existence in modern times
among the Indian thugs is fully substantiated), a number of instances of mysterious child-murder undoubtedly did occur in twelfth- and thirteenth-century England, at least ten being well authenticated between 1144 and 1290."
Harvey finds "unassailable" proof in public records and "in the poignancy
and pathos of the very considerable literature of the subject and its wide dis-
tribution. Best known is the reference in Chaucer's Prioress's tale, but the
memory survived longer and went further in a series of exquisite folk-songs,
of which 'Little Sir William' and 'Oh down, oh down in merry Lincoln' are
still well known."[45] We see in Harvey's analysis the process whereby myths

pass through English literature and emerge as historical fact. Tony Kushner notes that Harvey's "best-selling textbook was not withdrawn by its various publishers until the late 1980s" and that, more recently, there have been protests made about "local clergy . . . repeating the blood libel story to tourists in Lincoln cathedral."[46]

Why have these English writers continued to find this myth so irresistable? Why ritual murder and not some other charge? What exactly is it about this specific crime—or actually sequence of criminal acts beginning with abduction and circumcision and ending with crucifixion and cannibalism—that has made it so central, if only on a subconscious level, to English notions of Jewish identity? When Friar Bernardine in Marlowe's *The Jew of Malta* is about to reveal to his partner Friar Jacomo a terrible crime committed by Barabas "that makes [him] tremble to unfold," Jacomo interrupts, "What, has he crucified a child?"[47] It turns out that Barabas has not; but Jacomo's guess was not a bad one, since, for Elizabethan audiences, no Jewish crime seemed to have captured the imagination as powerfully as that of ritual murder. When Samuel Purchas researched this subject, he relied upon the public records assembled by the young antiquarian John Selden (who is reputed to have objected to Purchas's reworking of his information). Where Selden had gone back to archival records, other historians, including Purchas, were content to rely on the versions that were circulating and recirculating in major Elizabethan histories like Holinshed's *Chronicles*, Stow's *Annales of England* and Foxe's *Actes and Monuments*. These great rewritings of England's social, political, and religious identity, then, were also repositories of the history of this alleged Jewish crime against the English.

Holinshed, for example, describes the "heinous act committed by the Jews at Norwich" in 1144, "where they put a child to death" by "crucifying him upon a cross," and another in Lincoln in 1255 when over a hundred Jews were brought to Westminster and examined for conspiring to crucify another child. This was the famous case of Hugh of Lincoln, whose murder was revealed by the "diligent search made by the mother of the child, who found his body in a well on the backside of the Jew's house where he was crucified." Holinshed also indicates that this communal atrocity was an annual event: "They used yearly (if they could come by their prey) to crucify one Christian child or other."[48] While the Tudor historians also recounted many of the savage attacks by English barons and populace against the Jews, they justified these persecutions on the grounds that the Jews' ritual murders warranted retaliation. Defending one such attack, Foxe denies that "this plague of their's [was] undeserved," since "every year . . . their custom was to get some Christian man's child from the parents and on Good Friday to crucify him in despite of our religion."[49]

III. The origins of the myth

Historians of these accusations have traced the connection between ritual murder and Jews back to the writings of the Greek historian Posidinius in the second century B.C.[50] However, Gavin Langmuir, who has patiently tracked the complicated issue of the transmission of this narrative from antiquity up through the medieval period, has persuasively argued that when the charge resurfaced in the twelfth century in England there was virtually no possibility the medieval authors of the new accusations had any knowledge of the obscure and rare classical manuscripts that contained earlier accounts. The same holds true for an independent version of the story that tells of an incident said to have taken place in Syria in the fifth century. For practical purposes, then, the accusation first appeared in medieval Europe in Thomas of Monmouth's account of the death of William of Norwich in 1144. Langmuir has also shown that Thomas of Monmouth got his story secondhand, arriving in Norwich some six years after the alleged crime had occurred. In retelling the story, Thomas made the evidence more damning by putting "it in the mouth of a leading Jew of Norwich."[51]

The history of ritual murder accusations has been told many times, and the curious reader can consult a number of classic and more recent accounts.[52] My interest here is necessarily limited to why and how this story continued to circulate in early modern England. Some locales, such as Norwich, were celebrated for the miracles subsequently produced by the martyred boy, and pilgrimages (no doubt profitable ones to the community) soon followed. In the celebrated case of William of Norwich, Thomas of Monmouth's original manuscript almost immediately influenced accounts like the *Anglo-Saxon Chronicle* as well as later printed versions by John Capgrave and Wynkyn de Worde. For those unable to read these accounts, church paintings displayed the story of the Jews' crime to generations of parishioners. Among those that survived the Reformation and the wholesale destruction of saints' images at the time is the painting on the screen in Loddon Church, Norfolk, which probably dates from the first half of the fifteenth century. It shows young William, stretched out on the forks of two wooden uprights surrounded by the Jews who draw his blood into a basin, presumably to be used for ritual purposes (see illustration 1).[53]

The printing press did much to consolidate and popularize the myth of ritual murder,[54] especially after the publication of Hartmann Schedel's *Nuremberg Chronicle* of 1493, which describes and depicts in a gruesome woodcut how the Jews murdered Simon of Trent.[55] Simon's remains also became a tourist attraction and continued to draw visitors, including those from England, well into the seventeenth century. When the Catholic Englishman Charles Somerset passed through Trent in 1611–1612 he recorded in his travel diary that "there is in this town a child called St. Simon that was circumcised by a Jew, and killed, and this body is there unputrified. And there hath been many miracles wrought by this body, as the book makes mention that is printed of them."[56]

By the late sixteenth century a strand of the narrative of Jewish ritual murder unavailable to medieval writers—Socrates Scholasticus's account of the crime in fifth-century Syria—had found its way into print in England, complementing native accounts of this crime as well as those versions that had arrived over from the continent. Meredith Hanmer's frequently reprinted translation of Socrates Scholasticus's work, first published in 1577, describes how "the Jews for their horrible practices against the professors of the Christian faith, suffered punishment . . . in a certain place called Inmestar . . . in Syria." The story relates how Jewish plays attacking Christianity got out of hand, as the feigned stage violence turned into actual violence against the Christians: "At the time of their plays," the Jews "committed many absurd and shameful acts. At length through frenzy and furious motion they removed reason out of her seat, and like madmen they . . . derided in their plays not only the Christians but also Christ Jesus himself." The Jews then took hold of "a child of the Christians," and proceeded to "nail him to a tree." When "they had so done, first they deride[d] and laugh[ed] at him; immediately after, like madmen, they scourge[d] him as long as breath remained in his body." When the emperors heard "what a horrible act the Jews had committed," they ordered a "diligent search and inquisition for the authors and workers of so great a mischief," and the Jews who had committed these outrages "in jest, were punished in earnest."[57]

Another little-known version of the accusation from antiquity—as well as the first repudiation of the charge that Jews committed ritual murder—was made available to Elizabethans when Thomas Lodge translated Josephus's rebuttal of Appion's charges of Jewish ritual murder. This version was also pre-Christian. Lodge's translation describes how Antiochus, who invaded and desecrated the Jews' Temple in 168 B.C., came upon a man held prisoner in the Temple. The man told Antiochus that "he was a Grecian" who, "travelling in the country to get his living . . . was suddenly seized . . . and brought unto the Temple and shut up therein." He had been "fed or fatted with all dainties that could be provided," which "at first . . . made him joyful, but afterward he began to suspect it." Finally he demanded of one of his jailors why he was being kept there, and learned to his horror that "the Jews" annually take "a Grecian stranger and feed him" for "a year." At that time they "then carry him to a wood, and there . . . kill him and sacrifice him according to their rites and ceremonies, and . . . taste and eat of his entrails." Afterwards, they cast the "residue of the murdered man . . . into a certain pit." The story contains all of the defining features of native versions of the accusation circulating in Lodge's England: the yearly crime, the initial imprisonment of the victim, the cannibalistic devouring of the body, and the attempt to hide traces of the body and the crime.

What sets Lodge's book apart from earlier English accounts of Jewish ritual murder is his decision to include Josephus's repudiation of this "forged lie." This "fable," Josephus argues, "is not only stuffed full of all tragical cruelty" but is "also mingled with cruel impudency." Josephus contested the accusation on factual grounds, and asks "how it is possible that so many thousand people as are of our own nation, should all eat of the entrails of one man as Appion reporteth?" Josephus first refutes the charge point by point and then concludes that it is "ignominious . . . for a grammarian not to be able to deliver the truth of a history," and accuses Appion of "great impiety and a voluntary forged lie" in spreading this myth.[58]

Lodge's translation of Josephus's refutation went unheeded. In fact, English stories describing how Jews engaged in just such activities remained quite popular well into the seventeenth century, most of them based on the authority of the public records and various histories. In 1648, for example, the York minister Thomas Calvert was still citing John Foxe on the subject of Jewish ritual murder: "Our diligent Foxe hath given us notice that when England gave Jews harbour, they got our English children and sometimes crucified them in diverse places, as you may find in *Actes and Monuments*." Calvert also refers his readers to Foxe's "Latin sermon at the baptism of a Jew" for further proof.[59]

The controversy over the readmission of the Jews to England in 1656 rekindled popular interest in this myth. William Prynne describes in the opening pages of his *A Short Demurrer to the Jewes* how his book was motivated by a conversation with "Mr. Nye the Minister," who caught Prynne off guard by asking "Whether there were any law of England against bringing in the Jews amongst us? For the lawyers had newly delivered their opinions [that] there was no law against it." Prynne heatedly replied that "Jews had been formerly great clippers and forgers of money, and had crucified three or four children in England at least, which were principal causes of their banishment." The skeptical Nye replied that "the crucifying of children was not fully charged on them by our historians, and would be easily wiped off." Prynne angrily responded that Nye was "much mistaken" in this view and set off to find documentary evidence to prove it. In his investigations Prynne went back to medieval chronicles that "undeniably" show "the transcendent impiety, blasphemy, malice, persecution, and obloquy of the Jews against our Saviour Jesus Christ, and Christians, and their constant, usual practice of crucifying children almost every year."[60] In the "Second Part" of his *Demurrer*, Prynne further documents the Jewish crime of "circumcising and crucifying Christian children."[61]

So compelling (and presumably convincing) were these accusations that Menasseh ben Israel, the Amsterdam rabbi who served as emissary for the Jewish community of London in the 1650s, felt that he had to defend the Jews against these groundless charges of ritual murder before turning to more positive arguments for their readmittance to England. His *Vindiciae Judaeorum*, published in English in 1656, refutes the accusations of ritual murder point by point. In challenging these claims, Menasseh begins by showing how illogical the accusations were, especially the charge that Jews circumcised their victims before murdering them. If "it was intended that shortly after this child should be crucified," Menasseh demanded, "to what end was he first circumcised? If it shall be said it was out of hatred to the Christians, it appears rather to the contrary, that it proceeded from detestation of the Jews, or of them who had newly become proselytes, to embrace the Jews' religion." Surely, he concludes, "this supposed prank" seems more characteristic of the Catholic "Spaniards" who "first baptized the poor Indians and after out of cruel pity to their souls, inhumanely butchered them, than of strict law-observing Jews, who dare not make a sport of the seals of their covenant."[62]

Menasseh suggests instead that the accusations have been motivated either by a desire to account for unexplained murders or alternatively to find an easy culprit for murders that Christians themselves have knowingly committed: "I cannot but weep bitterly, and with much anguish of soul lament that strange and horrid accusation of some Christians against the dispersed and afflicted Jews that dwell among them, when they say (what I tremble to write) that the Jews are wont to celebrate the feast of unleavened bread, fermenting it with the blood of some Christians, whom they have for this purpose killed." It is far more likely, he writes, that the Christians "themselves have most barbarously and cruelly butchered some of them. Or to speak more mildly, have found one dead, and cast the corpse, as if it had been murdered by the Jews," into Jewish "houses or yards, as lamentable experience hath proved in sundry places."

One of the earliest writers to speculate upon the motivations underlying the blood libel, Menasseh offers the powerful insight that Christians, recognizing their deep similarity (or feared similarity) to Jews, project onto them the same hostility that was once directed at themselves: the "very same accusation and horrid wickedness of killing children and eating their blood was of old by the ancient heathens charged upon the Christians, that thereby they might make them odious, and incense the common people against them." This ancient charge against Christians was familiar to English writers, who derided the claim that "the Christians in the primitive Church . . . were slandered to kill children, to eat their flesh, and to drink their blood." As a final and no less futile line of defense, Menasseh concludes that even as Christians deny "the imputation of this cruelty" when it has been "falsely charged upon them," so "in like manner do we [Jews] deny it."[63]

IV. Why ritual murder?

Menasseh's discussion of why these charges had been leveled against the Jews invites further speculation as to why the myth of ritual murder was so widely accepted. Surely at some level the accusations of ritual murder have to do with what Gavin Langmuir, in his account of the medieval blood libels, describes as a "crisis of faith." While the nature of Christian belief in England may not have changed all that much in the four centuries following the earliest accusations in 1140, it assuredly would in the decades following the Reformation, when a sense of spiritual turmoil and instability was experienced by a good many English men and women. In the face of increasing doctrinal differences between Christian denominations, it was important to dispel doubts about Christianity by juxtaposing universally accepted Christian values with those of the stubborn, criminal, and misbelieving Jews.

Fundamental doubts about Christian belief could also be allayed by proving that the Jews secretly believed that Christ was the Messiah they had long awaited. In 1678 Richard Mayo offered English readers such a narrative, set in the "the days of Constantine the Great." In this story (told by a Protestant named "Mr. B." to the Jew whom he seeks to convert, "Rabbi J."), the protagonist, "Joseph the Jew," fell sick

> so desperately, that they had no hope of his life. The Jews coming about him to perform those ceremonies, and give that advice which they use to do to dying persons, one of the chief of them (an ancient man skilfull in their law) came to him, and whispered these words in his ear: "Believe that Jesus who was crucified under Pontius Pilate, being the son of God, and afterwards born of Mary, is the Christ of God, and was raised from the dead, and shall come again to judge the dead and the living." And thus Joseph came to know, that among their last mysteries, the Jews secretly persuaded dying men to believe.[64]

A more chilling version of this story, and one that hints at ritual murder, was quoted above in the Introduction: John Donne's sermon describing how the Jews always keep in readiness the blood of some Christian, with which they anoint the body of any that dies amongst them, with these words, 'If Jesus Christ were the Messiah, then may the blood of this Christian avail thee to salvation.' "[65] In Donne's example, ritual murder serves both as threat to and confirmation of Christianity.

It also helped resolve questions generated by the desire to show not only that other peoples were physically different, but why they were different. The most striking example, also mentioned earlier, is Thomas Calvert's suggestion that the loss of blood Jewish men experienced when menstruating led to the practice of "child crucifying among the Jews." In the twisted pathology of his argument, these Jewish men are caught in a terrible cycle of bleeding and replacing that lost blood by crucifying children for supplementary blood, blood that then leaks out of them. The feminized male Jew's leaky body, then, is inescapably bound to shame, dissolution, and crime, in contrast to the shameless, whole, masculine, and divine image of the Christian male.[66]

Setting aside for the moment biological and theological anxieties at the heart of the myth of ritual murder, it is also worth considering other kinds of social problems to which early modern cultures were reluctant to admit. One is the abandonment of children, a practice that John Boswell has recently shown to have been endemic in Western culture from classical antiquity through medieval times. We have already noted that a crucial component of the ritual murder accusation was the abduction of the young Christian child, a feature made much of in virtually every account of this crime. Boswell observes that "charges that Jews stole, bought, and killed Christian children, which became very widespread in the later twelfth century and did incalculable harm to Jewish communities for centuries thereafter, may be a further indication of abandonment [of children] among Christians." He adds that the "idea that Jews were responsible for any mysterious harm to Christian children captivated the imagination of the English public, and there were plenty of missing or dead children to fan the flames of paranoia and hostility."[67] Boswell might also have noted that at several points medieval Christians decreed that Jewish children were to be taken away from their parents and raised as Christians. Could it be that Christians projected onto the Jews activities that they themselves had engaged in? Anthony Wood writes in his history of Oxford that in 1236 "a Jewish child that had been converted and baptized was by the Jews . . . forcibly taken away" and "the said Jews . . . imprisoned."[68] And D'Blossiers Tovey draws on the chronicles for another thirteenth-century example, one occurring in response to a scandalous incident that arose when a priest fell in love with a Jewish woman and underwent circumcision (the story calls to mind the one told by Samuel Usque). He relates how "all the Jews in England were commanded" by King Henry III "to change their religion." The King also ordered that "their children" who were "under six years of age" were to be "taken from them and brought up Christians." This decree was "occasioned by the marriage of a Christian priest with a Jewish woman, whom he was desperately in love with, but could obtain from her parents on no other condition than circumcision." This "so enraged the populace that they would have burnt all the Jews alive, if the King, to pacify them, had not given the aforementioned orders."[69]

The deep fear of losing one's children (and of one's children losing their true identity) helps explains the tenacity of the ritual murder accusations. It it not surprising, then, to find Elizabethan dramatists delving into this subject in their depiction of relations between Jews and Christians. Both Marlowe, in *The Jew of Malta*, and Shakespeare, in *The Merchant of Venice*, include episodes in which Jewish daughters are more or less abducted from their Jewish fathers. The Abigail, Barabas's "seduced daughter," actually abandons her father and enters a "new-made nunnery" at her father's behest (he wants her to find the treasure he has hidden there).[70] In Shakespeare's play, the Christian Lorenzo has "lately stole [Shylock's] daughter." In making good her escape, Jessica is first "transformed to a boy" and then to "a Christian." The clownish servant Lancelot underscores the dark undercurrent of ritual murder accusations and the ensuing retaliations against Jews that circulate through Shakespeare's play when he punningly warns Jessica in the ominous and proverbial jingle: "There will come a Christian by / Will be worth a Jewess' eye." Lorenzo is indeed the Christian for whom Jessica waits, but the "worth" of the proverb has less to do with the value of a lover than the revenge exacted upon the Jewish community for its crimes.[71]

More typically in both myth and drama it is the Jews who are reputed to seduce and abduct Christian children.[72] When in 1627 King Charles I sat through a long Latin play called *Paria*, written by the young dramatist Thomas Vincent, he would have witnessed the abduction of a Christian boy by a scheming Jew, Eleazer. Vincent takes his plot from Eusebio Luchetti's Italian prose comedy *Le Due Sorelle Rivali* (1609). Notably, however, the depiction of the Jew is decidedly English and owes little to the Italian source, except perhaps for the Jew's stench. Steven Berkowitz, whose recent facsimile edition of the play has finally made it available to interested readers, notes that in "the Italian comedy there is no connection between Sciamoel [the Jew] and the theft of the [Christian] infant Fulvio," a central feature of Vincent's transformed plot.[73] The English "Argument" prefacing the published version of *Paria* makes this point clearly: "Lidonia a lady of Ancona had two twin-born sons, Archaicus and Fulvius, whereof the one was lost in his infancy, being stolen away by a Jew and sold to Laberio a merchant of Milan." In the denouement Eleazar admits to having "stolen and sold" one of the boys and is sentenced "to eat pork at the wedding feast."[74] This is another distinctly English touch, one that may owe something to the celebrated punishment inflicted in London on the Judaizer John Traske.

The Jews were also frequently charged with cannibalizing their victims, consuming their blood for ritual purposes. This part of the accusation required Christians to invert what they knew from Scripture: that Jews were strictly forbidden from drinking or eating blood. Once again the drama of the time explores this deep-seated cultural anxiety of having one's body eaten and identity absorbed by one's enemy. Take, for example, Shakespeare's description of Shylock's desire to feast upon his Christian enemies. We learn in Shylock's first appearance that he "will feed fat the ancient grudge" he bears Antonio, and he later adds that he'll "go in hate, to feed upon / The prodigal Christians."[75] When asked by Salario what possible use he could have for Antonio's flesh, Shylock replies, "To bait fish withal; if it will feed nothing else, it will feed my revenge." And Gratiano, calling Shylock "wolvish, bloody, starved, and ravenous," compares him to a predatory wolf who has fed on human flesh and is "hanged for human slaughter."[76] Other dramatists drew on this tradition as well. In John Day, William Rowley, and George Wilkins's collaborative *The Travels of the Three English Brothers* (1607), Zariph, the only Jewish character in the play, puts things bluntly when he says that "'it would my spirits much refresh / To taste a banquet all of Christian flesh," and, moreover, that "the sweetest part / Of a Jew's feast is a Christian heart."[77] The language of usury would even become entangled with this aspect of the ritual murder accusation. William Prynne, for example, quoting from the Tudor chronicler John Speed, writes that "by their cruel usuries" the Jews have "eaten" the English "people to the bones."[78] Moreover, exorbitant moneylending was often referred to as "biting" usury, and the elision of Jews as economic exploiters and literal devourers of Christian flesh was easily made. This may in part be explained by the philological determination of Elizabethan writers on usury, whose Hebrew was good enough to know that the biblical word for lending at interest, *neshech*, also meant "to bite."[79]

What may have intensified these fears about Jewish cannibalism were residual anxieties about Protestant England's own Catholic and therefore cannibalistic past. For, like other Catholics, the English before the Protestant Reformation believed that they were physically consuming the blood and body of Christ when taking Communion. Evidence that the Catholic rite was thought of in cannibalistic terms after the Reformation in England is provided by Reginald Scot, author of *The Discoverie of Witchcraft*, who speaks of the "cannibal's cruelty" when describing Catholic "sacrifices exceeding in tyranny the Jews or Gentiles." For Scot, the "incivility and cruel sacrifices of Popish priests do yet exceed both the Jew and the Gentile, for these take upon them to sacrifice Christ himself." The Catholics "are not ashamed to swear, that with their carnal hands they tear his human substance, breaking it into small gobbets; and with their external teeth chew his flesh and bones, contrary to divine or humane nature. . . . Finally, in the end of their sacrifice (as they say) they eat him up raw, and swallow down into their guts every member and parcel of him."[80] Scot's grim likening of the Catholic mass to Jewish ritual cannibalism once again suggests that the Jew continued to figure as a point of reference in early modern England for a wide variety of social and theological concerns that ultimately had little to do with Jews themselves.

Finally, the one feature of the myth of ritual murder most peculiar to English versions (it was nowhere near as central to accusations made elsewhere in Europe) was that Jews circumcised their young male victims. The early modern English obsession with this detail is nothing less than extraordinary. To give a sense of how great a preoccupation this could be, roughly a quarter of Samuel Purchas's account "of the Jews sometimes living in England" is given over to a record of "their circumcising alone,"[81] that is, without the murder that inevitably followed in ritual murder accusations. Raphael Holinshed and John Foxe also described how Jews were punished for having circumcised Christian boys (who were rescued before any other harm could be done to them).[82] And in his *History and Antiquities of the University of Oxford*, Anthony Wood similarly lists among the "enormities" performed by medieval Jews at Oxford "enticing the young scholars and the children of the inhabitants to be of their religion, forcing them also to be circumcised."[83]

Even when taken independently, the various parts of this "Jewish crime"— especially child abduction, circumcision, and cannibalism—appear to have touched deeply on fears that no doubt stretch across cultures but seem to have had a special urgency in early modern England. Each of these parts of the larger crime also effects an irreversible transformation of identity: familial, sexual, religious, and physical. It is not hard to imagine, then, why these various concerns should have cohered into a powerful and satisfying narrative, one with vast explanatory force and one that could explain both conscious and barely understood fears experienced by early modern English men and women. In trying to understand the complex role of literature in transmitting such myths, I turn now to *The Merchant of Venice*, reconsidering what it means for Shylock to cut a pound of Antonio's flesh and focusing more intently on the ways in which aspects of this Jewish crime haunt Shakespeare's play as they did his culture.

IV ⮑

"The Pound of Flesh"

What a matter were it then if I should cut of his privy members,
supposing that the same would altogether weigh a just pound?
—spoken by the Jew in the English translation of Alexander Silvayn's
The Orator, *1596*

I hope I shall never be so stupid as to be circumcised. I would
rather cut off the left breast of my Catherine and of all women.
—Martin Luther, c. 1540

Perhaps the least explicable feature of the ritual
murder accusations was the charge that Jews first
circumcised their victims before killing them. In
some ways it must have made perfectly good sense.
After all, it was well known that Jews circumcised
young boys, and it was not all that difficult to
imagine this practice as part of a more complex
and secretive Jewish ritual ending in human sacri-
fice. In other ways, however, it made no sense at all, for as Menasseh ben Israel
justifiably wondered, "to what end he was first circumcised" if "it was
intended that shortly after this child should be crucified?" The confusion is
understandable, since the ritual significance of what is described in the Bible as
cutting the "foreskin" of the "flesh" remains poorly understood even by Jews
and other peoples who have long practiced this rite. In the twentieth century
we stand doubly removed from appreciating the effect of circumcision upon
cultural identity. Even as circumcision is now routinely practiced in Western
cultures for hygienic and aesthetic reasons, an awareness of its symbolic meanings (aside from psychoanalytic ones) has been virtually lost. Current debate
about circumcision has focused almost exclusively on the pain it might cause
the child, or on its effects upon reducing the spread of certain diseases. A very
different situation prevailed in early modern Europe, where there was an
intense curiosity about the often unnerving implications of a ritual bound up

with theological, racial, genealogical, and sexual concerns. I am interested here not only in restoring a sense of the fascination and importance circumcision held for Elizabethans but also in arguing that an occluded threat of circumcision informs Shylock's desire to cut a pound of Antonio's flesh. Before turning to the presence of circumcision in *The Merchant of Venice* and its sources, it is important to consider what this ritual might have meant to Elizabethans, what their understanding of it was based on, and what light this casts on their cultural beliefs.

I. Elizabethan ideas about circumcision

In the twentieth century circumcision has often been described as a symbolic form of castration or emasculation. This association has undoubtedly been influenced by the theories of Sigmund Freud, who, in an argument that bears a striking resemblance to Maria Edgeworth's ideas about childhood trauma and the wellsprings of anti-Jewish feelings, writes in *Little Hans* that the "castration complex is the deepest unconscious root of anti-semitism; for even in the nursery little boys hear that a Jew has something cut off his penis—a piece of his penis, they think—and this gives them a right to despise Jews. And there is no stronger unconscious root for the sense of superiority over woman."[1] For Freud, the symbolic act of circumcision proves a vital source of both misogyny and antisemitism.[2] The notion that circumcision could easily slide into the more definitive cut of castration did not originate with Freud and in fact had long circulated in English culture. D'Blossiers Tovey, in his account of instances in medieval England in which Jews were charged with being "emasculators," cites a case from the reign of King John in which "Bonefand a Jew of Bedford was indicted not for circumcising, but totally cutting off the privy member" of a boy named Richard.[3] And Shakespeare's contemporaries used circumcision as a metaphor for castration: the poet Gabriel Harvey, for example, implores God to "circumcise the tongues and pens" of his enemies.[4]

For early modern English writers, though, the threat of circumcision did not begin and end with emasculation. In the sixteenth century circumcision was more than a cut, it was an unmistakable sign. But of what, exactly? When the Elizabethan preacher Andrew Willet tried to answer this question he found himself describing circumcision as not only a "a sign of remembrance or commemoration of the Covenant . . . made between God and Abraham" but also as a sign "distinguishing the Hebrews from all other people." To this genealogical, Jewish association, he added a few more that are distinctly Christian: circumcision prefigured "baptism" and demonstrated "the natural disease of man, even original sin."[5] To these Willet might have added yet another: that through circumcision, one "is . . . made a Jew,"[6] a troubling thought for a Christian who might find himself threatened with such a cut.

One such individual was Thomas Coryate, the celebrated Elizabethan traveler. Coryate describes how his efforts to convert the Jews of the Venetian ghetto soured, leading him to flee from the hostile crowd. Though this specific detail is never mentioned in the narrative itself, a picture of Coryate pursued by a knife-wielding Jew is included in a series of scenes illustrating the title page of his travel book, *Coryats Crudities* (see illustration 9).[7] For those who wrote commendatory poems to Coryate's book—including Laurence Whitaker—this Jew threatens not death but circumcision: "Thy courtesan clipped thee, 'ware Tom, I advise thee, / And fly from the Jews, lest they circumcise thee." Hugh Holland, too, draws attention to the danger to Coryate's foreskin: "Ulysses heard no Syren sing: nor Coryate / The Jew, least his prepuce might prove excoriate." Coryate's conversionary effort backfires, and instead of turning Jews into Christians he finds himself in danger of being religiously transfigured by means of a circumcising cut.[8] Holland, comparing Coryate to Hugh Broughton, the evangelizing Elizabethan Hebraist, makes this symmetrical relationship between baptism and circumcision explicit:

> He more prevailed against the 'excoriate Jews
> Than Broughton could, or twenty more such Hughs.
> And yet but for one petty poor misprision,
> He was nigh made one of the circumcision.[9]

With the exception of a handful of infants circumcised by the radical Puritan group led by John Traske around 1620, and a few self-circumcisors like Thomas Tany and Thomas Ramsey thirty years later, there is no evidence that circumcisions took place in early modern England. Nonetheless, the same post-Reformation interest that led to this Judaizing impulse also inspired a broader curiosity about a ritual not only central to the Old Testament accounts of the patriarchs but also crucial to the theological position maintained by the apostle Paul in that central text of the Protestant Reformation, Epistle to the Romans. One result of this new interest was that English travelers eagerly sought out invitations to circumcisions and recorded what they witnessed for the benefit of their contemporaries. As noted earlier, the resilient Coryate, who in the course of his extensive travels had long desired to observe a circumcision, finally had his wish granted in Constantinople, at the "house of a certain English Jew called Amis" [i.e., Ames]. The fact that Ames and his two sisters spoke English no doubt made it easier for Coryate to have various details of the ritual explained to him. Coryate describes how the Jews

> came into the room and sung certain Hebrew songs, after which the child was brought to his father, who sat down in a chair and placed the child being now

eight days old in his lap. The whole company being desirous that we Christians should observe the ceremony, called us to approach near to the child. And when we came, a certain other Jew drawing forth a little instrument made not unlike those small scissors that our ladies and gentlewomen do much use, did with the same cut off the prepuce or foreskin of the child, and after a very strange manner, unused (I believe) of the ancient Hebrews, did put his mouth to the child's yard, and sucked up the blood.[10]

English observers were particularly struck by how the rite symbolically enacted the male child's passage from his mother to the community of men.[11] Coryate observes that at the conclusion of the rite, the "prepuce that was cut off was carried to the mother, who keepeth it very preciously as a thing of worth," and Fynes Moryson, describing a circumcision he had witnessed in Prague, was alert to the fact that women were "not permitted to enter" the room and that they "delivered the child to the father" at the door. Like Coryate, Moryson records his surprise at witnessing another practice for which Scripture had offered no precedent, *metzitzah*, the part of the ceremony in which the circumcisor sucks the blood from the glans of the circumcized "yard" or penis of the infant. Moryson writes that "the rabbi cut off his prepuce, and (with leave be it related for clearing of the ceremony) did with his mouth suck the blood of his privy part."[12] Apparently, this innovative practice, introduced during the Talmudic period, though not universally practiced by Jews, must have seemed to these English observers to have sodomitical overtones.[13]

Coryate, Moryson, and other Elizabethan observers express surprise at the discrepancy between the ceremonies that they witnessed and that which they had expected to see based on the divinely ordained precepts set forth in the Bible.[14] There was also disagreement over whether the Jews were the first people to have practiced circumcision. At stake in this debate was whether circumcision should be viewed as something peculiarly Jewish. On one side there were those like Samuel Purchas, who had read too many accounts from too many foreign lands to accept the argument that all peoples who practiced circumcision had learned this rite from the Jews. Purchas insisted that the "ceremony and custom of circumcision hath been and still is usual among many nations of whom there was never any suspicion that they descended from the Israelites."[15] Opposing this minority view were those like Andrew Willet, who maintained that "circumcision was a peculiar mark of distinction for the Hebrews" and further urged that "some nations among the Gentiles retained circumcision by an apish imitation of the Hebrews, but they did abuse it superstitiously and did not keep the rite of institution as the Lord had appointed it."[16] Writers who sided with Willet's position used this as a basis for substantiating claims about the discovery of the ten lost tribes of Israel. When Thomas Thorowgood, for example, writes that "many Indian nations are of Judaical race," he offers as evidence that the "frequent and constant character of circumcision, so singularly fixed to the Jews, is to be found among them."[17]

While it was widely accepted that others—especially Turks—practiced circumcision, there was still considerable resistance to abandoning the idea that it was a distinctively Jewish rite. An unusual story regarding Turkish circumcision—and murder—made its way to England in February 1595 when John Barton, the English ambassador in Constantinople, forwarded to Lord Burghley a report describing the events surrounding the accession of the Turkish monarch Mohamet III. The narrative, written in Italian by a Jew named Don Solomon, describes how Mohamet consolidated his power by inviting his nineteen brothers, the eldest eleven years old, to greet him: Mohamet "told them not to fear, he meant no harm to them but only to have them circumcised according to their custom. . . . As soon as they kissed his hand, they were circumcised, taken aside by a mute, and dextrously strangled with handkerchiefs. This certainly seemed strange and cruel, but it was the custom of this realm."[18] The story offers yet one more instance, in the year preceding the first staging of *The Merchant*, of the association of circumcision with ritualistic and surreptitious murder.

II. Romans and the theological meanings of circumcision

This unprecedented interest in the physical act of circumcision was directly related to some of the theological preoccupations of post-Reformation England. Elizabethans knew that circumcision had caused something of an identity crisis for early Christians, especially Paul. Paul, who was himself circumcised and had circumcised others,[19] directed his epistles to communities for whom to circumcise or not to circumcise was a matter of great concern. But Paul's remarks on circumcision went well beyond approving or disapproving of the act itself: they offered a revolutionary challenge to what defined a Jew, and by implication, a Christian. Luther and Calvin both devoted themselves to explicating Paul's often cryptic remarks on circumcision, and a host of English translators, commentators, theologians, and preachers enabled the widespread circulation of these interpretations to the broadest community possible. More than anything else in the late sixteenth century—including firsthand reports like the ones described above—Paul's ideas about circumcision saturated what Shakespeare's contemporaries thought, wrote, and heard about circumcision. At times confusing and even contradictory, Paul's remarks, and the extraordinary commentary produced to explain and resolve various ambiguities contained in them, had an immeasurable impact on Elizabethan conceptions of Jews. This body of commentary, much of it gathering dust in a handful of archives, richly repays close examination.

The first problem confronting a Christian explicator of Paul's Romans was a fairly simple one. Since God had first ordered Abraham to undertake circumcision as a sign of the Covenant, what justified abandoning this practice? And what were the consequences of such a break? The immediate answer was that the Jews had misunderstood that this Covenant, like the Law, was not changed or abolished by Jesus, "but more plainly expounded . . . and fulfilled." "Surely," Philippe de Mornay wrote, in a text translated by Sir Philip Sidney, "in this point . . . we [Christians] be flat contrary to them." And sounding a bit like a modern deconstructive critic, Mornay adds, that the "thing which doth always deceive" the Jews is that "they take the sign for the thing signified," since circumcision was merely a "sign or seal of the Covenant, and not the Covenant itself."[20]

For John Calvin, the "disputation and controversy" over circumcision similarly masked a more consequential debate over "the ceremonies of the Law," which Paul "comprehendeth here under the particular term of circumcision." By equating circumcision with the Law and its supersession by faith, English Protestants drew an analogy between Paul's rejection of circumcision and their own repudiation of Catholicism's emphasis on justification through good works: it is "not circumcision, but faith [that] makes us wait for the hope of righteousness; therefore not circumcision but faith justifies."[21] Calvin's interpretation of Paul had made it clear that "circumcision" had lost its "worth,"[22] having been replaced by the sacrament of baptism. No longer even "a sign," it was "a thing without any use."[23]

But such an outright rejection of circumcision seemingly contradicted Paul's own assertion that "circumcision verily is profitable, if thou do the Law."[24] Confronted with such a claim, commentators had to work hard to show that Paul's words actually meant quite the opposite of what literalists might mistakenly imagine. In order to achieve this end, the gloss to the Geneva Bible takes Paul's wonderfully concise and epigrammatic phrase and turns it into a ponderous argument: "The outward circumcision, if it be separated from the inward, doeth not only not justify, but also condemn them that are circumcised, of whom indeed it requireth that, which it signifieth, that is to say, cleanness of heart and the whole life, according to the commandment of the Law."[25]

The commentator's overreading is enabled by the fact that Paul in the verses that follow introduces a crucial distiction between inward and outward circumcision. It is a distinction central to his redefinition of Jewish identity in a world in which circumcision has been superseded: "He is not a Jew which is one outward, neither is that circumcision, which is outward in the flesh. But he is a Jew which is one within, and the circumcision is of the heart, in the spirit, not in the letter, whose praise is not of men, but of God."[26] Paul here attacks

Jewish identity at its genealogical root.[27] If he can deny that outward physical circumcision alone defines the Jew from generation to generation, he can insist on a figurative reading of the Law in all other matters as well. For Joseph Hall, Paul's message is unambiguous: "He that would be a true Israelite or Jew indeed must be such inwardly" and must be "cleansed from all corrupt affections and greed." Moreover, this "circumcision must be inwardly in the heart and soul and spirit (in cutting off the unclean foreskin thereof) and not a literal and outward circumcision of the flesh."[28]

Before turning to the symbolic circumcision of the heart touched on here by Paul and his explicators—the most striking feature of his argument and the most relevant to a reading of *The Merchant of Venice*—it is important first to emphasize that Paul and his followers were reluctant to abandon the outward, physical implications of trimming the foreskin, in part because this surgical act so perfectly symbolized the cutting off of sexual desire. Andrew Willet, drawing on the work of Origen, remarks that even if "there had been no other mystery in circumcision, it was fit that the people of God should carry some badge or cognizance to discern them from other people. And if the amputation or cutting off some part of the body were requisite, what part was more fit then that . . . which seemed to be obscene?"[29] The gloss to the Geneva Bible reads this puritanical perspective back into Genesis 17.11, explaining there that the "privy part is circumcised to show that all that is begotten of man is corrupt and must be mortified." And the 1591 Bishops' Bible similarly stresses the connection between circumcision and the curbing of sexual desire, explaining that Deuteronomy 30.6—"And the Lord thy God will circumcise thine heart"—means that God will "cut away thy ungodly lusts and affections." These commentaries effectively rewrite Old Testament allusions to circumcision, infusing them with Paul's deep discomfort with human sexuality.[30]

John Donne was particularly drawn to this line of thought. In his New Year's Day sermon preached in 1624 commemorating the Feast of the Circumcision, Donne imagines himself in Abraham's place after having been commanded by the Lord to circumcise himself and all the men in his household. Given that it was to be done "in that part of the body," Donne surmises that this command must have struck Abraham as too "obscene a thing to be brought into the fancy of so many women, so many young men, so many strangers to other nations, as might bring the promise and Covenant itself into scorn and into suspicion." Why, Abraham must have wondered, "does God command me so base and unclean a thing, so scornful and misinterpretable a thing, as circumcision, and circumcision in that part of the body?" The answer, of course, is that in "this rebellious part is the root of all sin." The privy member "need[s] this stigmatical mark of circumcision to be imprinted upon it" to prevent Abraham's descendants from "degenerat[ing] from the nobility of their race."[31] Willet, Donne, and like-minded commentators never quite acknowledge that insofar as the cutting off of the foreskin effectively subdues that rebellious and sinful part of men's bodies, circumcision once again veers perilously close to the idea of a (partial) sexual castration and emasculation.

It was also clear to Christian theologians that for the Jews who literally circumcised the flesh, the Covenant could only be transmitted through men.[32] This helps explain why Jewish daughters like Jessica in *The Merchant of Venice* and Abigail in *The Jew of Malta* can so easily cross the religious boundaries that divide their stigmatized fathers from the dominant Christian community. The religious difference of Jewish women is not usually imagined as physically inscribed in their flesh, and the possibility of identifying women as Jews through some kind of incision never took hold in England, though for a brief time in the fifteenth century in northern Italy the requirement that Jewish women have their ears pierced and wear earrings served precisely this function. In her investigation of this sumptuary tradition, Diane Owen Hughes cites the Franciscan preacher Giacomo della Marca, who in an advent sermon said that earrings are jewels "that Jewish women wear in place of circumcision, so that they can be distinguished from other [i.e., Christian] women."[33] One wonders whether Pauline ideas about circumcising desire also shaped this bizarre proposal. Though this method of marking Jewish women was short-lived (other women also wanted to wear earrings) and apparently not widespread, a trace of it may possibly be found in *The Merchant of Venice*, when Shylock, upon hearing that Jessica has not only left him but also taken his money and jewels, exclaims: "Two thousand ducats in that and other precious, precious jewels. I would my daughter were dead at my foot, and the jewels in her ear!"[34] Shylock fantasizes that his converted daughter returns, and through her earring is reinscribed at last as a circumcised Jewess.

The problems that circumcision raise for issues of gender and sexuality persist into our own more secular age. To cite an unfortunate instance of this, modern medicine, when confronted with the extremely rare cases of botched circumcisions, has found it advisable to alter the gender of the child by reconstructing female rather than male genitalia.[35] Does this procedure confirm the kind of anxieties we have been exploring about the underlying castrating and feminizing threat of circumcision? Or does it suggest that doctors are perhaps so influenced by such deeply embedded cultural beliefs as to translate them into scientific practice? In either case it underscores how provisional the assignment of gender is, a point familiar enough to Shakespeare's audiences confronted in *The Merchant* with cross-dressing women and a hero who describes himself as a "tainted wether," or castrated ram. Circumcision, then, was an extraordinarily powerful signifier, one that not only touched on issues of identity that ranged from the sexual to the theological but, often enough, on the intersection of the two. The threat of Shylock's cut was complex, resonant, and unusually terrifying.

III. Circumcision in the sources of The Merchant

The foregoing analysis may help explain why *The Merchant of Venice*, more than any other depiction of Jews in this period, has continued to provoke such controversy and has also continued to stir long-buried prejudices against the Jews. I want to be careful here about being misunderstood. I am not proposing that Shakespeare is antisemitic (or, for that matter, philosemitic). *The Merchant of Venice* is a play, a work of fiction, not a diary or a polygraph test; since no one knows what Shakespeare personally thought about Jews, readers will continue to make up their own minds about this question. *The Merchant of Venice* is thus not "about" ritual murder or a veiled circumcising threat any more than it is about usury, or marriage, or homosocial bonding, or mercy, or Venetian trade, or cross-dressing, or the many other social currents that run through this and every other one of Shakespeare's plays. Plays, unlike sermons, are not reducible to one lesson or another, nor do they gain their resonance from being about a recognizable central theme. Surely, in the hands of a talented dramatist, the less easily definable the social and psychological currents a play explores, the greater its potential to haunt and disturb. We return again and again to Shakespeare's plays because they seem to operate in these depths and tap into the roots of social contradictions on a stunningly regular basis, leaving critics with the task of trying to explain exactly what these are and how Shakespeare's plays engage them. With this in mind, I offer the following interpretation of the pound of flesh plot.

Those watching or reading *The Merchant of Venice* are often curious about what part of Antonio's body Shylock has in mind when they learn of Shylock's desire to exact "an equal pound" of Antonio's "fair flesh, to be cut off and taken" in that "part" of his body that "pleaseth" the Jew. Those all too familiar with the plot may forget that it is not until the trial scene in act 4 that this riddle is solved and we learn that Shylock intends to cut from Antonio's "breast" near his heart.[36] Or partially solved. Why, one wonders, is Antonio's breast the spot most pleasing to Shylock? And why, for the sake of accuracy, wouldn't Shylock cut out rather than "cut off" a pound of flesh if it were to come from "nearest" Antonio's "heart"? Moreover, why don't we learn of this crucial detail until Shylock's final appearance in the play?

It is not immediately clear how for an Elizabethan audience an allusion to a Jew cutting off a man's "fair flesh" would invoke images of a threat to the victim's heart, especially when one calls to mind the identification of Jews as circumcisors and emasculators. On a philological level, too, the choice of the word *flesh* here carries with it the strong possibility that Shylock has a different part of Antonio's anatomy in mind. In the late sixteenth century the word *flesh* was consistently used, especially in the Bible, in place of *penis*. Readers of the Geneva Bible would know from examples like Genesis 17.11 that God had commanded Abraham to "circumcise the foreskin of your flesh," and that discussions of sexuality and disease in Leviticus always use the word *flesh* when speaking of the penis.[37]

Not surprisingly, popular writers took advantage of the punning opportunities made available by this euphemism. Shortly before writing *The Merchant of Venice* Shakespeare himself had played on the sexual possibilities of *flesh* in *Romeo and Juliet*. In the opening scene of that play the servant Samson, boasting of his sexual prowess, tells Gregory: "Me [the maids] shall feel while I am able to stand, and 'tis known I am a pretty piece of flesh." Playing on the contrast between erect flesh and flaccid fish, Gregory responds: "'Tis well thou art not fish." Mercutio returns to the same tired joke about the loss of tumescence when he says of Romeo's melancholy: "O flesh, flesh, how art thou fishified."[38] *The Merchant of Venice* is similarly replete with bad jokes about trimmed male genitals. As noted above, Antonio in the court scene speaks of himself as "a tainted wether" best suited to suffer the exaction of Shylock's cut.[39] In addition, Salerio's jibe about Jessica having Shylock's "stones," that is, testicles, "upon her" and Gratiano's tasteless joke about "mar[ring] the young clerk's pen" (i.e., penis) offer two other instances from the play of men's obsessive anxiety about castrating cuts.[40] It should also be noted that in Elizabethan England such a cut was not merely the stuff of jokes. As a deterrent to crime, convicted male felons were told at their sentencing to prepare to be "hanged by the neck, and being alive cut down, and your privy members to be cut off, and your bowels to be taken out of your belly and there burned, you being alive."[41]

Scholars have long recognized that Shakespeare drew upon a well established tradition in his retelling of the story of the pound of flesh. Among the printed sources Shakespeare may have looked at were Giovanni Fiorentino's *Il Pecorone* and Alexander Silvayn's *The Orator*. Other scholars have uncovered a range of analogues and antecedents, including popular English ballads like "Gernatus the Jew" and medieval works like the *Cursor Mundi* that bear a strong resemblance to Shakespeare's plot. Surprisingly little attention has been paid, however, to what part of the body the pound of flesh is taken from in these sources and analogues. In fact, when Shakespeare came to one of the main sources that we are pretty confident he consulted, Silvayn's *The Orator*, he would have read about a Jew who wonders if he "should cut of his [Christian victim's] privy members, supposing that the same would altogether weigh a just pound?" Before turning to this story and its curious reception, I want to consider another first, one that is even more revealing about the significance of the pound of flesh: Gregorio Leti's *The Life of Pope Sixtus the Fifth*.

Leti was a popular Italian historian, born in the early seventeenth century, who left Italy and took up residence in Northern Europe after converting to Protestantism. For a brief period in the early 1680s he lived and wrote in England. Although there are no recorded performances of *The Merchant of Venice* during his stay there, Leti may well have become familiar with the printed text of Shakespeare's play in the course of the extensive research he undertook on Elizabethan England.[42] The earliest edition of his biography of Sixtus V, first published in Lausanne in 1669, omits any reference to the celebrated pound of flesh story; the anecdote was only introduced in the revised version, published in Amsterdam after Leti's visit to England,[43] which may suggest that Leti drew on English sources for this addition.

After 1754, when Ellis Farneworth translated Leti's story,[44] those unable to read the Italian original could learn how in the days of Queen Elizabeth I it was "reported in Rome" that the great English naval hero, Sir Francis Drake, "had taken and plundered St. Domingo, in Hispaniola, and carried off an immense booty. This account came in a private letter to Paul Secchi, a very considerable merchant in the city, who had large concerns in those parts, which he had insured." Leti then relates that Secchi then "sent for the insurer, Sampson Ceneda, a Jew, and acquainted him with it. The Jew, whose interest it was to have such a report thought false, gave many reasons why it could not possibly be true; and, at last, worked himself up into such a passion, that he said, "'I'll lay you a pound of my flesh it is a lie.'" Secchi replied, "If you like it, I'll lay you a thousand crowns against a pound of your flesh, that it's true." The Jew accepted the wager, and articles were immediately executed betwixt them, the substance of which was "that if Secchi won, he should himself cut the flesh, with a sharp knife, from whatever part of the Jew's body he pleased."

Leti then relates that "the truth of the account" of Drake's attack "was soon after confirmed by other advices from the West Indies," which threw the Jew "almost into distraction, especially when he was informed that Secchi had solemnly sworn [that] he would compel him to the exact literal performance of his contract, and was determined to cut a pound of flesh from that part of his body which it is not necessary to mention." We move here from a cut "from whatever part of the Jew's body he pleased" to the more precisely defined "part of his body which it is not necessary to mention." The original Italian version conveys even more strongly a sense that only modesty prevents specifying that Secchi's intended cut will come from the unmentionable genitals of the Jew ("e che la modestia non vuo che io nomine").[45] The circumcised Jew faces a bit more surgery than he reckoned for.

The rest of the story should be familiar to anyone who has read Shakespeare's play, except, of course, that this time it is the Christian who is intent on cutting the flesh of the Jew. The Governor of Rome referred the tricky case to the authority of Pope Sixtus V, who tells Secchi that he must fulfill the contract and "cut a pound of flesh from any part you please, of the Jew's body. We would advise you, however, to be very careful; for if you cut but a scruple, or a grain, more or less than your due, you shall certainly be hanged. Go, and bring hither a knife and a pair of scales, and let it be done in our presence." This verdict led both Secchi and the Jew to agree to tear up the contract, though the affair was not fully settled until Sixtus V fined both of them harshly to serve as an example to others.[46]

Farneworth, in a note appended to his translation, states the obvious: the "scene betwixt Shylock and Antonio in Shakespeare's *Merchant of Venice* seems to be borrowed from this story, though the poet has inverted the persons and decently enough altered some of the circumstances."[47] Farneworth's comment that Shakespeare "decently enough . . . altered some of the circumstances" presumably alludes to the threatened castration of the Jew. And while we don't know why Leti in the version of the story has "inverted the persons," there is little likelihood that he did it out of love of the Jews. In his book on Great Britain published in England shortly before his departure, Leti reveals his familiarity with London Jewry, describes the services at the Bevis Marks Synogogue in London in somewhat mocking terms, and makes fun of the ridiculous gestures of the Jewish worshippers.[48] We can only speculate about the original source of Leti's seventeenth-century story. Did it antedate Shakespeare's play, and was Shakespeare familiar with versions in which the Jew was the victim? Or did it emerge out of a tradition that was itself influenced by *The Merchant of Venice*? Did turning the tables and having the Christians threaten to castrate or symbolically recircumcise the Jew ultimately prove more satisfying to Christian readers?

Farneworth's translation of Leti's story made a strong impression on eighteenth-century English interpreters of *The Merchant of Venice*. Edmond Malone reproduced this passage in his influential edition of Shakespeare's works in 1790,[49] and David Erskine Baker, though he does not acknowledge his source, wrote that Shakespeare's story "is built on a real fact which happened in some part of Italy, with this difference indeed, that the intended cruelty was really on the side of the Christian, the Jew being the happy delinquent who fell beneath his rigid and barbarous resentment." Tellingly, he adds that "popular prejudice, however, vindicates our author in the alteration he had made. And the delightful manner in which he has availed himself of the general character of the Jews, the very quintessence of which he has enriched his Shylock with, makes more than amends for his deviating from a matter of fact which he was by no means obliged to adhere to."[50] Again, we are left with a set of difficult choices: is it "popular prejudice" that "vindicates" Shakespeare reassigning the "intended cruelty" to Shylock? Or is it Shakespeare's play that by the late eighteenth-century is influential enough to perpetuate and channel this "popular prejudice"?

Familiarity with this inverted version of the pound of flesh story was given even broader circulation by Maria Edgeworth in her novel *Harrington*, where she allows the Jew, Mr. Montenero, to present what he believes to be the historically accurate version of the facts in his response to Harrington, who had recently attended a performance of Shakespeare's *Merchant of Venice*. Edgeworth, too, sees the issue of "popular prejudice" as a central one, and has Mr. Montenero politely acknowledge that while "as a dramatic poet, it was" Shakespeare's "business . . . to take advantage of the popular prejudice as a *power*," nonetheless "we Jews must feel it peculiarly hard, that the truth of the story should have been completely sacrificed to fiction, so that the characters were not only misrepresented, but reversed." Harrington "did not know to what Mr. Montenero meant to allude. He politely tried to "pass it off with a slight bow of general acquiescence," before Mr. Montenero went on to explain that in "the true story, from which Shakespeare took the plot of *The Merchant of Venice*, it was a Christian who acted the part of the Jew, and the Jew that of the Christian. It was a Christian who insisted upon having the pound of flesh from next the Jew's heart." Seeing how struck Harrington is by this revelation, Mr. Montenero magnanimously offers that "perhaps his was only the Jewish version of the story, and he quickly went on to another subject." Edgeworth adds her own authority to Montenero's when she provides a footnote to the words "true story" directing readers to "Steevens' Life of Sixtus V and Malone's Shakespeare," where the Farneworth translation appears. Strikingly, though, at the very moment that she insists on the original version, Edgeworth herself either misremembers or swerves away from a key features of Leti's "true story" in favor of Shakespeare's version of the events when she substitutes the words "having the pound of flesh from next the Jew's heart" for Farneworth's translation of Leti's original: "from that part of his body which it is not necessary to mention."[51]

Once nineteenth-century Shakespearean source-hunters like Francis Douce and James Orchard Halliwell-Phillipps pointed out that Leti's version could not have antedated Shakespeare's play, and, moreover, that this episode in Sixtus V's life was probably fictional, interest in Leti's narrative rapidly declined. H. H. Furness, in his still influential variorum edition of *The Merchant of Venice*, includes Farneworth's translation but then invokes the authority of those who dismiss it as a source. And though he quotes Farneworth's observation that Shakespeare's plot "is taken from this incident," he cuts off the quotation at the point where it leads Farneworth to point out that Shakespeare has also made the Jew the victim and left out indecent details.[52] Interest in pure sources—rather than near contemporary versions that might cast light on various aspects of the story—has been influential enough in Shakespeare studies in this century to account for the virtual disappearance of Leti's story from editions or even from collections of Shakespeare's sources.[53] Nowadays, Leti's version is no longer cited, mentioned, or even known to most Shakespeareans.

When we turn to Alexander Silvayn's *The Orator*, which these same source-hunters agree is one of Shakespeare's primary sources for the pound of flesh plot, we find a clear precedent for the argument that a Jew considers the possibility of castrating the Christian. The ninety-fifth declamation of *The Orator*, translated into English in 1596 shortly before the composition of *The Merchant*, describes "a Jew, who would for his debt have a pound of the flesh of a Christian."[54] In his appeal to the judge's sentence that he "cut a just pound of the Christian flesh, and if he cut either more or less, then his own head should be smitten off," the Jew insists that in the original agreement the Christian was to hand over the said pound:

> Neither am I to take that which he oweth me, but he is to deliver it me. And especially because no man knoweth better than he where the same may be spared to the least hurt of his person, for I might take it in such a place as he might thereby happen to lose his life. What a matter were it then if I should cut of his privy members, supposing that the same would altogether weigh a just pound?[55]

While Shakespeare's eighteenth-century editors included this source in unadulterated form,[56] a century later it would be partially suppressed, apparently proving too obscene for Furness to reprint in unexpurgated form. In a strange act of textual castration and substitution, Furness alters the line to read "what a matter were it then, if I should cut of his [head], supposing that the same would weigh a just pound."[57] This makes little sense, no matter how light-headed the victim might be, since in the next sentence the Jew continues, "Or else his head, should I be suffered to cut it off, although it were with the danger of mine own life,"[58] and in the sentence after that wonders if his victim's "nose, lips, his ears, and. . . . eyes . . . make of them altogether a pound."[59] Furness's textual intervention immediately influenced subsequent editions of the play; a year after his edition was published, for example, Homer B. Sprague wrote "head" (without brackets) in his popular school edition of the play.[60] The bowdlerization of this source, and the lack of interest in Leti, have effectively deflected critical attention away from aspects of the play that touch upon ritual Jewish practices.

IV. The circumcision of the heart

Why this bond is forfeit,
And lawfully by this the Jew may claim
A pound of flesh, to be by him cut off
Nearest the merchant's heart.
—The Merchant of Venice, *4.1.227–30*

When Paul declares that "the circumcision is of the heart" and is "in the spirit, not in the letter," we are presented with a double displacement: of the physical by the spiritual and of the circumcision of the flesh by the circumcision of the heart. Elizabethan commentators were well aware that Paul's metaphorical treatment of circumcision builds upon a preexisting tradition in the Old Testament, expressed particularly in Deuteronomy 10.16 and 30.6: "Circumcise the foreskin of your heart," and "The Lord thy God will circumcise thine heart."[61] Mornay, in Sidney's translation, also notes that when the Old Testament prophets "rebuke us, they call us not simply uncircumcised, but uncircumcised of heart or lips,"[62] and Peter Martyr simply confirms that "Paul borrowed" this "phrase touching the circumcision of the heart . . . out of the Old Testament."[63]

Hugo Grotius understood that this substitution of heart for flesh neatly defined the relationship between Christian fellowship and the genealogical Judaism it replaced, since the Covenant "should be common to all people." He even argued that the Old Testament prophets recognized this "mystical and more excellent signification contained" in "the precept of circumcision," since they in fact "command the circumcision of the heart, which all the commandments of Jesus aim at."[64] John Donne is particularly eloquent on this symbolic displacement: "The principal dignity of this circumcision was that it . . . prefigured, it directed to that circumcision of the heart." For Donne, "Jewish circumcision were an absurd and unreasonable thing if it did not intimate and figure the circumcision of the heart."[65]

The unexplained displacement of Shylock's cut from Antonio's "flesh" upward to his heart is now considerably clearer. Viewed in light of this familiar exegetical tradition, Shylock's decision to exact his pound of flesh from near Antonio's heart can be seen as the height of the literalism that informs all his actions in the play, a literalism that when imitated by Portia leads to his demise. Also echoing through the trial scene of *The Merchant* are the words of Galatians 6.13: "For they themselves which are circumcised keep not the Law, but desire to have you circumcised, that they might rejoice in your flesh," that is to say (as the gloss to this line in the Geneva Bible puts it), "that they have made you Jews." Shylock will cut his Christian adversary in that part of the body where the Christians believe themselves to be truly circumcised: the heart. Shylock's threat gives a wonderfully ironic twist to the commentary on Paul's Romans that "he is the Jew indeed . . . who cuts off all superfluities and pollutions which are spiritually though not literally meant by the law of circumcision."[66] Psychoanalytically inclined readers will immediately recognize how closely the terms of this Pauline displacement correspond to the unconscious substitution central to Freud's secular theories. Theodore Reik, a disciple of Freud's, interpreted Shylock's bond in just these terms, arguing first that the "condition that he can cut a pound of flesh 'in what part of your body pleaseth me'" is "a substitute expression of castration." Reik adds that when it is later decided that "the cut should be made from the breast, analytic interpretation will easily understand the mechanism of distortion that operates here and displaces the performance from a part of the body below to above."[67]

In repudiating circumcision, Paul's sought to redirect the Covenant, sever the genealogical bond of Judaism, distinguish Jew from Christian, true Jew from false Jew, and the spirit from the flesh (while retaining in a metaphorical sense the sexuality attendant on the flesh). Yet his actual remarks about circumcision are enigmatic and confusing. It is only mild consolation that they proved no less puzzling to the sixteenth-century theologians who tried to untangle the various levels of Paul's literal and symbolic displacements. Take, for example, the Geneva Bible's gloss to Romans, which reaches new depths of convolution in its attempt to iron out these difficulties by asserting that "Paul useth oftentimes to set the letter against the spirit. But in this place the circumcision which is according to the letter is the cutting off of the foreskin. But the circumcision of the spirit is the circumcision of the heart. That is to say, the spiritual end of the ceremony is true holiness and righteousness, whereby the people of God is known from profane and heathenish men." In their frustration, Paul's interpreters often turned against one another. Andrew Willet, for example, chastised Origen for misreading Paul and "thus distinguishing the circumcision of the flesh; that because there is some part of the flesh cut off and lost, some part remaineth still. The lost and cut off part (saith he) hath a resemblance of that flesh, whereof it is said, all flesh is grass. The other part which remaineth is a figure of that flesh, whereof the Scripture speaketh, all flesh shall see the salutation of God." Willet is sensitive to Origen's conflation of the two kinds of circumcision here, spiritual and fleshly—"Origen confoundeth the circumcision of the flesh and the spirit, making them all one"—but it is hard to see how to maintain hard and fast divisions when, on the one hand, commentators drive a wedge between the spiritual and the physical, while, on the other, they show how even in the Old Testament circumcision was used both literally and metaphorically. For Willet, then, the correct interpretation, and one that seems to require a bit of mental gymnastics, requires that we think not of the circumcision of the flesh and the circumcision of the heart "as though there were two kinds of circumcisions" but as "two parts of one and the same circumcision which are sometimes joined together, both the inward and the outward."[68]

V. Uncircumcision

If the distinction between inward and outward circumcision were not confusing enough, Paul further complicated matters by introducing the concept of reverse, or *un*circumcision. Even if a faithful Christian were circumcised in the heart, what if one's body still carried (as Paul's did) the stigmatical mark that revealed to the world that one was born a Jew? The seventeenth-century Scottish preacher John Weemse recognized that the early Christians were embarrassed by this Judaical scar: "When they were converted from Judaism to Christianity there were some of them so ashamed of their Judaism that they could not behold it; they took it as a blot to their Christianity."[69] Uncircumcision, then, was the undoing of the seemingly irreversible physical act that had been accomplished through the observance of Jewish law, and it was a topic that Paul would return to obsessively (in large part because it was a pressing issue within the new Christian communities he was addressing). Paul asks in Romans "if the uncircumcision keep the ordinances of the Law, shall not his uncircumcision be counted for circumcision? And shall not uncircumcision which is by nature (if it keep the Law) condemn thee, which by the letter and circumcision art a transgressor of the Law?"[70] In Galatians he writes in a similar vein that "in Jesus Christ neither circumcision availeth anything" nor "uncircumcision, but faith, which worketh by love."[71] His remarks in Corinthians on the irrelevance of this mark are even more forceful: "Is any man called being circumcised? Let him not gather his circumcision. Is any called uncircumcised? Let him not be circumcised. Circumcision is nothing, and uncircumcision is nothing, but the keeping of the commandments of God."[72]

Paul's shifts between literal and figurative uncircumcision in these key passages are dizzying, and the commentators had to scramble to keep up with him. Thomas Godwyn voices the question that must have been on many readers' minds: "Here it may be demanded how it is possible for a man, after once he hath been marked with the sign of circumcision, to blot out that character and become uncircumcised?"[73] He is responding to Paul's warning that one should not "gather" or reverse one's circumcision. The gloss to this line in the Geneva Bible also takes Paul in the most literal sense imaginable, explaining that this "gathering" is accomplished with "the help of a surgeon" who undoes the effect of the cutting of the foreskin by "drawing the skin with an instrument, to make it to cover the nut" or glans of the penis. The Geneva Bible even directs readers to the medical source for this procedure, the seventh book of Celsus's *De Medicina*.[74] Other writers explained that Paul forbids this literal uncircumcision in his letter to the Corinthians "because some that were converted to Christianity from Judaism did so renounce all their Judaical rites that they used means to attract the preputia again, which was an act of too much superstition and curiosity, and so is censured here."[75] It also needs to be stressed here that, uncircumcision, like circumcision, was understood by Paul's commentators to operate both spiritually and literally; Andrew Willet reminds his readers that "as there are two kinds of circumcision, so there is also a twofold uncircumcision, "an uncircumcision of the heart, and another of the flesh."

The belief that one could be uncircumcised, could have one's irreducible Jewish identity replaced with a Christian one, is also a fantasy that powerfully shapes the final confrontation between Shylock and Antonio in *The Merchant of Venice*. Antonio's consummate revenge upon his circumcised adversary, whose actions symbolically threaten to transform not just his physical but his religious identity, is to ask of the court a punishment that precisely reverses what Shylock had in mind for him. When Antonio demands that Shylock "presently become a Christian," a demand to which the Duke readily agrees, the "christ'ning" that Shylock is to receive will metaphorically uncircumcise him. The new covenant has superseded the old, as the sacrament of baptism, which has replaced circumcision, turns Jew into Christian.[76] In his commentary on Romans Peter Martyr offers up a summary of Paul's treatment of the Jews that ironically foreshadows Antonio's victory over Shylock at the end of the trial scene: "In civil judgments, when any is to be condemned which is in any dignity or magistrateship, he is first deprived of his dignity or office, and then afterward condemned. So the apostle first depriveth the Jews of the true Jewishness, and of the true circumcision, and then afterward condemneth them."[77]

Antonio and Shylock, who fiercely insist on how different they are from each other, to the last seek out ways of preserving that difference through symbolic acts that convert their adversary into their own kind. Paradoxically, though, these symbolic acts—a threatened circumcision of the heart and a baptism that figuratively uncircumcises—would have the opposite effect, erasing, rather than preserving, the literal or figurative boundaries that distinguish merchant from Jew.[78] It is just this fear of unexpected and unsatisfying transformation that makes *The Merchant of Venice* so unsettling a comedy, and that renders the even more deeply submerged and shadowy charge of ritual murder such a potent one. The desire to allay such fears produces a fantasy ending in which the circumcising Jew is metamorphosed through conversion into a gentle Christian. While this resolution can only be sustained through legal force in the play (Shylock's alternative, after all, is to be executed), its power was sufficiently strong for this spectacle of conversion to be reenacted in a number of English churches in late sixteenth- and early seventeenth-century England, as a handful of Jews were led to the baptismal font.

V 🍂

The Hebrew Will Turn Christian

This making of Christians will raise the price of hogs.
—*Lancelot Gobbo in* The Merchant of Venice, *1596*

When a mouse shall catch a cat, then a Jew converted to be a
Christian will remain a firm Christian.
—*Thomas Calvert, 1648*

Antonio's sardonic remark upon agreeing to Shylock's bond—the "Hebrew will turn Christian"[1]—proves to be unusually prophetic. Still, Elizabethan audiences might have been surprised that Shylock submits to this decree, not only because it goes against his character but also because in Shakespeare's sources the defeated Jew had simply torn up the bond and departed.[2] Moreover, coerced conversions were virtually unheard of in the various narratives circulating about Jews in sixteenth-century England. Shylock's conversion is not the only one in the play, nor is Antonio's request in act 4 that Shylock "presently become a Christian" the only point at which *The Merchant of Venice* confronts the issue of Jewish conversion.[3] There is an odd scene midway through the play, often cut in modern productions (perhaps because audiences find its banter about intermarriage, miscegeny, and illegitimacy disturbing) in which Lancelot teases Jessica about her recent conversion to Christianity. When he tells her that he fears for her soul because she is the daughter of a Jew, Jessica replies that she "shall be saved by my husband; he hath made me a Christian." Lancelot responds: "Truly, the more to blame he! We were Christians enough before, e'en as many as could well live, one by another. This making of Christians will raise the price of hogs." The joke is too good to drop, and it is repeated moments later with the entrance of Lorenzo. Jessica

reports to her husband that Lancelot "tells me flatly there's no mercy for me in heaven because I am a Jew's daughter, and he says you are no good member of the commonwealth, for in converting Jews to Christians, you raise the price of pork."[4] In a play in which the financial worries of the moneyed classes are so central—including the venture capital required to woo Portia, Antonio's risky overseas trade, Shylock's moneylending, and Venice's laws protecting foreign merchants—Lancelot's quip can easily pass unnoticed. It points, however, to a larger social concern shaping conversionary efforts at this time, what might be described as the economics of conversion, a topic that will be taken up again later in this chapter.

Also noteworthy is that conversion is not quite the same for Jewish women as it is for Jewish men. In the world of fiction, the marriage and conversion of Jewish women usually go hand in hand; as Jessica puts it, she shall become "a Christian and [Lorenzo's] loving wife."[5] The exception that seems to prove the rule is Abigail, in Marlowe's *The Jew of Malta*, who even after she enters a convent is pursued by Christian suitors (as Don Mathias puts it, "better would she far become a bed, / Embraced in a friendly lover's arms, / Than rise at midnight to a solemn mass").[6] In contrast, Jewish men who convert to Christianity are never married off to Christian women. And where Jewish women are always depicted as young and desirable, male Jewish converts are invariably old and impotent, condemned to remain unwed and at the periphery of the Christian community (a convention not easily reconciled with the concurrent belief that they were "insatiably given unto women").[7] To early modern Englishmen, the fantasy of Christian men marrying converting Jewesses was far more appealing than the idea of Jewish men, even converted ones, marrying Christian women. It is also worth noting that there were English laws dating back to the thirteenth century, technically in effect three centuries later, that condemned to death Christians who had sex with Jews (and linking this activity to the comparable crimes of sodomy and bestiality). In the 1640s Edward Coke once again made available this "ancient law of England, that if any Christian man did marry with a woman that was a Jew, or a Christian woman that married with a Jew, it was felony, and the party so offending should be burnt alive."[8]

While the desire to convert Jews was subtly shaped by economics and gender, it was influenced on a far greater scale by the Bible and Protestant millennial expectations. These were fostered in the late sixteenth century by Romans, where Paul assures his audience of the Jews' future calling to the Christian faith; by Revelation, which led millenarian interpreters to conclude that the conversion of the Jews was a necessary antecedent to Christ's Second Coming; and above all, by the prophesies of Daniel, whose obscure chronologies were cited as confirmation that Jesus Christ truly was the messiah the

Jews had long awaited. Here, too, Shakespeare's play provides a momentary if shadowy glimpse into the larger social and religious concerns intertwined with the conversion of the Jews, a glimpse that comes in the trial scene with Shylock's invocation of Portia as a "Daniel come to judgement, yea, a Daniel!" which is turned triumphantly back upon him by Gratiano, after Shylock is thwarted: "A second Daniel, a Daniel, Jew!" and again, "A Daniel, still say I, a second Daniel!"[9] Editors of the play uniformly note that the characters are alluding to the apocryphal story of Susannah and the elders, where Daniel is described as "a young child" who convicts the lying elders out of their own mouths. The explanations go no further, perhaps because the similarities between the young Portia and Daniel end there. It is worth considering what else the invocation of Daniel might have meant to Shakespeare's audiences, for even if the reference might have recalled the story of Susannah, Elizabethans did not consider this narrative as separate from the rest of Daniel: as the Geneva Bible notes, it was often joined "to the end of Daniel" to "make it the thirteenth chapter." In scores of sermons and tracts produced in the late sixteenth century, Daniel called to mind first and foremost the Jewish prophet who foresaw the final judgment, an event precipitated by the conversion of the Jews.

My interest here is not in forcing a line or two of a play to fit more snugly into a favored interpretation, but in exploring how *The Merchant of Venice* touches upon a number of aspects of what this "turning" of the Jews meant in post-Reformation England. Since surprisingly little has been written on this subject, much of this chapter is concerned with presenting contemporary evidence that shows the extraordinary interest Elizabethans had in the conversion of the Jews, an interest intensified by religious controversies that produced a crisis of faith, the severity of which, it was hoped, Jewish conversion might somehow alleviate.

I. English reformations and Jewish conversion

In the past twenty years or so the place of the Jews in the millenarian aspirations of seventeenth-century English men and women has been explored in great detail. We now have a much better sense of how this interest peaked in mid-century and "contributed to demands for a militant foreign policy which would expedite Antichrist's overthrow, the gathering of the Gentiles, and the conversion of the Jews."[10] To this end, by the 1650s dozens of pamphlets promising the imminent conversion of the Jews were circulating through England, with titles like *The Great Deliverance of the Whole House of Israel*, and *Light for the Jews, or, the Means to Convert Them*.[11] Building on this recent research, David Katz has shown how strongly these apocalyptic beliefs shaped English attitudes toward readmitting Jews in the 1650s.[12]

Since almost all of the scholars working on English millenarian beliefs have worked backward from their impact on the English Revolution or the Read-mission of the Jews, the pursuit of the roots of this tradition rarely extends beyond the early years of the seventeenth century, which witnessed the landmark work of Thomas Brightman, Thomas Draxe, Sir Henry Finch, and Joseph Mede. This is unfortunate, because this approach has created the misleading impression that English interest in the conversion of the Jews was not widespread during Elizabeth's reign. In fact, England's fascination with the conversion of the Jews had begun in earnest in the late 1570s and early 1580s and was quite well established by the time that Shakespeare wrote *The Merchant of Venice*. In reconsidering this topic I'd like to work forward in time from the Reformation, or, to be more accurate, from the series of reformations England experienced beginning with the reign of Henry VIII. Reformist theology, coupled with the crisis of religious identity produced by England's break from Catholicism, brought into question what before this time had been one of the least troubled aspects of social identity: what it meant to be Christian. The rapid transformations in English religious beliefs in the sixteenth century generated a demand for something that could reground faith in a world filled with challenges and counterchallenges to what had once seemed infallible doctrine. This demand was met in part by the idea of the stubborn Jew whose conversion not only revealed the truths of Christianity in general but also, many sects hoped, the rightness of their own particular beliefs.

A brief overview of this historical context is in order. Henry VIII's decision in the early 1530s to replace papal authority over the Church of England with his own was motivated in large part by his desire to divorce Catherine of Aragon.[13] His break with Rome led to further reforms, including ransacking the monasteries, translating the Bible into English, and ending many Catholic ceremonies (though it must be pointed out that in his last years on the throne Henry slowed the pace of reform and edged back somewhat toward traditional Catholic practices).[14] Upon Henry's death in 1547 his young son Edward VI came to the throne and greatly accelerated the pace of reform his father had set in motion. Revised prayer books were produced that rearranged the church calendar and transformed the popular experience of the mass, changes that helped provoke a Catholic uprising in 1549. Throughout England during Edward's reign parish churches sold off Catholic objects and replaced them with now mandated English Bibles and published homilies. But Edward's brief reign, though it had dampened traditional Catholic beliefs, had not extinguished them. Many objects that had been hidden away were brought back into churches after 1554 when Edward died and was succeeded by his Catholic sister, Mary I.[15]

Even as it is a mistake to see Henry VIII's break with Roman Catholicism

in absolute terms, it would be no less erroneous to see Mary's restoration of
Catholicism as marking a complete reversal of the changes that had taken place
in the previous decade. Nonetheless, Latin masses were heard again in England, and the publication of new religious primers replaced their reformist predecessors. There was also fairly severe punishment accorded to noncon-
formists: some three hundred Protestants were burned to death, and many others fled to the shelter of the continental Protestant communities in Geneva and
Basel. Despite Mary's Catholic reforms, a complete transformation of belief
could not be imposed in such a brief span of time. Moreover, the availability of
Protestant evangelical books and of English Bibles, sixty editions of which had
been published during Edward's short reign, enabled individuals to read and
interpret God's word independently. Reformist ideas were not and could not
be entirely suppressed.[16]

When Queen Elizabeth I followed her half-sister to the throne in 1558, English Christians experienced their third religious upheaval in a little more than a
decade. Elizabeth passed an Act of Uniformity and once again abolished the
Catholic mass. Yet resistance to her reforms was not insignificant, and to
"many folks . . . the distinctions between their Catholic faith and the Queen's
church remained comfortably vague" until the end of the 1560s and perhaps
longer.[17] Once again, as under Edward VI, there was a large-scale appropriation as well as the destruction of altars and vestments.[18] As Elizabeth's reign
stretched on into the 1570s and 1580s, the face of change became more permanent. Scholars are increasingly acknowledging that the real break with traditional Catholic practices did not occur until the late 1570s, midway through
Elizabeth's reign.[19] By "the end of the 1570s, whatever the instincts and nostalgia of their seniors, a generation was growing up which had known nothing
else, which believed the Pope to be Antichrist, the Mass a mummery, which did
not look back to the Catholic past as their own, but another country, another
world."[20] The Elizabethan Settlement preserved the peace but stopped well
short of resolving the differences that now separated English Christians across
a broad spectrum that ranged from an adherence to an ancestral Catholicism at
one extreme to radical Puritanism on the other. It was within such a climate
that interest in the conversion of the Jews flourished.

If these were the social and political conditions that helped generate this
interest, the intellectual and theological seeds were planted back in the 1540s
and 1550s by continental reformers influenced by the writing of Paul. They
were particularly struck by Paul's explicit declaration in Romans that "all
Israel shall be saved."[21] The commentary accompanying this epistle in the
Geneva Bible explains that "God appointed this casting off of the Jews that it
might be an occasion to call the Gentiles; and again might turn this calling of
the Gentiles to be an occasion to restore the Jews."[22] The "blindness of the

Jews" was neither universal nor for all time: "as the prophets have fore-warned" there "shall be a time" when the Jews "shall effectually embrace that which they do now so stubbornly for the most part reject and refuse." The commentary to Romans is unambiguous on this point: Paul "beateth this into their heads that the nation of the Jews is not utterly cast off without hope of recovery."[23] It was also a belief that evangelical preachers and writers contin-ued to beat into the heads of Elizabethan parishioners.

The forewarning of the prophets spoken of here is primarily an allusion to Daniel and Revelation, texts to which sixteenth-century reformers tirelessly returned. Daniel "was concerned with the specific and visible monarchies in world history." Its two visions, in which four monarchies are portrayed—the "vision of the idol and the vision of the four beasts"—stood for the four empires, usually understood to signify Babylon, the Medes and Persians, Greece, and Rome.[24] The prophesies found in the Revelation of St. John offered a history of Christianity that neatly dovetailed with Daniel's history of the world, and mapped it out in three distinct stages: from "the time from Christ to Constantine; the millennium of Satan's bondage; and the final forty-two months of the world's history during which the final plagues and trials prepared the Church for the second coming to judgment."[25]

The Protestant reformers' interest in the historical rather than symbolic interpretation of these prophesies can be traced back to Luther's decision in the 1540s to reject the allegorical readings Augustine had successfully imposed upon these works. Augustine had himself reversed the millenarian perspective of the early Church, insisting on a metaphorical approach in which the "thou-sand years' reign became merely the work of the church on earth."[26] In place of these readings, Luther, Melanchton, and their successors discovered in the prophesies of Daniel and Revelation the veiled story of their own struggle against the Antichrist, Rome. For them, Daniel and Revelation "were genuine, if obscure, historical prophesies." This model of history was easy for Protes-tant reformers to accept, since they were convinced that the Pope was Antichrist and they needed to explain why God had allowed the papacy to per-secute the faithful for a thousand years.[27] As historical events in the wake of the Reformation forced these reformers to place themselves in history, they responded by searching out and discovering the appropriate scriptural confir-mation that their Church had always been true and visible. Out of this scrip-tural justification—in both Old and New Testament texts—also came a need to address some peripheral issues raised by these prophesies, including the con-version and restoration of the Jews.

An unanticipated difficulty was how daunting a task interpreting the obscure prophesies of Daniel proved to be, especially when the historical chronologies predicting the last days had to be perfectly reconciled with the scriptural authority of Revelation. The Gordian knot that historical chronologists struggled to cut was the notoriously problematic prophesy of Daniel's "seventy weeks."[28] Careers were made—and wasted—elaborating upon the smallest details of this crux. The Cambridge classicist and Hebraist Edward Lively is a typical case. He published a dense volume in 1597 in which he limited himself to the historical problems raised in the last four verses of the ninth book of Daniel. Lively points out that not merely a knowledge of Hebrew and of rabbinical scholarship is required to "to unlock the shut and hid meaning of Daniel's oracles" but also a command of such classical authorities as "Pliny, Pausanius, Solinus, Horatius, Homer, Sophocles, Herodotus, Euripides, Xenaphon, Plutarch, Quintus Curtius, Festus, Pompeieus, Cicero, Galen, [and] Stabo."[29] It is no wonder that this text attracted some of the most ambitious and brilliant minds of the period.

This was no matter of how many angels could dance on the head of a pin. At stake for Protestants was a reading of Scripture that confirmed the historical legitimacy of their church, the defeat of the papal Antichrist, and the imminent end of the world (though most writers, at least until the early seventeenth century, cautiously avoided predicting the precise date that the world would end). English scholarship on historical chronology proliferated from the 1540s onward.[30] Interest in these matters was not limited to scholars and divines; King James himself was busy writing about "this our last age."[31] A further great prize awaiting the scholar able to unlock the secrets of Daniel was the irrefutable evidence, produced by a prophet even the stubborn Jews accepted, needed to persuade Jews that Christ really was the messiah. To this end, one of the most debated issues raised by Daniel was, as Andrew Willet succinctly puts it, "Whether all the Jews shall be called before the coming of Christ?" Willet, theologically a centrist, found himself between the more extreme positions of those who argued that only a few Jews would be called and those who believed in a universal calling. He concluded that "the safer opinion is" that it is not likely that "the whole nation is like to be called," and that Paul had only meant that "the greater part" of the Jewish people "shall be converted and believe."[32]

That this controversy extended beyond the study and pulpit into a wider public sphere is made clear enough in Ben Jonson's *The Alchemist* (1610), where the playwright's parody depends upon his audience's familiarity with these interpretations. Jonson pokes fun at the more recondite scholarship by having Dol Common in the midst of a fit speak bits and pieces of it: "after Alexander's death . . . that Perdiccas and Antigonus were slain, the two that stood, Seleuc', and Ptolomy. . . . made up the two legs, and the fourth beast," while at "last Gog-dust and Egypt dust . . . fall in the last link of the fourth chain."[33] These incoherent fragments derive from historical chronologies that had for several decades now been the basis of sermons and commentary. The fact that the ideas Jonson parodies are so foreign to our own sensibilities (and are simply cut in modern productions) should not diminish the fact that they represented a herculean effort on the part of Protestant reformers to rewrite the history of the Church and show that the Protestant one was both true and visible.

These polemical objectives were of incalculable importance in the struggle between Protestants and their Catholic opponents for much of the late six-teenth century. In their enthusiasm to undermine the positions of their adver-saries, Protestant and Catholic writers alike hunted down instances of how their opponents had betrayed their own faith. Matthew Sutcliffe, for example, accused the Catholic writer Robert Parsons of being an apostate who could "turn like a weathercock and renounce religion," and he asks whether Parsons would "have all his countrymen to prove apostates like himself?"[34] The polemic turned even nastier when both Catholics and Protestants uncovered examples of how their opponents had converted to Islam or Judaism. The Catholic writer William Rainolds composed a thousand-page Latin tract, *Calvino-Turcismus*, showing how similar Protestant beliefs were to those of Islam.[35] Two could play at this game; Matthew Sutcliffe's *De Turco-Papismo* refuted these charges, insisting that it was Catholics, not Protestants, who so closely resembled the Turks in their beliefs, rites, ceremonies, and feasts.[36]

These exchanges proved little besides the fact that both sides were vulner-able to apostasy and that it did not take much for Christians to turn Turk or Judaize. This point is made especially clear in one of the books spawned by this controversy, *The Converted Jew*, written by Catholic writer Roger Ander-ton under the pseudonym John Clare in 1630. The book consists of an imag-inary dialogue set in Oxford between a Jewish convert to Catholicism named Micheas and his three Protestant interlocutors, Ochinus (an early English Protestant), Heuserus (chief pastor of Heidelberg), and John Rainolds (a Puritan and brother of the Catholic writer who had written *Calvino-Turcis-mus*). The convert Micheas methodically uncovers the instability of the grounds of the Protestants' faith, a religion, he points out, not more than sev-enty years older than he himself, and is so devastating in his critique that Ochinus and Heuserus, finding the basis of all their beliefs undermined, abandon their faith in Christ in favor of Islam and Judaism, respectively (as in fact these historical figures had done in their own lives). Micheas cannot resist providing additional examples of famous Judaizing Protestants, such as the "impious Jew" David George, once "a chief Protestant and . . . professor" at Basel, and Alamanus, a disciple of Zwingli and friend of Beza, who also became a "blasphemous Jew." And he tells Rainolds that to read of other "Protestants, who became Turks and Jews," he need only consult "a book written by his own brother, William Rainolds, called *Calvino-Turcismus*," and helpfully provides references to specific passages where these apostasies are described.[37]

By the second decade of the seventeenth century a related genre emerged in England: narratives in which Protestants and Catholics celebrated their renunciation of their previous false faith, and their providential submission to the true one. What is striking about these testimonies is how belated they are, appearing decades later than one might have expected, given that the Reformation had begun nearly a century earlier. Why didn't these works start pouring from the presses in the 1570s? Or at least by the 1590s? Looking back, it is easy to argue that the Reformation was irreversible after Henry VIII, or Edward VI, or surely after the Catholic Northern Rebellion of 1569 under Elizabeth I. But to contemporaries the gulf between Catholicism and Anglican Protestantism would only be unbridgeable after the 1580s and 1590s. Given the extent of doctrinal overlap between the Church of England and the Roman Catholic Church, it is easy to see how there may have been confusion about what really distinguished the two forms of worship, once one moved beyond the question of royal versus papal authority and the use of the vernacular. Only in the 1590s, with the publication (and repeated reprinting) of works like Andrew Willet's *Synopsis Papismi, That Is, a General View of Papistrie* (1592), were Elizabethans finally able to identify point for point exactly what distinguished Anglican from Catholic doctrine and practice.

In the course of the years 1609–1625 a score of these conversion tracts poured from various presses,[38] including those describing Protestant conversions to Catholicism by Humphrey Leech,[39] Francis Walsingham, the Cambridge divine Benjamin Carier,[40] and the Anglican minister Theophilus Higgons, who then apostasized again, returning to the Protestant fold.[41] On the other side, among those who published tracts upon renouncing Catholicism in favor of the reformed faith were Richard Shelton,[42] the Carthusian monk Christopher Musgrave,[43] John de Nicholas,[44] Ferdinand Texeda,[45] and the Catholic Archbishop of Spalato, Marco Antonio de Dominis, who broke with Rome and made his way to England in 1616 before subsequently returning to the Catholic fold.[46] The end result of this series of exhausting and confusing conversions and apostasies was that, rather than proving for all time and all readers the rightness of a particular set of Christian doctrines, the narratives revealed as never before since the early history of the Church how unstable Christian religious identity could be. The language of antitheatricalism, itself largely the product of Puritan polemicists, had begun to color theological controversy as well: Robert Burton, for example, speaks of the papacy as "a new scene of superstitious imposters and heretics, a new company of actors,"[47] perhaps raising in some minds the possibility that these new actors were merely challenging a temporarily more established troupe.

In such a climate public interest in the conversion of Jews also flourished, for given the indecisive outcome of these doctrinal battles, what could confirm the rightness of Christian doctrine more than the conversion of a Jew? The styles of the Protestants and the Catholics in converting Jews differed in predictable ways: for continental Catholics in this period of Counter-Reformation it constituted an exciting theatrical event; for Protestants in England the Jew's printed confession of Christian faith following a sober sermon proved more appropriate.

The best surviving account by an Elizabethan of Counter-Reformation Catholic methods of converting Jews is Gregory Martin's unpublished "Roma Sancta."[48] Martin, a Catholic who had fled Protestant England, is best known for his translation for English Catholics of the Old and New Testaments. His unpublished guide to Rome includes a long chapter on "Preaching to the Jews for Their Conversion." Martin, who believed that the main reason that the Jews are "suffered to live" is "for the confirmation of our faith," explains that Jews in Rome "are not forced" to convert, but rather are "invited and persuaded to forsake obstinate Judaism." In practice, this meant obligatory attendance at conversion sermons every Saturday afternoon "to hear what may be said for Christianity against their Judaism." Gathered at this proceeding were not only leading church officials, but also "noble citizens and strangers . . . of all countries and states, flocking hither so thick as to no other exercise besides."

In this great spectacle of conversion, the "converted and the late baptized Jews have their place among the Christians." Eloquent converts then debated with the remaining Jews, trying to "confound them by their own peevish opinions and absurd imaginations." Part of the entertainment was watching how irritated the Jews in attendance became at having the prophesies of Daniel turned against them. The end result of all this activity was that "now one, and now another, and sometime a whole household, sometime of the rabbis themselves, feel compunction and remorse. . . . and so signifying their mind, they are received and baptized."[49] The Protestant Henry Blount, who questioned Levantine Jews about these conversions to Catholicism in Rome, skeptically reports that the Jews "pretend" that these supposed apostates are actually "poor Christians hired from other cities, to personate that part."[50] Either way, it was impressive theater.

This Roman Catholic spectacle was paralleled in London by a more modest and scripturally grounded Protestant conversion of a Jew, something that was not so easily arranged, given how few Jews were living in England and how few of them were known to be Jews and willing to convert. On April 1, 1577, Londoners gathered at the small parish church of All Hallows in Langbourn Ward to witness the conversion of Yehuda Menda, who had been living in

London for the previous five years. Following his baptism Menda took on a new name, Nathaniel, and no less a figure than John Foxe then provided a stirring sermon to mark the event. Foxe praises God for "glorious work begun with this Israelite stranger," and asks for His help "to allure the whole remnant of the circumcised race, by this example."[51]

Foxe's sermon, based on Paul's Romans, encapsulates the major Protestant ideas about the conversion of the Jews circulating in England in the 1570s. Addressing Menda (and a fictive Jewish audience) in his sermon, Foxe says: "I hope well of your amendment. For why should I not hope, when as I find St. Paul to conceive so well of your return again," for the same sermon that Paul had preached "concerning the falling away of the Jews . . . also very plainly disclose[s] that high mystery touching that blessed and joyful return of the Jews." Foxe's sermon also makes clear how central a text Daniel was for the conversion of the Jews. Foxe tells his (imagined) Jewish listeners that this "heavenly prophet doth in few words comprehend the whole estate of your commonweal. . . . together with the utter abolishment of the observances and sacrifices of the ceremonial Law, by such special marks and tokens so evidently, that it can by no means possible be gainsaid."[52] Foxe is no philosemite, however, and he rails against the Jews' "intolerable scorpion-like savageness, so furiously boiling against the innocent infants of the Christian Gentiles," as well as their other "heinous abominations, insatiable butcheries, treasons, frenzies, and madness."[53]

While Foxe directly addresses the Jews in his sermon, his real target is undoubtedly fellow Christians, not only the Catholics (whom Foxe derides for their "stagelike gestures and pelting trumperies") but also all Christians whose faith has been undermined by Reformation and Counter-Reformation polemic: "For howsoever Christian divinity is tossed and turmoiled to and fro, with innumerable, intricate, entangled, and wandering questions, yet remaineth faith one self-same nevertheless both pure and simple: and as it is but one, so aught all men necessarily be induced therewith wholly." Yet even as Foxe asserts the bedrock foundation of this single true faith, he concedes that even this needs some bolstering: "Admit that a man stand assured and steadfast in the certainty of his faith, yet what faith is there so sure, constant and unvanquishable, but may be more stable and perfect?"[54] For Foxe, there was no better way to buttress the shaky foundation of this "true and sincere" faith, making it even more "stable," than Menda's public conversion.

Menda, for his part, dutifully delivers a *Confession of Faith* in which he promises to "utterly forsake my former ways and the steps that my nation walketh in, leaving with them not only that false looking for another Christ, but my name also which was given me at my circumcision (being Yehuda) though in itself it be honourable; desiring that as I have received a new gift from the Lord, so in token thereof I may be called Nathaneal."[55] Menda had learned well the anti-Catholic views of his converters, explaining that "had it not been for the great and manifold idolatry that is committed and used amongst the Christians almost in all places where His name is professed, many of our nation had repented in sackcloth and ashes and had come to this man Jesus."[56] Sir Francis Walsingham, the influential Puritan Privy Councillor and Elizabeth's Principal Secretary, missed the service due to illness, and had Foxe deliver the sermon again in his presence. Menda retired to London's Domus Conversorum, where he lived for the next thirty years, signing for his stipend in Hebrew. His confession of faith and Foxe's sermon were soon published together. A Latin version of Foxe's sermon was also published that year, presumably for a wider European audience.[57]

Millennial hopes for the conversion of the Jews increased considerably in England in the years following this celebrated conversion. An interesting example that has escaped attention is a manuscript on the "Conversion and Restoration of Israel" completed in 1580 by Roger Edwards. While in prison in the Tower of London because of the offense taken at a previous manuscript (in which he had presumed to advise Queen Elizabeth on the sensitive topic of "the establishment of the succession of the crown"),[58] Edwards gave himself "wholly to read God's book" that "affirmeth the general conversion and restitution of the house of Israel."[59] Eager to share this knowledge and desperate for patronage, Edwards dedicated his manuscript to a number of prominent figures, including the Lord High Treasurer Burghley, the Earl of Bedford, the Earl of Leicester, the Bishop of London, and Sir Francis Walsingham. We also know from his correspondence with John Dee that Edwards had first taken his ideas about the conversion and restitution of the Jews to religious leaders, but they were not sufficiently enthusiastic, "either through malice or ignorance."[60] Edwards's surviving correspondence gives us some sense of how widespread belief was in the conversion of the Jews: the Bishop of Lincoln, for example, wrote back to Edwards that he "never impugned that opinion of the general restitution of Israel," and Dee too foresaw a "paradoxical restitution Judaical."[61]

Edwards's millenarian views—though more intensely felt than those quietly held by leading intellectuals and church figures—were nowhere near as politically threatening as his manuscript on royal succession had been. But there were others writing in England in the 1580s whose apocalyptic fantasies about the conversion and restitution of the Jews did cross over the line of what was considered permissible. One of these was Ralph Durden, a Cambridge-educated minister, who was imprisoned in 1586 for "predicting the downfall of the Tudor monarchy" and for prophesying that "he would lead the Jews and all the saints to rebuild Jerusalem."[62] A good deal of what we know about Durden's beliefs comes from a confiscated letter he had written to a tailor in Cambridge named Robert Williamson, "one of his party" who had been also been imprisoned and interrogated. In this letter Durden explains that he had been chosen by God to fulfill the scriptural prophesies of Daniel, Revelation, Isaiah, and Romans. Durden believed that "the Jews are to be brought from among the Gentiles, even unto the land of Judea," and that he was "ordained of God to be their deliverer." Apparently, Durden thought of the English Puritans as the true Israelites, for he writes that "we are the same Israelites, whom this land doth persecute" and who "shall be sent unto the land promised us" in "this Queen's days, that now reigneth." Shortly after that, he concludes, "all the kings of the whole world shall be gathered together, to fight against us in Judea, where we shall have the victory; and all the kings of the world shall be obedient unto us, and pay us tribute." [63] In his examination and confession Robert Williamson asserted that Durden said that "all that tarry in England shall be damned, except they go with him . . . to build Jerusalem."[64] Durden soon retracted these seditious claims and remained a minister in Essex for many years.

While Durden escaped severe punishment for his fantasy of leading the "Jews" to Jerusalem, Francis Kett in 1589 was not so fortunate. He reputedly claimed that "whosoever will be saved, must before he die go to Jerusalem," that "Christ with his apostles are now personally in Judea gathering of his Church," and that "the faithful should miraculously be preserved at Jerusalem with a wall of fire, and be fed with angels' food from heaven." William Burton, a contemporary preacher, writes of Kett that these dreams "caused him to plunge himself over head and ears in most damnable heresies." For these and other beliefs (including his claim "that Christ is not God, but a good man as others be"), Kett was condemned to death. The Bishop of Norwich charged him with heresy and wrote to the Lord High Treasurer Burghley, urging that Kett be executed; Kett was burned in the castle ditch at Norwich on January 14, 1589.[65] Within a year of Kett's death Andrew Willet completed the first book on the conversion of the Jews to be printed in England.[66] In this Latin work Willet compares the notorious Kett with a recent false messiah, the Marrano Solomon Molko, who earlier in the century had generated considerable support among European Jewry before he was executed by Charles V in Italy in 1532. Willet first speaks of Molko's heretical belief in the restoration of the Jews before turning to "Kett, our Englishman, who was justly sentenced to the fire and flames and burned at Norwich, having been caught in the same heresies and obstinately persisting in them."[67]

While a good deal of attention has been focused on the more radical millenarians like Durden and Kett, other individuals, like Andrew Willet and the Cambridge teacher and preacher William Perkins, represent a more mainstream strand of those in England who wrote about the conversion of the Jews. In 1587 Perkins wrote *A Fruitfull Dialogue Concerning the Ende of the World*, in which he responds to the popular report that the following year would usher in the Final Judgment.[68] The *Dialogue* consists of an exchange between a scholar named Christian and a wealthy man named Worldling whom he meets on the road to Cambridge. Their conversation turns to the topic of prophesies, and Worlding asks the young scholar whether the world shall come to an end "this next year?" Christian responds "that it is not possible for any to find out the time of the end of the world," and even "if it were possible to appoint that time," such prophesies "were not lawful." The skeptical Wordling is sure that the young scholar is hoarding his knowledge: "Everybody thinketh that unto learned men it is both possible and lawful" to know. Like Roger Edwards, Worlding also points out that all "the signs of the coming of Christ are past. Oh, what earthquakes have there been? What famine? What wars and hurly-burlies among men? What signs in the sun and moon? What flashing in the air? What blazing stars? Surely, surely, the world can not last long." Christian calmly responds that while some of the signs of Christ's coming have already taken place——the preaching of the gospel, the "spreading abroad of errors, heresies, and schisms," the Pope revealed as Antichrist, and "the afflictions of the world by earthquakes, wars, pestilence, famine, and such like"——the last crucial sign, "the conversion of the Jews unto that religion which now they hate," has not yet come to pass: "this sign which goeth immediately before the coming of Christ to judgment is not yet fulfilled, for anything I can tell."[69] Their fictional dialogue provides unusual access into the kinds of popular beliefs rarely encountered in historical documents: the conviction, based on natural signs, that the end of the world was near, coupled with the belief that only the conversion of the Jews stood in the way of the final judgment. If Perkins's *Dialogue* is any indication, the force of Reformist theology concerning the prophesies contained in Daniel and Revelation had by the late 1580s begun to shape not only intellectual battles but popular beliefs as well.

The late 1570s also witnessed the translation into English of Socrates Scholasticus's stories of large-scale conversions of Jews "a thousand years ago."[70] One of the more vivid stories in this history describes how "the Jews in Crete," having been deceived by a false messiah, "embraced the Christian faith." A "certain Jew, being a subtle knave, feigned himself to be Moses and said that he came down from heaven for to lead the Jews which inhabited the isle through the sea into . . . the land of promise." This description might have struck a resonant chord with Elizabethans who had recently been warned about the apocalyptic preachings of heretics like Kett. When the appointed day came, this false messiah then "brought them to a certain mountain" from which the Jews were to "cast themselves into the sea." The outcome was terrible to behold: "some were crushed tumbling down the hill," while others "were drowned in the sea." Christian fishermen and merchants, seeing what was happening, "drew up some which were almost choked with water and saved their lives." The victimized Jews, shaken by this turn of events, decided then and there to "forsake Judaism and cleave unto the Christian faith."[71]

This and other such stories continued to circulate in England well into the early seventeenth century and proved a source of excitement and comfort to those who fervently believed in the imminent conversion of the Jews. Among those cheered by such reports was Joseph Mede, a leading millenarian writer who believed that just as "Paul [was] no sooner converted, but was immediately inspired with the knowledge of the mysteries of Christ, without the instruction of any apostle or disciple," so too, the "Jews with their miraculous calling shall be illuminated also with the knowledge of the mysteries of the Christian faith, even as it is taught in the Reformed churches, without any instructors from them or conference with them."[72] Mede's fantasy of the Jews' sudden and Pauline conversion reveals just how powerfully the Jews figured in the minds of Protestant reformers desperate for some irrefutable confirmation of their beliefs.

When another millenarian, William Twisse, wrote to Mede to express some reservations about the idea of this sudden Pauline conversion of the Jews, Mede wrote back insisting that the Jews "will never believe that Christ reigns at the right hand of God, until they see him; it must be invincible evidence which must convert them after so many hundred years of settled obstinacy," though he acknowledges that there may be some "converted upon other motives, as a forerunner of the great and main conversion." While Mede admits to Twisse that his argument is not yet strong enough "to build a firm assent upon," his is nonetheless optimistic, for he recently discovered a history, until then unknown in England, "of the greatest multitude of Jews that ever, I think, were converted since the apostles' times," a discovery that confirms for him the rightness of his belief in "a miraculous apparition" that will convert the multitude of Jews. The narrative he had stumbled upon described an event that had occurred in the year 570 following a public disputation between Jews and Christians in which the side that lost agreed to convert to the others' faith. On the third day of the disputation Jesus miraculously intervened, descending "from heaven with beams of glory," whereupon "the Jews were all stricken blind, and received not their sight till they were baptized." Mede admits that he himself has some doubts about the varacity of this report: "If this story be true, it makes much for a probability of such a conjecture for the future. If it be counterfeit, at least it argues that some many ages ago thought such a mean not unlikely; for poets themselves are wont to feign."[73] This last touch is a nice one: it show how narratives of conversions, even if fictional, nonetheless signal a larger truth. The lines between fictional and factual conversion narratives would be crossed time and again in their retellings in early modern English books, sermons, and confessions of faith.

With Joseph Mede we have jumped too far ahead, several decades beyond the 1580s and 1590s or how what was written in those decades might have shaped Elizabethan attitudes toward the conversion of the Jews. Up until this point I have dealt primarily with reformist millenarian thinking and the related issue of confirming doctrinal truths, issues that would continue to engage English theologians, as Mede's letters to Twisse clearly show. But there were other advantages to converting Jews, economic ones, about which Elizabethans were especially alert.

III. The economics of conversion

When Peter Martyr, the noted sixteenth-century continental reformer and Oxford lecturer, spoke of Jewish conversion, he did so in language drawn from the worlds of agriculture and commerce: "This scattering of them abroad in the world" is not "unprofitable unto the Christians," because the Jews' punishment serves as a warning to the Christians who are "grafted in their place." He adds that "there is another commodity which cometh unto us by the dispersing" of the Jews, and that is the preservation of "the holy Bible."[74] While Martyr thinks of commodity and profit in theological terms, others would quickly capitalize on the more tangible gains that conversionary plans made possible. By the early seventeenth century, merchants trading in foreign ports were even encouraged to carry with them pocket-sized guides for converting non-Christians, so that they could be prepared when "in their long voyages they commonly met with "Pagans" in China, "Mahometans" in the "Turkish empire," or "Jews, who as they are now professed enemies of Christians, so are dispersed through the greatest part of the world."[75] Less well known are plans that predate these seventeenth-century efforts, including Hugh Broughton's efforts to combine "policy with religion" in 1596, the same year that Shakespeare's *The Merchant of Venice* was first staged. Broughton hoped to convert all the Jews of Constantinople to Protestantism, thereby winning for England control of the lucrative Turkish trade.

The origins of this enterprise reach as far back as the early editions of John Foxe's *Actes and Monuments*. Foxe recounts an incident that took place in 1528 in which "a Christian Jew in Constantinople [was] martyred by the Turks." Foxe tells how the Jew after "receiving the sacrament of baptism was converted and became a good Christian. The Turks, fearing lest his conversion should be a detriment to their Mahometical law . . . sought means how to put him to death, which in short time after they accomplished." When "they cast his dead corpse into the streets, commanding that no man should be so hardy as to bury the same," the "marvelous glory and power of Christ" manifested itself: for "the dead corpse lying so by the space of nine days in the midst of the streets, retained so his native color and was so fresh, without any kind of filthiness or corruption, and also not without a certain pleasant and delectable scent or odor, as if it had been lately slain, or rather not slain at all. Which when the Turks beheld, they were thereat marvelously astonished, and being greatly afraid, they themselves took it up, and carried it to a place near without the town and buried it."[76] The apocryphal story and accompanying woodcut (see illustration 4) nicely capture the spirit of English attitudes towards Jewish conversion in the 1560s. We have here a sense of the radical otherness of the Jews (even a converted one is called a "Christian Jew") whose religious transformation aromatises him but does not completely erase his fundamental Jewishness. Jewish conversion exists here simply to confirm "the marvelous glory and power of Christ."

Foxe's account was first published not long before English interests in Constantinople and its Jews expanded beyond the theological to include foreign trade and diplomacy. Only after giving up on the difficult overland trade route through Russia into Persia that they had explored from 1566 to 1581 did the English turn their attention to Turkey.[77] The extent to which Elizabethan merchants and their agents worked through Jewish intermediaries tends to be underplayed in twentieth-century accounts of Elizabethan expansionism. Both the first English ambassador, William Harborne, who arrived in Constantinople in 1583, and his successor, Edward Barton, who replaced him in 1588, had extensive dealings with Turkish Jews, some of whom they employed. Barton even wrote home to Francis Walsingham describing how indebted he was to Jews in Constantinople during the time of the Spanish Armada for their support "against the false information of our adversaries."[78] These dealings appear to have led in turn to the forwarding of a letter from a rabbi in Constantinople named Abraham Reuben to the Puritan writer and preacher, Hugh Broughton (the correspondence was probably promoted by Barton, who wrote to Richard Stapers, a London alderman, that the Jew's letter "might turn to the benefit of Christendom").[79] Stapers, who was at this time the Governor of the Levant Company, had reportedly heard rumors that "the Turks were willing to grant to the Englishmen the temple of Sophia if Mr. Broughton would go hither and read and preach in Hebrew or Greek."[80]

Broughton was probably the finest Hebrew scholar in England. He had studied the language at Cambridge under the French scholar Antoine Rodolphe Chevallier and was soon teaching Hebrew himself. Broughton was neither a philosemite nor a millenarian. What distinguishes his work is his refusal to dismiss Talmudic and other rabbinic authorities out of hand. Instead, Broughton tried to reconcile them and their chronologies with New Testament ones. In the words of one historian, he approached "the New Testament as a Talmudist."[81] After years of painstaking study in Greek and Hebrew he produced in 1589 *A Concent of Scripture*, an impressive and controversial genealogical treatise based on the prophets, which, as far as Broughton was concerned, permanently resolved the cruxes that had divided Jewish and Christian apocalyptic tradiions. One of the practical ends of his scholarship was to facilitate the conversion of the Jews, since presumably Jews could not refute Broughton's conclusive proof that Christ was the messiah whom the Jews had long awaited.

Though he spent much of his adult life abroad, having alienated powerful churchmen, Broughton was a figure well enough known in London to be satirized on the popular stage. In Ben Jonson's *The Alchemist*, for example, Dol Common, mentioned above in connection with other historical chronologies, is described as having "gone mad, with studying Broughton's works."[82] Shortly thereafter, Dol begins speaking garbled lines conflated from a number of Broughton's notoriously obtuse works. Jonson makes her lines even more incomprehensible by having two other characters continue speaking through the course of Dol Common's rant:

> And so we may arrive by Talmud skill,
> And profess Greek, to raise the building up
> Of Helen's house, against the Ishamaelite,
> King of Thogarma, and his Habergions
> Brimstony, blue, and fiery; and the force
> Of King Abaddon, and the Beast of Cittim:
> Which Rabbi David Kimchi, Onkelos,
> And Aben-Ezra do interpret Rome.[83]

Broughton's forbidding prose and genealogical obsession were familiar enough to Jacobean audiences to warrant other casual allusions as well: earlier, in *Volpone* (1606), Jonson's Peregrine, impressed with the dizzying rhetoric of the mountebank Volpone, compares this "rare" language to that found in "Broughton's books."[84]

When Abraham Reuben's letter to Broughton arrived in London in 1596 none "could so much as read the endorsement," since the letter was written in a script unfamiliar to English Hebraists. It was finally forwarded to Broughton, who was then in Germany.[85] Despite what he interpreted as Reuben's request that Broughton "teach in our country" and "be our guide,"[86] Broughton hesitated to undertake the conversion of Turkish Jewry without official authorization and financial support. Moreover, as Broughton was unfamiliar with the flowery and hyperbolic style of his correspondent, he read into the letter far more interest than Reuben intended.

Seeking royal support for his plan to travel to Constantinople and convert Reuben and the rest of the Jews there, Broughton first published a brief letter addressed to Queen Elizabeth in which he argued that the "Jew seemeth by his epistle to be of great authority, not only among the Jews which are at Constantinople the chiefest of the world." Broughton believed that with Reuben "carrying them after him, the rest" of the Jews throughout "the East will sooner follow."[87] And elsewhere, following a similar tack, Broughton suggests that Reuben could not have been acting without official sponsorship: "I have reason to think that by the [Turkish] King's commandment, and not of himself, he would write as he did."[88]

Broughton's published requests were greeted with considerable skepticism in London, and rumors circulated that a self-promoting Broughton had made the whole thing up.[89] While conceding that the letter might be genuine—"suppose it were true, that a Jew had written"—Broughton's critics nonetheless ridiculed Broughton's conviction that the "Jews desired to have [him] sent to all the synagogues in Constantinople, if it were but to see [his] angelical countenance."[90] Broughton, bitterly complained that many "in London are persuaded that the Jew's epistle was forged,"[91] and that this libel followed him to Geneva and "altered princes from great promises" of support.[92] At stake was not simply Broughton's reputation or the afterlife of converted Turkish Jews but, more immediately, the possibility of enhancing English trade in its struggle to compete with other European nations more solidly established in foreign ports.

Embittered by these accusations and having failed to move the Queen, Broughton next appealed to her Privy Council, arguing that he should be "sent to . . . direct the Jews willing to learn Christianity." This mission was not only "honorable" for the Queen to perform, but "such as she may not deny without open contempt of Christianity."[93] This pamphlet too went unanswered, as did many others. Broughton unsuccessfully appealed to Parliament, warning that no "kingdom ever condemned such a request. . . . So the petition should profit us; which to deny, if wit or policy suffer not, religion will less suffer. And God will send a recompense according to the greatness of fault. . . . Thus hoping that policy with religion will bear sway in you."[94]

Broughton saw a crucial connection between conversion and commerce. He writes in 1591 that English "merchants that pass over all nations cannot carry into the East more noble merchandise from the West" than books that resolved theological issues, books that would also "move any Jews" by demonstrable proofs, and thereby turn trade to England.[95] So insistent was Broughton that English merchants stood to profit from his labor that he demanded that they assume the financial burden of subsidizing his conversionary efforts. To this end, he later wrote that having recently translated "the Apocalypse into

Hebrew" for the benefit of the Jews, he would expound it only if English merchants trading with Turkey "pay the charges." "If they refuse," Broughton warns, he "will leave them to try, whether strange shipwreck shall revenge them." He also dedicated his *A Require of Consent* to "the famous company of Merchant Adventurers."[96] Since they were barely meeting the financial demands of their own agents abroad, it should come as no surprise that these London merchants chose to ignore Broughton's requests.

After Elizabeth's death Broughton turned to King James. Prompted by reports of the "honorable bent of the King" for a translation of the Apocalypse into Hebrew, he advised James of a potential beneficiary of this project, a Turkish Jew curious to learn about Christianity from the English. The connection here was made by "Edward Crain, a shipper of Newcastle" who "was long in Thrace," and who reports that Jews there hope "to learn from us salvation." Apparently this Jew had accompanied Crain first to Venice and on to Leyden in search of Broughton, for, Broughton writes, he "would be fully instructed of me that he might return to save his nation." Broughton's latest plan was to "have the Jew sent to England . . . unbaptized" so that he might be converted before King James following a sermon by Broughton himself.[97] The narrative was by now well-worn. One last time, his designs were ignored. Defeated, he wrote of Abraham Reuben and the "Turkey cause" that "if I went to the couch of my bed, if I give sleep to my eyes, or slumbering to my lids, without thinking upon an answer unto the Jew, for the praises of our God, let my hand forget to rule my pen."[98] He quietly returned to England in 1612 and died shortly thereafter.

While his great hopes came to naught, the efforts of Broughton and others to exploit the economics of Jewish conversion left an impact on English foreign trade. For example, while Broughton never made it to Constantinople, John Harrison, Groom of the Privy Chamber to Prince Henry, who had been sent on a mission to Morocco in 1610, was at least able to attempt to convert the Jews there.[99] Harrison depended upon the millenarian arguments derived from Broughton and others—in this instance a book called *The Christian Directorie or, Resolution*—to win the Jews, and trade, for England.[100] Harrison writes that the Moroccan "king, at that time of my arrival," was away in Fez, and he had to wait six months for his return. During that time, "one of the chief rabbis" named "Rabbi Shimeon," visited him regularly, "for my better instruction in the Hebrew (whereof I had a little taste before)." No doubt drawing upon his *Resolution*, Harrison began "arguing and reasoning" with Rabbi Shimeon "of the Messiah," who the Jews "say [is] yet to come," but which the Christians "are able to prove, by invincible arguments and demonstrations, both out of your own law and rabbis [is] already come." Later in his mission Harrison spent an additional three and a half months with Moroccan Jews, "where also

I grew familiarly acquainted with" the members of the Jewish "nation, and was presented at sundry times (especially at . . . marriages, and solemn feasts) . . . which I took very kindly." Yet he also witnessed "the great and grievous oppression, under which" the Jews "groan": "taxations, vexations, exactions . . . not only in Barbary, but in all other parts of the world besides, as a fatal effect, of that heavy curse laid on" them by their "own forefathers long ago, upon the death of Christ."[101] Harrison also attempted to combine policy with religion: he conducted negotiations with Moroccan officials and attempted to convert the Moroccan Jews who were important middlemen in both the sugar trade and in the fitting out of the galleys, thereby hastening the apocalyptic goal of "the conversion of the Jewish nation, the very period of all prophecies."[102] His experience offers yet another instance of the confluence of millenarian thought, nascent capitalism, increasing knowledge of Hebrew, and exposure to actual Jews, at a time before the more radical strand of apocalyptic thought developed in early seventeenth-century England.

IV. Confessions of faith

Complementing efforts to convert foreign Jews were sporadic attempts to convert Jews living in England. When Judah ben Meir forsook Judaism and entered the Church of England in 1709, he noted that it was "the constant practice of the Jews converted to the Christian faith in all places where I have travelled to publish some small treatise containing the reasons of their conversion," that "it may have some blessed effect upon the unconverted."[103] And Moses Marcus, some fifteen years later, followed the same "common rule, that all those who are converted to another religion should give the reasons and motives of their conversion, as well to clear themselves to this censorious world."[104] Between Yehuda Menda's confession of faith in 1577 and Judah ben Meir's and Moses Marcus's accounts of their conversion a century and a half later, a dozen or so of these testimonies were published in England, most of them concentrated in the closing decades of the seventeenth century.[105]

These treatises, with few exceptions, follow a straightforward formula, telling much the same story despite the promise to provide both "reasons and motives." An Augustinian exploration of the psychology of the convert is eschewed in favor of a conversion experience based on a careful reading and reconsideration of key scriptural passages. The experience of Daniel ben Alexander, who was baptized in Rouen and whose conversion tract was published in English in 1621, is typical. He speaks of how a chance perusal of the Gospels led to his "conferring the New and Old Testament together," his "neglecting the Talmud," and eventually his decision to "utterly forsake the Jewish religion and to become a Christian."[106] The prophesies of Isaiah had an unusually strong conversionary force among Jews who compared Old and

New Testament passages. Thomas Calvert cites the example of Johann Isaacs, a German Jew who converted in 1558 and admitted that "the fifty-third of Isaiah did draw me to the Christian Faith." For Isaacs, this chapter of Isaiah contained "more mystery concerning Christ ... in the Hebrew text than can be found in any other translation."[107]

At the risk of anachronism, I have chosen to draw upon a number of these tracts written as late as a century or so after Shakespeare's day, largely because the genre barely changed in the century following Foxe's conversion of Yehuda Menda and because they cast at least some light on what earlier attitudes might have been like. The similarities between these various conversion narratives are all the more remarkable when one considers not only the different backgrounds of each convert but also the wrenching social and religious changes England had experienced in the course of the many decades in which they were written. The value of these narratives, then, resides less in the insight they provide into the hearts and minds of individuals wrestling with religious choices than in what, when viewed collectively, they reveal about the expectations of converting Jews held by early modern English Christians. Taken together they also mark a sharp break from medieval conversion tracts in which apostate Jews spent more time heaping abuse upon their former coreligionists than they did confessing their faith in Christ. It is also worth noting that as a genre the confession of faith had a fairly limited life span: originating in post-Reformation England with Menda's tract, the genre peaked in the 1660s, 1670s, and 1690s before gradually trailing off in the mid-eighteenth century. Collectively these treatises demarcate a time in early modern Protestant England when certain biblical texts, especially Romans, Daniel, Revelation, and Isaiah, were touchstones for how both faith and history were understood. They also suggest that into the early eighteenth century, Christian identity was still vulnerable enough in England to warrant these periodic testaments to the true faith.

A roll call of Jewish converts also begins to appear in a number of seventeenth-century English works, confirming the regularity with which at least a remnant of the Jews had abandoned their faith and embraced some form of Christianity. A good example of such a litany appears in Richard Mayo's otherwise fictional *Conference Betwixt a Protestant and a Jew*, in which a Protestant invokes these precedents as a way of persuading a Jew to convert: "What if you should from this day forward become a Christian? . . . . Let me tell you, you are not the first of your nation that hath so done." His list of converts goes back to "the year 1310" when "Nicholas de Lyra . . . became a Christian" and wrote "an excellent treatise proving by irrefragable arguments that the Messiah is come and that no other is to be expected." Other examples also emphasize those whose conversion was followed by publications excoriating the Jews, including Paulus Burgensis, who "turned Christian also, and wrote against Judaism," and Elias Levita, who "left his rabbinism and entered the Church of Christ by baptism, bringing some thirty Jews more with him to be baptized, about the year 1517." Another was "Hieronymus de Santa Fide," who "was converted to Christianity and wrote a book called *Hebraeomastix*, or *The Jew's Scourge*." After this book was published in Spain, "above five thousand Jews were turned to the faith." Among other famous Jews who turned Christian were Paulus Ricius, who "wrote many things against his old misbelief," Antonius Margarit, who "converted in heart and baptized," turning "his hand and pen against the Jews," and Ernestus Ferdinandus, who wrote *Flagellum Judaeorum*. Mayo's Protestant interlocutor tells the prospective convert that he looks "upon these and such like particular converts amongst the Jews to be only as first fruits. We Christians expect ere long a full harvest in the conversion of your whole nation."[108]

Each individual act of conversion provided yet another indication that these "first fruits" would ultimately yield a bumper crop. This was not merely a battle over souls but over the narrative or story central to each religion. If the Jewish narrative was one in which the arrival of the messiah remained imminent, the Christian one needed to show that the Jews had misconstrued the plot entirely, for Christ had already come. In this sense the conversion of the Jews was an acknowledgment that the Christian narrative and sense of history, both past and future, was correct. This may help explain why, in virtually all of the post-Reformation treatises, the converting Jew habitually warns his fellow Jews to "stay for no other Messiah than He that is come."[109] Since the promise of the literal conversion of the Jews remained critical to early modern Protestant notions of history, these conversion tracts at once provided evidence of this historical process while allowing the Jews themselves to refute their own misguided reading of history in the Bible.

The fantasy of Jews rejecting their own beliefs in favor of Christian ones was so strong that it gave rise to stories of deathbed confessions by rabbis. Sir William Brereton, traveling in Holland in 1635, writes in his diary of having heard that at "Basel . . . there died one of the Jews' most learned rabbis" who "desired upon his death bed that his will and testament might be published and proclaimed to all the Jews his brethren in all parts." The "substance of his will was that the Jews had long "expected a Messiah and Saviour, and if he came not within thirty-four years or thereabouts . . . that then they should not expect any longer, but rather embrace the Saviour of the Christians."[110] Given the difficulty of proving to the stubborn Jews that the messiah had already come, such reports were highly prized.

Seventeenth-century English writers drew on an increasingly rich history of false messiahs, a history that exposed the Jews' vain hopes. Thomas Calvert offers such an "account of the notablest delusions that that people has groaned under in this kind," even drawing upon rabbinical authorities for support, including Maimonides, who "reckons up four more obscure false Christs, that did arise among the Jews in Spain and France." For Calvert, the evidence can only point to one conclusion: the Jews "have been so often gulled, they will hearken to no conjectures any more," though he dismissively adds that it "were well they would make this resolution as brass, and strong as iron."[111] The story of the most famous "Counterfeit Messiah" of the Jews—Sabbatai Zevi—was especially popular in the second half of the seventeenth century.[112] Yet, as Richard Popkin has recently shown, the story was used to deride not only Jewish but also contemporary English millenarian delusions.[113]

English writers were also busy rationalizing why Jews had up to this time in history refused to convert. The most frequent explanation was that the Jews were horrified by Catholic practices, especially the violation of the second commandment concerning the worshipping of images. Samuel Purchas, in his chapter on "the hopes and hindrances of the Jews' conversion," also blamed the practice of forcing Jews to give up their riches. "This alone to the world-bewitching Jew is such a partition-wall to keep him from Christianity that he will venture soul and all rather than thus betray himself, his wife, and children, to extreme beggary and want."[114] And James Howell, echoing the position taken by Hugh Broughton, added to these two obstacles a third: the absence of suitable translations has meant that the Jews "are debarred from the use of the New Testament, the means of their salvation. And thus we leave them in a state most pitiful, and little pitied."[115]

Jews like Yehuda Menda were few and far between in late sixteenth- and early seventeenth-century England. Proselytizers like Hugh Broughton knew that the most dependable way to insure a Jewish conversion was to import a willing foreign Jew for the purpose. And in the case of Daniel ben Alexander, a translated version of the confession of faith, rather than the actual convert, was imported from the continent. Only after the tacit readmission of the Jews into England did these treatises proliferate, beginning in earnest with Moses Scialitti's conversion testimony in the summer of 1663.[116] A disappointed D'Blossiers Tovey wrote that this Florentine's conversion "was likely to have brought in the whole flock," yet "nothing more came of this promising example than the conversion of three or four."[117] Five years later Solomon Franco's *Truth Springing Out of the Earth*[118] relies less on traditional Old Testament citations to refute the Jews because "of late years, merely to contradict the Christians," the Jews "have studied and found out such other expositions thereof as suffice to satisfy their minds. And I, having full notice of them, judge that not to be the way to convince them, since they presently save themselves with another interpretation." Taking a slightly different tack, Franco argues that since the Jews "believe that the immediate Providence of the Lord was never yet enjoyed by any nation except their own," if "we can evidently prove that the Lord appeared to the Christians of Israel, who can doubt but their religion and manner of service is accepted of the Lord." The recent restoration of King Charles II clinches his argument: "Hath not the Lord manifested himself with his particular care over them in all ages? Who is so brutish and devoid of reason that doth not consider the miraculous restoration of our Sovereign Lord King Charles?"[119] Franco's conversion tract was followed by Monsieur de Bréval's (François Durant) in 1671,[120] John Jacob's in 1678,[121] John Alexander's in 1689,[122] and Theodore John's in 1693.[123] The content of these tracts, written over a century after Menda's, had barely changed. In each instance the convert invokes the same set of scriptural proofs, appeals to the stubborn Jews, and recites a catechism confirming his knowledge of the true Christian faith.

By the time Shalom ben Shalomoh entered the Church of Christ at the meeting house in Rosemary Lane in London in 1699, cracks in the tired genre were beginning to show.[124] Thomas Humphrey, who stage-managed the conversion and wrote the pamphlet himself, was painfully conscious of just how many objections skeptical readers might have to "the truth of this Jew's conversion." Unearthed here are many of the doubts that had been silently suppressed in the first-person accounts, and while Humphrey believed that by raising them he would be able to exorcise each in turn, one is left with a strong sense that his readers' skepticism was not so easily allayed. Humphrey himself acknowledges that some may wonder how is "it possible that a person so unacquainted with the Christian religion and so vicious in his life and conversation should so suddenly arrive to such a strong persuasion of his interest in a crucified Saviour?" And if a Jew turns once, what is to stop him from turning again, and returning to his abandoned faith? Like the proverbial weathercock, Shalom ben Shalomoh is described as turning first from Judaism to the sway of the "Duke of Brandeburg's minister," then to a "minister in . . . Ryneburg," next to a life of "revelling in all manner of wickedness" in England, followed by a brief flirtation with the Quakers ("but alas! there I found nothing to my satisfaction, so that I was at a loss again"), before finally coming to rest in the truth revealed by the careful instruction of Humphrey himself. In his quoted testimony Shalom ben Shalomoh puts his finger on the problem of the proliferation of Protestant denominations eager to win over Jewish converts: "I heard there were many churches; one cried, 'Here is Christ,' another cried, 'Here is Christ.' "[125] Shalom ben Shalomoh's dizzying turns suggest that lurking deep within every earnest Jewish convert to the Christian faith is an apostate, counterfeit Christian. It was a stigma that could not be erased, partly because of the long Marrano tradition of dissimulating belief in Christ, partly because to believe that Jews could convert was to accept that religious identity, even the true faith of a Christian, was not natural or essential, but something that individuals could try on or put off, much like an actor dressing for the stage.

Even as published confessions of faith circulated celebrating the convert's acceptance into the Christian community, competing narratives also in circulation took the story one step further, concluding with the Jew's eventual apostasy. There were both fictional and historical precedents for Jewish reversion. One of the more popular examples was to be found in Hanmer's 1577 translation of Socrates Scholasticus, where the fifth-century historian describes "the miracle wrought at the baptizing of the deceitful Jew" by Paul the Novatian Bishop. The story recounts how a "certain dissembling Jew feigning he would embrace the Christian faith, was often baptized, through the which wiles he got much money." After "he had guilefully deceived many men of sundry sects and opinions . . . having no more whose eyes he might blear, at length he comes to Paul the Novatian Bishop and protesteth unto him that gladly he would be baptized, and prayeth him that he may obtain it at his hand." Pleased by this Jew's apparent eagerness to convert, Paul "made all things ready for baptism," first providing him with "a white garment," then having the baptismal "font . . . filled with water." Miraculously, the rite was prevented when the baptismal "water by a certain divine power and secret operation which the outward eye could not attain unto, was suddenly dried up." Though the font was refilled and "all the holes and chinks on every side" stopped up, when the Jew was brought to the font a second time "the water again vanished." Paul was wise enough to interpret these divine signs correctly, and thereupon exposed the Jew's treachery.[126]

For Shakespeare's contemporaries, stories of dissembling Jews exploiting gullible Christians were not merely the stuff of moldy old tales. Consider, for example, the case of the Jew taken from London by Sir James Lancaster on his East India voyage of 1601.[127] Sometime in September or October 1601, the English voyagers "had a sermon and a communion. . . . And after noon one of our men," who "was a Jew, was christened and called John, our general being his godfather."[128] This was not to be "John's" last conversion. The travel diary of the Frenchman François Pyrard de Laval, who met up with these English voyagers, picks up the story where the English accounts leave off. He describes how he encountered "a man who was a Jew in faith and race, and knew a large number of languages; among others, he spoke Arabic and the Indian tongues well. . . . The English had taken him to England, where he had learnt English well." Pyrard de Laval notes that with "the English he was of their religion; with the Mahometans, of theirs; whereas he was all the while a Jew." His religious infidelity was matched by his other actions; he robbed Lancaster and fled with his ill-gotten money, "married a wife wherever he happened to be," and was a "scoundrel" and a "liar."[129] One of the more telling signs of how suspicious Christians were about apostasizing Jews is the frequency with which writers mentioned the practice among the Turks of never allowing a Jew to convert to Islam without first turning Christian. As Thomas Scales puts it in his notes on the history and practices of the Jews: "Neither will the Turk at any time receive a Jew into the fellowship of their Mohametan superstition except first he hath passed from his Judaism through the purgatory of a Christian profession."[130]

V. Cat and mouse

Each successful conversion narrative seems to have had concealed within it the latent threat of apostasy.[131] As Marlowe's *The Jew of Malta* makes clear, this holds true for converting Jewish women as well. In exploring the improvisational basis of Jewish conversion, Marlowe has Abigail convert not once but twice to Christianity in the course of the play. Barabas has earlier rejected the possibility of his own conversion—"I will be no convertite"—when Ferneze invites him to "be Christened" to avoid losing his entire estate for refusing to pay the Turkish tribute.[132] To recover his extorted wealth, hidden in his house (which has been turned into a convent), Barabas persuades Abigail to ask the abbess to accept her into the convent as a novice, and instructs his daughter on why this Jewish dissembling is preferable to Christian hypocrisy:

> As good dissemble that thou never mean'st
> As first mean truth, and then dissemble it;
> A counterfeit profession is better
> Than unseen hypocrisy.[133]

Thus instructed, Abigail plays the part of the "distressed maid" to perfection, telling the abbess of her desire to "pass away my life in penitence, / And be a novice in your nunnery, / To make atonement for my labouring soul."[134] The scene does not end with the abbess agreeing to "admit [her] for a nun," for Barabas has his own role to play: that of the Jewish father appalled by the apostasy of his daughter. He, too, fulfills all generic expections: "Why, how now, Abigail, what makest thou / Amongst these Christians?" And when told that his daughter has been "admitted to the sisterhood," he charges her on his "blessing" that she "leave / These devils, and their damned heresy," and asks his "seduced daughter" whether it "[b]ecomes it Jews to be so credulous?" (all the while signaling to her where his wealth is hidden).[135]

In a later scene, after Abigail has successfully rescued her father's riches and has left the convent, Barabas invokes Christian polemic in order to persuade Abigail that Jewish deception and apostasy are justified:

It's no sin to deceive a Christian,
For they themselves hold it a principle,
Faith is not to be held with heretics:
But all are heretics that are not Jews:
This follows well, and therefore, daughter, fear not.[136]

But her father's treachery proves too great even for her, and upon discovering that Barabas plotted the death of her two suitors, she once again asks to "be admitted for a nun." This time, however, the Christians are wary. Friar Jacomo reminds her—and us—that "it is not yet long since / That I did labour thy admission, / And then thou didst not like that holy life." Abigail defends her new resolve, explaining that

Then were my thoughts so frail and unconfirmed,
And I was chained to follies of the world;
But now experience, purchased with grief,
Hath made me see the difference of things.
My sinful soul, alas, hath paced too long,
The fatal labyrinth of misbelief,
Far from the Son that gives eternal life.

Her confession of faith is *too* good—provoking Friar Jacomo's suspicious reply: "Who taught thee this?" Abigail persists, and Friar Jacomo finally agrees to take her back into the convent, but with the warning that this turning must stop: "See thou change no more, / For that will be most heavy to thy soul."[137] Barabas makes sure of this, for he poisons her, along with all the other nuns, and Abigail dies insisting that in her case there will be no deathbed reversion: "Witness I die a Christian."[138] While there is no reason to doubt her sincerity at this moment, her very need to insist that she is no apostate draws attention to the popular belief that, with death imminent, Jewish converts repudiated the Christianity they had once willingly embraced.

Shakespeare provides the slightest hint of the possibility of such turning in his depiction of Jessica's conversion to Christianity. This hint appears in the scene at the beginning of act 5 of *The Merchant of Venice* in which Jessica and Lorenzo engage in an exchange ill-suited to newlyweds, where Jessica remarks how "In such a night / Medea gathered the enchanted herbs / That did renew old Aeson," to which Lorenzo sharply replies, "In such a night / Did Jessica steal from the wealthy Jew / And with an unthrift love did run from Venice."[139] Even a cursory knowledge of the story of Medea would have enabled Elizabethan theatergoers to recognize that she was an emblem of a daughter who abandoned her father and her culture in marrying her husband (whom she would soon betray and abandon, after his own betrayal of her). Those familiar with John Studley's 1581 English translation of Seneca's *Medea* may also have remembered the chorus's lines asking Medea, "Why for his sake from father hast thou fled, / And thrust thyself out from thy native soil?" and Medea's own wish that "Full gladly will I get me home, if he that brought me thence, / Vouchsafe to bear me back again."[140] Having been reminded of Jessica's infidelity to her father, Shakespeare's audience may have wondered how long her own vows of faith, religious and marital, would remain firm.

Jessica served as something of an archetype of the female Jewish convert for the next century or so. There are certainly strong similarities between her case and that of Eve Cohan, a convert to Christianity in 1680 whose story was told by Bishop Gilbert Burnet in *The Conversion and Persecutions of Eve Cohan*.[141] Eve was a young Dutch Jew who decided to convert to Christianity despite parental objections: "She was oft beaten by her mother, and not suffered to come to the door or look out at rose windows that opened to the street, lest being in a Christian country she might have discovered her designs to such as would have assisted her in bringing them to perfection." Like the cloistered Jessica, she was only able to escape in the context of marriage to a Christian, with whom she fled to England. Unlike Jessica, though, she did not abscond with her parent's wealth, "being more concerned to preserve her life and to save her soul than careful how to live, she did not so much as carry away the jewels that were in her possession." The Jews of London who tried to take action against her were frustrated by the Lord Mayor, who warned them that "he would carry the matter as far as the law would allow him against their whole sect." In an action recalling Portia's legal triumph over Shylock, he even gave "order to some to bring him an extract of all the laws in force against the Jews." Perhaps the most unusual detail of this conversion narrative concerns her pregnancy, which had begun before Eve's baptism. Left unresolved is the question of whether a child conceived while she was still a Jew would be a Christian if it were born after her baptism. The question turned out to be moot, for she miscarried.[142]

Lorenzo's exchange with Jessica at the beginning of act 5 of *The Merchant* raises the possibility that the obedient and converted Jewess who had to disobey one man and one set of religious principles to embrace another might revert to her true Jewish nature. A fictional instance of a converted Jewess revealing these buried traits appears in a little-known novella of 1729, *The Fair Hebrew*, by the popular writer Eliza Fowler Haywood.[143] Though written long after Shakespeare's play, *The Fair Hebrew*, like the late seventeenth-century narrative of Eve Cohan, may nonetheless provide a belated glimpse into the darker side of the female Jewish convert in early modern England.

Haywood's story begins with a handsome young Christian man named

Dorante entering a synogogue where he sees a glove drop from the women's section. Impetuously rushing up to the woman who dropped the glove, he unveils her before being escorted out by the Jews whose service he had disrupted. After discovering where this young and beautiful woman lives, Dorante sends a messenger with a profession of his love. Her name is Kesiah and she is the only daughter of an old Jewish father. Like Jessica and Eve Cohan before her, "the strict restraint she was kept in by her parents had heightened her desire of liberty. . . . To add to all this, she had an aversion not only for all the men of her religion but also for the laws and customs of the religion itself, and desired nothing more than to become a Christian."[144] Dorante agrees to marry her and they elope.

Up to this point the story reads very much like earlier narratives: the handsome young Christian man, as yet without a fortune, in love with a Jewess, the Jewish parent who tries to protect her from the Christian world, the decision of the young woman to convert and abandon her family and take her jewels with her, and, finally, the young couple's flight. But where *The Merchant of Venice* and *The Conversion and Persecutions of Eve Cohan* stop, *The Fair Hebrew* pursues the darker side of the Jewess's conversion to its tragic end. After Kesiah's father discovers that she is missing, he finds Dorante's father, who is no less aggrieved. When Dorante approaches his own father, he is rejected, and when Kesiah tries writing to her Christian father-in-law, things get worse. As the situation deteriorates, "the real disposition of Kesiah began to show itself." When her husband is thrown into debtor's prison, she refuses to join him, and, after Dorante disinherits himself in favor of his younger brother in order to raise desperately needed funds, she absconds with the money. Kesiah's treachery reaches new depths when she falls for another man and flees the country with him. Justice prevails, however, when "the ship which bore Kesiah, her lover, and the plunder of her deceived husband was taken by a Sallee pirate, and all the passengers carried to Madagascar," where they lived out their days "in a hard and perpetual slavery." The moral is clear: Dorante, in marrying this Jewess, mistook her outward beauty and failed to see how it concealed her essential "hypocrisy and ill nature."[145]

It is tempting to see this not as an alternative narrative to the kind we are offered by Shakespeare but as a completion of it. Consider, in this regard, Thomas Calvert's comparison of the act of Jewish conversion to that of a rebellious, fallen woman penitently returning to her "first husband," basing his argument on a bizarre and unprecedented reading of Jeremiah 31.22—"The Lord shall create a new thing upon the earth, a woman shall compass a man"—which Calvert takes to mean that a "wonderful and new thing will the Lord bring to pass: the Church of the Jews, that like a wandering and strange woman is departed from the Lord by rebellion and idolatry, to whom she was betrothed once . . . shall come with bitter repentance, returning to her first husband, and embracing him again graciously whom she had vilely forsaken."[146] Scriptural and popular ideas about the infidelity of Jewish women reinforce each other and are strengthened by historical accounts that described how Jewish women who converted to Christianity deviously married first one man, then another.[147]

161

ı5.

The

Hebrew

Will Turn

Christian

A potential counterexample to this image of the Jewess is found in Maria Edgeworth's early nineteenth-century novel *Harrington*, discussed earlier in chapter 3, which flirts with the possibility that a marriage between an English man and a Jewish woman can provide satisfying closure.[148] But not even Edgeworth, in a work that she deliberately undertook to compensate for an anti-Jewish bias in her earlier work, could go this far. We are offered instead a fantasy solution when we learn in the last three pages of the novel that Harrington's beloved Berenice, daughter of a foreign Jew, Mr. Montenero (and referred to scores of times in the novel as "the Jewess"), turns out to have been born of a mother who was a Christian as well as the "daughter of an English gentleman of good family." Berenice's mother also insisted that her daughter be "bred in her faith—a Christian—a Protestant." On learning of this in the novel's denouement, Harrington's father happily exclaims: "Not a Jewess! . . . Not a Jewess!—give you joy, Harrington, my boy!" and he cannot help repeating that she is an "English Protestant! . . . English! English!" It appears that poetic justice is not fully served until we learn that she is not only Christian but Protestant; not only Protestant, but an English Protestant, and descended of English gentry. Edgeworth's protagonist falls in love as a result of his sympathy for a Jewess's feelings, indeed, is attracted to her because of her Jewishness, but they only marry after the happy discovery that she has been a good English Christian all along.[149] Lancelot Gobbo's exchange with the converted Jessica comes to mind here: "Marry, you may partly hope that your father got you not, that you are not the Jew's daughter"; to which she replies, "That were a kind of bastard hope indeed!"[150] While Edgeworth steers clear of making Berenice illegitimate, the surprising last-minute revelation of her Christian birth and upbringing accomplishes the same end of maintaining firm boundaries between Christian and Jew (that Berenice is nonetheless the offspring of a Jewish father is quietly avoided by Edgeworth).

No less than her male counterpart, the converted Jewess of early modern English culture could not erase her essential Jewish nature. *Castle Rackrent* (1800), Edgeworth's earlier and celebrated Gothic tale, provides yet another example of the unregenerate Jewess: in fact, she is actually called Jessica. The narrator, an old garrulous servant named Thady Quirk, describes how his young Irish master Kit Rackrent, having run up gambling debts, marries a young heiress in Bath, and returns with her and her jewels to his estate in Ire-

land. He goes on to describe how his master used to call his bride "his stiff
necked Israelite, though before he married her" he "used to call her . . . 'my
pretty Jessica.'" The similarities to Jessica's elopement with Lorenzo are obvi-

ous. To Thady Quirk his master's new bride is a "foreigner" and, at first sight,
"little better than a blackamoor." Edgeworth never makes clear whether "Jessica" really is Jewish (as Thady Quirk, who clearly never met a Jew, keeps saying) or, like her Shakespearean namesake, whether she converted to Christianity when she eloped with jewels in hand. The otherwise unnamed bride is soon
punished for refusing to turn over her jewels (especially a diamond cross) to
her profligate husband. He locks her in her room and orders that at his table
only "pig meat in some shape or other" (which she refuses to touch) be served.
Seven years goes by and she is near death, but still refuses to turn over her jewels. When Kit Rackrent suddenly dies in a duel (fought over which of three
potential brides is to be his next wife), she recovers and departs for England,
ungenerously giving nothing to the servants at her parting, "notwithstanding
the old proverb of 'as rich as a Jew.'" To the end, this "Jessica" reverts to her
"Jewish" ways, and the narrator concludes that her "diamond cross was, they
say, at the bottom of it all."[151]

While these eighteenth- and early nineteenth-century fictional accounts, in
the absence of other evidence, help clarify how both male and female Jewish
conversion were understood, they are considerably removed from the lived
experience of Shakespeare's contemporaries. In bringing this chapter to a
close, I'd like to return to an episode that occurred in England in 1612, one that
confirms how easily the Christian desire to convert the Jews could be exploited
by a Jew cunning enough to play upon these millennial expectations. The best-
known version of this event appears in Anthony Wood's *History and Antiquities of the University of Oxford*, where he writes of "Joseph Barnet, a Jew both
by nation and superstition, who read Hebrew to diverse young students," and
who "had cunningly pretended and held forth that he embraced and believed
Jesus to be the true Messiah." Wood recounts how Barnet "professed that he
was seriously and heartily grieved for his former blasphemies against Him,"
and "mournfully bewailed that the eyes of his brethren and countrymen were
so blinded, and their hearts so hardened." Barnet understood the conversion
genre and played his part in it to perfection. He "seemed to desire nothing
more earnestly than that he might be judged worthy to be admitted into the
Christian Church by the sacrament of baptism." Among those he deceived by
"these tricks were . . . many . . . learned doctors, especially Dr. Lake, Warden
of New College, afterwards Bishop of Bath and Wells." The climax of the
story occurred when a "Sabbath was appointed publicly wherein baptism
should be administered to this new disciple in St. Mary's Church." The congregants of St. Mary's were in for a disappointment, for "the very day before

he was to be baptized this dissembling Jew ran away. Dr. Lake being informed thereof, sent some on horseback, others on foot to pursue him, who overtaking him, brought him back, though against his will." Barnet then "on his own accord . . . professed that he was returned to his old Judaism, which he had foresworn. He jeered at Christ and despised baptism, for he had now filled his purse." Reacting quickly to this turn of events, "Dr. Twisse laid aside the sermon which he had prepared and instead . . . preached an excellent sermon upon [the] occasion of Barnet's revolt." The sermon "showed God's just judgment upon that perverse nation and people whom he had given up to a reprobate sense even to this very day."[152] News quickly traveled to the Privy Council in London, which directed the Vice-Chancellor of Oxford to take the "Jew now lately committed by you" and send him "hither unto us under safe custody, to be disposed of as shall be thought meet."[153] Nine days later, on November 16, the Privy Council sent an "open warrant directed to all his Majesty's officers," ordering that it is "his Majesty's express pleasure and commandment . . . that Jacobus Bernatus, a Jew, be presently conveyed to the seaside to be sent out of the realm."[154]

That would be about all that we know of Jacob Barnet, except for the fact that buried in the eleventh edition of Andrew Willet's *Synopsis Papismi* (1634) is an account of the events leading up to this denouement as recalled by Willet's son-in-law, Peter Smith (while Barnet is never mentioned by name, the date, people involved, and details of the case conclusively point to him). In his account, Smith writes how many strangers passing through England visited Willet, including an occasional guest that took advantage of Willet's hospitality. The most notorious of these was "a certain Jew, born (as he said) in Italy, and I think in Venice, who in his journey pretended to Cambridge, came to his doors and inquired the way thither." Barnet is described as "a young man of comely presence, a smiling countenance, and of graceful behavior. Smith adds that he "was no stranger in the Old Testament, but most familiarly acquainted with the letter of it." Needless to say, his "company was very delightful" to Willet, who had "written in his youth a Latin treatise . . . touching the general and last calling of the Jews" and "believed that some" Jews "were called every day and instructed in the faith of Christ." Cheered that Providence had directed this young Jew to him, Willet "hoped he might be able to help forward that good work by the conversion of this man."

Smith's account illuminates what leading preachers like Willet thought would bring about Jewish conversion. He describes how for a month or so the two men debated "'whether Christ be already come and whether he was the same who suffered once upon the cross, which the Jews deny.'" Gradually, Willet "so powerfully prevailed with him by enucleating the prophecies concerning Christ, discovering the kernal that before lay hidden in the shell to him, that he confessed his sight was cleared, and the veil was now removed from his eyes." Either out of newfound conviction or cunning villainy based on a perfect ear for what evangelizing Christians desired, Barnet thereupon called Willet "father," Willet's wife "mother," and "gave the titles of brother and sister to his children, challenging a spiritual alliance with them." All that remained was for Barnet to be baptized.

But the narrative proved to be one of apostasy, for "such is the obstinacy of that nation and such their perfidious disposition and dissimulation." Barnet's treachery triggered in Smith a litany of past apostates, some of whom pretended to convert and undergo baptism in order to "deceive and pervert the simple." Smith recalls those in the days of Emperor Leo who washed off their baptism, as well as apostates during the reign of King Childeric who, "violating their Christian vow, returned to their former vomit." The same apostasizing pattern held true for Barnet, "who though he carried it out fairly for a time, yet dissimulation, we know, lasts not, and the ape . . . clothed like a young gallant and taught to behave himself mannerly, if you throw him but a nut will presently shew himself an ape." Barnet, having exhausted Willet's hospitality, then exploited his patronage. With Willet's recommendation in hand, Barnet visited first Cambridge, then Oxford. Rather than undergo baptism at Willet's hands at his living in Barley, it was decided that it should be done at Oxford "with more solemnity in the sight of many doctors and learned clerks."[155]

The story does not end with Barnet's deportation. Arthur Lake, mentioned briefly in Anthony Wood's account, was at the time Warden of New College, Oxford. Sometime after the summer of 1614, Lake preached five sermons to the congregants of St. Mary's in Oxford who had expected to witness Barnet's conversion.[156] The subject of his sermons was the treachery of the Jews, and the text, fittingly, was Luke 3.7: "Then said he to the people that were come to be baptized of him, O generation of vipers, who hath forewarned you to flee from the wrath to come?" The furiously anti-Jewish slant of Lake's sermons is best explained by the recent events at St. Mary's. Lake speaks of "the Jew, than whom none is more properly the brood of the serpent" and elaborates at considerable length on the "error of the Jews." With Barnet's recent flight no doubt in mind, Lake notes that while the "corporal [flight] will be attempted" by the Jews, it is "all in vain," for only "spiritual flight . . . is the remedy"; that is to say, the only "flight from the wrath to come is the benefit of baptism," a message clearly lost on Barnet. Lake's dark sermons give some inkling of the sting of repudiation still felt by the parishioners of St. Mary's.[157]

Barnet's story, like many of the others recounted in this chapter, reveals some of the practical difficulties posed by the conversion of the Jews, especially the problem of trusting that Jews were sincere in embracing Christianity. Thomas Calvert, disgusted with reports of Jewish apostasy, tells the story of a Jewish convert in Colagne who "a little before his death . . . rejected with execration the Christian religion and professed his Jewish misbelief which, it was judged, he had abandoned." Having learned their lesson, the Christians of Colagne raised a monument to memorialize this paradigm of Jewish apostasy. "They made this emblem to be infixed in his tomb: a mouse is represented pursuing a cat, with this inscription: *When a mouse shall catch a cat, then a Jew converted to be a Christian will remain a firm Christian.*" For Calvert, the moral is clear: it is unthinkable "that any Jew will heartily convert and turn to Christ."[158]

There is no way of knowing whether Elizabethans witnessing a performance of *The Merchant of Venice* left the theater doubting the sincerity of either Jessica's or Shylock's conversion. For some, perhaps, instances of Jewish apostasy they had read or heard about or seen onstage left open the possibility that these "Christian Jews" would turn once again; no doubt, for others, the conversions of Jessica and her father were irreversible and confirmed the rightness of the Christian faith. Yet even if Jewish conversion to Christianity was sincere, theoretical hurdles remained. Did converted Jews retain a racial distinction that prevented their inclusion as political members of the commonwealth? If not, what stood in the way of one who chose to be Christian choosing to be English as well? Did conversion really put Jews on equal footing with foreign-born Christians seeking to become naturalized or endenized English subjects? As the following chapter argues, these were extraordinarily difficult issues to resolve, for answers to these Jewish questions were contingent upon, and therefore demanded, a more precise definition of English national, racial, and political identity than the English were ready to agree upon.

VI

Race, Nation, or Alien?

Jews have never been grafted onto the stock of other people.
—*Andrew Willet, 1590*

 In 1590, a few years before he emerged as one of England's more respected and prolific theologians, Andrew Willet found himself wrestling with one of the unresolved issues raised by Paul's remarks about the conversion of the Jews. How was one to reconcile Paul's declaration in Romans that "all Israel shall be saved" with the knowledge that in the many centuries since he had written these words the Jews had been dispersed to the four corners of the earth, no doubt in the process commingling with other peoples? If such a national mixture had indeed occurred, which of their descendants were to be counted among those to be saved, and which, having thoroughly intermingled with other peoples, were not?

The effort to answer this Jewish question led Willet and others to reexamine much more broadly how racial and national difference was constituted. In order to define the Jewish nation, Willet compares it to a racial and national history that he and his readers understood somewhat better: their own. Setting aside Romans, Willet turns his attention in his Latin treatise to England's hybrid past: "Our England was first inhabited by the Britains; then the Saxons conquered her, and these were the people who afterwards became the Britains, with only their name changed."[1] He adds that the "French afterwards crossed over into England," invading it "by force of arms."[2] England's past experience of racial contamination and dissolution was no different than that of other European nations: "History makes it plain that the same sort of upheavals have often befallen other kingdoms, whose populations have frequently been changed or wiped out."[3]

These assertions about cultural and national dissolution led Willet into even murkier depths, as he tried to pinpoint the extent to which emigration altered national identity. He first suggests that if "an Englishman should go to Spain, his heirs will be counted as Spaniards, though it is allowed that he himself does not lose his connection by blood." But what, exactly, does that connection by blood entail? Searching for a better example, he argues next that "if a Scot should move from his kingdom and transport his household into France, his descendants would reek of French customs, no longer accustomed to Scottish ones."[4] But setting aside customs, are the descendants of the Scot living in France still Scottish by blood? Willet sidesteps this and other obstacles in order to stress his main point: people eventually assimilate. The trajectory of Willet's argument seems to lead directly to the conclusion that the Jews, who after all have been subject to greater dispersion than any nation on earth, are also subject to this assimilative process. It is a little disconcerting, then, to discover that Willet had offered the Englishman and the Scot as counter-examples to the Jews: "a Jew, though, whether he journeys into Spain, or France, or into whatever other place he goes to, declares himself to be not a Spaniard or a Frenchman, but a Jew."[5]

In making this claim, Willet invokes a metaphor derived from Romans, one that is repeated again and again in early modern English discussions of racial and national difference: "Jews have never been grafted onto the stock of other people."[6] Paul had introduced this image in order to explain to the Gentiles how they, like a wild scion, had been grafted onto the root of Abraham, replacing the natural branches of the Jews that had broken off. But Paul also made clear that the Jews one day "shall be grafted in, for God is able to graft them in again." Indeed, this reingrafting will be even stronger than that of the Gentile scion since the Jews were of the original stock.[7] But how, Elizabethan commentators wondered, was one to reconcile Paul's insistence that Christianity was fraternal with his seemingly contradictory claim that Christians had been grafted onto the root of Abraham? The Geneva Bible compounded the problem by also conflating genealogy with nationality in explaining that Paul "showeth that the time shall come that the whole *nation* of the Jews, though not every one particularly, shall be joined to the Church of Christ."[8] This racialized sense of the Jewish nation (or to view it another way, this nationalized sense of the Jewish race) suited sixteenth-century theologians, since adopting the alternative—that the Jews, like all nations, were subject to dissolution and intermingling—rendered Paul's claims about the conversion and restoration of the Jews incoherent. It also fit well with popular stereotypes that Jews looked, smelled, and really were racially different.

Yet to accept the fact that a Jew, in Willet's terms, always remained a Jew, produced a whole new set of potential contradictions. If the Jews were truly unlike other nations insofar as they were racially distinct, how could they ever fully be joined into the Church of Christ? The Spanish had belatedly realized the disastrous consequences of such thinking when earlier in the sixteenth century they had tried to assimilate large numbers of New Christians into their culture. Ultimately, social pressures led the Spanish to abandon a fraternal model of Christianity in favor of one based on blood and racial origins, and Jewish converts, who had begun to occupy a wide range of social positions that had been denied to them as Jews, were once again subject to various prohibitions.[9]

Andrew Willet's racially grounded solution to the problem raised by the national identity of the Jews proved attractive to subsequent writers, including Increase Mather, the Boston Congregational minister who would figure largely in the religious and political controversies of New England. Mather's account of the racial purity of the Jewish nation, published in London in 1669, is patterned closely on Willet's:

> The providence of God hath suffered other nations to have their blood mixed very much, as you know it is with our own nation: there is a mixture of British, Roman, Saxon, Danish, [and] Norman blood. But as for the body of the Jewish nation, it is far otherwise. Let an English family live in Spain five or six hundred years successively, and they will become Spaniards. But though a Jewish family live in Spain a thousand years, they do not degenerate into Spaniards (for the most part).[10]

This last parenthetical concession reveals a deep crack in the façade of this racial argument.

Mather goes on to reveal one of the reasons why Christian theologians needed to insist that the Jews had long been genealogically distinct: how else would it have been possible to prove that Christ was truly the Messiah, a lineal descendant of the tree of Jesse? Yet the coming of Christ would seem to raise new problems, since with his arrival the "genealogical distinction amongst the Jews is now perished." Nonetheless, Mather concludes, though "there is not now . . . any need of such distinction, yet a national distinction there still remaineth." His final words on the topic indicate that there was no other easy way to reconcile ideas of national identity with Paul's declaration about the Jews: "whence some conclude, that there will be in due time a national conversion of that people."[11]

The conclusions reached by Willet, Mather, and others at this time did not disappear with the Enlightenment. In fact, they can be found as late as the Victorian period, where we find the historian E. A. Freeman writing that the "Jew must be very nearly or absolutely, a pure race, in a sense in which no European nation is pure. The blood remains untouched by conversion, it remains untouched even by intermarriage."[12] The fact that nineteenth-century Anglo-Jewish writers similarly perpetuated the myth of a Jewish race did not help; Lucien Wolf, for example, writes in the *Fortnightly Review* that "it is too little known that the Jews are as a race really superior physically, mentally and morally to the people among whom they dwell."[13] In the sections that follow I explore how early modern notions of race, nation, and alien began to emerge in relation to confused and often contradictory ideas about the Jews.

I. Race

> I knew you to be a Jew, for you Jews have a peculiar colour of face different from the form and figure of other men. Which thing hath often filled me with admiration, for you are black and uncomely, and not white as other men.
> —*Paul Isaiah, 1655*[14]

Contemporary scholars have traced the origins of modern racism and nationalism back to the sixteenth century, a time when European nations were coming into contact on an unprecedented scale with other peoples. Indeed, they are quick to point that the words themselves—*race* as well as *nation*—only began to acquire their current meanings at this time.[15] Much of this research is flawed, however, by its secular bias: it has been remarkably slow to acknowledge the extent to which theology shaped the way people thought about both racial and national difference in early modern times. As a result, this scholarship has necessarily ignored the place of the Jew in the formation of early modern European ideas about race and nation, despite the fact that so much theorizing about these topics in the sixteenth and seventeenth centuries was produced in response to theoretical problems posed by the Jews. Perhaps one reason why contemporary theorists have avoided Jewish questions is that, as their early modern predecessors discovered, the Jews confound and deconstruct neat formulations about both racial and national identity. In fact, one of the implications of this chapter is that ideas about race, nation, and religion are inextricably and hopelessly intertwined and that these identities are always multiple and overlapping.

It was one thing to claim that Jews were, as John Foxe and others put it, aromatized by their conversion; it was quite another to figure out what happened to their racial otherness when they converted and entered, or tried to enter, a Christian commonwealth. The complications raised by conversion disturbed

English commentators, some of whom offered vague theories of racial assimilation to explain away the problem. Richard Baxter, for example, proposed that once converted, the Jews "would be no Jews immediately in a religious sense nor within sixty to eighty years in a natural sense."[16] But Baxter never explains what that "natural" difference is, or how the Jews will lose it, and his solution is more or less an updated model of the aromatized convert, except in this case, a more reasonable three or four generations are needed to eliminate the taint of Jewishness.

Increasingly, seventeenth-century English travelers, whose views of racial difference were grounded in a curious amalgam of what they read and what they saw firsthand (which was almost always skewed by what they had first read about the Jews), expressed skepticism about claims for the purity of the Jewish race. Henry Blount, for example, closely interrogated Jews in his Levantine travels about their racial degeneration in the years after the ten tribes "were led captives beyond Euphrates." Blount writes that he "asked if they had there degenerate[d] into the race, and gentilism of the heathen, as our Christians have done in the Holy Land, whom now we know not from other Turks but by some touch of language." Blount notes that the Jews were loathe to admit to this racial intermingling: "ashamed of such apostasy, [they] told me that those ten tribes are not found anywhere" and were "either swallowed" up or "blown away with a whirlwind."[17]

The accumulated experience of over a hundred years of travel, trade, and conquest had convinced Europeans that some of the accepted stereotypes of Jewish racial otherness, including the belief that Jews were black, needed to be qualified. When William Brereton jotted down his impressions of the Jews in the synagogue in Amsterdam in 1635, he noted that the Jewish "men [are] most black . . . and insatiably given unto women," drawing here on contemporary prejudices linking blackness and licentiousness.[18] And when the Scottish minister Robert Kirk toured London in January 1690, he also paid a visit to the synogogue there, where he observed over two hundred Jews worshipping. He noted in his journal that "they were all very black men, and indistinct in their reasonings as gypsies."[19] By the end of the seventeenth century works like the English translation of François Maximilien Misson's *A New Voyage to Italy* make clear that it is "a vulgar error that the Jews are all black. This, Misson observes, "is only true of the Portuguese Jews, who, marrying always among one another, beget children like themselves." Consequently, "the swarthiness of their complexion is entailed upon their whole race, even in the northern regions. But the Jews who are originally of Germany, those, for example, I have seen at Prague, are not blacker than the rest of their countrymen."[20] Even Menasseh ben Israel, in his plea for the readmission of the Jews into England, offered evidence that some of the Jews in distant lands differed racially. In his

Humble Address, Menasseh mentions in passing how one group of Jews of Cochin, India, are "of a white colour and three of a tawny," the latter being "most favoured by the King."[21] Unlike Misson, though, Menasseh assumes

that the Portuguese Jews are "white," raising predictable questions of what constituted blackness. *The Merchant of Venice* provides another instance of this identification of Jews with blackness in naming Shylock's "countrymen" Tubal and Chus, the latter Biblical name immediately recognizable to Elizabethan audiences as the progenitor of all Black Africans.[22]

The most rigorous English challenge to the position that the Jewish nation was biologically distinct appears in Thomas Browne's consideration of whether "Jews stink naturally," in his *Pseudodoxia Epidemica*, published in 1646. Browne's opening words—"That the Jews stink naturally, that is, that in their race and nation there is an evil savour, is a received opinion we know not how to admit"—attack the question head on, though they dodge the issue of whether the Jews constitute a race or a nation. While Browne acknowledges that some plants and animals can be distinguished by their smell, he is unwilling "to fasten a material or temperamental propriety upon any nation." Rejecting a model of essential otherness, Browne assumes that environmental factors explain why races and nations differ. He next challenges the argument advanced by theologians that the Jews have somehow retained their racial and national purity, arguing that while the Jews have "pretended to be pure," they "must needs have suffered inseparable commixtures with nations of all sorts; not only in regard of their proselytes, but their universal dispersion." He even jokes that if Jews could "be smelled out, [it] would much advantage, not only the Church of Christ, but also the coffers of princes."[23]

Not content merely to challenge this myth, Browne proceeds to explain how it developed though a literalization of metaphors about the Jews: "The ground that begat or propagated this assertion, might be the distasteful averseness of the Christian from the Jew, upon the villainy of that fact, which made them abominable and stink in the nostrils of all men. Which real practice and metaphorical expression did after proceed into a literal construction." Browne's essay stands as a warning about the dangers of using metaphors carelessly, especially in the company of those who out of ignorance might take them in their literal sense: "How dangerous it is in sensible things to use metaphorical expressions unto the people, and what absurd conceits they will swallow." It is important to stress that Browne's interest in not in the Jews themselves but in the way that they offer an outstanding case study for how his contemporaries misunderstood and misrepresented national identity, for in "assenting hereto, many difficulties must arise."

Browne's digression on metaphor and misunderstanding brings us back to the world of Shakespeare's *The Merchant of Venice*, one in which casual and often misguided assumptions about cultural otherness predominate. In this respect, the conventional critical view that what sets Shylock apart is his religion has deflected attention away from the more complex ways in which Shakespeare situates Jews within a larger, confused network of national and racial otherness. For Shakespeare's contemporaries, Jews were not identified by their religion alone but by national and racial affiliations as well. We ought to remember that this is a play in which the heroine laughingly dismisses her dark-skinned suitor, the Prince of Morocco, with the words, "Let all of his complexion choose me so." Some recent editors have felt so uncomfortable with these racist sentiments that they have labored in explanatory notes to exonerate Shakespeare's heroine. Her allusion to Morocco's complexion, they explain, does not necessarily refer to the color of his skin, but to his personality or temperament. Perhaps they hope that readers will already have forgotten the first words of love the "tawny Moor" speaks to Portia, when he asks that she not reject him simply because his skin is black: "Mislike me not for my complexion, / The shadowed livery of the burnished sun . . . I would not change this hue, / Except to steal your thoughts, my gentle queen."[24] Editors have been equally uncomfortable glossing Lorenzo's words to Lancelot about the latter's having impregnated a Black serving girl. Perhaps stung a bit by Lancelot's remark that he is "no good member of the commonwealth" for having married and converted a Jewess, Lorenzo responds that he "shall answer better to the commonwealth than you can the getting up of the Negro's belly."[25] Their banter barely conceals the fact that both men are aware that by marrying or impregnating women of foreign races, they threaten to sully the purity of their white, Christian commonwealth.[26]

II. Nation

> They say we are a scattered nation.
> —*Barabas in Marlowe's* The Jew of Malta, *1.1.120*

In the course of the sixteenth and seventeenth centuries English writers increasingly turned their attention to the national status of the Jews, partly in response to unprecedented challenges to their own national identity and destiny. Insofar as the political and ecclesiastical structures of the Jewish nation had been divinely ordained, that newly elect Protestant nation, England, looked to Jewish practices as a model for its own.[27] English writers began with the Bible, which provided a rich portrait of the origins, history, wars, traditions, laws, prophets, kings, and ultimately exile, destruction, and diaspora of this godly nation. Interest in the Old Testament narrative soon stimulated curiosity about its postbiblical fate. In 1555 William Waterman provided an appendix summarizing "the orders and laws of the Jews' commonwealth" in his *The Fardle of Facions*.[28] Three years later Peter Morwyng surely spoke for many when he asked: "Who would not be very much delighted and desirous to understand the end, and what became at length upon such a people, that he hath

heard so much of, as every man hath read and heard of the Jews in the Bible?"[29] To satisfy that desire, Morwyng published *Jossipon*, a best-selling history of the postexilic fate of the Jewish nation that passed through a score of editions by the end of the seventeenth century.[30] Others also wrote about the "miserable destruction and dispersion of the Jews from the time of the desolation of their city and temple to this day."[31] A sense of Jewish history as discontinuous (and in which the experience of the Israelites was viewed separate from that of modern Jews) was slowly being displaced by a more fluid, continuous narrative of the fate of the Jewish people.[32] Meanwhile, prominent legal minds from Richard Hooker to John Selden drew on the example of the Jewish nation in order to resolve controversies over issues as diverse as ecclesiastical authority, the Sabbath, and divorce. In drawing on Jewish precedents, a number of these writers moved beyond scriptural evidence and drew upon the Talmud and even upon medieval Anglo-Jewish history, thereby further collapsing any simple distinction between the ancient Israelite and the modern Jewish nation.[33]

Books about the commonwealth of the Jews began circulating through Europe, as political theorists began to pay serious attention to what could be learned from the former practices of the Jewish nation.[34] By 1596 Thomas Morton found it difficult to offer "a bare and historical narration" of the ancient Israelite kingdom without raising suspicions that his work was politically seditious; he adds a disclaimer that "everyone" should be "content with that government which is already established in the place where he liveth, not thinking of any alteration which is very dangerous and bringeth with it as always great troubles, so often a final overthrow to the people."[35] A half-century later, following the execution of King Charles I, the rejection of monarchy, and the institution of a commonwealth, English writers were producing revolutionary tracts squarely based on the example of the Jewish nation.[36]

As English interest in the history of the Jewish nation grew, theologians, historians, and legal authorities found themselves mulling over an ever-widening set of theoretical and practical questions about the national status of the present-day Jews. Were they still were a nation? Were these Jews to be restored to their national homeland?[37] And in the meantime, what legal status should they be granted in Christian commonwealths? There was something deeply troubling to Elizabethans about the fact that the Jews who were scattered everywhere had somehow retained their racial purity and yet lacked a homeland. The diplomat Giles Fletcher, for example, writes that the Jews are "diffused (though not confused) and dispersed in small numbers here and there, deprived of all save their name . . . that they may be known by other nations to be that people whom God hath punished and rejected." But Fletcher also believes that the Jews had been kept racially intact as a sign of God's "infinite mercy in preserving that people from commixture and confusion with other nations."[38] This residual belief that Jews constituted a nation that was racially intact even in its dispersion left Elizabethan political theorists with two alternatives: either the Jews were to remain forever homeless and landless vagabonds or the remnants of the Jewish nation were to be restored to their homeland. Each of these alternatives proved unsettling in its own way.

Martin Luther was one of the first to warn that ideas about the restoration of the Jews were being taken too literally both by Jews and reformers alike. Henry Bull translated for English readers Luther's explanation that while the Jews "see great and ample promises concerning their land and their kingdom," they refuse to see that these promises "are conditional" and refer only to a "spiritual kingdom."[39] A number of English writers echoed this view, including Arthur Lake, who writes that the Jews are "much deceived" if they "think they shall ever become a nation again," for they "may neither breath in their own air nor tread on their own ground." Like "the brood of Cain," they are "continual vagabonds" who are "never suffered long in any one place, neither entertained otherwise than as mere strangers."[40] To be a vagabond in Elizabethan England was to be a criminal, one who had no fixed geographical or social position within the state.[41] Sixteenth-century statutes directed against vagabonds who threatened the English countryside warned that itinerants must be whipped and returned to their place of origin; but to what locale would one send a whole nation of Jewish vagabonds? As Anne Dennis observed in 1703, "other outlandish people may be sent to their own country, if we have no room for them; but the Jews have no country."[42]

This connection between Jews and lawless vagabonds had been in currency since the mid-sixteenth century, when, for example, Thomas Becon wrote that from "the destruction of Jerusalem unto this day, the Jews have ever lived like the most vile vagabonds and abominable abjects, having no country, no commonweal, no kingdom, no priesthood."[43] John Donne likewise preached from his pulpit at St. Paul's Cathedral in London that "ever since the destruction of Jerusalem the Jews have been so far from having had any king, as that they have not had a constable of their own in any part of the world."[44] For Samuel Purchas, too, the Jews have lived "like Cain, wandering over the world, branded with shame and scorn." Purchas concludes that the Jews are, paradoxically, "strangers where they dwell, and travelers where they reside."[45] One can only wonder whether Purchas was aware of how easily the same description could be applied to the many English voyagers whose journeys throughout the world were celebrated in his *Hakluytus Posthumus, or Purchas His Pilgrimes* (1625). In his discussion of Mandeville's *Travels*, Stephen Greenblatt has suggested that Mandeville's hostility toward the Jews can best be explained by the fact that the Jews were his "rivals in the dream of repossession" of Jerusalem as well as "rivals in the dream of wandering."[46] Mandeville was fic-

tional; Purchas's explorers were not. Perhaps, for these merchant adventurers, and for the English investors who financed their expeditions, the Jews had truly become rivals in their dream of wandering (not to mention rivals in international commerce). It was certainly easier to insist that Jews were international vagabonds than to acknowledge that in the outposts of a nacent empire it was the English themselves who were fast becoming strangers where they dwelled and travelers where they resided.

Early modern English writers were also prepared to show why the Jews would always retain this status as a nationless nation. According to Henry Blount, there were "two causes," why the Jews "can never cement into a temporal government of their own." The first is that "the Jewish complexion is so prodigiously timid as cannot be capable of arms." Coupled with this lack of martial prowess is the Jews' "continual cheating and malice among themselves." They could never attain "that justice, and respect to common benefit" upon which "civil society" must "stand."[47] And Samuel Purchas stresses that since their dispersal the Jews have been incapable of exercising political authority; and where they have held power they have only done so by buying "dignities" from rulers. Purchas explains that he belabors this point "lest any should think the Jews had simple freedom or power in this time of their malediction in any place."[48]

Others argued that the vagabond Jews could never be reincorporated into any nation because they were constitutionally subversive of the social order. William Prynne reminds his fellow countrymen of "the Jews themselves in all ages having been principle firebrands of sedition both in their own land and all places where they have dispersed,"[49] while Thomas Calvert writes that the criminal nature of the Jews has "made kingdoms cast them out and throw them forth like poisons, and sometimes murder them like beasts. Such virtues as these have made it a much canvassed question in politics, whether the Jews and Jewish synagogues are to be suffered in Christian commonwealths, and there are many reasons urged by some why they should not be endured." Calvert ends his warning by quoting a popular "proverb used to this purpose, 'Happy is that commonwealth, in which there is neither an Abraham, a Nimrod, nor a Naaman': that is, which is neither troubled with a Jew, nor a tyrant, nor a leper."[50]

A legend that gives some indication of the strength of feeling about endlessly itinerant Jews is that of the Wandering Jew. It is surely no coincidence that the early seventeenth century witnessed his return to England. The changes that this legend underwent from its origins in the thirteenth century through the course of the seventeenth century provide access into these and other concerns Christians had about the international nation of the Jews. Thus, while the earliest versions of this legend had limited nationalist overtones, in the wake of the great waves of Jewish and Marrano migration from Spain and Portugal in the fifteenth and sixteenth centuries the legend increasingly figured in the identification of Jews as vagabonds. In the earliest versions of the legend (which, notably, made its first European appearance in print in England, in Roger of Wendover's thirteenth-century *Flores Historiarum*,[51] and was copied and elaborated upon by Matthew Paris),[52] the man who abuses Christ and is condemned to wander is not even a Jew, but a Roman named Cartiphulus. Paris's influential account was printed in England (in Latin) in 1571.[53] By the late sixteenth and early seventeenth centuries Cartiphulus had been effectively supplanted by another incarnation of the legend, now imagined as a wandering Jew named Butadeus. A German pamphlet of 1602 was responsible for yet another transformation of the legend, in which the wandering Jew was renamed Ahasuerus.

Ahasuerus soon made his way into England. In 1612, a license was issued for a prose version of the myth and a ballad (both lost).[54] John Aubrey and Francis Peck record reputed sightings of the old wanderer in the English countryside.[55] A version of the legend was copied into a commonplace book by Richard Shann around 1620, describing how ever since that moment when "Jesus Christ, oppressed with the heavy burden of his cross would have rested himself against" this Jew's house, and "he churlishly thrust" Christ away, the Jew has "ever remained in life wandering through the world, for a penance imposed upon him for insolence he had committed against our Saviour," who "said unto him, 'I will rest, but thou shalt walk.'" At that instant, "leaving a child which he had in his arms," the Jew "could never return to the place where whence he parted to see his wife and children but had always been a vagabond."[56]

The cultural traces of this legend turn up in some unexpected places. Londoners apparently had a chance to see a play called *The Wandering Jew* on the public stage; unfortunately, the manuscript of this play, which survived into the late seventeenth-century, is now lost.[57] And in the early 1620s John Donne delivered a sermon based on Micah 2.10, "Arise and depart, for this is not your rest," a passage whose relevance to the fate of the Wandering Jew—"I will rest, but thou shalt walk"—is plain to see. Donne extrapolated from this scriptural verse the lesson that the Jews are condemned to wander, never to resettle in their homeland. Nationalist, theological, and mythical strands intersect as Donne preaches that "God precludes them from any hope" and thus "reveals His purpose, His decree, and consequently His inexorableness." The Jews "must lose their rest, they must have no rest," not "here" and not even "in the land of promise itself," for "there is no intimation, no hope given, that they should have rest anywhere else, for as they were to rise, only to depart, so they were to depart into captivity." [58] Any hope of restoration and resettlement in their ancient homeland is a delusion, precluded by divine will. The return of the Wandering Jew into seventeenth-century England reinforced conceptions of the Jews as vagrants, moving from country to country, without a land of their own, denied even the resting place of their old home, the now desolate Jerusalem. The Wandering Jew stood for the whole Jewish nation: unassimilable, unchanged, living witness to the historical truths of Christianity, an example of the severity of the punishment the Jews had suffered for rejecting Christ, condemned to wander until the end of time.

Even as some writers underscored the impossibility of the restoration of the Jews to a homeland, others began advocating it in earnest. Here, too, the ideas of Jews as racially different played an important role. Patrick Forbes, an early advocate of the Jews' national restoration, is struck by the fact that for the past "fifteen-hundred years" the Jews have not possessed "one foot of property in the earth, yet are kept a separate people." Though at first cautious—"Now, whether they shall be brought to inhabit again their own land, albeit I dare not determine"—Forbes admits that his "heart inclineth" to a territorial restitution, for "their solemn conversion must bring with it, the removing of their reproach, and so, of necessity, a gathering from their dispersion, to brook a state in the eyes of the world."[59] Why else would God have miraculously kept the Jews racially distinct if He did not intend their restoration?

It was one thing when an Aberdeen preacher broached such ideas, quite another when one of the most prominent legal figures in London, Sir Henry Finch, did in 1621 in *The Worlds Great Restauration*, provoking the ire of his monarch. Finch, a Puritan lawyer, imagines not only a religious conversion of the Jews but their political reenfranchisement as well. Finch first acknowledges the Jews' exiled, institutionless, and formless state: there is no "people so dispersed, without government, without religion, without form, either of church or commonwealth."[60] Yet, Finch believes, an ingathering of the Jews will occur and include not just the "Ten Tribes" but "the rest of the Jews" as well. Finch is adamant that these apocalyptic hopes "and such like are not allegories" but "meant really and literally of the Jews. . . . Wherefore we need not be afraid to aver and maintain that one day they shall come to Jerusalem again, be kings and chief monarchs of the earth, sway and govern all, for the glory of Christ that shall shine among them."[61]

Finch made the subordination of Christian kings to this Jewish commonwealth even more explicit in his dedicatory epistle—directed to "all the seed of Jacob, far and wide dispersed"—where he flatly states that all "the kings of the Gentiles shall . . . fall down before thee."[62] Yet once the restoration of the Jews moved from a world of millenarian hope to political possibility, it began to raise all kinds of unforeseen problems about the relationship between the powers of western Europe and this newly reformed Jewish state. Who would be subject to whom? King James I did not like the implications of Finch's argument and had him imprisoned. The aging King did joke about being "so old that he cannot tell how to do his homage at Jerusalem." James, who loved a good royal procession as much as any monarch, was less than thrilled with Finch's claim that he and other "kings of the Gentiles" would have to crawl to Jerusalem to throw themselves prostrate before the Jews. Puritan millenarianism, England's sense of itself as God's elect nation, even geopolitical fantasies of the Jews as a buffer against Catholic and Turkish foes all clearly contributed to the impulse to restore the Jews to Palestine. Yet one is still left wondering if these rational explanations stretch quite far enough. After all, these efforts to restore the Jews to their ancient homeland remained far more palatable to English writers than the idea of restoring Jews to England itself.[63]

The failure of the Jews to conform to acceptable notions of nationhood rendered equally unsatisfactory the alternatives of assimilating these vagabonds into Christian commonwealths or providing them with their own land so that they could rule their own nation once more. There were those who could at least entertain a third possibility. Sir Thomas Shirley grasped at it in 1607 when he urged King James to settle the Jews in Ireland, thereby solving both Irish and Jewish questions and reaping the benefits of heavy taxation. This would eliminate, and at the same time draw a profit from, two unacceptable claimants to national status.[64] The idea was not as farfetched as it may now seem. In 1656 the political theorist James Harrington proposed a similar solution in his utopian tract, *The Commonwealth of Oceana*. In his introduction Harrington describes the land of "Panopea," his allegorical name for Ireland, which he calls "the soft mother of a slothful and pusillanimous people . . . anciently subjected by the arms of Oceana," that is, England. Harrington writes of Ireland as "almost depopulated for shaking the yoke, and at length replanted with a new race," the victorious English. Ireland, according to Harrington, while "rich in the nature of the soil and full of commodious ports for trade," is nonetheless populated by a people that "come still to degenerate." Harrington's belated proposal—"which in my opinion (if it had been thought upon in time) might have been best done"—attempts to resolve the nagging Irish problem "by planting" Ireland "with Jews, allowing them their own rites and laws, for that would have brought them suddenly from all parts of the world, and in sufficient numbers. And though the Jews be now altogether for merchandise, yet in the land Canaan (since their exile from whence they have not been landlords) they were altogether for agriculture; and there is no cause why many should doubt but, having a fruitful country and good ports too, they would be good at both."

Like Shirley before him, Harrington recognizes the economic advantages that would accrue from such an arrangement:

> Panopea, being farmed out unto the Jews and their heirs forever, for the pay of a provincial army to protect them during the term of seven years, and for two millions annual revenue from that time forward—beside the customs, which would pay the provincial army—would have been a bargain of such advantage, both unto them and this commonwealth, as is not to be found otherwise by either.

Harrington's solution to the Irish and Jewish problems was to imagine a land without a people for a people without a land. His recommendation is also grounded in the Pauline arboreal metaphor of "planting" Ireland with the unassimilable Jews: to "receive the Jews after any other manner into a commonwealth were to maim it; for they of all nations never incorporate but, taking up the room of a limb, are of no use or office unto the body, while they suck the nourishment which would sustain a natural and useful body."[65] This final metaphor returns us to a world in which the unassimilable nation of the Jews must "suck" (that familiar trope again) on others. But if Harrington's plan were enacted, the Jews' parasitic preying upon the "natural and useful body" of others would ultimately serve to nourish a "new race," the English. While Harrington acknowledges that his proposal comes too late to be acted upon, his work nonetheless reveals how strong an impact Paul's ideas about Jewish racial difference had upon English conceptions of the nation.

III. Alien

If it be proved against an alien . . .
—The Merchant of Venice, 4.1.345

Every Jew who stepped foot in England in the late sixteenth and early seventeenth centuries—Joachim Gaunse of Prague, Roderigo Lopez of Portugal, Yehuda Menda of Barbary, Jacob Barnet of Italy—was an alien. Menda died an old man at the Converts' House. Lopez was publicly executed, the crowd jeering at his insistence that he loved Queen Elizabeth as much as he did Jesus Christ. Gaunse and Barnet, as professing Jews, were banished the realm; while not charged with any crime, as aliens they had no legal recourse. The borders of England were permeable, and these Jews were only a small part of the vast stream of thousands of immigrants who entered England in the course of the late sixteenth and early seventeenth centuries. England (especially London) was far from the homogeneous world that is all too often nostalgically imagined. Like other successful centers of international trade at this time, London was full of outsiders: French, Dutch, Italians, Spaniards, Portuguese, and even a small number of Blacks and Jews were crowded within London's walls. Scholars have estimated that aliens comprised roughly four or five percent of London's population in the late sixteenth century, somewhere between five and ten thousand individuals.[66] They were officially referred to as "aliens," or more typically as "strangers." "Foreigners," odd as it may sound to us, was the term Londoners usually reserved for the men and women (including Shakespeare himself) who had abandoned the English countryside and who swelled the size and strained the resources of the metropolis in the late sixteenth century. To these two groups may be added a third: the fellow inhabitants of the British isles, the Welsh, Scots, and Irish then dwelling in London.

All these aliens had one thing in common: they were not English, and, as such, provide some access into understanding exactly what being English meant, at least in terms of various legal and economic rights. Aliens also found themselves situated at the crossroads of contested authorities in early modern England, subject to "Statutory Law, Common Law, Lex Mercatoria, Custom of the City and local parish regulations and so forth."[67] To define the shifting status of the alien was thus one way of understanding the complex levels of authority in the realm. When Sir Edward Coke in his *Institutes* defined an alien as "one born in a strange country under the obedience of a strange prince or country," he put his finger on the basic problem of the place of aliens within the community: to whom did an immigrant owe allegiance?[68]

Complicating matters still further was the fact that aliens, if they had the financial resources, could become English by means of royal patent (denization) or by parliamentary act (naturalization), raising again interesting questions about authorization and allegiances. There were slight differences between the rights one obtained through denization and naturalization, ones that subsequently proved critical to Jews seeking the rights of native-born subjects in the seventeenth and eighteenth centuries (only a parliamentary act "could make the person a subject from birth" retroactively, crucial for issues of inheritance).[69] Even if one were a denizen, though, one was not necessarily a "free" denizen, that is, one who had the freedom of the City of London to conduct one's economic affairs on an equal basis with native-born English competitors. The status of aliens was thus made up of a patchwork of overlapping and sometimes conflicting jurisdictions, confusing then as now, with even the simplest opposition of native/alien complicated by instances in which an English couple bore a child abroad or aliens long-established in England bore children while residing there. In these cases the tension between where one was born and to whom one owed allegiance was particularly strained.[70]

While the status of aliens remained unstable, the threat that these stranger communities posed was imagined by some English subjects to be far greater than their actual power or numbers. Sixteenth-century England was at times a haven and, less frequently, a hell for these strangers. Memories of the infamous May Day riots of 1517, in which London's alien community was brutally attacked by apprentices, remained alive. Even as skilled alien artisans and religious refugees—predominantly Dutch and French Protestants—found safety in London in the post-Reformation years, their presence was not always welcomed by the local population. For example, as Andrew Pettegree notes, in "the spring of 1551, a time of particular tension and rumbling discontent, a deputation of citizens made a formal complaint to the Lord Mayor against the strangers, and a plot to attack the foreigners was nipped in the bud by the city authorities. It was being put about that there were forty or fifty thousand strangers in London . . . an absurd exaggeration." Eight years later a similar rumor circulated "that there were now forty thousand strangers in London,"[71] probably ten times their actual number. Given that London's population at this time was somewhere between seventy and ninety thousand,[72] this rumor is quite remarkable for what it reveals about Londoners' fears of being overwhelmed by strangers. In response, civic authorities took the unprecedented step of compiling a census of aliens residing within London's walls, a procedure that would be repeated periodically in the course of the late sixteenth and early seventeenth centuries, and one that helped underscore the difference between strangers and citizens. While these "returns" were not comprehensive, they reassured Londoners that there were far fewer aliens in their midst than some had feared.[73] Nonetheless, the knowledge that there were fewer aliens did not put an end to local xenophobia. In 1567 libels showing "gallows, and, as it were, hanging of strangers" appeared in London, while in 1586 libels again circulated, and a plot to destroy the strangers was discovered.[74]

Another return was completed in 1593, probably the most comprehensive one, at a time when concerns over London's alien population had reached new levels of intensity. In addition to this accounting, vigorous legislative attempts to control the alien population were also undertaken.[75] On March 1, 1593, a bill for the control of merchant strangers was introduced into Parliament. Five days later Queen Elizabeth commanded the Lord Mayor to instruct the Aldermen to make with "as great secrecy as may be . . . diligent search . . . within all parts within your ward what and how many foreigners are residing and remaining within the same, of what nation, profession, trade or occupation every of them are of."[76] There were those like Edward Dymock, William Hurlle, and Walter Walker who wanted the government to go beyond mere "returns of strangers" and to organize a better way of providing "surveyance and registration."[77] The ostensible grounds for this request: the economic and political threat posed by these aliens not only to the nation at large but to native-born artisans. According to John Strype, among the other arguments "used to persuade the Queen to grant a register" was that it "was commonly urged against the strangers, that a greater number might repair hither, than with good policy were fit to be endured. That very many might justly be supposed to resort hither, not so much out of zeal to religion, or love to the Queen, as to practice against her and her state and to rob the English of their commodities to enrich themselves." There was also fear that English "artisans and mechanical persons might be impoverished by the great multitude of strangers being of their trades and faculties," besides the fact that "there were many rich men among them, that lived obscurely, to benefit themselves by usury and exchange of money, without doing any good to the commonwealth," as well others who, "having gotten into their hands great riches and treasure, by engrossing out commodities," have "suddenly departed the realm, and many times stole away with other men's goods, without any notice given thereof." And finally, "that under the color of merchandise and religion, many intelligencers and spies [have] adventured to come hither."[78]

Parliamentary proceedings indicate that attitudes toward London's alien population were polarized. Before Parliament was dissolved by the Queen on April 10, 1593, the House of Commons had passed a bill against merchant strangers (preventing them from retailing foreign wares), a bill that was then rejected in the House of Lords. In opposition to those who wanted to restrict alien activities were economic pragmatists, like Privy Councillor John Wolley, who argued that the proposed anti-alien legislation would ultimately harm the city: "This Bill should be ill for London, for the riches and renown of the City cometh by entertaining strangers, and giving liberty unto them. Antwerp and Venice could never have been so rich and famous but by entertaining of strangers, and by that means have gained all the intercourse of the world."[79]

Wolley's remarks are akin to those not long after expressed in *The Merchant of Venice* about the freedom of the city accorded Venice's alien population. It was no secret to Elizabethan legislators, especially those with any first or secondhand information about the economy of Antwerp or Venice, that Jews figured prominently in international trade. Even Edward Dymock, who had advocated closer surveillance of the aliens, noted cautiously that in "Venice any stranger may buy, sell, or purchase house or lands and dispose thereof by his will, or otherwise at his pleasure, as freely as any citizen. And this we may do then in some sort."[80] Venice, clearly, stood as a model for an ideal economic coexistence between subjects and aliens, but when mapped onto an English landscape, the contradictions generated by an alien policy of toleration and equality, on the one hand, and legislation, restraint, surveillance, and suspicion, on the other, were not easily reconciled.

Marlowe had anticipated Shakespeare in identifying Jews as aliens, and Elizabethan theatergoers in 1593 would surely have been alert to how closely Barabas's activities in *The Jew of Malta* resembled those attributed to the dangerous aliens in their midst. Barabas is, after all, an alien merchant residing in the "Port-Town" of Malta who happily engrosses commodities into his own hands; he is also quick to brag that he is "on every side enriched" by trade (and that he has "as much coin as will buy the town").[81] Marlowe draws attention to Barabas's alien status in Malta early on, in the scene where Ferneze and the Knights ask that Barabas and his fellow Jews subsidize the tribute to the Turks. When Barabas asks, "Are strangers with your tribute to be taxed?" he is sharply rebuked by the Second Knight, who reminds him that along with the rights of strangers come obligations as well: "Have strangers leave with us to get their wealth? Then let them with us contribute." These lines must surely have struck a resonant chord with theatergoers in the early 1590s aware of the ongoing tensions between London's native and alien artisans. When Barabas later turns spy and enables Calymath and his forces to "surprise the town," he may well have confirmed the worst fears English subjects had about strangers as "intelligencers and spies."[82]

The association of aliens and Jews resurfaced in a libel posted in London in May 1593, setting in motion a strange set of events that led to the arrest and torture of Thomas Kyd and the house arrest (and, shortly thereafter, the murder) of Christopher Marlowe. Given these circumstances, it would be surprising if the incident had escaped Shakespeare's notice. In the month since Parliament had dissolved without enacting legislation against London's aliens, popular agitation against strangers had increased. On April 16 the Privy Council noted hostility directed against "Flemings and Strangers," and a week later a note calling for the expulsion of aliens within three months was read into the Council's minutes. On May 4 the Council dealt with the complaint of London shopkeepers against illegal trading by aliens. A day later the libelous poem mentioned above—one that threatened the lives of London's aliens—was found on the wall of the Dutch Churchyard. The Privy Council's response to this last offense was decisive: it not only ordered a search and apprehension of those suspected of writing the poem, but sanctioned the use of torture at Bridewell prison, "by the extremity thereof" to "draw them to discover their knowledge of the said libels."[83]

Until a public auction at Sotheby's in June 1971, only the first four lines of the poem, quoted by John Strype, had been recorded. The discovery at this sale of a contemporary transcription made by John Mansell of a 53-line poem in couplets entitled "A Libel, Fixed Upon the French [i.e., Dutch] Church Wall, in London, Anno 1593," provides a remarkable example of how the alien threat shifts easily into anti-Jewish discourse:

Ye strangers that do inhabit in this land,
Note this same writing do it understand,
Conceit it well for safeguard of your lives,
Your goods, your children, and your dearest wives.
Your Machiavellian merchant spoils the state,
Your usury doth leave us all for dead,
Your artifex and craftsman works our fate,
And like the Jews you eat us up as bread.
The merchant doth ingross all kind of wares
Forestalls the markets, whereso'er he goes
Sends forth his wares, by peddlers to the fairs,
Retails at home, and with his horrible shows,
    Undoeth thousands.[84]

"And like the Jews you eat us up as bread"—an enigmatic line that resonates with the discourse of host desecration on the one hand and, on the other, the cannibalism associated with Jews in late sixteenth-century discussions of usury. The counterfeiting Machiavellian merchant who spoils the state, whose usury leaves citizens for dead, who engrosses all kinds of wares and forestalls the markets, and, finally, who as a Jew devours the Christians (and yet who is himself cooked to death in a cauldron) all point back to Marlowe's merchant stranger, Barabas. Whoever had written the offensive poem may well have been inspired by recent performances of *The Jew of Malta* at the Rose Theater just a few months earlier, when the playhouses had opened again briefly from December 29 until February 1, 1593. Three of the twenty-nine performances staged during this period were of *The Jew of Malta*. Allusions in the libel to two other Marlowe plays, *Tamburlaine* and *The Massacre at Paris*, link his drama with anti-alien sentiment even more closely. Small wonder that the Privy Council had sought out Marlowe in their hunt for the source of the libel.

Contemporary playwrights recognized that the issue of London's aliens was of considerable interest to their audiences, and around this time several of them, including in all probability Shakespeare, submitted a draft of *Sir Thomas More* to the Master of the Revels, Edmund Tilney, for his approval. Given the fact that their play contained scenes that literally reenacted the bloody anti-alien riots of 1517, Tilney found much worth censoring. Tilney not only told the playwrights to "leave out the insurrection wholly and the cause thereof... at your own perils"[85] but also struck out again and again passing references to that loaded word, *stranger*. Indeed, in the scene generally accepted as Shakespeare's the offensive word appears seven times.[86]

The scene in *Sir Thomas More* attributed to Shakespeare attempts to undermine the anti-alien rebellion in the very course of staging it, reminding the English rioters that one day they too might be strangers in a strange land:

> Would you be pleased
> To find a nation of such barbarous temper
> That breaking out in hideous violence
> Would not afford you an abode on earth,
> Whet their detested knives against your throats
> Spurn you like dogs, and like as if that God
> Owned not nor made not you, not that the elements
> Were not all appropriate to your comforts,
> But chartered unto them? What would you think
> To be thus used? This is the strangers' case,
> And this your mountainish inhumanity.[87]

Yet it remains difficult to determine what Shakespeare's own views were about aliens here, and scholars remain divided over this question.[88] My own sense is that Shakespeare does seem to be repudiating the arguments that had appeared in anti-alien libels while at the same time retaining the dramatic excitement of staging, rather than merely narrating, the insurrection and anti-alien attacks (and thereby potentially inflaming anti-alien sentiment). It is also worth noting that Shakespeare leaves himself open here to the same risk of appropriation that Marlowe had experienced. After all, what was to prevent the next libeler from quoting Shakespeare's words approvingly to bolster the claim that "the removing of strangers . . . cannot choose but much advantage the poor handicrafts of the city."[89] Of course, Shakespeare also writes a speech repudiating this idea, but who would know that if the first passage had been quoted out of context?

A valuable lesson to be learned from the censorship of *Sir Thomas More* was that Tilney appears to have been content with simply substituting less offensive terms: for example, he replaced the words *stranger* and *Frenchman* with *Lombard*, and did the same with the phrase *saucy alien*. There were only a very few Lombards in London at this time, and the association was less national than professional, as the word connoted moneylender, usurer, or banker. After the expulsion of Jews from England, the Lombards had assumed the role of moneylenders and, by extension, the reputation of extortionate usurers. Apparently, as far as Tilney was concerned, a simple act of substitution legitimated topical allusions: he specified in the directions written into the left margin of the opening lines of the manuscript that the attacks should be represented as directed "against the Lombards only." There was no problem redirecting hostility against a largely fictive minority popuation that was an easy target and peripheral to the real object of anti-alien sentiment. Marlowe had apparently mastered this lesson in his representation of strangers in *The Jew of Malta*: by identifying the Jews as strangers he is able to use the politically sensitive term *stranger* with impunity. While Shakespeare had chosen not to engage in this act of deflection and substitution in *Sir Thomas More*, he certainly did so a few years later when he came to write about the *alien* in *The Merchant of Venice*.

The steps taken by civic leaders in 1593 were insufficient to quell anti-alien sentiment. Two years later, in "the year 1595, the poor tradesmen made a riot upon the strangers in Southwark, and other parts of the City of London . . . [and] the like tumults began at the same time within the Liberties (as they are called) where such strangers commonly harboured."[90] This apprentice riot at Tower Hill on June 29, 1595, in which a crowd of a thousand or so stoned the city officers who tried to pacify them,[91] was an unusual event and one that would not have easily slipped from the minds of Elizabethans a year or so later when, at the Globe Theater in the same Liberty of Southwark, they paid to see Shakespeare's new play, *The Merchant of Venice*, in which the plot turns on the conviction of an alien who had threatened the well-being of a citizen. What disturbed the rioters of 1595 so much about the aliens they attacked was that these strangers were "seen as forming an inward-looking society of their own deliberately cutting themselves off from their hosts."[92] While the violence was directed against the well-established and successful Dutch and French Protestant communities, the terms of the complaint against these strangers resonate with those brought against the Jews of England before their expulsion and after their resettlement: "Though they be demized or born here amongst us, yet they keep themselves severed from us in church, in a government, in trade, in language and marriage,"[93] a charge that calls to mind Shylock's declaration that "I will buy with you, sell with you, talk with you, walk with you and so following: but I will not eat with you, drink with you, nor pray with you."[94]

It was the economic strength of resident aliens, not usury, that was making Londoners increasingly nervous about their own financial well-being. Clearly, like Marlowe's Barabas, Shakespeare's "alien" Shylock cannot really be understood independent of the larger social tensions generated by aliens and their economic practices in London in the mid-1590s. Consider the trial scene in act 4 of *The Merchant of Venice*, which appears to come to an end after Portia's brilliant defense that Shylock's bond specifies a pound, no more nor less, of Antonio's flesh:

> if thou tak'st more
> Or less than a just pound, be it so much
> As makes it light or heavy in the substance,

Or the division of the twentieth part
Of one poor scruple—nay, if the scale do turn
But in the estimation of a hair,
Thou diest and all thy goods are confiscate.[95]

Shylock, content at this point with receiving just his "principal," is divested even of that. Portia dismisses him, warning: "Thou shalt have nothing but the forfeiture / To be so taken at thy peril, Jew." Defeated, Shylock turns to go. His parting words are: "Why then the devil give him good of it! / I'll stay no longer question."[96] The play has seemingly arrived at a moment of satisfying comic closure: marriages and finances are (marginally) in order and the threat to Antonio's life has been breathtakingly eliminated by Portia's legal skill. Jessica has eloped, taking with her some of Shylock's wealth. Moreover, Shylock's principal, which has bankrolled Bassanio's successful wooing of Portia and which led in turn to his courtroom defeat, is now forfeited to his Christian adversaries.

Yet the scene does not end there. A sufficiently disturbing threat remains, one that provokes Portia to call the departing Shylock back:

Tarry, Jew,
The law hath yet another hold on you.
It is enacted in the laws of Venice,
If it be proved against an alien
That by direct or indirect attempts
He seek the life of any citizen,
The party 'gainst the which he doth contrive
Shall seize one half his goods; the other half
Comes to the privy coffer of the state,
And the offender's life lies in the mercy
Of the Duke only, 'gainst all other voice.[97]

Many readers, and I count myself among them, have found something troubling about this speech. Through the precedent of old laws still on the books—but apparently unknown to Antonio, Shylock, the Duke, and all other interested parties—Venetian society is able to have it both ways: while the city's charter guarantees equality before the law, a feature that has attracted foreigners to Venice, it retains legislation that renders this equality provisional, if not fictional. The trial scene thus offers a fantasy resolution to the conflicting and overlapping jurisdictions intrinsic to such trials by invoking a law that effectively supersedes the city's charter (a charter that more closely resembles the kind one would find in an English city under a feudal monarch than in the

Venetian Republic).[98] As much as it might want to, given its charter, Venetian society cannot punish Shylock simply because he is a Jew. But in the terms of the play it can convict him as a threatening alien. In order to accomplish this delicate maneuver in the space of these dozen lines, the nature of Shylock's difference is reconstituted: a Jew at the start of the speech, three lines later he is an alien. Yet once Shylock is convicted as an alien, he can be punished, not as an alien, but as a Jew, who must "presently become a Christian."

For this brief and crucial moment in the play, Shylock is both Jew and alien. This momentary slippage is vital, for it allows Shakespeare to represent not simply theological questions, but pressing social ones, even as Elizabethan London confronted an ongoing crisis over its own alien communities. *The Merchant of Venice* thus serves a complex social function for its audiences. It raises the issue of anti-alien sentiment, in a theater playing to a cross section of the population that probably included some of the artisans and apprentices who a year before had sought to inflict violence upon London's alien community. Yet the play also takes an alien's threat of violence (rather than any direct act of violence against a citizen) and reverses the actual threat existing in London's liberties. That is, we have in the play not a community's attack upon an alien, but the conviction of an alien on the grounds that he violated a preexisting law against citizens. The hostility is reimagined as originating with the aliens and directed against the citizenry and is enacted in a way that does not contradict the more tolerant laws governing the freedom of the city that guarantee equality before the law to strangers.

To the extent that *The Merchant of Venice* reproduces the practice of translating anti-alien into anti-Jewish sentiment, we are left with a view of the play as a cultural safety valve. Seen in this light, Shakespeare's play actively draws on and partakes of two of the ways in which the alien crisis was dealt with in London in the 1590s: first, the playing out of violence in the courts, and second, the deflection of anti-alien sentiment into anti-Jewish feeling. If Elizabethan England was a society built upon certain legal fictions, they were enabling fictions that allowed it—like the imaginary Venetian "state" of Shakespeare's play—to promise equal treatment to aliens in strengthening the economy and building foreign trade and to restrict that freedom when social policy deemed it necessary to do so.

IV. The unresolved status of Jews in England after their return

It should be clear at this point that residency in England was insufficient to make one English, nor, as Jews discovered in 1656, did resettlement accomplish this either. By the early seventeenth century a handful of Jewish merchants had availed themselves of the opportunity of becoming denizens.[99] Denization, though a less attractive alternative than the retroactive act of naturalization, was the only avenue open to practicing Jews. For after 1609, "an Act of Parliament was passed forbidding anyone to be naturalized or restored in blood unless within a month before the introduction of his Bill he received the Sacrament of the Lord's Supper, and before the second reading of his Bill had taken the oaths of supremacy and allegiance in the Parliament House," oaths that included the wording "on the faith of a Christian."[100] This act was directed against the Catholic, not Jewish threat, coming only a few years after the Gunpowder Plot. Legal barriers thus continued to stand between Jews living in England and natural-born subjects, and these barriers persisted long after tacit readmission.

The Whitehall Conference of late 1655 had left the legal status of the Jews in England unresolved. The issue was almost immediately put to the test when, in March 1656, following the outbreak of hostilities with Spain, the Council of State issued a proclamation declaring all Spanish goods and shipping to be lawful prize. As Spanish or Portuguese nationals, many of the wealthiest Jews residing in England stood in danger of having their goods confiscated by the state. The threat was realized when one of the richest, Antonio Roderigues Robles, had his ships seized. In response, the Jewish community chose the unprecedented legal tactic of repudiating their Spanish nationality and claiming instead that, like Robles, they were "of the Hebrew nation and religion."[101] A sympathetic Cromwell saw to it that the warrants issued against Robles were dropped and that others were not pressed against members of this small Jewish community that had sought his protection. No longer Spanish and yet not English (except for the handful that were denizens), England's Jews were neither citizens nor aliens.

The privileges that Cromwell may have privately granted the Jews—to worship privately, trade freely, and bury their dead in a Jewish cemetery—did not resolve the problem of the Jews' legal status. In fact, they only exacerbated it, for hard upon Cromwell's death the opponents of the Jews in London petitioned (unsuccessfully) to overturn these privileges, urging Richard Cromwell to expel the Jews and confiscate their property. And upon Charles II's accession to the throne similar proposals were advanced "for the expulsion of all professed Jews out of your Majesty's dominions and to bar the door after them." In submitting one of these petitions, the Lord Mayor and Alderman of London charged that Jews, once readmitted, will seduce the "ignorant and indigent" to their beliefs, betray state secrets, and deceive Christians with their unscrupulous business practices (the petitioners asserted that the Jews had already "prostituted" the price of English goods in foreign ports). Moreover, they claimed, the Jews who has recently settled in England had begun to contaminate English national purity, having "already debauched some necessitous ones of the weaker sex, to the abominable taint of the English blood and bringing on us the infamy of a mixed nation."[102] The King's decision to ignore these petitions—as well as two others subsequently submitted by Thomas Violet, the first of which reminded the King that it was a felony for any Jew to be found in England[103]—only deferred the problem of the Jews' status. From a legal standpoint their identity remained troublingly indeterminate, not English, but not exactly "not-English."[104]

With the accession of each English monarch in turn in the late seventeenth century, new attacks were made on the Jews' ambiguous legal status. In 1685 Samuel Hayne, a patriotic provincial customs officer at Falmouth, morally outraged that English Jews were conniving to avoid paying alien duty on their goods, took them to court. But his Jewish opponents were far more powerful than he, and Hayne served time in Fleet Prison and suffered financially for his unsuccessful efforts.[105] That same year the Beaumont brothers, Thomas and Carleton, citing the recusancy laws of Queen Elizabeth I dating back to 1581 and still on the statute books, had forty-eight of London's Jewish merchants charged with recusancy, thirty-eight of whom were "taken off the Exchange and obliged to give bail."[106] In response, King James II ordered his attorney general to stop these proceedings against the Jews, who "should not be troubled, upon this account, but quietly enjoy the free exercise of their religion, whilst they behave themselves dutifully and obediently to his government."[107] Since this royal intervention did nothing to clarify the Jews' ambiguous legal status, it should come as little surprise that following the Glorious Revolution of 1688 and the accession of King William to the throne, the Jews of England once again found themselves having to defend their status. Faced with a parliamentary bill for special taxation of the Jews in November 1689, the Jewish community printed a petition, *The Case of the Jews Stated*, which tried to solidify the earlier claim that their rights as subjects, unlike those of all other foreign nationals, were based on their belonging to a homeless Jewish nation: "That the Jews being a nation that cannot lay claim to any country, do never remove from any part where they are tolerated and protected. And therefore may be looked upon to be a greater advantage to this kingdom than any other foreigners, who commonly, so soon as as they got good estates, return with them into their own countries."[108]

A fundamental change had occurred since Robles and his fellow Jews had earlier claimed to be of the Hebrew nation *and* religion in 1656. Three decades later the Jews living in England decided to abandon the religious part of the argument in favor of one based solely on national identity: since Jews were an anomalous international nation, it was impossible for them to owe allegiance to a foreign prince. Their parliamentary opponents recognized in this petition an attempt by the Jews to claim the rights of full English subjects, and when Paul Foley tried to deliver the Jews' petition, a member of Commons named

Hampden challenged him, saying: "I hear some of these Jews are naturalized, but I would know how they came to be naturalized!. . . . There is a great deal of difference betwixt being subject to the laws and enjoying the benefit of the laws."[109] While this parliamentary effort to tax the Jews did not carry, the "failure of the Jews to agree to special taxation," as David Katz notes, "also brought about a renewal of efforts made to cancel exemptions they had received from the payment of alien duties, and to have them reclassified as foreign residents rather than as resident nationals of an international nation." As long as the government needed to extract money from Jews residing in England—and they sought to do so at this time not only through this proposed tax but also through a "forced loan, alien duties," and "a special poll tax"—the problem of the Jews' unresolved status remained a sore spot and a point of contention.[110]

In his analysis of the events leading up to 1688, David Katz confronts the question that is central to my discussion here, the status of Jews as aliens. Having acknowledged that Jews "were neither alien nor citizen," Katz notes that they

> simply did not fit comfortably into any of the existing categories. They were undoubtedly "strangers," in religion, in language, in appearance, and in habits. But so were the Scots, and in any case the problem went far deeper. The Jews in England were often described as "aliens": the Sephardim presented themselves as belonging to an international nation. A good number had been endenized and were thus on the road to full citizenship, but they would not get there until the middle of the nineteenth century, for the Christian oath still barred the way to Emancipation, even if the the notion of "alien" must surely wear thin after two centuries.

Katz's final stab at the question shifts the terms of the argument considerably, momentarily (and I think mistakenly) relocating Jews under the rubric of Christian dissenters: "So were the Jews of England 'Dissenters'? In a strictly formalistic sense they were, since they did not take communion according to the rites of the Church of England. But so much divided Anglo-Jewry from the Presbyterians, Congregationalists, and even Unitarians who fell under this heading, that the use of the term must surely muddle rather than enlighten."[111] This last claim misses the point, I think, because it does not recognize the extent to which the Jews in *The Case of the Jews Stated* had themselves sought to define their own legal status in England on national, rather than narrowly religious grounds, and this would clearly distinguish their fate from that of other religious minorities, Dissenters or Catholics.

Another problem with this conclusion is that while the notion of alien (and again, they were not simply aliens) might have worn thin, it had not worn out. It is possible to detect a bit of wishful thinking here, too. The claim that after 1688 the presence of the Jews in England was "an undisputed matter of fact"[112] might surely have surprised readers of the 1703 *Historical and Law Treatise Against the Jewes and Judaism*. This work, written by "B. B.," continued to insist that the Jews are "mere aliens." Moreover, the tract reminds its readers, "the banishment of the Jews" in 1290 "was by the full consent of King and Parliament, and not by the King alone" and that the expulsion order was never repealed. Accordingly, "all the Jews in England may be cut off," though B. B. cautions, "God forbid Christians should be so unmerciful as to do any such thing to the Jews." The desire of Jews resident in England to move beyond their ambiguous alien status and assume that of full-fledged subjects was countered by native-born Englishmen who believed that these Jews were not and could not be English and, furthermore, that they were parasitic on English society. For B. B., "as locusts are to corn, so are the Jews to Christians; the former consume the grain, and the latter undermine the commonwealth."[113] B. B.'s work was reprinted twice in the early eighteenth century and was joined by scores of other tracts having to do with the issue of naturalizing foreigners. Remarkably, not until 1846 were the *Statutum de Judeismo*, technically in force since the thirteenth century, formally repealed. Even in that year a disability still remained: Jews could not fully partake of English political life.[114] Historians have since felt a strong need to iron out these inconsistencies and ambiguities.[115] These efforts, however, cannot disguise how poorly defined the status of the Jews remained in early modern England. The problem did not go away, in part because the identity of the English was bound up with that of the non-English. And it would return with a vengeance during the controversy over the Jewish Naturalization Act of 1753, the subject of the following chapter. That *The Merchant of Venice* was a catalyst in that controversy over naturalization should not be surprising; for what remained latent in English society's unresolved attitude toward the Jews' ambiguous alien status resonated with something embedded deep within Shakespeare's play.

VII ↜

Shakespeare and the Jew Bill
of 1753

Old Shylock the Jew, whom we mean to restore ye,
 Was naturalized oft by your fathers before ye;
Then take him tonight to your kindest compassion,
 For to countenance Jews is the pink of the fashion.
—*John Cunningham, 1753*

If you consider rightly, it will be very hard to answer the question,
"What is an Englishman?"
—*Anon., 1748*

The English have naturally interwoven in their constitution a
peculiar kind of national self-love, and the least attempt to dispense a favour to foreigners alarms their fears, and awakens that
jealousy which is natural to their very frame. It is to this we owe
the general discontent which has broke out among all ranks of people upon the late occasion. . . . As it is apparent from what has been
observed already, that the Christian religion has no longer a footing in this country, it may not be improper to repeal the Sacramental Test and to substitute in its room the Act of Circumcision.
—*Arthur Murphy, 1753*

The "late occasion" that provoked this "general
discontent" was the Jewish Naturalization Act or
Jew Bill (as virtually everyone at the time called it)
of 1753. The facts of this parliamentary legislation
hardly explain the hue and cry that led to its swift
repeal. At first glance the legislation seemed harm-
less enough: a slight alteration in the requirements
for how foreign Jews could become naturalized
British subjects. Considerably more proved to be at stake, however, than revis-
ing alien laws that had remained unchanged since the reign of King James I.
While the acceptance of Jews in eighteenth-century England might in retrospect appear undisputed, to contemporaries the legal status accorded these
Jews remained confusing and, for some, disturbing. Were they aliens,
denizens, subjects, or something else entirely? What place, if any, should Jews
have in a Christian commonwealth? Could they own and inherit land, including church holdings? Should they pay alien duties? And why should Jews be
permitted to worship freely when Catholics and Dissenters were prevented
from doing so? By the middle of the eighteenth century the number of Jews

living in England had grown to almost eight thousand,[1] and their role in the economic life of the country was perceived as far greater than their numbers would warrant, a factor that drew attention to their indeterminate status. Robert Liberles is surely right in arguing that the "Jew Bill provided the first real opportunity since Readmission for a public debate in England on the status of the Jews," and that all "the doubts and apprehensions concerning the Jews' position now came to the fore as the controversy extended far beyond the limited intent of the bill itself."[2] The controversy not only touched upon what legal rights should be extended to these foreigners but also called into question what is "naturally woven" into what Murphy, in his satiric essay, calls the English "constitution." Insofar as Englishness was being reconstituted socially, politically, economically, and religiously at this time, the attempt to naturalize Jews—and thereby do away with that which distinguished Englishness from Jewishness—proved explosive. Even the most levelheaded commentators understood that a bill perceived as encouraging "Jews abroad to come over in great numbers and to settle in this country" would "most certainly" produce "a general uneasiness and discontent throughout the nation."[3]

The facts of this alien legislation and the ensuing controversy have been well documented.[4] In January 1753, after some debate within the Jewish community itself, a successful Jewish banker named Joseph Salvador decided to petition the government to modify slightly the process whereby foreign-born Jews could be naturalized (which would relieve them of having to pay expensive alien duties). The major obstacle for Jews seeking to be naturalized was the Sacramental Test. Since practicing Jews could not take the Holy Sacrament, Salvador proposed that they be allowed to substitute the Oath of Supremacy and Oath of Allegiance.[5] With the support of the ruling Whig party, especially of Prime Minister Henry Pelham and his brother, the Duke of Newcastle, a bill to this effect was introduced on April 3 into the House of Lords, where it was rapidly approved. The bill soon passed through Commons as well.[6] But, unexpectedly, opposition gradually mounted and then erupted; the clamor for repeal reached a deafening roar by autumn. Before November 15, when Pelham and his party led the way in repealing the bill that they themselves had first advocated, more than sixty pamphlets, endless newspaper columns, various satiric illustrations, sermons, and an assortment of related books had been printed, pro and con, on the Jew Bill. Almost as rapidly, the controversy disappeared from print and public scrutiny.[7] Historians have since puzzled over what the controversy was really about.

Two broad explanations have been offered.[8] The first maintains that the events of 1753 were a product of traditional English antisemitism. Opposition to the legislation thus provided an opportunity for Jew-baiting that was not to be missed. Central to this thesis is a largely essentialized notion of Jewish his-

tory in western Europe, in which periods of tolerance are predictably inter-
rupted by outbreaks of virulent antisemitism and persecution. Not surprisingly, this has been the interpretation given to the Jew Bill crisis by a number
of Anglo-Jewish historians. There is certainly enough evidence in the Jew Bill
controversy of the crudest sort of racial prejudice. For example, the idea that
Jews were black-skinned resurfaced in the facetious preface to *Some Considerations on the Naturalization of the Jews*, where the author jokingly suggests that
those of his English readers who might want to appear Jewish should, "in
order to bring the skin to a lively complexion like that of a new Negro from the
coast of Guinea," take "the peeling" of "walnuts" and "carefully rub the flesh
night and morning for three weeks together. Afterwards rub yourselves with a
flesh-brush," and "it will make it shine exactly like the back of an old base-viol,
and will fix such an indelible hue that will not come off in six weeks with all the
water and soap you can use to it, and this in order to make you complete olive
beauties."[9] Charges of Jewish ritual murder reappeared as well: the anonymous author of *The Rejection and Restoration of the Jews* reminded readers of
the Jews' "insatiable thirst for the blood of Christians, especially of Christian
children, which they often steal and solemnly crucify," which explains why
"they have been so often expelled out of so many Christian countries."[10]
Another author, writing under the pseudonym "Britannia," similarly describes
how the Jews have engaged in "crucifying several Christian children on Good
Friday, as could be instanced by seven or eight facts in England alone, of which
they were detected."[11]

The great majority of British historians, for their part, have until quite
recently ignored this embarrassing episode from their national past, overlook-
ing as well evidence from contemporary accounts that would lend support for
this antisemitic perspective, including the report in the *London Evening Post*
from mid-November 1753 that on the previous "Saturday night amidst the
rejoicings for the celebrating his Majesty's birthday in the borough of Southwark, the populace dressed up the effigy of a Jew and burnt him in a large bonfire."[12] Such incidents cannot simply be excused as a by-product of local politics and are ignored at some risk. So too are the bizarre claims that the controversy spawned, such as the one that appeared in *Read's Weekly Journal* in "An
Answer to the Apology for Naturalization of the Jews":

The Jews, though they have underwent a great many changes, yet are still a people; this is no reason that they should be restored. But that the contrary may be
drawn from thence, and that they are reserved as a living monument of divine
vengeance, may be reasonably supposed, if we consider the red mark which some
of the Jews now have upon their foreheads. The mark appears when they are in a
passion, which is in some two, in some, three streaks ending in a point upward,

joining at bottom to a dash about two inches square, as Cain had a mark on his forehead for killing his brother Abel.[13]

While some early Anglo-Jewish historians who have written about the Jew Bill may have focused too narrowly on a transhistorical model of anti-semitism in Europe, their insistence that the Jew Bill was a product of—and in turn produced—anti-Jewish sentiment should not be dismissed out of hand. This position has recently been reinforced by the scholarship of Todd Endelman, whose incisive work on the place of Jews in eighteenth-century English culture shows that what happened in 1753 was part of a much broader anti-Jewish sentiment, both religious and secular, prevalent in English society at this time.[14]

An opposing, revisionist view nonetheless maintains that what was ulti-mately at stake in this conflict was no more nor less than a political struggle in an election year between entrenched Whigs and the aggressive out-of-power Tories who seized on a convenient issue to wrest more parliamentary seats. This reading of events is compellingly advanced by Thomas Perry in the only book-length study of the Jew Bill controversy. Perry maintains that "party politics rather than raw bigotry was the impelling force behind most of the anti-Semitic propaganda of the clamor. The clamor was meant to pre-pare the ground not for a pogrom, but for a general election."[15] For Perry, "its real targets were the Court Whig politicians, not the Jews; and its vio-lence, at bottom, was that of unrestrained political partisanship rather than anti-Jewish hysteria." In redefining the uproar as a by-product of aggressive eighteenth-century politics, Perry quickly dismisses those Anglo-Jewish scholars (most of them, he notes, are not professional historians after all) who incorrectly stressed the antisemitic content of the polemics spawned by the Jew Bill. According to Perry, these writers, "knowing little about the tone of eighteenth-century political controversy, but being familiar with the language of anti-Semitic bigotry in all ages, naturally tend to see, in the extravagant and cruel attacks on the Jews and their bill, conclusive evidence that England in 1753 went through a period of rabid anti-Jewish hysteria." He concludes that "at bottom the violence of most of the propaganda against the Jew Bill simply reflects the normal level of eighteenth-century partisan debate, which was deplorably low."[16] For Perry, the Jew Bill was never really about the Jews.

Perry's position has been supported and modified by recent scholars like Nicholas Rogers, who also locates the controversy within the "shifting temper of City politics" and who finds the "lasting impact of the agitation" nonethe-less "negligible." For Rogers, as for Perry, the Jew Bill debate was "an episode in party politics," one that reveals "at the very least," a "sign of the lingering vitality of Toryism in the country at large." Rogers also points out that opposition in the provinces derived from "an ingrained anti-semitism and xenophobia," while City opposition was "directed at the Jewish merchants and financiers who formed part of the metropolitan plutocracy, whose speculative deals on behalf of the foreign fund-holders troubled merchants and tradesmen of different political colors." Ultimately, for Rogers, "the agitation touched raw nerves about the potentially corrosive influence of the moneyed interest in society and politics and the likely increase of Jewish participation in the funds as a result of Naturalization." To this was added yet another fear: that of a "massive immigration of foreign traffickers [that] would prejudice the trade of the local shopkeepers."[17] And Paul Langford astutely observes that the "peculiar weakness" of the Jew Bill "was that it permitted a junction between two elements which had often been kept apart by the problem of Jacobitism: popular, patriotic, xenophobic Whiggism, and High Church Toryism."[18]

Problems with each of these two main interpretations persist, however: why fight so heatedly over the place of Jews in England, if this was merely partisan political struggle? On the other hand, if this was really about anti-semitism, what accounts for the absence of anti-Jewish violence or slander? To these binary and partial positions, both of which contain arguments of considerable merit, I offer a third and supplementary one that tries to be sensitive to the nuances of contemporary English politics while at the same time taking seriously what the polemicists actually wrote.[19] I'd like to suggest that the buried threat occasioned by the naturalization of Jews had to do with the surprising vulnerability of English social and religious identity at this time: if even a Jew could be English, what could one point to that defined essential Englishness? The anonymous author of the satiric tract *The Exclusion of the English*, written five years before the Jew Bill, may well be the first English writer to ask in print that most nagging of questions: "If you consider rightly, it will be very hard to answer the question, 'What is an Englishman?' "[20] And a poem that appeared in the popular *Gentleman's Magazine*—"The Jew naturalized, or the English alienated"—makes much the same point in 1753: "Such actions as these most apparently shews, / That if the Jews are made English, the English are Jews."[21]

In support of this interpretation of the Jew Bill and Englishness, I'm interested in showing how sixteenth-century ideas about the racial, national, and criminal nature of the Jews left their mark upon the Jew Bill debate. I have argued at considerable length that some of the darker currents of early modern English attitudes toward the Jews informed Shakespeare's *The Merchant of Venice*: Jews were aliens, they were a separate nation, racially set apart, and, most ominously, they secretly desired to take the knife to Christians in order to circumcise or even castrate them. With the Jew Bill of 1753 these same cultural stereotypes were dusted off and tried out again on an English public. Insofar as these projections needed to be presented in a culturally sanctioned form, Shakespeare, the national poet, and *The Merchant of Venice*, the best-known English work about the Jews, provided confirmation of the insidious threat Jews posed to the economic, sexual, and religious life of the nation.

I. Naturalization and toleration

The controversy over the Jew Bill needs to be situated within the broader context of eighty years of English debate over alien immigration and naturalization. Powerfully intertwined with and greatly complicating the economic and legal questions about admitting larger numbers of strangers into the land was a related debate over toleration: should England be a place where those of different religious orientations—Protestant dissenters, Catholics, even non-Christians—are permitted to practice their faith freely? Insofar as most of the desired immigrants were Protestant refugees, the two issues crossed at many points. Taken together, toleration and naturalization struck at the very heart of the twin pillars of English identity: the true-born Englishman and his Anglican faith.

While the xenophobia that characterized the attitude of many in sixteenth-century England—from the May Day riots of 1517 to the libels against strangers in the closing decades of the century—never disappeared, a more organized anti-alien movement did not really develop until 1660 or so, with the Restoration of the monarchy. In that year two anti-alien broadsides and a pamphlet were published that attacked the exemption from alien duties granted to those naturalized. In the mid-1680s a more widespread effort was undertaken to challenge naturalizing foreigners; at that time dozens of broadsides and pamphlets were published in London, the center of anti-alien sentiment. Despite this opposition, economists and parliamentarians continued to promote the advantages of a large-scale naturalization. By 1709, when a bill for a general naturalization was finally passed by Parliament, over a dozen attempts had been made to enact such legislation. But opposition to the passage of this bill was too strong, and the bill was repealed just three years later. Still, proponents of naturalization did not give up, and there were subsequent attempts to promote naturalizing foreigners well into the mid-eighteenth century. In fact, in several of the years immediately preceding the Jew Bill debate—1747, 1748, and 1751—such legislation over immigration had again been debated, and the 1751 bill had only narrowly been defeated.[22] The Jew Bill thus comes toward the end of a long, tired battle over naturalization where the lines of engagement had been firmly drawn.

Early proponents of naturalization had been spurred by fears of declining population, since contemporary economists believed that only with a large population could England, or for that matter any nation, prosper. Thus, for example, the author of the 1673 tract *The Grand Concern of England* declared that "a general naturalization of all foreign Protestants" was "absolutely necessary at this time," since "nothing" was "so much wanting in England as people."[23] Authors like John Toland extended this argument to include the Jews, maintaining that the Jews (like other strangers) ought to be naturalized because England needed people to work and populate the land. Moreover, because the Jews had no country of their own, they would bring economic strength to England, where they would leave their wealth.[24] One of the most eloquent defenses of general naturalization on these grounds in the early eighteenth century was Daniel Defoe's *The True-Born Englishman*, first published in 1700. For Defoe, England's economic health depended on large-scale immigration: in an earlier work he had maintained that "no number of foreigners can be prejudicial to England."[25] Defoe argued that foreigners had always assimilated rapidly into English society. In fact, England's greatness was a result of this hybridity, a characteristic that Defoe traces back to England's medieval past:

> We have been Europe's sink, the jakes where she
> Voids all her offal outcast progeny.
> From our fifth Henry's time, the strolling bands
> Of banished fugitives from neighb'ring lands,
> Have here a certain sanctuary found:
> The eternal refuge of the vagabond.

Having arrived in England, these "true born" immigrants soon pick up the habits of the natives, and having acquired "new blood and manners from the clime," they display their true Englishness by their xenophobic response to all foreigners:

> Proudly they learn all mankind to condemn,
> And all their race are true-born Englishmen.[26]

While Defoe made a virtue of England's diversity, opponents of naturalization mocked England's willingness to open herself to foreign penetration. The author of *The Exclusion of the English* agreed with Defoe's sense of the past but disagreed over the consequences, seeing interbreeding as a sign of contamination, not health. Invoking the familiar Pauline trope, the author maintains that the latest naturalization bill would "engraft the branches of all nations upon one solid stock and make Great Britain an epitome of the universe."[27] For eighteenth-century English men and women, granting naturalization was not only about extending legal and economic rights to others; it was also about rendering their identities and communities vulnerable to that which was un-English and even un-Christian. When Samuel Johnson came to define the term "to naturalize" in his famous *Dictionary of the English Language*, the first meaning in which he understood it was precisely this: "to adopt into a community; to invest with the privileges of native subjects."[28] Outsiders, including Jews, discovered that attempts at making inroads into that community could provoke stiff resistance.

Even as political economists praised the benefits of large-scale immigration, English philosophers and theologians debated the wisdom of extending the limits of English toleration so far as to allow Dissenters, Catholics, and even non-Christian groups like Muslims and Jews to worship freely. For advocates of toleration like Edward Bagshaw, it made no sense that England allowed Jews to pray according to their own rites but denied the same freedom to non-conformist Protestant groups such as the Quakers, Congregationalists, and Baptists. As Bagshaw puts it: "'tis agreed that a Christian magistrate cannot force his religion on a Jew or a Mahomedan, therefore much less can he abridge his fellow Christian in things of lesser moment."[29] The story of how religious toleration emerged in late seventeenth- and early eighteenth-century England is no less complex than that of the history of naturalization, and the thumbnail sketch of both movements which I offer here can only begin to account for their effect on the 1753 controversy. It must be remembered that, like all late seventeenth-century and early eighteenth-century regimes, England's was one in which religious, no less than political, conformity was expected. Toleration, then, "was not simply about religious beliefs and practices but about a loosening and eventual severing" of the "tight bond between the temporal and spiritual realms."[30] Toleration and disestablishment constituted a threat not only to the Crown but to the newly restored Anglican hierarchy. In this respect, we also need to keep in mind that "Restoration England was a persecuting society," the "last period in English history when the ecclesiastical and civil powers endeavored to secure religious conformity by coercive means."[31] A landmark event that broke with this past was the passage of the so-called "Act of Toleration" in 1689. This Toleration Act was actually not much more than an act of indulgence that "did not provide general toleration or confer unencumbered citizenship on Dissenters" but merely exempted them from various penalties demanded by existing penal laws.[32] Still, to advocates like John Locke, it gave hope: "Toleration has now at last been established by law in our country. Not perhaps so wide in scope as might be wished for. . . . Still, it is something to have progressed so far."[33] Even with the passage of the Toleration Act, the Test Act and the Corporation Act (both of which required those holding public office to take communion in accordance with Anglican rites) were still in place, denying non-Anglicans the right to participate fully in English political life.

John Locke was the most prominent theorist of the value of religious tolerance, and his most celebrated text was the *Letter of Toleration* (1689), published anonymously and soon translated from Latin into English. Some decades before this publication, Locke had already drafted an essay on toleration in 1667, in the final manuscript version of which he first invokes the example of the Jews as a precedent for tolerating Protestant dissenters: " 'Tis strange to conceive upon what grounds of uniformity any different profession of Christians can be prohibited in a Christian country, where the Jewish religion (which is directly opposite to the principles of Christianity) is tolerated; and would it not be irrational, where the Jewish religion is permitted, that the Christian magistrate, upon pretence of his power in indifferent things, should enjoin or forbid any thing, or any way interpose in their way or manner of worship?"[34] As Nabil Matar has recently shown, this argument marks a crucial shift in Locke's thought, in which "rational consistency" (rather than the absence of a threat to the state) justified that Jews be tolerated, and "although the Jews were not pivotal to the political debate in 1667, they constituted for Locke the yardstick against which toleration in England was to be measured."[35]

Two decades later, in his *Letter of Toleration*, Locke went even further, rejecting compulsion in matters of faith and urging freedom of worship for Dissenters and Jews (although he excluded atheists as well as Catholics, whose loyalty to Rome precluded their toleration): "If we allow the Jews to have private houses and dwellings amongst us, why should we not allow them to have synagogues? Is their doctrine more false, their worship more abominable, or is the civil peace more endangered, by their meeting in public, than in their private houses? But if these things may be granted to Jews and pagans, surely the condition of any Christian ought not to be worse than theirs, in a Christian commonwealth."[36] Locke emphasizes that even if "a Jew does not believe the New Testament to be the word of God, he does not thereby alter any thing in men's civil rights."[37] Curiously, Locke's anonymously published tract and its defense of the Jews was partially misunderstood by a major respondent, Jonas Proast, who thought that the tolerationist argument advanced in the *Letter* was merely a front for "the advancement of trade and commerce (which some seem to place above all other consideration)."[38] It was not easy to keep the strands of naturalization, immigration, trade, and toleration apart, especially when Jews were invoked as examples.

The influential doctrines of toleration and disestablishment advanced by Locke did not lead inexorably toward the birth of a tolerant English society. Intolerance toward Catholics, extreme Protestant sects, and atheists, as well as the xenophobia revealed in episodes like the Jew Bill controversy, provide more than enough evidence to the contrary. It is important to emphasize that even nominally liberal and enlightened ideas like Locke's attitudes toward the Jews were rooted in post-Reformation beliefs about the restitution of the Jews, beliefs that remained extraordinarily influential. As late as 1753 many of the early modern ideas about Jews still exercised a very powerful force on English thought, insinuating themselves into and reshaping what scholars would prefer to think of as Enlightenment attitudes. Not even Locke was immune from these forces, and our natural desire to read our best secular impulses back into his expressions of tolerance for the Jews is held in check by a final and radical shift in his attitude toward Jews as English subjects, one that is conveniently suppressed in studies that lionize his contribution to the philosophy of toleration. Locke's competing, conversionist impulse is already apparent in *A Second Letter Concerning Toleration* (1690), a work in which Locke maintained that "only full naturalisation could direct the Jews of England towards Christ."[39] By the time that Locke completed his *Paraphrase and Notes on St. Paul's Epistle to the Romans* (1707), his desire for the conversion and restitution of the Jews had quietly replaced his call for tolerating them.

Locke, explicating the enigmatic verse of Romans 11.23—"And they also, if they abide not still in unbelief, shall be grafted in; for God is able to graft them in again"—goes well beyond simple paraphrase: "The Jews also, if they continue not in unbelief, shall be again grafted into the stock of Abraham, and be re-established [as] the people of God. For, however they are now scattered, and under subjection to strangers, God is able to collect them again into one body, make them his people, and set them in a flourishing condition in their own land." If this elaboration were not enough, Locke adds a long note making the restorationist claim he sees implicit in Paul even more explicit: "This grafting in again seems to import that the Jews shall be a flourishing nation again, professing Christianity in the land of promise, for that is to be reinstated again in the promise made to Abraham, Isaac, and Jacob. This St. Paul might, for good reasons, be withheld from speaking out here; but, in the prophets, there are very plain intimations of it."[40] It is striking that into the early years of the eighteenth century Locke was still arguing for the conversion and restitution of the Jews, in a tradition that can be traced directly back to Joseph Mede and before him Henry Finch. Matar has shown how this tradition was powerful enough to redirect the course of Locke's toleration of the Jews, whose residence in the Christian commonwealth he had come to regard as temporary.[41] Even for Locke, toleration had to give way to the more compelling claims tied to the conversion and restoration of the Jews.

Locke's final understanding of the Jews' place within the nation thus underwent an about-face: for Locke "the Jews were not to regard England as a permanent home. Whether they became citizens or not, Locke affirmed that the Jewish home was not England."[42] The idea that England was and needed to be defined as a Christian commonwealth died hard; nevertheless, it was a point to which polemicists in the 1753 debate habitually returned. George Coningesby spoke for many when he claimed that the Jews had no place in England for precisely this reason: "The members of our community are supposed, by the whole tenor of its laws, to be Christians, and none other. For which reason our common law has all along from the beginning looked upon the Jews as aliens and incapable of being otherwise while Jews."[43] But there were others writing during the Jew Bill debate who invoked Locke's earlier defense of the Jews on the grounds that there could be no security for Protestant dissenters if the Jews were threatened. The anonymous author of the *The Crisis, or An Alarm to Britannia's True Protestant Sons* was quite explicit about this Lockean point: the "pretext" of opponents of religious toleration "would be to begin with the Jews as the weakest. But they would be happy could they extend their restrictions unto all, and make the Anglican a second Popish church." The author concludes with a warning: if it "were once admitted, that it is proper for the public to examine people's private rights on account of their religion, none can answer where that would end."[44] At stake here, as in immigration debates, was not the Jews themselves so much as the broader social principles embodied in accepting them into the social fabric.

It may well be that these extreme pressures to accommodate new ways of thinking about both immigration and religious toleration—forces that in fact redefined the English nation—required some sort of cultural release. In this case, the example of tolerating and naturalizing foreign Jews, while legislatively and practically of minor significance, served as a lightening rod for the unfocused anger and confusion that could not easily be articulated or directed at its intended targets. The fact that the social and legal status of England's Jews remained so unresolved at this time only intensified the habit of projecting deeper anxieties about the changing face of Englishness upon a group that some felt to be unassimilable into an English commonwealth; only by such insistence on difference could what remained truly and transcendently English be confirmed. As one anonymous polemicist put it, "Is it not true, that every kingdom upon earth has been shaken to pieces and undergone such violent shocks and dissolutions, that the . . . primitive inhabitants" have been "so absolutely absorbed and lost in the inundations that have been poured in on them from other nations?" In contrast, "How has it fared with the Jews?" The answer is predictable: "Though they have been thus broken and dissipated, though they have lost their civil polity as a nation, and are become subject to every kingdom upon earth, still they are a people, distinct from others. . . . They have not mixed their blood with the natives of any other country."[45]

The need in 1753 to maintain clear-cut differences between the English and the Jews found its most powerful expression in the polemical writing of William Romaine, for whom the "Jews stand outlawed, both by the common law and express statutes."[46] Ironically, Romaine was himself the younger son of a French Protestant immigrant to England, the kind of patriotic true-born Englishman Defoe had satirized. Where Defoe a half-century earlier had insisted that "A true-born Englishman's a contradiction, / In speech an irony, in fact a fiction,"[47] Romaine would counter, "Who ever heard of a natural-born vagrant?" or "of a natural-born Jew-English-Foreign-Jew?"[48] Rejecting the tolerationist position, Romaine urged that principles of exclusion were a defining feature of the English nation: "Our state can have no natural-born subjects but Christians, and a natural-born Jew-Christian-Foreign-English-man, is such a medley of contradictions, that all the rabbis in the world will never be able to reconcile them."[49]

II. The Jew Bill and Englishness

Recent scholars of English nationalism and of the emergence of Englishness have focused on the eighteenth century as the period in which a "sense of British national identity was forged," and how "the manner in which it was forged has shaped the quality of this particular sense of nationhood."[50] Building upon Benedict Anderson's useful concept of nations as "imagined communities," Linda Colley, one of the more influential of these scholars, argues that "we can plausibly regard Great Britain as an invented nation superimposed, if only for a while, onto much older alignments and loyalties."[51] For Colley, this emerging sense of nation needed to be defined against an Other, and for Great Britain this Other was France:

> War with France brought Britons . . . into confrontation with an obviously hostile Other and encouraged them to define themselves collectively against it. They defined themselves as Protestants struggling for survival against the world's foremost Catholic power. They defined themselves against the French as they imagined them to be, superstitious, militaristic, decadent and unfree.

And, Colley adds, "increasingly as the wars went on, they defined themselves in contrast to the colonial peoples they conquered, peoples who were manifestly alien in terms of culture, religion, and colour.[52] Of course, as the preceding chapters have made clear, the English did not need to look beyond the Jews they had once expelled and who had now returned to their shores to find a people "manifestly alien" not only in their culture, religion, and physiognomy but also in their confused and confusing national identity. I'm not suggesting that Colley or others who cast their gaze across the English Channel have got it wrong;

rather, I believe that a far more complex set of projections, ones that include first and foremost the Irish as well as the Jews, the French, the Spanish, and the peoples colonized in these early years of the British Empire, collectively combine to redefine British and English identity. What was especially pernicious about the Jewish Other was that it kept trying to claim for itself a part of Englishness and indeed had already met with considerable success.

In exploring the response to such Jewish incursions during the course of the Jew Bill controversy, it is easiest to begin with the crudest sort of claims, ones that depended on showing the racial inferiority of those who were not English. Perhaps the most skilled at this in the 1753 debate was James Ralph, who concluded that Jews "cannot be incorporated with Englishmen without violating whatever Englishmen hold sacred."[53] Their "very breed," he writes, "is in general of the lowest, basest, and most contemptible kind, distinguishable to the eye by peculiar marks, odious for that distinction, and what, if once communicated to a family becomes indelible." Arguing that Jews should be excluded on racial grounds, Ralph points to the example of the Portuguese, who had degenerated as a race because of their contamination with the "impure blood of the Jews."[54] Similar racial arguments appear in the *London Evening Post*, where a writer using the pseudonym "Old England" suggests that "had there been a law to innoculate the leprosy upon every man, woman, and child, throughout his Majesty's British dominions, there had been less to complain of, than of the impure conjunction with Jewish blood, at the expense of all that can be called Christian amongst us."[55] A popular ballad published at this time charged that the Jew Bill would turn the Jews into masters and the English into their servants; according to this logic, the bill thus threatened to transform "True Blue" Englishmen into "Negroes and slaves":

> Lord how surprised when they heard of the news,
> That we were to be servants to circumcised Jews,
> To be Negroes and slaves, instead of True Blues.[56]

Other writers were careful to distinguish the unassimilable Jews from more acceptable immigrant groups. In the proceedings of the "Political Club," published in the *London Evening Post*, one speaker argues that "the Jews are not like French refugees, or German Protestants," for these "in a generation or two become so incorporated with us, that there is no distinguishing them from the rest of the people: their children, or grandchildren, are no longer French, or Germans, or of the French or German nation, but become truly English, and deem themselves to be of the English nation." In contrast, "the unconverted Jews can never incorporate with us. They must for ever remain Jews, and will always deem themselves to be of the Hebrew, not the English nation."[57]

Such racial explanations were not limited to the margins of English political discourse. In fact, they were invoked in parliamentary debate during the effort to repeal the Jew Bill. When the Duke of Newcastle, who had initially supported the bill but recognized the political necessity of its repeal, nonetheless insisted that he "knew that every Jew born here was, by the common law, a natural-born subject," and knew as well "that such as were not born here might be naturalized by residing for seven years in our plantations in America, or by engaging in some particular sorts of manufactures here at home," his opponent, the Duke of Bedford, would have none of it: "Whatever opinion the noble Duke may have of our common law, with respect to Jews born in this kingdom, and I have the best authorities for my opinion, that no Jew born here can be deemed a natural-born subject whilst he continues to be a Jew."[58]

Bedford refused to accept that a Jew could ever be a natural-born English subject, and he urged that the English never "naturalize such foreigners whose latest progeny must always continue a people separate and distinct from the people that naturalize them." Bedford supports this racial line of attack by arguing that Jewishness was an essence even more ineradicable than the blackness of colonial slaves. His unusual argument is worth quoting at length:

> I shall suppose, that for strengthening our sugar colonies, and for peopling them with subjects instead of slaves, a scheme were proposed for naturalizing all the blacks born in any of them without any other condition whatsoever: I will say that our adopting such a scheme would be ridiculous, because their progeny would continue to be a distinct people. But if the conditions were added that no blacks should be naturalized unless they declared themselves Christians, and that no such black man should be naturalized unless he married a white woman, nor any black woman unless she married a white man, the ridicule of the scheme would be very much softened, because their progeny would in time unite and coalesce with the rest of the people. It might a little alter the complexion of the people of these islands; but they would all be the same people and would look upon themselves in no other light than as subjects of Great Britain. This must show the imprudence, and even the ridiculousness, of our adopting the doctrine, that all Jews born here are to be deemed natural-born subjects, for their latest posterity whilst they continue Jews, will continue to be, and will consider themselves as a people quite distinct and separate from the ancient people of this island.[59]

The claim that the chasm separating Black slaves from their colonialist masters was more easily bridged than the racial lines separating Jews from the "ancient" English people is remarkable and gives some sense of just how different Jews were felt—or claimed—to be by members of the educated and ruling classes.

This insistence on Jewish racial difference carried in its wake the fear of racial contamination. Even a supporter of the Jew Bill could half-jokingly allude to the concern that—given the foppishness of English gallants—English women might turn their attention to the influx of Jewish men: "At this time there are not a few of our British females who begin to bewail their virginity. But least this should be misconstrued to proceed from an approaching nearer the connection with the Jews . . . it may not be amiss to hint that . . . this seems to arise from the fashionable gallants' negligence in marriage.[60] A contemporary satirist connected the Jew Bill with the other controversial piece of legislation enacted in 1753, the Marriage Bill: "It is shrewdly suspected by several deep politicians that the Marriage Bill lately passed was principally intended to favour some of the iniquitous purposes of this [Jewish Naturalization] Act, viz., to enable parents and guardians to compel their daughters to marry the rich Jews that are daily expected here, and who by this Act are enabled to make (what was the chief thing before wanting) a proper *landed* settlement upon them."[61]

English men were repeatedly warned to guard their threatened foreskins. One popular broadside, titled *Circumcision Not Murder, but Jews No Christians*, underscored the importance of the prepuce as a sign of the "true born Briton":

> Though circumcision now will be
> Within this realm made known,
> Yet every true born Briton he
> Will surely keep his own.[62]

It is not particularly memorable verse, but the message is clear enough.

Another representative and disturbing text is the anonymous pamphlet *The Christian's New Warning Piece: Or, A Full and True Account of the Circumcision of Sir E. T. Bart.*, which describes how an ambitious young Englishman, seeking the financial support of the Jews in a parliamentary bid, submits himself to the circumciser's knife:

> Then Mr. Moses Ben-Amri approached with great solemnity with the forceps in one hand and the circumcision knife in the other, and having muttered some words in Hebrew . . . he lifted up the flaccid prepuce and at one dextrous stroke severed it—never more to return to the stump on which it grew.
>
> It is the observation of Galen, that the passion of fear, when worked up to its highest pitch, is very apt in some constitutions to evacuate itself through the urinary passages and to drive all it find there before it. It happened thus in the case of this unhappy victim, and the curiosity of Mr. J—k—n (who though, like a provident general, he had secured the rear, was, at the same time unaccountably

negligent of what might happen in the front) having hung his head directly over the jet *d'eau*, he had the good luck to catch the whole stream in his mouth.[63]

In exploring the emasculation accomplished by the Jews, the passage flirts not only with the circumcising stroke, separating flesh from "stump," but with the perversity of Sir E. T.'s urinary ejaculation into the mouth of the overcurious "Mr. J—k—n."

Those defending Englishness from the taint of Jewishness turned for support to English historians. In maintaining that the Jews have never been "natural-born subject[s]," Willaim Romaine challenged "any Jew advocate to produce from history one authority of the Jews being considered as the natural-born subject of this realm."[64] Other writers scoured ancient archives in support of their opposition to Jewish incursions upon the rights of natural-born English subjects. For example, in November 1753 the *London Magazine* made available for the first time in English an act from the reign of Henry III declaring that "no Jew shall from henceforth have a freehold in any manors, lands, tenements, fees, rents, or tenures whatsoever, either by charter, gift, feoffment, confirmation, or other grant, or by any other means whatever." The contributor of this information insinuates that English Jews may have conspired to tamper with this and other key documents from England's past: "This act of Henry III was stolen from the rolls by the Jews or some of their agents before Lord Coke's time, or that it was so mislaid that neither he nor any one since could ever find it. And if there was any statute in the 28th [year of the reign] of Edward I for banishing all the Jews out of England, it has met with the same fate."[65]

Topical poems written at this time similarly defined England's past greatness in terms of its repudiation of the Jews. In a poem anthologized in *A Collection of the Best Pieces and Verse Against the Naturalization of the Jews* (a collection that "cannot be too much read by every Briton who thinks a very valuable part of his birth-right is in danger"), we are offered a nationalistic myth of the Jews' place in medieval English history, one that reduces their role to clippers of coins and foreskins:

> In brave Edward's days they were caught in a gin,
> For clipping our coin, now to add sin to sin,
> As they've got all our pelf, they'd be clipping our skin.
> Those foes to the pork of old England,
> Oh! the old English roast pork.

And the stanza that follows defines the greatness of the Elizabethan era in terms of it having been an England free of Jews:

When good Queen Elizabeth sat on the throne,
When Jonathan's jobbers and Jews were unknown,
Each Briton might then call his birthright his own,
And feed on the pork of Old England,
Oh! the old English pork.[66]

For these writers, England had emerged as a great nation not simply because it was a nation free of Jews, but because it was a nation that had defined itself as one that had expelled its Jews, denying them the right to own English land or share in its birthright.

Insofar as England was also defined by who could own a piece of it, one of the features of the Jew Bill that provoked the greatest hostility was that it implicitly validated the rights of Jews to own English land (paradoxically, by a clause added to the bill that denied them the right to own Church holdings). Moreover, it emerged in the course of the debate that this right had already been granted by virtue of a little-known naturalization act that had been passed by Parliament in 1740, specifying that it "is enacted that foreigners living seven years in any of our colonies in America shall be deemed natives on taking the Oath . . . It is further enacted that each qualified person shall receive the Sacrament, except Quakers and Jews," and "that the the Jews in taking the oaths may omit the words *upon the true Faith of a Christian*."[67] Fewer than two hundred Jews had availed themselves of this process of naturalization, the majority of them residents of Jamaica, where there was a thriving congregation.[68] By means of this legislation these naturalized Jews had won the right to own land and pass it on to heirs, a right denied to their coreligionists who were only denizens. The consequences were not lost on those committed to restricting English land to English ownership. Joseph Grove, in a detailed account of English law related to this topic, exaggerates the number of Jews naturalized by this act, and concludes that the measure, like the Jew Bill itself, was "anti-constitutional": the

> very circumstance of several hundred Jews being naturalized by Act of Parliament in so short a space of time as thirteen years [1740–1753] is the greatest shock that this or any other *free* nation ever sustained in time of profound peace and tranquility. For the Jews so naturalized can, by the laws of this kingdom, purchase and hold lands . . . [that] will ever remain in perpetuity to them.[69]

While the scores of polemical pamphlets disappeared from bookstalls after the repeal of the Jew Bill, the controversy left a more lasting impression on the formation of English identity through the work of the celebrated British engraver and artist William Hogarth, who memorialized aspects of the Jew Bill in one of the major works of his last decade, *The Election*, a series undertaken after 1754 and completed in 1758. Hogarth integrated some of the most telling features of the controversy into this series, the subject of which was a "fictional election" that, as one recent critic puts it, "is being fought over keeping Britain British." For Richard Dorment, the work is characterized by Hogarth's tolerance for intolerance, his "xenophobia and his love of liberty," which gives Hogarth his "real claim to the title of the 'Father of British Painting.'"[70] The telling details in *The Election* are easy to spot. The "central figure in the Tory parade outside the window" in the first print, "An Election Entertainment," is "the effigy of a Jew."[71] The words on his breast read: "No Jews" (see illustration 15). The second plate is similarly explicit. According to Ronald Paulson, "Hogarth's strongest statement appears in the juxtaposition of the triangle of the Jewish peddler, Tory candidate, and pretty young ladies with the grenadier who wears the star of David in his cap" in this print.[72] The fourth and final plate shows the Jews (and the Christian politicians who serve their interests) as victorious, even though the Jew Bill had in fact been repealed. In this print a Jewish fiddler leads the successful Tory candidate as pigs flee in the other direction; the collapse of Brittania's chariot in the intervening plate had made inevitable this last transformation. Paulson argues that for Hogarth, whose work deliberately recalls the facetious newspaper columns from 1753 describing a Judaized England a hundred years hence, "England has become Jewish."[73] These and other elements in the prints reveal how Hogarth's patriotic output reduced the Jews to easy caricatures.[74] Hogarth's work also suggests how difficult it is to define the emergence of English and British national identity at this time, in part because the formation of this identity depended on fears and projections that are more often revealed in works of art and literature than in the archival records that historians have long relied on. Imaginative works, then, become a powerful lens through which these cultural processes can be examined, and in the Jew Bill controversy it was not only Hogarth's art, but the drama of the national poet, Shakespeare, that provided a vehicle for expressing some of the most powerful anti-Jewish sentiments. Tellingly, the two are joined together in the *Poetical Description of Mr. Hogarth's Prints* written by John Smith in 1759, with, he claims, Hogarth's "sanction and inspection." Describing the encounter in the second plate between the Tory candidate, the young ladies, and the Jewish peddler, Smith writes:

> Yet hush!—for see his honour near;—
> Truly a pretty am'rous leer,
> The ladies both look pleasant too;
> "Purchase some trinkets of the Jew."
> One points to what she'd have him buy;
> The other casts a longing eye;

And Shylock, money-loving soul,
Impatient waits to touch the cole.[75]

As we shall soon see, this would not be the first nor the last time that Shakespeare and the protagonist of *The Merchant of Venice* found their way into the Jew Bill controversy.

III. The place of The Merchant of Venice in eighteenth-century England

One of the most exciting developments in recent Shakespeare scholarship has been the attention paid to Shakespeare's place in eighteenth-century English culture. An emergent English nation badly needed a national poet, and Shakespeare's reputation expanded to fill that need, so much so, as one critic has put it, that Shakespeare had "become as normatively constitutive of British national identity as the drinking of afternoon tea" (a practice that, for the record, also caught on in England at this time).[76] The relationship between this newly elevated national poet and the emergent nation he spoke for was thus a reciprocal one. As Jonathan Bate neatly puts it, "Shakespeare was constituted in England in the eighteenth and early nineteenth century," and "cultural life during that period was by constitution Shakespearean."[77] The revisionist works of scholars like Bate and Michael Dobson do not address the issue of Shakespeare and the Jews, no doubt because the leading historians whose research they have necessarily relied on for their knowledge of the period have themselves ignored the Jew Bill. As a result, the role of *The Merchant of Venice* in this controversy remains a curious blank in accounts of appropriations of Shakespeare in the eighteenth century. In redressing that omission, it is important first to reconsider the history of *The Merchant of Venice* in the hundred and fifty years since its inception, for, like both its creator and English culture itself, the play, too, had a complicated history.

Given its immense popularity in the eighteenth, nineteenth, and twentieth centuries (as well as its popular appeal shortly after its initial staging both in London and on the continent), the stage history of *The Merchant of Venice* in the seventeenth century stands as a strange, almost inexplicable, blank. Texts of the play continued to be available, not only in the four folios produced in the seventeenth century but also in the unusual 1653 quarto of the play (one of only three quartos published during the Interregnum), a publication that was probably intended to capitalize on Readmission interest. Not until the early eighteenth century was the play again staged in London, and then only in the radically altered version offered by George Granville, under the title *The Jew of Venice*.[78] This revision, which was produced sometime during the 1700–1701 season, was first performed on June 23, 1701. First printed in that year, it went through six editions in the next thirty-five years and was staged more than forty times, with six different actors playing Shylock by 1738.[79] The prologue to Granville's revision, written by Bevill Higgons, offers an inkling of the topical connection between the fate of English Jewry and the possibly renewed interest in the play at the close of the seventeenth century. The prologue, spoken by the ghost of Shakespeare, explains:

> Today we punish a stock-jobbing Jew,
> A piece of justice, terrible and strange;
> Which, if pursued, would make a thin Exchange.[80]

What helped bring Shakespeare's play into prominence (and into the canon of plays regularly staged for the next three centuries) was the brilliant version first offered on the London stage by Charles Macklin on February 14, 1741. Macklin went a long way to restoring something approximating what had been staged in Shakespeare's day, and his first run was an enormous success: between opening night and May 1741 the play was performed twenty-two times, and Macklin, amazingly, continued to play the role for almost fifty years, until his retirement from the stage. A contemporary anecdote (attributed to Alexander Pope) said of Macklin: "This is the Jew / That Shakespeare drew."[81] Contemporaries noted that when Macklin first undertook the role of Shylock, "he made daily visits to the center of business, the 'Change and the adjacent coffee-houses, that by a frequent intercourse and conversation with the 'unforeskinned race' he might habituate himself to their air and deportment."[82] William Cooke, Macklin's biographer, also reports that Macklin had taken pains to learn what Jews wore.[83] It is not easy to determine whether Macklin was more successful at imitating Jews or at creating an image of them that was more real to his fellow countrymen than the numbers of Jews they passed on the streets of London.

I offer this brief digression on the stage history of the play in the early eighteenth century because it is necessary to get some sense of what the play might have meant to English audiences when it was subsequently invoked as part of the polemic surrounding the Jew Bill of 1753. Two written versions competed in circulation: Shakespeare's (through the surviving quartos and folios and through the editions of Rowe, Pope, Theobald, Hanmer, and Warburton) and Granville's *The Jew of Venice*. In the theater, though a half-dozen actors played Shylock in these years, Macklin's frequently staged version clearly predominated (although he himself did not perform the play in 1753, having briefly retired for a time from the theater during this year).

One other feature of its stage history, unnoted in the accounts of the play in performance, is also relevant: audience expectations about when they might see the play in the course of the theatrical season. Since *The Merchant of Venice*, starring Macklin, had been staged at the opening of Drury Lane on September 15, 1747, an informal tradition emerged that the play would be performed near the start of each fall season at Drury Lane, along with *The Beggar's Opera*. Thus, after a fairly late appearance in 1748 (November 3), it was the fourth play performed in 1749 (September 9), the opening play in 1750 (September 8), and the second play in both 1751 (September 9) and 1752 (September 19). In the months leading up to the Jew Bill debate the play remained in repertory, appearing on January 4, 1753, at Covent Garden, a week later at Drury Lane, once again at Covent Garden on January 26, 1753, and on Shakespeare's birthday, April 23, at Covent Garden, before the controversy developed in earnest by May.[84]

When the fall season came around once more in early September, 1753 the patrons of Drury Lane must have been looking forward to the return of *The Merchant of Venice* with unusual interest. The controversy over the Jew Bill was reaching its peak; another two months would pass before Parliament met to discuss its repeal. A column in the politically neutral *Cambridge Journal* on August 25, 1753, two weeks before the theaters reopened in London, reported that "we are credibly informed, that some of the most eminent among the Children of Israel, have made interest with the patentee of Covent Garden Playhouse, not to engage Mr. Macklin for the ensuing season, to prevent his playing the character of Shylock in the *Merchant of Venice*, which it is apprehended will certainly be called for by the public."[85] Though perhaps tongue-in-cheek about the Jews' attempt to silence Macklin, the *Cambridge Journal* was correct in suggesting that Shakespeare's play would most certainly be called for. Yet on opening night the management of Drury Lane refused to stage *The Merchant of Venice*, offering instead *The Beggar's Opera*. The disappointment was strong enough to elicit protest. We learn from the manuscript diary of the theater manager Richard Cross from September 8 that the public clamor for the play was ignored: the "Naturalizing Bill having made some noise against the Jews, some people called out for the *Merchant of Venice*, and a letter was thrown upon the stage desiring that play instead of *The [Beggar's] Opera*, but we took no notice of it, some little hissing but it died away."[86] It would not be too hard to guess what the letter contained. Cross draws the obvious connection between the "noise" over the "Naturalization Bill" and the "hissing" in the theater, but the call for Shylock went unheeded. There were no performances of *The Merchant* at either Drury Lane or Covent Garden that fall. Not until April 6, long after the bill had been repealed and interest in the controversy had died down, did the play reenter the repertory, this time at Covent Garden (April 6, May 8, and, once again at the start of the season, September 9, 1754). Some form of censorship was clearly at work.

A hint as to the source of this censorship can be found in an unusual manuscript note included in the Gabrielle Enthoven Theatre Collection in the Victoria and Albert Museum, placed in the Drury Lane file: "Last Sunday—8th July, 1753. An order came from the Lord Chamberlain's office to the managers of both theaters, forbidding them under the severest penalty to exhibit a certain scandalous piece, highly injurious to our present happy establishment, entitled *The Merchant of Venice*."[87] This seems to clinch the case, except, as L. W. Conolly has argued, the entry is highly irregular. Conolly notes that while the Lord Chamberlain would no doubt have been receptive to Pelham's desire not to let the controversy spill over onto the stage, it is highly unlikely that he would send an order on a Sunday. Furthermore, since May 26 marked the end of the 1753 theater season and since, with the exceptions of a few plays and entertainments during Bartholomew Fair, the theaters remained closed until the second week of September, why would the Lord Chamberlain send such a note in July?

Conolly finds the answer in a newspaper column called "News for One Hundred Years hence in the *Hebrew Journal*," which first appeared in the *Craftsman* and was reprinted by other newspapers, including the *London Evening Post*. This "News" column offers a glimpse at life in a future England ruled by Jews and includes the following entry: "Last Sunday an order came from the Lord Chamberlain's office to the managers of both theaters, forbidding them under the severest penalties, to exhibit a certain scandalous piece, highly injurious to our present happy establishment, entitled *The Merchant of Venice*."[88] Clearly, in the Judaized England of 1853 imagined in this column, there could be no place for Shakespeare's anti-Jewish play. Capitalizing on how prescient this forecast for a hundred years in the future would prove, the issue of the *London Evening Post* immediately following the reopening of the theaters made much of the suppression of Shakespeare's play: "It is shrewdly suspected that one part of the '*Hebrew Journal* for one hundred years hence' will be fulfilled this winter, by the neutrality of both our theatres, in not obliging the town with *The Merchant of Venice*."[89] What may be most interesting about this column is the inference on the part of the partial pro-Tory newspaper that it was the "neutrality" and self-censorship of the theaters, rather than bias toward the Jews or the Whigs who had initially supported the Jew Bill, that accounted for the suppression of *The Merchant* at this time. Apparently the theaters were simply trying to stay out of the political crossfire.

Capping the above-mentioned column in the July issue of the the *London Evening Post* was an advertisement from Gamaliel Ruben's Shylock, addressed "To the gentlemen, rabbins, and freeholders of the county of Canaan," in which Shylock offers himself as "a candidate," there "being a vacancy in the great sanhedrin." He "entreat[s] the favour of your votes and interest, assuring you, that if I am so happy as to be returned, I shall take every opportunity of manifesting the sincerest attachment to the cause of Israel, the warmest zeal for the interest of the whole Jewish people, and a particular attention to the rights and privileges of the county of Canaan."[90] By now the name *Shylock* had become synonymous with a rapacious Jew and Shakespeare's play was thoroughly identified with anti-Jewish sentiment. Additional entries from this column imagining England's Jewish future reflect some sense of the cultural anxieties produced by the Jews: "Last week twenty-five children were publickly circumcised at the lying-in hospital in Brownlow Street." And "Last night the bill for naturalizing Christians was thrown out of the Sanhendrin by a very great majority."[91] The fears are not all that different from the kind expressed over a century earlier: St. Paul's Cathedral is now a synagogue, smugglers running pork into Sussex are captured, and the Christian uprising in North Wales is a false rumour. It is a malicious piece of journalism, and the editors of the *London Magazine* attached an apology: "We look upon the forgoing to be a low piece of burlesque, and not quite free from profaneness. All the use of our inserting it" is "to show with what spirit some things may be opposed, which indeed ought to be opposed. But then it should be done only in a sober and manly way. For though we ought not by too great an indulgence to encourage any set of men in their unbelief, yet thus to lampoon them may only tend to harden them, and is far from being agreeable to the true spirit of Christianity."[92] Conolly rightly concludes that the manuscript note "in the Enthoven Collection is nothing more than a copy of the paragraph from the anti-Jewish propaganda first published in the *Craftsman*." He adds that the item was meant "to persuade Englishmen to believe that they would be deprived of one of Shakespeare's best-loved plays once the Jews became naturalized and infiltrated positions of influence and power in British society."[93]

The polemical literature includes additional traces of how *The Merchant of Venice* was appropriated by opponents of the Jew Bill. "J. E., Gentleman," the author of *Some Considerations on the Naturalization of the Jews*, in the midst of a long diatribe against Jewish naturalization, turns to the matter of the Jews' "exorbitant avarice." The subject immediately put him "in mind of a passage in the *Merchant of Venice*," and he begins by citing Shylock's hatred of Antonio: "I hate him for he is a Christian." He then proceeds to quote at length from *The Merchant of Venice*, including the lines from the trial scene where Shylock gloats over having been awarded a pound of Antonio's flesh. Shakespeare's play reveals just what kind of threat awaits the English if they naturalize the Jews. After three uninterrupted pages of quotation from Shakespeare's play, he demands of his readers: "And now, Englishmen and countrymen, judge ye, what advantage it can be to you to have these Jews naturalized! What can you get by them? They are all griping usurers. And what can they get out of you, but your very blood and vitals? It can never be your temporal interest to see such persons made Englishmen."[94] The words of Shakespeare, that exemplary Englishman, provided powerful support for those opposed to Jewish naturalization.

Additional evidence of how Shakespeare's play was invoked in opposition to the bill appears in the anonymous *The Repository*, an anthology that includes several allusions to Shylock. Thus, we find "The Prophecies of Shylock," a passage in biblical prose addressed to the Jews about the English, which reads in part: "Therefore, thus saith the Lord, I will destroy them in mine anger, and give you their land for a possession. I will establish you as their rulers, and strengthen you by the word of my power, that you may punish them for their transgressions, and scourge them for their sins."[95]

Another allusion to Shakespeare's protagonist comes near the end of the anthology, in a poetic dialogue called "Shylock and Zimri." Shylock's last verses likewise turn on Jewish revenge against the Christians:

> How sweet are the thoughts of that glorious scene,
> When none but a Jew over Jewry shall reign!
> No ruler, nor king, over Jews shall have place,
> But who is descended from David's great race.
> From around all the globe each nation shall meet
> And the Gentiles shall lick up the dust of his feet.[96]

A similar invocation of Shylock appears during the election campaign in an attack on one of the supporters of the Jew Bill, Sir William Calvert. A note in *Gray's Inn Journal* describes an imaginary cabal of Jewish stock-jobbers and other "Children of Israel" who support the candidate "on account of his attachment to our cause in the last Parliament." Predictably, one of the signers is "Josephus Shylock."[97] In political cartoons, too, Shylock exemplified the Jewish involvement in English economic affairs: one of those in circulation at this time—"Shylock's Race from the Chequer Inn to Paris"—depicts Samson Gideon's involvement in the 1753 lottery and shows Shylock riding on a pig's back with the devil.[98]

Shylock also appears as a ringleader in fantasies of Jewish attempts to take over England. In a column entitled "London, the 1753rd Chapter of the Jews" in *Read's Weekly Journal* we come across the "Acts of Shylock":

> In those days the Children of Jerusalem were scattered abroad upon the face of the whole earth. And behold no man received them; howbeit with much subtilty they gained very great riches. Nevertheless, the Lord had not given them a land where they might go over to possess it. . . . Now, there was a man among them

named Shylock, and he was a strong man, and powerful, having very many talents. . . . And he stood among the Jews, and said, "Oh my countrymen! this is the only fitting land for us to possess; seeing the people are pleased with us, and with our money." And they answered, and said, "O Shylock, live for ever! . . . Do thou, O grand director of our ways and pattern of our cunning, establish us, we beseech thee, in this promised land!" . . . Now the rest of the Acts of Shylock, and the words he spake, and the doings of the other people, verily shall be found in the following chapters.[99]

This triangulation of Shylock, the Bible, and contemporary politics became increasingly explicit as the controversy heated up in October of 1753. In a column entitled "The Thirty-fourth Chapter of Gen[esis]" that first appeared in the *London Evening Post* and which subsequently ran in the *Cambridge Journal*, Shylock is introduced along with real figures in the controversy, such as the Pelhams and Salvador, supplanting Jacob's sons in a parodic version of the rape of Dinah (one that is expected to take place ten years hence, after the Jews are allowed free reign):

And it came to pass, in the year seventeen-hundred sixty-three, that the daughters of the Britons, which their wives bear unto them, went into the synagogues of the Jews, to see the daughters of the Israelites. And when the sons of Gid[eon], of Shylock . . . and Salv[ador] saw them, they took them, and defiled them. . . . And Gid[eon] and Shylock came to the gate of the [Ex]change, and communed with the men of their own nation. . . . And unto Gid[eon] and Shylock hearkened all the Jews that went unto the [Ex]change. And they told the Pelh[ami]tes, who ordered every male to be circumcised. . . . And it came to pass on the third day, whilst their private parts were sore, that the Jews took their swords, and slew every male of the Britons."[100]

Here, the biblical and Shakespeare narratives are conflated, with Shylock taking the role of father of the rapists, and then (since the story is revised so that the Jews are both violators and revengers) as one who first arranged for the Britons to be circumcised, then slain. By now Shylock has become more than simply a dramatic character and is aligned here with actual figures in the controversy.

A good number of these allusions turned on a knife-wielding, circumcising, castrating Shylock. In "The Prophesies of Shylock" that appeared in the *London Evening Post*, there is a notice of an "advertisement was found placed against the meeting house at Dartford in Kent" that reads: "to all Jews . . . pensioners and others whom it may concern: this is to give notice that this evening will be held at the Bull Inn a private circumcision feast, . . . Benjamin Shylock,

Scribe."[101] Examples can easily be multiplied.[102] The anonymous author of the satiric tract *Seasonable Remarks on the Act Lately Pass'd in Favour of the Jews* offers Shakespeare's play (which by now no longer needs to be explicitly named) as "proof" that the Jews "have not forgot their old practices of circumcising, crucifying, etc.," reminding his readers of "an instance on record with regard to a Jew at Venice" that "seems to show that nothing less than our flesh as well as our money will satisfy their unchristian appetites."[103]

We witness in a number of these examples a shift from Shylock as stage character to one who steps out of the theater into the daily lives of English men and women, whose influence extended out of the City into the countryside. In the *London Evening Post*, for example, an account appeared of "a gentleman," who, "travelling on the Uxbridge Road overtook a farmer who looked very disconsolate. . . . He asked him the matter," and

> the farmer replied: "Lord, Sir, I have had no sleep for these three nights, the thoughts of the Jews ever running us distracting me. For we hear in the country that the Jews will circumcise all their tenants. And my landlord having ruined himself by cards and dice, is about selling my farm, and several others in the neighborhood, and we hear, to a Jew. For last week two strange-looking men (one they called Shylock) came to look at mine."[104]

Further evidence that these examples offer not simply a "Shylock" abstracted and separate from *The Merchant of Venice*, but one very much based on the character of Shakespeare's play is apparent from allusions in the pamphlet literature to Lancelot Gobbo, Shylock's servant. In a column called "More News for One Hundred Years hence, in the *Hebrew-Journal*" an advertisement appears, dated August 29, 1853, and signed Lancelot Gobbo, that reads:

> Gentlemen, having had the honour to be put in nomination, by a large majority of gentlemen, rabbi[s], and freeholders, met this day at Lewes, to represent you, in the ensuing Sanhedrin, I beg the favour of your votes and interest, and am, gentlemen, your most obedient servant, Lancelot Gobbo.[105]

The attack is probably aimed at Prime Minister Henry Pelham, and the joke is straightforward enough: like Gobbo, Pelham is merely a servant—and a lowly one at that—of Jewish masters. The attack was sufficiently popular to be reprinted in the *London Evening Post* three days later. Yet another allusion to Shylock, this time as a "Christian Imposter," immediately follows in the advertisement below the allusion to Gobbo: "By desire, at the Theater-Royal in Drury-Lane, on Sunday next, will be presented a comedy called, I believe . . .

The Christian Impostor. The Part of Dr. Tillotson to be performed by Rubens Shylock."[106] These allusions to Shylock persisted long after the furor over the Jew Bill had passed. By 1765 Shylock has become not simply a character but an author, offering the second and third books of *The Jew Apologist*, a strange verse narrative, written "when Roman Catholics, a sort of men far more obnoxious to government than the Jews, have lately pressed so hard for the repeal of the penal laws."[107] Three years later a defeated Shylock would take up his pen again in defense of Jewish naturalization, this time offering *The Rabbi's Lamentation Upon the Repeal of the Jew Act.*[108]

Despite the decision to refrain from staging *The Merchant of Venice*, London's theaters were not immune from anti-Jewish outbursts. In recounting the "only instance of actual public unpleasantness towards Jews" that he found "in any contemporary source"[109]—a definition narrow enough to exclude the personal violence recorded against itinerant Jewish peddlers, one of whom was slain[110]— Thomas Perry cites the following account from the *London Evening Post*:

> After the second music, some Jewish ladies and gentlemen were noticed in one of the balconies, when the cry immediately began, "*No Jews, out with them, circumcise them*, etc., etc.," and was followed with showers of apples, etc., with great rudeness, till the company were obliged to leave their seats. But upon remonstrance from a gentleman that sat next to them, to some others in the pit, a loud clap ensued, the company were reinstated, and met with no other molestation.[111]

Why members of the audience would call for the circumcision either of Jewish men or women is not entirely clear. The incident perhaps casts further light on why London's theater managers were loathe to stage *The Merchant of Venice* or any other plays about Jews at this time. The pressure of the Jew Bill nonetheless made its presence felt in small ways on the London stage. A good instance is in the prologue, written by Garrick and "Spoken by Mr. Foote, at his first apppearance on Drury-Lane Stage," on October 20:

> The many various objects that amuse
> These busy curious times, by way of news
> Are, plays, elections, murders, lott'ries, Jews,
> All these compounded fly throughout the nation,
> And set the whole on one great fermentation.[112]

The self-censorship that prevented Shakespeare's play from being staged within London during the course of this controversy did not extend to the provinces. While standard stage histories of *The Merchant of Venice* and of English provincial touring companies offer no extant records of performances of the play outside of London in 1753, I was fortunate to stumble upon an account of a touring production, probably staged in late spring or summer of 1753 in the north of England, or perhaps in Edinburgh. The evidence of this production survives in John Cunningham's *Poems, Chiefly Pastoral*, published in London in 1766. According to the *Dictionary of National Biography*, Cunningham, after "travelling about a great deal as a strolling actor . . . eventually appeared at Edinburgh, where he became a great favorite with the manager, Mr. Digges, and the leading lady, Mrs. George Anne Bellamy, and wrote many occasional prologues for them." Included in his collected verse is one such occasional piece, composed by Cunningham at the age of twenty-four: "A Prologue, Spoke by Mrs. G——, in an Itinerant Company, on Reviving *The Merchant of Venice*, at the Time of the Bill Passing for Naturalizing the Jews."

We have no other record of the performance or performances. There is little doubt that "Mrs. G——" is Mrs. George Anne Bellamy, a leading actress of the 1750s. While Mrs. Bellamy makes no reference in her multivolume memoirs to this touring production (or to any other performance of *The Merchant of Venice*), entries recorded in *The London Stage* indicate that she was in London from February 1753 through at least May 7, where she played the leading roles in *Lady Jane Gray, The Brothers, Venice Preserved, Othello, The Orphan*, and *Macbeth*, all at Drury Lane. She only resumed playing in London, this time for Rich's company at Covent Garden, sometime in September or October 1753.[113] In sum, one of the stars of the London theater apparently went on tour to the north sometime between late May and September, at the height of the uproar over the Jew Bill. Presumably, she played the part of Portia, and, as befitted the leading performer, recited the special prologue that Cunningham had written for the occasion:

'Twixt the sons of the stage, without pensions or places,
And the vagabond Jews, are some similar cases;
Since time out of mind, or they're wronged much by slander,
Both lawless, alike, have been sentenced to wander;
Then faith 'tis full time we appeal to the nation,
To be joined in this bill for na-tu-ra-li-za-ti-on;
Lord, that word's so uncouth!—'tis so irksome to speak it!
But 'tis Hebrew, I believe, and that taste, as I take it.
Well—now to the point—I'm sent here with commission,
To present this fair circle our humble petition:
But conscious what hopes we should have of succeeding,
Without (as they phrase it) sufficiently bleeding;
And convinced we've no funds, nor old gold we can rake up,
Like our good brothers—Abraham, Isaac, and Jacob;

We must frankly confess we have nought to present ye,
But Shakespeare's old sterling—pray let it content ye.
Old Shylock, the Jew, whom we mean to restore ye,
Was naturalized oft by your fathers before ye;
Then take him tonight to your kindest compassion,
For to countenance Jews is the pink of the fashion.[114]

It is an unusually rich document, one that powerfully connects the anxieties circulating in Shakespeare's play with those that surfaced during the Jew Bill controversy. The prologue also partakes of the self-contradiction characteristic of many of the polemical pamphlets, not least of all in the itinerant actors' simultaneous denigration of and identification with Jews in the opening lines. The legal status first assigned to wandering players in the late sixteenth century—vagabonds—is here applied, as elsewhere in the pamphlet literature of 1753, to the wandering Jews as well. In the witty tone that pervades the entire prologue, Mrs. Bellamy protests that the similarity with the Jews stops there: that the actors hope to win audience approval without having to be circumcised, that is "(as they phrase it) sufficiently bleeding." The self-deprecating vein may extend to a misreading of the play itself: for in a play whose casket scene warns of the dangers of silver no less than of gold, the actors protest that, since unlike Jews they cannot rake up gold, they must offer instead "Shakespeare's old sterling."

In the most telling lines of the prologue, Mrs. Bellamy recited how "Old Shylock, the Jew, whom we mean to restore ye, / Was naturalized oft by your fathers before ye." A remarkable conflation of naturalization and conversion takes place here, for Shylock is not naturalized after all, but agrees to be converted to Christianity. There is a precedent for figuratively equating naturalization with conversion as early as 1622, when John Donne spoke of "persons . . . not naturalized by conversion . . . from another religion to this."[115] Shakespeare's play is reimagined here as one that depicts the legal and political transformation of the Jews rather than their religious conversion—not surprising in a culture in which national affiliations were gradually superseding religious ones, though in the heady polemic of 1753, these overlapping aspects of English identity were not so easily separated. A final ironic twist appears in Moses Margoliouth's nineteenth-century *The History of the Jews in Great Britain*, where Margoliouth (a Jew who converted to Christianity) urges the English to take a sympathetic view of Shakespeare's character on the grounds that as "Shylock has been so long exhibited on the English stage, he must be considered as a naturalized Englishman."[116]

Cunningham's lighthearted prologue, like much of the polemic produced during the Jew Bill debate, first imagines and then quickly insists upon fundamental differences between Englishmen and Jews. Yet the more Cunningham elaborates upon these differences, the faster they threaten to collapse: differences between itinerant actors and wandering Jews, between circumcision and castration, between Christian subjects and Jewish aliens, between Shakespeare's "old sterling" and the silver casket in Shakespeare's play whose reward is as much as one deserves, and, finally, between the political act of naturalization and the religious one of conversion. The unstable elements buried deep within the texture of Shakespeare's play—including predatory aliens, and the sexual and conversionary threat embodied in Shylock's desire to cut a pound of Antonio's flesh—resonated powerfully with the fantasies about the Jews generated by the Jew Bill, and were thus immediately recognizable to eighteenth-century Englishmen. In this case, no major revision of Shakespeare's work was needed to bring it into line with contemporary taste, for its post-Reformation ideas about the Jews still cast a dark shadow over this Enlightenment world. Insofar as these unstable elements suffuse *The Merchant of Venice*, it is hard to imagine how, in the performance that followed, Mrs. Bellamy and the rest of the itinerant troupe could have put these anxieties to rest.

In retrospect, this book has explored what happens when "facts of history" are grounded in "idle tales." I have tried to account for why some of Shakespeare's contemporaries told stories about how Jews threatened to contaminate or transform the English body and body politic. And I have tried to connect this to stories told by historians who claim that there were no Jews or Jewish questions in Shakespeare's England. Stories retain their currency because they tell us what we want to hear, even if at some level we know them to be untrue. The fantasy that when Jews "were unknown . . . each Briton might then call his birthright his own" will no doubt continue to appeal to those who long for this imaginary golden age. Anglo-Jewry has been no less fond of sentimentalizing the past. Until quite recently its historians had celebrated a romantic version of the past that traced a more or less direct line from Expulsion to Readmission to Emancipation; this triumphant march toward toleration and emancipation ignored a good many complications and ended all too abruptly in the 1850s, before things began to unravel under the pressure of large-scale immigration.[1]

Stories not only allow insight into the complex processes through which cultural identities are formed but also help define the boundaries that mark major cultural shifts. I have argued in these pages that one such shift, beginning with the English Reformation and lasting until the mid-eighteenth century, brought with it a change in English attitudes toward Jews and Jewishness as the opposition of Christian and Jew was slowly overtaken by that of Englishman and Jew. Only gradually are historians acknowledging the extent to which

English Reformation thought was preoccupied with Jewish questions, and how, as a result, emerging political, social, and religious institutions were influenced by Jewish models.[2] Modern theorists of the discourses of race and nation continue for the most part to ignore how profoundly these modes of thought were shaped by Reformation theology; what would have been obvious to sixteenth-century writers remains anathema to their twentieth-century interpreters. Surely, to speak of race and nation as primarily class-based, or as emerging independent of each other, or, for that matter, independent of conceptions of Jewish racial and national identity, is to arrive at a very distorted notion of early modern thought and of its influence on our own ways of thinking. Race, nation, and gender not only need to be read in conjunction with religion but also read through it if we are to make sense of the categories of thought that the early modern world has bestowed upon us.

I do not pretend to have plucked out the heart of the mystery of Englishness in the early modern period; if anything, the idea of Englishness, no less than that of Jewishness, remains, for me, as elusive as ever. But I do think that by holding Englishness and Jewishness up to each other a clearer sense of both of their contours becomes possible. I also want to stress that my focus on issues of criminality, conversion, race, alien status, and national identity is not meant to suggest that these are the only ways in which Jewish questions informed early modern English attitudes and policies—they are simply the ones that circulate most forcefully through *The Merchant of Venice*. English men and women interested in rethinking the institution of marriage, for example, turned to Jewish precedent, from Henry VIII's consultation with Jewish authorities regarding his plans to divorce Catherine of Aragon, to Elizabeth Cary's *The Tragedie of Mariam, Faire Queene of Jewry* (1613), to John Selden's *Uxor Ebraica* (1646), to the Marriage Act of 1753.[3] And I have only touched upon the place of Jewish questions in early modern English political theory, from the Jewish antecedents that inform Richard Hooker's *Of the Lawes of Ecclesiasticall Politie* ([1594]–97) to the complicated ways in which Jewishness and republicanism were conflated by royalists. Recent and forthcoming scholarly investigations into the ways in which Jewish practices shaped English social and political values (and were taken up onstage in plays on Jewish subjects) will surely complicate and extend the interplay of Englishness and Jewishness explored here.

In the course of writing this book I have developed a good deal of respect for the vitality of irrationality, and of the power of stories to lead people to act in ways that are difficult to comprehend. Consider, for example, the disturbing report from 1621 found in the State Papers describing how "Grey, an Irish fanatic, has murdered his own child, with the idea of procuring the restoration of the Jews, by shedding innocent blood." Grey, about whom we know little

else, placed a letter "on the body of his child challenging inquiry into the murder . . . in order that in his trial he may expose the judges, and plead the cause
of the Jews."[4] Instances like this should remind us that modern, rational, and
secular frames of reference make it difficult, if not impossible, to grasp the
impact of Jewish questions in the early modern world.

Another argument that has been advanced in these pages is that racist fantasies continue to compel belief because they tap into some of the deepest fears
people have of "turning"—especially of physical, sexual, or religious transformation. Dig deep enough and one discovers that the affirmation of cultural
identity too often rests on the slippery foundations of prejudice and exclusion.
Even as stories feed our hunger to imagine others as inferior, evil, and dangerous, they succeed in masking the extent to which the storytellers' identities are
formed (and often deformed) in the act of recounting such tales. A different
kind of deformity, one that derives from the cult of victimization, occurs when
one group can hear only the stories others tell about it and is deaf to the stories
it tells about others. This may seem obvious enough, but in a world in which
an increasing number of identity groups compete for the status of greatest victim, the point is easily forgotten. In that sense, this book will have been badly
misunderstood if it is taken as another cry of Jewish victimization, or read as
a condemnation of England, of Christianity, or for that matter, of Shakespeare. I have tried to explore the place of the Jews in the formation of early
modern English identity without, on the one hand, dismissing the Jews as irrelevant or, on the other, reflexively accusing the English of harboring anti-Jewish sentiments, and I have done so in order to understand English history and
culture, and the place of Jews in it.

One way of showing what stories can reveal about cultural prejudices is to
turn those stories against the storytellers. Menasseh ben Israel tried to do this
in the 1650s when he reminded Christians that in telling stories about Jewish
ritual murder they were accusing Jews of the same crime that they themselves
had been charged with centuries earlier.[5] Richard Hole adopted a similar strategy in 1796 when he offers by way of experiment a revision of the scene in *The
Merchant of Venice* in which Tubal tells Shylock of Jessica's extravagances in
Genoa. He substitutes two Christian merchants in place of the Jews in order to
show that the "mirth" that the scene provokes "at the expense of these unpop-
ular characters" has more to do with English prejudices against Jews than with
anything inherent in the dialogue. Hole goes on to explore what it would be
like if the Jews were "again settled in their former territories" and even offers
a sample review of Shakespeare's play that in this future Jewish state might
appear in the *Jerusalem Daily Advertiser*. His approach allows him to ponder
what *The Merchant of Venice* (which the Jews in their future state have renamed
Shylock and consider a "tragedy") reveals not about the Jews but about the

English. Hole's Jewish reviewer of the future notes that English theatergoers had often cheered when learning of Jessica's plan to abandon her father and steal his gold and jewels, and wonders what impression this gives of "the English nation when such sentiments could be applauded!"[6]

A final example of this strategy of reversing roles occurs in the 1986 film *Avanti Populo*, by the Israeli director Rafi Bokai. The climax of the film, which is in Hebrew and whose action takes place in the Sinai desert during the fighting between Egyptian and Israeli soldiers, occurs when two Egyptian soldiers, dying of thirst, surrender to an Israeli platoon and ask for water. When the Israeli soldiers refuse to share this precious commodity, one of the Egyptians lunges for an Israeli's canteen, only to be thrown aside. He lunges again, only to be thrown back once more. At last the Egyptian pulls himself up and stands face to face with the Israeli. One speaks Arabic, the other Hebrew; their only shared language is that bestowed upon them by the British who have occupied their lands. The Egyptian soldier looks his Israeli counterpart in the eye and begins to recite in English Shylock's famous speech about the otherness of the Jew: "I am a Jew. Hath not a Jew eyes?" An Israeli soldier witnessing this harrowing encounter states the obvious: "He has changed the parts." It is an agonizing confrontation, but also a liberating one for both Israelis and Egyptians, for the performance of Shylock's speech enables the soldiers to transcend the vast differences that had until that moment separated them. But this achievement is shortlived, for in the film's tragic denouement, the soldiers, as well as the hope (implicit in the film's title) of people going forward together, are obliterated. The message is clear enough: while the words may be Shakespeare's, the destructive prejudices are our own, and always have been.

From its first staging in the 1590s to its quotation in *Avanti Populo*, the story that has never been far from the center of this book has been Shakespeare's *The Merchant of Venice*. I have tried to show that much of the play's vitality can be attributed to the ways in which it scrapes against a bedrock of beliefs about the racial, national, sexual, and religious difference of others. I can think of no other literary work that does so as unrelentingly and as honestly. To avert our gaze from what the play reveals about the relationship between cultural myths and peoples' identities will not make irrational and exclusionary attitudes disappear. Indeed, these darker impulses remain so elusive, so hard to identify in the normal course of things, that only in instances like productions of this play do we get to glimpse these cultural faultlines. This is why censoring the play is *always* more dangerous than staging it. *The Merchant*'s capacity to illuminate a culture is invariably compromised when those staging it flinch from presenting the play in its complex entirety, which is what occurred when Nazi directors, in the fifty or so productions they staged between 1933 and 1945, omitted the intermarriage of Jessica and Lorenzo, and which also occured when the British director Barry Kyle in a 1980 production in Israel was persuaded to omit Shylock's acceptance of conversion to Christianity, since it was so disturbing for Jewish audiences.[7] I leave to others the task of exploring the place of *The Merchant of Venice* in the cultural identities of Germany,[8] Israel,[9] the United States,[10] and even Japan,[11] investigations that will surely reveal much about the ways in which different nations have appropriated Shakespeare's work for their own political and social ends—and will no doubt continue to do so. One thing remains certain: as long as anxieties about racial, national, sexual, and religious difference continue to haunt the way we imagine ourselves and respond to others, Shakespeare's words will remain "not of an age, but for all time."

⚡ Notes

1.   Following the lead of historians, in the past decade literary critics have largely abandoned the term *Renaissance* in favor of *early modern*. The boundaries of the early modern period remain only slightly less precise than those of the Renaissance. For my purposes, early modern England covers the period extending from approximately 1550 to 1750.

2.   John Donne, "A Sermon Preached at Saint Dunstan's Upon New-Years-Day, 1624," in *The Sermons of John Donne*, ed. George R. Potter and Evelyn M. Simpson, 10 vols. (Berkeley: University of California Press, 1953–62), vol. 6, pp. 333–34.

3.   Samuel T. Coleridge, *The Collected Works of Samuel Taylor Coleridge, Marginalia II*, ed. George Whalley (Princeton: Princeton University Press, 1984), p. 247.

4.   Consider, for example, the British historian David Cannadine's remark that in "the context of international Jewry, the history of British Jewry is neither very interesting nor very exciting. In the context of British history, it is just not that important," in his review, "Cousinhood," *London Review of Books*, July 27, 1989.

5.   See Neil Hirschson, "The Jewish Key to Shakespeare's Most Enigmatic Creation," *Midstream* (February/March 1989), pp. 38–40; and David Basch, *The Hidden Shakespeare: A Rosetta Stone* (West Hartford, Conn.: Revelatory Press, 1994).

6.   Alan Marlis, *Queen Elizabeth Tudor: A Secret Jewess* (n.p., 1978).

7.   Anon., ed., *A Collection of the Best Pieces and Verse Against the Naturalization of the Jews* (London, 1753), p. 77.

8.   See Elliott Baker, *Bardolotry* (London: Holofernes, 1992), especially pp. 29–33.

9.   Jane Austen, *Mansfield Park*, ed. R. W. Chapman, 3rd ed. (Oxford: Oxford University Press, 1934), p. 338.

10.   My understanding of Jewish identity in the pages that follow is influenced by the work of Michael Krausz. Following Krausz, I distinguish "being a Jew by descent from Jewishness by assent," and believe "that Jewishness by assent should be understood in terms of identification with Jewish history." In this sense, being Jewish depends on one's willingness to

share in the preservation of Jewish memory and in sustaining the story of the Jewish people: it "involves embracing certain beliefs and seeing oneself as a character in a valued Jewish narrative that one both occupies and fashions. One who assents to his or her Jewishness at least partly understands himself or herself in terms of the historically emergent threads of the fabrics of Jewish histories" (Michael Krausz, "On Being Jewish," in _Jewish Identity_, ed. David Theo Goldberg and Michael Krausz [Philadelphia: Temple University Press, 1993], p. 277).

11. While there is considerable overlap in these terms, I have generally retained _New Christian_ to describe those whose conversion was probably sincere, _Converso_ where the question of apostasy is an open one, and _Marrano_ in cases where Jewish identity is predominant, though disguised.

12. William Prynne, _A Short Demurrer to the Jewes_, part 1 (London, 1656), pp. 94–95.

13. Jonathan I. Israel, _European Jewry in the Age of Mercantilism, 1550–1750_, 2d ed. (Oxford: Clarendon Press, 1989), p. 71.

14. Israel, _European Jewry_, pp. 31, 35.

15. Israel, _European Jewry_, pp. 70–86.

16. _The Diary of Ralph Josselin 1616–1683_, ed. Alan Macfarlane, Records of Social and Economic History, n.s. 3 (London: Oxford University Press, 1976), p. 337.

17. Sir Richard Burton, _The Jew, The Gypsy, and El Islam_, ed. W. H. Wilkins (London: Hutchinson, 1898), p. 21.

18. The Duke of Bedford, in the "Debate for the Repeal of the Jewish Naturalization Act, November 1753," _The Parliamentary History of England_, vol. 15 (1753–1765), (London: Hansard, 1813), p. 106.

19. Ben Jonson, _Every Man in His Humour_ (1601), 3.1.40, in C. H. Herford and Percy and Evelyn Simpson, eds., _Works_, 11 vols. (Oxford: Oxford University Press, 1925–52), vol. 3, p. 233; Anon., _Blurt, Master Constable_ (1601), 1.2.138; John Day, _Law Tricks_ (1608), in John Crow, ed., Malone Society Reprints (Oxford: Oxford University Press, 1950), line 613.

20. Shakespeare, _Much Ado About Nothing_, 2.3.253–54. Quotations from Shakespeare's plays (with the exception of _The Merchant of Venice_) are cited from _The Complete Works of Shakespeare_, 3rd ed., ed. David Bevington (Scott, Foresman, 1980).

21. Shakespeare, _The Merchant of Venice_, 2.2.105.

22. Shakespeare, _1 Henry 4_, 2.4.177.

23. Burton, _The Jew, The Gypsy, and El Islam_, p. 25.

24. Burton, _The Jew, The Gypsy, and El Islam_, pp. 36–37.

25. Tudor and Stuart plays that deal centrally with Jews include the lost _The Jew_ (1578); Christopher Marlowe, _The Jew of Malta_ (c. 1589); the lost _The Jew of Venice_, possibly by Thomas Dekker; William Hemming, _The Jews' Tragedy_ (1626); Richard Brome, _The Jewish Gentleman_ (1640), now lost; the lost _The Wandering Jew_; and two plays performed by English touring companies abroad: _Joseph the Jew of Venice_, in 1626 in Dresden; and _The Jew_ in 1607 in Passua. A number of other English plays from this period contain Jewish characters, including Robert Greene, _Selimus_ (1592); Robert Wilson, _The Three Lords and Three Ladies of London_ (1588); John Day, William Rowley, and George Wilkins, _The Travels of the Three English Brothers_ (1607). Two Latin dramas that contain Jewish characters are also worth noting: Nathaniel Wiburne, _Machiavellus_ (1597); and Thomas Vincent, _Paria_ (1627). For a more comprehensive list, see Edgar Rosenberg, "The Jew in Western Drama: An Essay and a Checklist," _Bulletin of the New York Public Library_ 72 (1968), pp. 442–91, rpt. in Edward Coleman, _The Jew in English Drama: An Annotated Bibliography_ (New York, 1970), pp. 1–50. For accounts of the representation of Jews in early modern English literature, see, for example, Jacob Lopes Cardozo, _The Contemporary Jew in the Elizabethan Drama_ (Amsterdam: H. J. Paris, 1925); Hijman Michelson, _The Jew in Early English Literature_ (Amster-

dam: H. J. Paris, 1926); Montagu Frank Modder, *The Jew in the Literature of England* (Philadelphia: Jewish Publication Society of America, 1939); Harold Fisch, *The Dual Image: The Figure of the Jew in English and American Literature* (London: World Jewish Congress, British Section, 1959); Fisch, *Jerusalem and Albion: The Hebraic Factor in Seventeenth-Century Literature* (London: Routledge and Kegan Paul, 1964); and Edgar Rosenberg, *From Shylock to Svengali: Jewish Stereotypes in English Fiction* (London: Peter Owen, 1961).

26. See in this regard Raphael and Jennifer Patai, *The Myth of the Jewish Race*, rev. ed. (Detroit: Wayne State University Press, 1989). The literature on race and racism is vast. For a useful point of entry into the problem of racialized discourse, see David Theo Goldberg, *Racist Culture: Philosophy and the Politics of Meaning* (Oxford: Blackwell, 1993).

27. For the only complete English translation of Luther's *Von den Juden und Iren Lugen* (Wittenburg, 1543), see Martin H. Bertram, trans., *On the Jews and Their Lies*, in Jaroslav Pelikan and Helmut T. Lehmann, gen. eds., *Luther's Works*, 55 vols. (Philadelphia: Fortress Press, 1971), vol. 47, pp. 121–306. That Elizabethans were not unaware of Luther's anti-Jewish polemic is clear from Samuel Purchas, who in a chapter on the conversion of the Jews in his *Purchas His Pilgrimage* (London, 1626), cites in the margin "a whole book" of Luther's *"Cont[ra] Judaeos"* (p. 212, n. "e"). See, too, William A. Clebsch, "The Earliest Translations of Luther Into English," *Harvard Theological Review* 56 (1963), pp. 75–86; and Basil Hall, "The Early Rise and Gradual Decline of Lutheranism in England (1520–1600)," in Derek Baker, ed., *Reform and Reformation: England and the Continent c. 1500–c. 1700* (Oxford: Basil Blackwell, 1979), pp. 103–31.

28. Surprisingly little work has been done on printed pictorial images of Jews in early modern England. See Eric Myles Zafran, "The Iconography of Antisemitism," Diss., New York University, 1973. See, too, Ruth S. Luborsky, "The Pictorial Image of the Jew in Elizabethan Secular Books," forthcoming in *Shakespeare Quarterly*. For a helpful account of the iconography of otherness, see Ruth Mellinkoff, *Outcasts: Signs of Otherness in Northern European Art of the Late Middle Ages*, 2 vols. (Berkeley: University of California Press, 1993); Mellinkoff's work is especially helpful on the iconography of the Jew in medieval illustrated manuscripts.

Those who have examined early modern English woodcuts know that a good many of them reappeared in different books in markedly different contexts. I have deliberately included among the illustrations that appear in this book woodcuts that were initially used to depict a Christian and were subsequently reused in another context to depict a Jew (see, for example, the picture of a Jew that appears in Andrew Borde's *Fyrst Boke of the Introduction of Knowledge* [London, 1562]; illustration 2). I have done so because these woodcuts, taken together, confirm that English readers (or even illiterate individuals perusing pictures in printed books) did not expect Jews to look all that different than Christians, except perhaps in their dress, nor did printers reusing these images alter them to exaggerate the physical features of the Jews. Indeed, English prints did not represent Jews with distinctive physical traits until well into the eighteenth century. Thus, to rule out woodcuts because the individuals in them do not look "Jewish" (though they are clearly labeled as Jews in the accompanying texts) is a misleading and mistaken approach. Put another way, woodcuts in early modern English books do not distinguish Jews from Christians except in terms of their garb—the few exceptions include Gad ben Arad, pseud., *The Wandering-Jew, Telling Fortunes to English-men* (London, 1640), where the Jew is distinguished not just by his garb but by a Jewish badge as well (see illustration 13); and the portrait of Erra Pater, which appears to depict a Jew with what contemporaries called "goggle eyes" (see, for example, the title page of Erra Pater, pseud., *A Prognostication for Ever, Made by Erra Pater, a Jewe, Borne in Jewrie, Doctor in Astronomie and Phisicke* [London, c. 1630]; illustration 11).

1. False Jews and Counterfeit Christians in Early Modern England

Sources for the epigraphs to chapter 1 are the following: John Florio, *Queen Anne's New World of Words* (London, 1611), p. 300; Prynne, *Short Demurrer*, part 1, p. 73; James Howell, *Lexicon Tetraglotton, an English-French-Italian-Spanish Dictionary* (London, 1660), sig. ZZ1r.

1. On the institution of the Jewish badge in England, see Cecil Roth, *A History of the Jews in England*, 3rd ed. (Oxford: Oxford University Press, 1964), p. 40.

2. The literature on the Inquisition is extensive. See, for example, H. C. Lea, *A History of the Inquisition of Spain*, 4 vols. (New York: Macmillan, 1922); Yitzhak Baer, *A History of the Jews in Christian Spain*, 2 vols. (Philadelphia: Jewish Publication Society, 1961); and Henry Kamen, *Inquisition and Society in Spain in the Sixteenth and Seventeenth Centuries* (Bloomington: Indiana University Press, 1985). See, too, Perez Zagorin, "The Marranos and Crypto-Judaism," in his *Ways of Lying: Dissimulation, Persecution, and Conformity in Early Modern Europe* (Cambridge: Harvard University Press, 1990), pp. 38–62. For an overview of the Marrano experience, see Elie Kedourie, gen. ed., *Spain and the Jews: The Sephardic Experience 1492 and After* (London: Thames and Hudson, 1992).

3. The figure that historians offer for the number of Jews expelled from Spain varies widely from fifty thousand to five hundred thousand. For Henry Kamm, despite "the unanimous opinion of contemporary chronicles that most Jews left Spain, the probability now appears that, over the whole period 1492–9, only a minority did. Many, as we shall see, chose to convert" ("The Mediterranean and the Expulsion of Spanish Jews in 1492," *Past and Present* 119 [1988], p. 39). Henry Kamen writes that as "evidence accumulates of the relatively small size of Jewish communities, it is very likely that the real figures [for those who went into exile from Spain] will turn out to be only half those cited" (*Inquisition and Society*, p. 16).

4. See John Edwards, "Mission and Inquisition Among *Conversos* and *Moriscos* in Spain, 1250–1550," in *Persecution and Toleration*, Studies in Church History 21, ed. W. J. Scheils (Oxford: Blackwell, 1984), pp. 141–45. Edwards notes that only on rare occasions, such as the ritual murder trial concerning 'the holy child of La Guardia' in 1491, were unconverted Jews tried by the Inquisition (p. 145).

5. See Marc Shell, "Marranos (Pigs), or From Coexistence to Toleration," *Critical Inquiry* 17 (1991), pp. 309–12; as well as his *The End of Kinship: "Measure for Measure," Incest and the Idea of Universal Siblinghood* (Stanford: Stanford University Press, 1988).

6. Yitzhak Baer, *A History of the Jews in Christian Spain*, as cited in B. Netanyahu, *The Marranos of Spain* (New York: American Academy for Jewish Research, 1966), p. 2. Baer thus concludes that "essentially the Inquisition was right in evaluating the character of the *conversos*" (as cited in Netanyahu, p. 3). For an excellent discussion of the formation of Converso identity, see Miriam Bodian, "'Men of the Nation': The Shaping of Converso Identity in Early Modern Europe," *Past and Present* 143 (1994), pp. 48–76.

7. Netanyahu, *The Marranos of Spain*, p. 3. According to this critical school, economic and racial rather than religious motivations led to the establishment of the Inquisition at a point where the Marrano population had all but lost touch with its Jewish roots, ironically causing something of a resurgence of marranism in response to this persecution.

8. As quoted in Yosef Kaplan, "Haim Beinart and the Historiography of the *Conversos* in Spain," in *Exile and Diaspora: Studies in the History of the Jewish People Presented to Professor Haim Beinart* (Jerusalem: Ben-Zvi Institute and the Hebrew University of Jerusalem, 1991), pp. 14–15. Kaplan writes that even though Beinart "did not ignore the existence of many Conversos who 'sought to make every effort to assimilate into the Christian public,' he accepted the theoretical position of Yizhak Baer, that 'Conversos and Jews were one people'" (pp. 14–15).

9. Haim Beinart, "The Conversos Community of Fifteenth-Century Spain," in R. D. Barnett, ed., *The Sephardi Heritage*, vol. 1 (London: Valentine, Mitchell, 1971), p. 452.

234

1. False Jews and Counterfeit Christians

10. In sum, "the Inquisition took as its test for crypto-Judaism adherence to a variety of ethnic practices common to earlier generations of Spanish Jews rather than actual belief in Judaism" (Jerome Friedman, "Jewish Conversion, the Spanish Pure Blood Laws and Reformation: A Revisionist View of Racial and Religious Antisemitism," *The Sixteenth Century Journal* 18 [1987], p. 15).

11. See Salo Wittmayer Baron's acccount of H. J. Zimmel's research on rabbinical responsa, in his *A Social and Religious History of the Jews*, 18 vols. (New York: Columbia University Press, 1952–1983), vol. 13, pp. 154–55.

12. It "was really a measure of the centrality of circumcision in the eyes of those very Marranos that they regarded it as the crucial event separating their Jewish from their Marrano lives" (Yosef Yerushalmi, *The Re-education of Marranos in the Seventeenth Century*, The Third Annual Rabbi Louis Fienberg Memorial Lecture in Judaic Studies [Judaic Studies Program, University of Cincinnati, 1980]).

13. As quoted in Yosef Kaplan, "Wayward New Christians and Stubborn New Jews: The Shaping of a Jewish Identity," *Jewish History* 8 (1994), p. 36.

14. Kaplan, "Wayward New Christians," p. 36. See, too, Isaiah Tishbi, "New Information on the 'Converso' Community in London Acording to the Letters of Sasportas from 1664–1665," in *Exile and Diaspora: Studies in the History of the Jewish People, Presented to Professor Haim Beinart*, ed. A. Mirsky et al. (Jerusalem: Hebrew University of Jerusalem, 1988), pp. 470–96 [Hebrew].

15. Consider, for instance, the case of Martin Soza, the endenized York goldsmith and sheriff who was born in Spain and emigrated to England in 1528, where he died in 1560. David M. Palliser has speculated that Soza was a "Christian Jew" and a committed Catholic, discouraged by the Protestant Reformation in England (Soza's Catholicism is strongly suggested by his desire to have prayers said for his soul after his death when such practices were no longer appropriate in Protestant England). See David M. Palliser, "Martin Soza—A Tudor Jewish Convert," in *Clifford's Tower Commemoration* (A Programme and Handbook, York, 1990), p. 56.

16. Yirmiyahu Yovel, *Spinoza and Other Heretics*, 2 vols. (Princeton: Princeton University Press, 1989), pp. 22, 28.

17. John Foxe, *Actes and Monuments* (London, 1596–1597), p. 849.

18. James Howell's letter, dated June 3, 1633, is cited in B. B., *A Historical and Law Treatise Against the Jewes and Judaism* (London, 1732), p. 41.

19. Henry Blount, *A Voyage Into the Levant* (London 1636), pp. 120–21.

20. Florio, *New World of Words*, p. 300.

21. John Florio, *A Worlde of Wordes* (London, 1598), p. 216. Florio's definition curiously concludes that *Marrano* "hath also been used for a kind of pinnace or fly-boat, or such ship." By the mid-seventeenth century English dictionaries were defining *Marrano* as "a Jew counterfeitly turned Christian" (Howell, *Lexicon Tetraglotton*, Sig. ZZ1r).

22. Some sense of how much of a threat renegades posed to cultural identity is to be found in plays staged at this time that offered reassuring depictions of their return to Christianity. See N. I. Matar, "The Renegade in English Seventeenth-Century Imagination," *Studies in English Literature* 33 (1993), pp. 489–505. For plays in which English renegades renounce Islam see, for example, Robert Daborne, *A Christian Turn'd Turke, or the Tragicall Lives and Deaths of the Two Famous Pyates, Ward and Danisker* (1612), and William Rowley, *All's Lost by Lust* (c. 1619–20).

23. Mayerne Turquet, Louis de, *The Generall Historie of Spaine* (1583), trans. Edward Grimeston (London, 1612), pp. 946–47, 958.

24. Thomas Browne, "That Jews Stink," in *Pseudodoxia Epidemica* (London, 1646), p. 202.

25. Donne, *Sermons*, vol. 7, p. 169, from a sermon preached at St. Paul's, May 21, 1626. Donne

notes that the only place where Jews write of rituals for the dead is in The Book of Maccabees.

26. Prynne, *Short Demurrer*, part 1, pp. 94–95.

27. Thomas Platter, *Journal of a Younger Brother*, trans. and ed. Seàn Jennett (London: Frederick Muller, 1963), p. 75.

28. Purchas, *Pilgrimage*, pp. 213–14.

29. Lancelot Addison, *The Present State of the Jews* (London, 1675), pp. 31–32. He also writes of "another Jew who in Malaga conterfeited Christianity so well as to be entrusted with the sale of indulgences; having made a good market thereof in Spain, [he] came with what he had left to a Christian city in Barbary, where his indulgences being all bought up by the Irish and others of the papal persuasion, he declared his religion. The Papists who had bought his indulgences impeach[ed] him to the government for a cheat, and clamour[ed] to have him punished according to demerit. The Jew pleaded the laws of the free port, that he had neither imported not sold any thing but his professed merchandise, and therefore desired (and obtained) the liberty and privileges of such as trafficked in that port. I report nothing but matter of personal knowledge" (p. 31).

30. *Calendar of State Papers, Spanish* (1550–1552), pp. 236, 254.

31. "*De Judaismo Nunquam Cogitavi*," in James M. Aitken, ed., *The Trial of George Buchanan Before the Lisbon Inquisition: Including the Text of Buchanan's Defences Along with a Translation and Commentary* (Edinburgh: Oliver and Boyd, 1939), pp. 5–7, 118–19, 56n1, and 36–37. I quote here from Aitken's translations; he does not reproduce the original Latin text of the Second Examination and explains that he has "slightly condensed" this exchange.

32. Arthur H. Williamson, "British Israel and Roman Britain: The Jews and Scottish Models of Polity from George Buchanan to Samuel Rutherford," in Richard H. Popkin and Gordon M. Weiner, eds., *Jewish Christians and Christian Jews from the Renaissance to the Enlightenment* (Dordrecht, The Netherlands: Kluwer Academic Publishers, 1994), pp. 99–100; and John Durkan, "Buchanan's Judaising Practices," *Innes Review* 15 (1964), pp. 186–87.

33. Martin Luther, *A Commentarie of M. Doctor Martin Luther Upon the Epistle of S. Paul to the Galatians* (London, 1575), fol. 96v. See, too, M. T.'s English translation of Charles Drelincourt, *The Roote of Romish Rites and Ceremonies: Shewing That the Church of Rome Hath Borrowed Most Part of Her Ceremonies of the Jewes and Ancient Pagans* (London, 1630).

34. Andrew Willet, *Synopsis Papismi, That Is, a General View of Papistrie*, 11th ed. (London, 1634), pp. 1298–99. First published in 1592.

35. Robert Parker, *A Scholasticall Discourse Against Symbolizing with Antichrist in Ceremonies* (London, 1607), p. 119.

36. Thomas Calvert, in his annotations to *The Blessed Jew of Morocco; Or a Blackmoor Made White*, by Rabbi Samuel, a Jew Turned Christian (York, 1648), pp. 185–86.

37. John Warner, *The Devilish Conspiracy* (London, 1648), pp. 15, 21, 35.

38. David Katz, *Sabbath and Sectarianism in Seventeenth-Century England* (Leiden: E. J. Brill, 1988), p. 1; as cited from E. C. S. Gibson, *The Thirty-Nine Articles* (London, 1898).

39. See "The Manuscripts of the Dean and Chapter of Windsor," ed. R. L. Poole, in *HMC Report on Manuscripts in Various Collections*, vol. 7 (London, 1914) p. 35. Bruern was also accused of adultery and homosexuality. See David Katz, *Philo-Semitism and the Readmission of the Jews to England, 1603–1655* (Oxford: Clarendon Press, 1982), p. 17; and John Fines, "'Judaising' in the Period of the English Reformation—the Case of Richard Bruern," *Transactions of the Jewish Historical Society of England* 21 (1968), pp. 323–26. Henceforth *TJHSE*.

40. As cited in Katz, *Philo-Semitism*, p. 16; see *The Works of John Whitgift*, ed. J. Ayre (London: Parker Society, 1851–52), vol. 1, p. 271. Katz refers to another example at Cambridge, where in 1585 John Smith was "cited before the University for advocating a Jewish observance of the Lord's Day" (*Philo-Semitism*, p. 16).

41. Peter Heylyn, *The History of the Sabbath* (London, 1636), vol. 2, p. 250. John Strype writes in a similar vein that "the chief of the inventors of this Sabbatarian doctrine was one Bound, who wrote a book in the year 1595 that the commandment for keeping the Sabbath was moral and perpetual, and that Christians were bound to rest upon the Sabbath, and to keep it, as the Jews did." He adds that in 1599 "(as well as before) did Archbishop Whitgift, by his letters and officers at synods, call in books on that subject, and forbade any more to be printed. And Sir John Popham, Lord Chief Justice of England, at Bury St. Edmonds in Suffolk, anno 1600, did the like" (Strype, *The Life and Acts of John Whitgift*, 3 vols. [Oxford: Clarendon Press, 1822], vol. 2, pp. 414–16.) See, too, Patrick Collinson, "The Beginnings of English Sabbatarianism," *Studies in Church History* 1 (1964), pp. 207–21.

42. Heylyn, *Sabbath*, vol. 2, pp. 250–51. Those sympathetic to Sabbatarianism could not have been pleased with an anecdote that appeared in medieval chronicles and that was endlessly retold at this time about a Jew who fell into a privy on the Jewish Sabbath and whose religious scruples prevented him from being pulled out. In some versions the story took place in thirteenth-century Tewksbury; in others it was said to have taken place in Germany. In every version local Christian authorities refuse to rescue the Jew on Sunday out of respect for their own religion, and by Monday the Jew has died. Thomas Calvert records parts of a ballad on this theme in which the Jew calls out from the privy, "I honour holy Sabbath's rest, / I will not rise from my foul nest," only to be told by a Christian, "Lest from your holy rule you swerve, / You shall our Sabbath too observe" (Calvert, *The Blessed Jew of Morocco*, pp. 41–42).

43. Heylyn also cites the more recent example of "Theophilus Braborne" (*Sabbath*, vol. 2, p. 259).

44. I draw in the paragraphs that follow on the excellent account of David Katz, who has told Traske's story at some length (*Philo-Semitism*, pp. 18–39). See, too, Henry E. I. Phillips, "An Early Stuart Judaising Sect," *TJHSE* 15 (1946), pp. 63–72; and D. B. [John Falconer], *A Briefe Refutation of John Traskes Judaical and Novel Fancyes* (n.p., 1618).

45. See John Chamberlain's letter of February 14, 1618, to Sir Dudley Carleton, in Norman E. McClure, ed., *The Letters of John Chamberlain*, 2 vols. (Philadelphia: The American Philosophical Association, 1939), vol. 2, p. 65.

46. For an account of the Star Chamber sentence, see "Trask in the Star-Chamber, 1619," *Transactions of the Baptist Historical Society* 5 (1916–17), pp. 8–14.

47. "Trask in the Star-Chamber," p. 11.

48. As cited in Katz, *Philo-Semitism*, p. 24, from *The Court and Times of James the First*, ed. R. F. Williams (London, 1848), vol. 2, p. 77.

49. "Trask in the Star-Chamber," p. 9.

50. Even Francis Bacon took Traske seriously. Notes of his speech in Star Chamber in June 1618 read: "New opinions spread very dangerous, the late Traske a dangerous person. Apprentices learn the Hebrew tongue" (as cited in Katz, *Philo-Semitism*, p. 25, from James Spedding et al., eds., *The Letters and the Life of Francis Bacon* (London, 1872), vol. 6, p. 315. King James himself warns of the "zeal" that leads one to "become a Judaized Traskite," in his *A Meditation Upon the Lords Prayer* (London, 1619), p. 18 (as cited in Katz, *Philo-Semitism*, p. 25).

51. Edward Norice, *The New Gospel, Not the True Gospel* (London, 1638), p. 2; as cited in Katz, *Philo-Semitism*, p. 23.

52. E. Pagitt, *Heresiography* (6th ed.; London, 1661), p. 178; as cited in Katz, *Philo-Semitism*, p. 23.

53. As cited in Katz, *Philo-Semitism*, p. 24.

54. Katz, *Philo-Semitism*, p. 38; quoting *Oeconomy of the Fleete*, ed. A. Jessopp, *Camden Society*, n.s. 25 (1879), p. 47.

55. Prynne, *Short Demurrer*, part 2, p. 133.

56. Prynne, *Short Demurrer*, part 1, sig. A3v.

57. The debates in the House of Commons in 1621 convey a sense of the extent to which Traske's Judaizing and Sir Henry Finch's recent call for the restoration of the Jews in his *The Worlds Great Restauration. Or the Calling of the Jews* (London, 1621), entered the English political arena. On May 28, 1621, notes for "Sir Edward Coke's report for the Sabbath" read that there "was nothing objected to the body of the bill of the Sabbath but to the title. They would have the word Sabbath put out because many were inclined to Judaism and dream that the Jews shall have regiments and kings must lay down their crowns to their feet. Therefore it should be styled the Lord's day commonly called Sunday." An entry for May 25, 1621, makes explicit the impact of the Traskites: "The other was a Bill concerning the Sabbath, to the body of which there was no exception but only to the word Sabbath in the title. The reasons whereof were declared by the Archbishop, first the aptness of diverse [individuals] to incline to Judaism as the new sect of the Traskites [note: other manuscripts read here "Israelites"] and other opinionists concerning the term 'Kingdom of the Jews'" (Wallace Notestein, Frances H. Relf, and Hartley Simpson, eds., *Commons Debates, 1621*, 4 vols. (London: Oxford University Press, 1935), vol. 2, p. 397, and vol. 4, pp. 377–78.

58. Katz, *Philo-Semitism*, pp. 28–29; see too Pagitt, *Heresiography*, p. 168.

59. *Calendar of State Papers, Domestic* (1635–1636), p. 132.

60. For an excellent account of Tany's activities, see Katz, *Philo-Semitism*, pp. 107–20.

61. Lodowicke Muggleton, *The Acts of the Spirit* (London, 1699), pp. 20–21.

62. Anthony Wood, *Athenae Oxonienses* (London, 1817), vol. 3, p. 599.

63. From Thomas Tany, *Theauraujohn His Theousori Apokolipikal* (London, 1651), p. 42, as cited in Katz, *Philo-Semitism*, p. 111. Katz (p. 116) also notes that Tany and the millenarian John Robins are cited along with the false Jew of Hexham in the anonymous broadsheet, *A List of Some of the Grand Blasphemers* (London, 1654).

64. As cited in *Middlesex County Records*, ed. J. C. Jeffreson (Middlesex County Records Society, 1886–1892 [1888], vol. 3, pp. 186–87.

65. Prynne, *Short Demurrer*, part 1, p. 83.

66. From Montaigne's essay "De Dementir": "Car la Dissimulation Est de Plus Notable Qualitez de Ce Siècle," as cited in Perez Zagorin, *Ways of Lying: Dissimulation, Persecution, and Conformity in Early Modern Europe*, p. xi.

67. Gad ben Arad, pseud., *The Wandering-Jew*. The woodcut on the title page of *The Wandering-Jew* draws on some of the iconographic details found in Borde's *Fyrst Boke of the Introduction of Knowledge*, in which a bearded Jew appears in cloak, gown, and hat, though without any distinctive badge or any other distinguishing characteristic other than a staff. It also bears a resemblance to the portrait of another prognosticating Jew, Erra Pater, woodcuts of whom adorned the popular almanac that went through many editions in the late sixteenth and early seventeenth centuries (see illustration 11). If the woodcut of "Erra Pater's Prophesy, or Frost Faire, 1685" is any indication, the iconographic identification of Erra Pater and the Wandering Jew continued to be strong well into the late seventeenth century (note that Erra Pater appears barefoot here, as the Jew does in the woodcut on the title page of *The Wandering-Jew*; see illustration 14).

68. Gad ben Arad, *The Wandering-Jew*, sig. C2v.

69. W. M., *The Man on the Moone, Telling Strange Fortunes, or The English Fortune Teller* (London, 1609), reprinted in James O. Halliwell, ed., *Notices of Fugitive Tracts, and Chapbooks*, Percy Society Reprints, vol. 29 (London: Percy Society, 1849).

70. Thomas Collier, *Brief Answer to Some of the Objections and Demurs Made Against the Coming in and Inhabiting of the Jews in This Commonwealth* (London, 1656), R. Radin, ed., in Occasional Papers, English Series No. 3, Pamphlets Relating to the Jews in England during

the Seventeenth and Eighteenth Centuries (San Francisco: California State Library, 1939), p. 43.

71. Prynne, *Short Demurrer*, part 1, p. 73.

72. Prynne, *Short Demurrer*, part 1, pp. 72–73, 83–84.

73. [Paul Isaiah], Eleazar Bargishai, pseud., *A Brief Compendium of the Vain Hopes of the Jews Messias* (1652); [Paul Isaiah], Eleazar bar Isaiah, pseud., *The Messiah of the Christians, and the Jewes* (1655); and Paul Isaiah, *A Vindication of the Christian Messiah* (1653).

74. Wilfred S. Samuel, "The Strayings of Paul Isaiah in England," *TJHSE* 16 (1952), pp. 77–87.

75. Isaiah writes in *A Vindication of the Christian Messiah* that "I was by birth such a one as men commonly call a Jew, and was likewise circumcised upon the eighth day, as the manner of such people yet is" (sig. A4r).

76. The account that follows draws on the groundbreaking analysis of David Katz, in "The Case of the False Jew and After," *Sabbath and Sectarianism in Seventeenth-Century England* (Leiden: E. J. Brill, 1988), especially pp. 21–33.

77. Anon., *The Converted Jew: Or, The Substance of the Declaration and Confession Which Was Made in the Publique Meeting House at Hexam* (Newcastle, 1653); and Anon., *The Counterfeit Jew* (n.p., 1653). See, too, the version printed in Thomas Weld, Samuel Hammond, William Durant, et al., *A False Jew: Or, a Wonderfull Discovery of a Scot* (Newcastle, 1653).

78. *The Converted Jew*, sig. B4r.

79. *The Converted Jew*, sig. D1r.

80. *The Converted Jew*, sigs. Div, D2r, D2v.

81. From the 1620 entry in the commonplace book of Richard Shann, as cited in George K. Anderson, *The Legend of the Wandering Jew* (Providence: Brown University Press, 1965), pp. 64–65.

82. *The Converted Jew*, sigs. D4v, B3v, B4v.

83. *The Counterfeit Jew*, pp. 1–2.

84. *The Converted Jew*, sigs. B4v, C3r.

85. After "the converted Jew" acts "his last scene" in this earlier narrative, he unmasks himself and takes his leave "in the plain and natural dialect of an English priest" (John Clare [Roger Anderton], *The Converted Jew* [n.p., 1630], pt. 3, p. 142).

86. *The Counterfeit Jew*, p. 7.

87. See Katz, *Sabbath and Sectarianism*, p. 33. Fake Jews would persist into the eighteenth century, though in a literary guise. A good example is *The Complaint of the Children of Israel*, 7th ed. (London, 1736), published under the pseudonym of Solomon Abrabanel but in fact written by William Arnall, a young Whig political pamphleteer in Robert Walpole's service. See Paul Radin, ed., *Two Pamphlets on the History of the Jews in England*, Occasional Papers, English Series No. 4 (San Francisco: California State Library, 1940), pp. i–ii.

88. Sanderson kept two copies of his *Diary*; one survives in the British Library MS. Lansdowne 241; the other, now lost, was given to Samuel Purchas along with various papers, which were reprinted in Purchas, *Hakluytus Posthumus, or Purchas His Pilgrimes* (London, 1625). The materials given to Purchas provide the only source for anecdote described here.

89. Purchas, *Pilgrimes*, p. 1633, note h.

90. Sir William Foster, ed., *The Travels of John Sanderson in the Levant (1584–1602)*, Hakluyt Society, series 2, vol. 67 (London: Hakluyt Society, 1931), pp. 95, 124–25.

91. See, too, Edwin Sandys, *A View or Survey of the State of Religion in the Westerne Parts of the World* (London, 1632), where Sandys writes that some of the Jews he has known were "men of singular virtue and integrity of mind, seeming to want no grace but the faith of a Christian" (p. 226). Yet Sandys also draws on conventional stereotypes when he shortly thereafter describes the Jews as "obstinate within and scandalized without; indefatigable in per-

suasion, worldly, yet wretched; received of their enemies, but despised and hated; scattered over all countries, but nowhere planted" (p. 232).

92. See Joshua Trachtenberg, *The Devil and the Jews* (New Haven: Yale University Press, 1943).

93. See Sander Gilman, *The Jew's Body* (New York: Routledge, 1991); and Howard Eilberg-Schwartz, ed., *People of the Body: Jews and Judaism from an Embodied Perspective* (Albany: State University of New York Press, 1992).

94. Robert Burton, *The Anatomy of Melancholy* (Oxford, 1628), p. 57. Burton cites Buxtorf as his source. A similar claim, ostensibly based on first-hand observation, was offered in Edwin Sandys, *A Relation of a Journey* (London, 1615), where Jewish women are described as for the most part "goggle eyed" (p. 149).

95. Burton, *The Anatomy of Melancholy*, p. 57.

96. For a representative caricature, see the reproduction from the frontispiece of the "Roth 'Hake' Manuscript" in *Remember the Days: Essays on Anglo-Jewish History Presented to Cecil Roth*, ed. John Shaftesley (London: Jewish Historical Society of England, 1966). The tradition that those who played the part of Jews on the Elizabethan stage wore large false noses derives from three references. The first allusion appears in "The Forfeiture," a ballad first printed by the one-time actor Thomas Jordan in his *Royal Arbor of Loyal Poesie* (London, 1664). Modeled loosely on the plot of *The Merchant of Venice*, the ballad describes how the Jew's "beard was red," and "His chin turn'd up, his nose hung down, / And both ends met together." To conclude, as many early critics did, that these lines offer a portrait of Shylock as the role was originally performed, is to make an unwarranted leap from page to stage (for the ballad and its reception, see H. H. Furness, ed., *The Merchant of Venice, A New Variorum Edition* (Philadelphia: J. P. Lippincott, 1888), pp. 461–62. The second is found in William Rowley's fictional *A Search for Money* (1609), which describes a usurer with "an old moth-eaten cap buttoned under his chin, his visage (or vizard) like the artificial Jew of Malta's nose" (as cited in Marlowe, *The Jew of Malta*, N. W. Bawcutt, ed. [Manchester: Manchester University Press, 1978], p. 2). The third apppears in Marlowe's play itself, when Ithamore describes Barabas as "the bravest, gravest, secret, subtle, bottle-nosed knave." Bawcutt notes that the same phrase is used in Lupton's *All for Money* and George Chapman's *The Blind Beggar of Alexandria*—and in neither case do scholars conclude that these usurers were physically depicted onstage in this disguise. Nonetheless, scholars—such as G. K. Hunter—conclude on the basis of this hyperbolic description that this false nose was "used to present the Jew of Malta on the stage" (G. K. Hunter, "Elizabethans and Foreigners," *Shakespeare Survey* 17 [1964], p. 51). A better case needs to be made that this was the standard practice, or even the occasional practice, of companies using Henslowe's stage properties.

97. Peter van Rooden writes, in his "Conceptions of Judaism as a Religion in the Seventeenth-Century Dutch Republic," that even with the presence of a vibrant Jewish community, Christians nonetheless conceived of the Jews in their own theological image: "Dutch Christian theologians and scholars, whether Orthodox or dissenting, generally described Judaism as a kind of mirror-image of Christianity. They considered it to be a creed-oriented religion, attempting to found its principles on revelation. The ethical and legal rules, rituals, and ceremonies, the core of normative Judaism, were judged to be secondary" ("Conceptions of Judaism as a Religion in the Seventeenth-Century Dutch Republic," *Christianity and Judaism*, Studies in Church History 29, ed. Diana Wood [Oxford: Blackwell, 1992], p. 306).

98. Purchas, *Pilgrimes*, p. 144.

99. See Yovel, *Spinoza and Other Heretics*, vol. 1, p. 19–21. See too Yosef Yerushalmi, "Marranos Returning to Judaism in the Seventeenth Century: Their Jewish Knowledge and Psychological Readiness," *Proceedings of the Fifth World Congress of Jewish Studies* (Jerusalem, 1969), vol. 2, pp. 201–9 [Hebrew].

100. See Leone Modena, *The History of the Rites, Customes, and Manner of the Life of the Present Jews Throughout the World*, trans. Edmund Chilmead (London, 1650); Menasseh ben Israel, *Hope of Israel*, trans. Moses Wall (London, 1650); Menasseh ben Israel, *To His Highnesse the Lord Protector of the Common-wealth of England, Scotland, and Ireland, the Humble Addresses of Menasseh ben Israel* (1655?); and Menasseh ben Israel, *Vindiciae Judaeorum, or a Letter in Answer to Certain Questions Propounded by a Noble and Learned Gentleman, Touching the Reproaches Cast on the Nation of the Jewes; Wherein All Objections Are Candidly, and Yet Fully Cleared* (n.p., 1656). Menasseh's works are collected and reprinted in Lucien Wolf, ed., *Menasseh ben Israel's Mission to Oliver Cromwell* (London: MacMillan, 1901), from which subsequent references to his work are cited. See, too, Cecil Roth, "Leone da Modena and England," *TJHSE* 11 (1928) pp. 206–27; and Roth, "Leone da Modena and His English Correspondents," *TJHSE* 17 (1953), pp. 39–43.

241

↖

1. False Jews

and

Counterfeit

Christians

101. Blount, *Levant*, p. 113.

102. Blount, *Levant*, pp. 113–14. In terms of their modern professions, Jews were also identified at this time not only as merchants and usurers but also as secondhand clothes sellers, as a reference in Lewis Machin (?), *Every Woman in Her Humour* (1609) indicates. In the play a woman suggests to her neighbor that she "hire a good suit at a Jew's or a broker's; it is a common thing, and especially among the common people" (as cited in Sidney Lee, "Elizabethan England and the Jews," *New Shakspere Society Transactions* [1887–90], p. 148).

103. Blount, *Levant*, p. 123.

104. Blount, *Levant*, p. 119. A similar claim is made by James Howell in his "Epistle Dedicatory," dated February 5, 1650, to Joseph ben Gurion, *The Wonderful and Most Deplorable History of the Later Times of the Jews: With the Destruction of Jerusalem* (London, 1678), where he writes that the Jewish "nation is grown cowardly and cunning, even to a proverb, which must be imputed to their various thraldoms, contempt and poverty (which though it use to dastardize, and depress the courage, yet it whets the wit), for besides qualities, they are commonly light, and giddy-headed, much symbolizing in humor with some of the apocalyptical zealots of these times and bold expounders of Daniel, with the other prophets" (sig. B1v).

105. As cited in Friedman, "Jewish Conversion," pp. 16–17.

106. Purchas, *Pilgrimes*, p. 205.

107. Henry Buttes, *Dyets Dry Dinner* (London, 1599), sig. k8r. I am indebted to Mario Digangi for this reference.

108. See Israel Levi, "Le Juif de la Légende" *Revue des Études Juives* 20 (1890), pp. 249–52, and vols. 19 and 20 (1889–90), p. 239 and 101ff., respectively. Allusions to Jewish smell can be traced back to classical writing in the work of Martial and others.

109. Howell, "Epistle Dedicatory," *The Wonderful and Most Deplorable History*, sig. B2v.

110. Marlowe, *The Jew of Malta*, 2.3.45–47.

111. Thomas Dekker, *The Whore of Babylon* (London, 1607). As cited from Fredson Bowers, ed., *The Dramatic Works of Thomas Dekker*, 4 vols. (Cambridge: Cambridge University Press, 1953–1961), vol. 2, p. 557.

112. Browne, *Pseudodoxia Epidemica*, pp. 201–5.

113. As cited in Robin Robbins, ed., *Sir Thomas Browne's "Pseudodoxia Epidemica,"* 2 vols. (Oxford: Clarendon Press, 1981), vol. 2, p. 922.

114. Calvert, "Diatriba of the Jews' Estate," prefacing *Blessed Jew of Marocco*, p. 20.

115. Calvert, *Blessed Jew of Marroco*, p. 31. This needs to be located within a larger discussion of Jewish effeminacy, one that would include Cervantes, who calls the Jews "gente afeminada" (Baron, *Social and Religious History of the Jews*, vol. 11, p. 154).

116. Thomas de Cantimpré, *Miraculorum et Exemplorum Memorabilium Sui Temporis* (Duaci, 1597), p. 245, in the section that describes "Cur Judaei Christanum sanguinem effundant

242

.x̯

1. False Jews

and

Counterfeit

Christians

quotannis." For a valuable discussion of the notion of Jewish male menstruation (especially its influence on late nineteenth-century thought) see Sander L. Gilman, *The Case of Sigmund Freud: Medicine and Identity at the Fin de Siècle* (Baltimore: Johns Hopkins University Press, 1993), pp. 96–99. Gilman also cites a number of recent studies that cast light on the anthropological implications of this issue: Herbert Ian Hobgin, *The Island of Menstruating Men: Religion in Wogeo, New Guinea* (Scranton: Chandler, 1970); and James L. Brain, "Male Menstruation in History and Anthropology," *Journal of Psychohistory* 15 (1988), pp. 311–23. Brain argues that the practice of bloodletting as a form of symbolic menstruation—"based on the premise that female menstruation carries out the function of ridding the body of 'bad blood' so common in primitive societies" (such as that of Wogeo)—has "its counterpart" in western Europe in the practice of phlebotomy, or medicinal bleeding (p. 314). The practice was familiar enough to the Elizabethans, as is clear in works like Simon Harward's *Harward's Phlebotomy: Or a Treatise of Letting of Blood* (London, 1601). One of the points Harward makes in his treatise is that children should not be bled, a point underscored by almost all writers on the subject (pp. 72–76). Since illustrations of Jews committing ritual murder—such as the most influential one, which appeared in Hartmann Schedel's *Nuremburg Chronicle* (1493)—show Jews bleeding Simon of Trent from the genital area, it is worth speculating on whether at some deep level these representations of Jews bleeding Christian children are informed not only by the symbolic circumcision that is enacted, but also by the effeminizing act of extensive bleeding. See, too, Gail Kern Paster, "Laudable Blood: Bleeding, Difference, and Humoral Embarrassment," in *The Body Embarrassed: Drama and the Disciplines of Shame in Early Modern England* (Ithaca: Cornell University Press, 1993), pp. 64–112.

117. Heinrich Kormann, *Opera Curiosa I: Miracula Vivorum* (1614; Frankfurt, 1694), pp. 128–29; on Franco da Piacenza, see Leon Poliakov, *The History of Anti-Semitism*, trans. Richard Howard, 4 vols. (New York: Vanguard Press, 1965–1975), vol. 1., p. 143n.

118. See Shell, *The End of Kinship*, p. 157.

119. Alexander Ross, *A View of All Religions in the World* (London, 1672), p. 51.

120. Purchas, *Pilgrimage*, p. 182.

121. D'Blossiers Tovey, *Anglia Judaica: Or, the History and Antiquities of the Jews in England* (Oxford, 1738), p. 104.

122. A. Fernandez de Otero, *Tractatus de Officialibus Republicae* (1700), p. 158, as cited by Joseph Kaplan, "Jews and Judaism in the Political and Social Thought of Spain in the Sixteenth and Seventeenth Centuries," in Shmuel Almog, ed., *Antisemitism Through the Ages* (Oxford: Pergamon Press, 1988), pp. 153–60.

123. John Donne, from a sermon "Preached at Saint Paul's Cross, 6 May 1627," *Sermons*, vol. 7, p. 427.

124. Howell's "Epistle Dedicatory" to *The Wonderful and Deplorable History* is probably the first place where the belief is recorded that "it is thought diverse families of these banished Jews fled then to Scotland [after the 1290 Expulsion], where they have propagated since in great numbers, witness the aversion that nation hath above others to hog's flesh" (sig. A5v).

125. *The Athenian Mercury* (London, 1691), vol. 1, no. 1, question 13, as cited in Arthur H. Williamson, "'A Pil for Pork-Eaters': Ethnic Identity, Apocalyptic Promises, and the Strange Creation of the Judeo-Scots," in Raymond B. Waddington and Arthur H. Williamson, eds., *The Expulsion of the Jews: 1492 and After* (New York, 1994), p. 249.

126. Williamson, "A Pil for Pork-Eaters," pp. 246–47.

127. For an excellent discussion of the Scots as "a sort of Jews" see Arthur H. Williamson, "The Jewish Dimension of the Scottish Apocalypse: Climate, Covenant, and World Renewal," in Y. Kaplan, H. Méchoulan, and R. H. Popkin eds., *Menasseh ben Israel and His World* (Leiden: Brill, 1989), pp. 7–30; Williamson, "Latter-day Judah, Latter-day Israel: The Millen-

nium, the Jews, and the British Future," in *Chiliasmus in Deutschland und England im 17. Jahrhundert*, ed. Klaus Deppermann et al. (Göttingen, 1988), pp. 119–49; and Arthur H. Williamson, "Scotland, Antichrist, and the Invention of Great Britain," in *New Perspectives on the Politics and Culture of Early Modern Scotland*, ed. John Dwyer et al. (Edinburgh: J. Donald, 1982), pp. 34–58.

128. This covenant promised to realign Anglo-Scottish relations according to the precedent established by the twelve tribes of Israel. As an anonymous writer puts it in 1648: "Although we heartily desire to be one with you, one in religion, one in affection, and one in assistance, yet let us remain two kingdoms, through we hold parity of interest in things spiritual . . . yet like united Israel, covenanted Israel of old (in the dividing of lands of Canaan among their tribes) let you and we rejoice in our distinct portion" (Anon., *The Scottish Mist Dispell'd . . . by an English Covenanter* [London, 1648], p. 5, as cited in Williamson, "A Pil for Pork-Eaters," p. 243).

129. Williamson, "A Pil for Pork-Eaters," p. 244. Williamson underscores the point that for "a great many Scots, the Hebrew experience provided a vocabulary by which to imagine alternative institutions and an alternative union" (p. 244).

130. Toland also repeats the claim that the Jews fled to Scotland: a "great number of them fled to Scotland, which is the reason so many in that part of the island have such a remarkable aversion to pork and black-puddings to this day, not to insist on some other resemblances easily observable" [i.e., that the Scots were tightfisted] (John Toland, *Reasons for Naturalizing the Jews in Great Britain and Ireland, on the Same Foot with All Other Nations* (London, 1714), Dedication and pp. 37–38.

131. Thomas Thorowgood, *Jews in America, or, Probabilities, That Americans Are of That Race* (London, 1650).

132. Indeed, the young boy only spoke Hebrew, which meant that "his mother would sometimes be ready to weep, when he came to do his duty to her, or to ask any thing from her, and must not speak to her in English, so that she might have conferred with him, and talked to him again" (as cited in John Lightfoot's Preface to Hugh Broughton, *Works* [London, 1662], sig. B1r).

133. See G. Lloyd Jones, *The Discovery of Hebrew in Tudor England: A Third Language* (Manchester: Manchester University Press, 1983).

134. Simon Sturtevant, *Dibre Adam, or Adams Hebrew Dictionarie: A Rare and New Invention, for the Speedie Atteyning, and Perfect Reteyning, of the Hebrew, Chaldee, and Syriack* (London, 1602), p. 25.

135. Thomas Ingmethorpe, *A Short Cathechisme, by Law Authorized in the Church of England, for Young Children to Learne: Translated into Hebrew* (n.p., 1633).

136. Robert Wakefield, *On the Three Languages* (London, 1524), ed. and trans. with an intro. by G. Lloyd Jones (Binghamton, N.Y.: Medieval and Renaissance Texts and Studies, 1989), p. 178.

137. Borde, *Fyrst Boke of the Introduction of Knowledge*, p. 221.

138. William Lithgow, *The Total Discourse of the Rare Adventures and Painefill Peregrinations of Long Nineteene Yeares Travayles from Scotland* (London, 1632), pp. 115–16. First published in 1612.

139. Gilman, *The Case of Sigmund Freud*, p. 30. See too, Gilman's excellent discussion of "The Secret Tongue of the Jews," in *Jewish Self-Hatred: Anti-Semitism and the Hidden Language of the Jews* (Baltimore: Johns Hopkins University Press, 1986), pp. 139–48.

140. As Thomas Browne makes clear (notably, in the course of his discussion of Jewish difference), by the seventeenth century there was already considerable skepticism that "the immunity of Ireland from any venomous beast" could be attributed to "the staff or rod of Patrick" (Browne, *Pseudodoxia Epidemica*, p. 205).

243

1. False Jews and Counterfeit Christians

1. Hugh A. MacDougall, *Racial Myth in English History: Trojans, Teutons, and Anglo-Saxons* (Hanover, New Hampshire: University of New England Press, 1982), p. 7. The account that follows is deeply indebted to MacDougall's work.

2. MacDougall, *Racial Myth*, p. 26. The question of "British" as opposed to "English" identity is an extremely complex one, with much overlap between the terms, especially after 1603 and the accession of a Scottish king to the throne of England. While not conflating Britishness with Jewishness, my book is primarily concerned with Englishness, in large measure because it was Englishness rather than Britishness that was juxtaposed with Jewishness (hence the alignment of the Jews with the Scots and even the Irish). As such, this book tries to provide some historical context for the view that Britain today is experiencing not only "an unravelling of the current form of union between Britain's component nations" but also "an unravelling of English national culture itself, as the English struggle to shake off the inherited mythologies which distort their perception of themselves and their relations with neighbouring peoples" (John Gray, "Whatever Happened to Englishness?" *TLS*, November 4, 1994, p. 26).

3. As cited in MacDougall, *Racial Myth*, p. 47.

4. See MacDougall, *Racial Myth*, pp. 31–70.

5. MacDougall, *Racial Myth*, p. 127.

6. W. J. Jackson, "Ethnology and Phrenology as an Aid to the Biographer," *Anthropological Review and Journal* 2 (1864), pp. 126–40, as cited in Richard Halpern, "Shakespeare in the Tropics: From High Modernism to New Historicism," *Representations* 45 (1994), pp. 2–3.

7. Peter Aldag, *Juden in England* (Berlin: Nordland Verlag, 1941), pp. 9–10. I am grateful to Ursula Heise for her help translating this material.

8. Edward Brerewood, *Enquiries Touching the Diversity of Languages, and Religions Through the Chiefe Parts of the World* (London, 1614), p. 92.

9. Colin Richmond, "Englishness and Medieval Anglo-Jewry," in Tony Kushner, ed., *The Jewish Heritage in British History: Englishness and Jewishness* (London: Frank Cass, 1992), p. 44.

10. For a useful overview, see Robert Stacey, "Recent Work on Medieval English Jewish History," *Jewish History* 2 (1987), pp. 61–72.

11. Vivian D. Lipman, "The Anatomy of Medieval Anglo-Jewry," *TJHSE* 21 (1968), p. 64.

12. Lipman, "Anatomy," p. 64–67. See, too, Roth, *History*, pp. 276–77.

13. See Zephira Entrin Rokeah, "The Expulsion of the Jews from England in 1290 A.D.: Some Aspects of Its Background," Diss., Columbia University, 1986, pp. 40–49.

14. Purchas, *Pilgrimage*, p. 153.

15. Anon., *The Case of the Jewes Stated: Or the Jewes Synagogue Opened* (London, 1656), sig. A2r.

16. Thomas Scales, "The Original, or Moderne Estate, Profession, Practise and Condition of the Nation of the Jewes," Huntington Library MS. 205, "Scales's Abridgment," (c. 1630), fol. 20.

17. Roth, *History*, p. 87.

18. Raphael Holinshed, *The Chronicles of England, Scotlande, and Ireland*, 3 vols. (London, 1587), vol. 3, p. 285.

19. Holinshed, *Chronicles*, vol. 3, p. 285.

20. Edward Coke, "Of Usury," *The Third Part of the Institutes of the Laws of England* (London 1644), pp. 151–52.

21. Roth, *History*, pp. 275–76.

22. See Issac Hayyim Contarini's *Pahad Yitzhak* (Amsterdam, 1685); cf. Cecil Roth's "England and the Ninth of Ab," in *Essays and Portraits in Anglo-Jewish History* (Philadelphia: Jewish Publication Society of America, 1962), pp. 63–67.

23. Roth, *History*, p. 90.

24. Tovey, *Anglia Judaica*, pp. 232–34. Cf. Charles Egan, who observes a century later that "as both English and Jewish writers have stated very different and conflicting opinions as to the cause of the departure of the Jews from England, we are naturally led to inquire, whether their emigration hence did not arise from causes quite different from those hitherto affirmed" (Egan, *The Status of the Jews in England, from the Time of the Norman Conquest to the Reign of Her Majesty Queen Victoria, Impartially Considered* [London, R. Hastings, 1848], p. 13).

25. Barnett Lionel Abrahams, *The Expulsion of the Jews from England in 1290* (Oxford: Blackwell, 1895), pp. 74–75. See, too, his essay "The Condition of the Jews of England at the Time of Their Expulsion in 1290," *TJHSE* 2 (1895), pp. 76–105.

26. Samuel Usque, *Consolation for the Tribulations of Israel* (Ferrara, 1553), trans. from the Portuguese by Martin A. Cohen (Philadelphia: Jewish Publication Society of America, 1965), pp. 181–84.

27. Usque, *Consolation*, pp. 183–84.

28. Lucien Wolf, "Jews in Tudor England," *Essays in Jewish History*, ed. Cecil Roth (London: Jewish Historical Society of England, 1934), pp. 87–89.

29. As cited by Tovey, *Anglia Judaica*, p. 234.

30. John Stow, *A Survey of London* (London, 1603), p. 283.

31. Samuel Daniel, *The Collection of the History of England*, 4th ed. (London, 1650), p. 190.

32. Prynne, *Short Demurrer*, part 1, sig. A3v.

33. Prynne, *Short Demurrer*, part 1, pp. 61–63.

34. Tovey, *Anglia Judaica*, p. 252.

35. On the problems raised by Jewish immigration in Victorian England, see, for example, Bernard Gainer, *The Alien Invasion: The Origins of the Aliens Act of 1905* (London: Heinemann, 1972); John Gerrard, *The English and Immigration 1880–1910* (London: Oxford University Press, 1971); Lloyd Gartner, *The Jewish Immigrant in England 1870–1914* (Detroit: Wayne State University Press, 1960); Eugene C. Black, *The Social Politics of Anglo-Jewry* (Oxford: Blackwell, 1988); Sharman Kadish, *Bolsheviks and British Jews: The Anglo-Jewish Community, Britain, and the Russian Revolution* (London: Frank Cass, 1992); and David Feldman, *Englishmen and Jew: Social Relations and Political Culture 1840–1914* (New Haven: Yale University Press, 1994).

36. Roth, *History*, pp. 72–73. Roth echoes B. L. Abrahams, who wrote in 1895 that the "Expulsion was a piece of independent royal action, made necessary by the impossibility of carrying out the only alternative policy that an honourable Christian king could adopt" (Abrahams, *The Expulsion of the Jews*, p. 74).

37. Colin Richmond, "Englishness and Medieval Anglo-Jewry," pp. 44. The same term is used by Rokeah, who writes that in 1290 "the whole of the Jewish community was expelled from England, producing a *Judenrein* state that lasted for some 350 years" ("The Expulsion," p. 1).

38. Richmond, "Englishness and Medieval Anglo-Jewry," p. 56.

39. See, for example, Robert Hewison, *The Heritage Industry: Britain in a Climate of Decline* (London, 1987); Patrick Wright, *On Living in an Old Country: The National Past in Contemporary Britain* (London, 1985); and Tony Kushner, "Heritage and Ethnicity: An Introduction," in Kushner, ed., *The Jewish Heritage in British History*, pp. 1–28.

40. An early advocate of the claim that the Expulsion was also about "nationalism" is Salo Baron, who writes that a "preoccupation with the Jewish problem deeply affected English national thinking." Baron's sense of nation here is based on ethnicity: "Edward is rightly considered the monarch under whose regime the Franco-Norman and Anglo-Saxon ethnic strains were finally fused into the new English nation, creating a fairly cohesive national

state" (*Social and Religious History of the Jews*, vol. 11, pp. 208–10). Cecil Roth adds that the emergence of British constitutionalism may also have been a by-product of the Expulsion, since from "this date the detailed regulation of finance by the representatives of the people became possible. It was thus not without its significance—though the importance of this fact should not be exaggerated—that the Model Parliament of Edward I assembled, and the English constitution received its shape, four years [1294] after the Expulsion" (*History*, p. 90).

41. In his essays Robert Stacey is more interested in establishing the political, legal, and economic changes that brought about the Expulsion than in the nationalist implications of these changes. His forthcoming book promises to address a wider set of concerns. See Stacey, "The Conversion of Jews to Christianity in Thirteenth-Century England," *Speculum* 67 (1992), pp. 263–83; "Thirteenth-Century Anglo-Jewry and the Problem of the Expulsion, in *Exile and Return: Anglo-Jewry Through the Ages*, ed. David Katz and Yosef Kaplan (Jerusalem: Zalman Shazar Center for Jewish History, 1993 [note: this essay is in Hebrew; I quote from an earlier unpublished English version Stacey generously provided]); "Royal Taxation and the Social Structure of Medieval Anglo-Jewry: The Tallage of 1239–42," *Hebrew Union College Annual* 56 (1985), pp. 175–249; "1240–1260: A Watershed in Anglo-Jewish Relations?," *Historical Research* 61 (1988), pp. 35–50; and Stacey's as yet unpublished and untitled talk delivered at the Association for Jewish Studies, December 14, 1992 (cited here as "Association").

42. Stacey, "Association," p. 1.

43. Stacey, "Association," pp. 2–4, 10–12.

44. Stacey, "Thirteenth-Century," pp. 11–12, 21.

45. Kenneth Stow, *Alienated Minority: The Jews of Medieval Latin Europe* (Cambridge: Harvard University Press, 1992).

46. Stow, *Alienated Minority*, pp. 285–86, 295.

47. Tovey, *Anglia Judaica*, p. 274.

48. Roth, "The Resettlement of the Jews in England in 1656," in V. D. Lipman, ed., *Three Centuries of Anglo-Jewish History* (London: W. Heffer and Sons, for the Jewish Historical Society of England, 1961), p. 15.

49. Josselin, *Diary*, p. 337.

50. Tovey, *Anglia Judaica*, pp. 245–46.

51. Stow, *Survay of London*, p. 39.

52. Tovey, *Anglia Judaica*, p. 269.

53. See for example, David S. Katz, "English Redemption and Jewish Readmission in 1656," *Journal of Jewish Studies* 34 (1983), pp. 73–91; Nathan Osterman, "The Controversy Over the Proposed Readmission of the Jews to England (1655)," *Jewish Social Studies* 3 (1941), pp. 301–28; Don Patinkin, "Mercantilism and the Readmission of the Jews to England," *Jewish Social Studies* 8 (1946), pp. 161–78. The definitive work on the subject remains David Katz, *Philo-Semitism*.

54. Prynne, *Short Demurrer*, part 1, pp. 89, 99.

55. Edgar Samuel, "The Readmission of the Jews to England in 1656, in the Context of English Economic Policy," *TJHSE* 31 (1990), p. 167.

56. Roth, *History*, p. 85.

57. Prynne, *Short Demurrer*, part 1, pp. 61–63. For an even more vehement attack upon the Jews, see W. H., *Anglo-Judaeus, or the History of the Jews Whilst Here in England* (London, 1656).

58. Tovey, *Anglia Judaica*, p. 274. For reaction to Menasseh ben Israel's presence, see David S. Katz, "Edmund Gayton's Anti-Jewish Poem Addressed to Menasseh ben Israel, 1656," *The Jewish Quarterly Review* 71 (1981), pp. 239–250. See, too, *Menasseh ben Israel and His World*, ed. Yosef Kaplan, Henry Méchoulan, and Richard H. Popkin; Popkin, J. E., *The Great*

Deliverance of the Whole House of Israel . . . in Answer to a Book Called, "The Hope of Israel," Written by a Learned Jew of Amsterdam Named Menasseh ben Israel (London, 1652); and Margaret Fell, For Menasseh ben Israel. The Call of the Jewes out of Babylon (London, 1656).

59. Roth, "The Resettlement of the Jews in England in 1656," p. 15.

60. For some examples of this, see Calender of State Papers, Domestic (1655–56), including the letter from H. Robinson on December 31, 1655, that the "Jews, we hear, will be admitted by way of connivency, though the generality oppose" (p. 82). See, too, the correspondence between Captain Francis Willoughby and Robert Blackborne that touches upon Jewish readmission during the month of December: Willoughby was clearly against the proposal; he writes from Portsmouth on December 10, 1655, that "I observe that the great business of the Jews is under consideration; I hope the Lord will direct in a matter of such concernment. If the first question should pass in the affirmative, whether a Jewish nation shall be admitted to live in this commonwealth, I hope the next will be whether a nation shall be suffered by a law to live amongst us to blaspheme Christ" (p. 51).

61. H. S. Q. Henriques, The Return of the Jews to England (London: Macmillan, 1905), p. 37, who cites this from The History of the Independency (London, 1649).

62. For scholarship on this period of Anglo-Jewish history, see Lucien Wolf, "Crypto-Jews Under the Commonwealth," TJHSE 1 (1894), pp. 14–48; M. Woolf, "Foreign Trade of London Jews in the Seventeenth Century," TJHSE 24 (1973), pp. 55–88; A. S. Diamond, "The Community of the Resettlement, 1654–1684: A Social Survey," TJHSE 24 (1973), pp. 134–50; Roth, "The Resettlement of the Jews in England," pp. 1–25; Isaiah Tishbi, "New Information on the 'Converso' Community in London," pp. 470–96; and David S. Katz, The Jews in the History of England, 1485–1850 (Oxford: Clarendon Press, 1994), pp. 107–89.

63. As cited in Roth, History, p. 160.

64. Wilbur Cortez Abbott, ed., The Writings and Speeches of Oliver Cromwell, 4 vols. (Oxford: Clarendon Press, 1947, rpt. 1988), vol. 4, p. 34.

65. Browne, Pseudodoxia Epidemica, p. 202.

66. Tovey, Anglia Judaica, p. 49.

67. Isaiah, The Messiah of the Christians, sig. B3r.

68. Henry Jessey, A Narrative of the Late Proceedings at White-Hall Concerning the Jews (London, 1656).

69. Tovey, Anglia Judaica, p. 270.

70. As cited in Henriques, Return of the Jews, p. 43.

71. For subsequent versions of these events, see, for example, Nathaniel Crouch [published under the pseudonym Robert Burton], "The Proceedings of the Jews in England in the Year 1655," in Two Journies to Jerusalem (London?, 1730), pp. 169–76.

72. Michael Roberts, ed., Swedish Diplomats at Cromwell's Court 1655–1656: The Missions of Peter Julius Coyet and Christer Bonde, Camden fourth series, vol. 36 (London: Royal Historical Society, 1988), p. 224.

73. Henriques, Return of the Jews, p. 46.

74. Jessey, Narrative, p. 10.

75. Calender of State Papers, Venetian (1665–66), pp. 160–61, as cited in Katz, Philo-Semitism, pp. 226–27.

76. Josselin, Diary, p. 358.

77. Henriques, Return of the Jews, p. 67; cited from Nicholas Papers, vol. 3, p. 255. Cromwell's editor also mentions the contemporary rumor that Jews had offered Cromwell two hundred thousand pounds as a gift or loan for his support (The Writings and Speeches of Oliver Cromwell, vol. 4, p. 52). See, too, Lucien Wolf, "Cromwell's Jewish Intelligencers," in Roth, ed., Essays in Jewish History, pp. 91–114.

78. Henriques, Return of the Jews, p. 51. See, too, Harold Pollins, Economic History of the Jews in

England (London: Associated University Presses, 1982), p. 33. An attempt to reconcile the contradictory positions of the society on the issue of Readmission appears in the pages of its *Transactions*: "The Fourth of February was last year [1894] celebrated by the Society as 'Resettlement Day.' It is proposed to make this an annual commemoration, for though Jews were living in England between 1290 and the time of Cromwell, yet the real modern history of the Jews of England commences from the formal toleration by the Protector in the middle of the seventeenth century." *TJHSE* 1 (1894), p. 161.

79.   David Cesarani, "Dual Heritage or Duel of Heritages? Englishness and Jewishness in the Heritage Industry," in Kushner, ed., *The Jewish Heritage in British History*, p. 35.

80.   As cited in Cesarani, "Dual Heritage," p. 35 and p. 40 n. 20, from *TJHSE* 5 (1908), pp. 278–79. Cf. The *Jewish Chronicle*, April 21, 1899, pp. 17–18.

81.   *TJHSE* 6 (1908), pp. 281, 296.

82.   See Tony Kushner, "Anti-Semitism and Austerity: The August 1947 Riots in Britain," in Panikos Panayi, ed., *Racial Violence in Britain, 1840–1950* (Leicester: Leicester University Press, 1993), pp. 149–68, which explores how the riots (primarily in Liverpool, Manchester, and Glasgow) have been written out of modern British history and consciousness.

83.   *Three Hundred Years: A Volume to Commemorate the Tercentenary of the Re-Settlement of the Jews on Great Britain, 1656–1956* (London: Vallentine Mitchell, 1957). This tradition continues: David Cesarani notes that when "Manchester Jewry organized a celebration of its bicentenary in 1988, the major event took place in the grounds of Chatsworth House—home of the Duke of Devonshire. The Duke is a firm and generous friend of Israel, but otherwise there was no reason for the choice of location other than the desire to identify with rural aristocratic English heritage in its classical form" ("Dual Heritage," p. 38).

84.   Hughes, *Anglo-Judaeus*, pp. 49, 34.

85.   Prynne, *Short Demurrer*, part 1, p. 103. Prynne also writes that "it was a very ill time to bring in the Jews, when the people were so dangerously and generally bent to apostasy . . . and would sooner turn Jew than Jews Christian." The fascination with "turning" Jewish, evident in Josselin's dream, finds a place in Prynne's account as well, not only in this last quotation, but in his citation of "maimed soldiers" in the streets of London who complain that "we must now all turn Jews, and there will be nothing left for the poor," and further, that they "are all turned devils already, and now we must all turn Jews" (sig. A3v).

86.   Prynne, *Short Demurrer*, part 1, pp. 103–4.

87.   Howell, *The Wonderful and Most Deplorable History*, as cited in Katz, *Philo-Semitism*, p. 191.

88.   John Richard Green, *A Short History of the English People* (London, 1884), p. 205.

89.   Lucien Wolf, "A Plea for Anglo-Jewish History," *TJHSE* 1 (1894), p. 6.

90.   Baldwin Smith, *A History of England*, 3rd ed. (New York: Scribners, 1966), p. 97.

91.   Sidney Lee, "Elizabethan England and the Jews," pp. 143–66.

92.   Green, *Short History of the English People*, p. 205; cf. the later edition, rev. by Alice Stopford Green (New York: American Book, 1916), which repeats this verbatim.

93.   Green, *Short History of the English People*, pp. 337–39.

94.   J. M. Rigg edited the 1902 selection as well as the first two volumes of the *Calendar* in 1905 and 1910; H. Jenkinson edited the third in 1929; and H. G. Richardson completed volume 4, taking the records up to 1277, in 1972. The most recent scholarly analysis of the Plea Rolls by Barrie Dobson emphasizes that not only Jewish men but many Jewish women as well were involved in business relations with Christian neighbors. See Dobson, "The Role of Jewish Women in Medieval England," in *Christianity and Judaism*, Studies in Church History 29, ed. Diana Wood (Oxford: Blackwell, 1992), p. 155.

95.   Arthur Quiller-Couch, *On the Art of Writing* (Cambridge: Cambridge University Press, 1916), pp. 139–40, as cited in Brian Doyle, *English and Englishness* (London: Routledge,

1989), p. 21.

96.   Luke Owen Pike, *A History of Crime in England Illustrating the Changes of the Law in the Progress of Civilization* (London: Smith, Elder, 1873), pp. 184–85.

97.   Sidney J. Low and F. S. Pullin eds., *Dictionary of English History* (London: Cassell, 1897). The *Dictionary* was a popular work, first published in 1884 and reprinted in 1885 and 1889, before a newly revised edition was published in 1896 and reprinted in 1897, 1904, and 1910.

98.   Low and Pullin, *Dictionary of English History*, 1910 ed., p. 628.

99.   Indeed, one can still search in vain for any trace of the Jews in England's past in recent surveys like Geoffrey Elton's *The English* (Oxford: Blackwell, 1992). This is all the more remarkable, since Elton, an eminent British historian, acknowledges that he himself was a European Jewish refugee. His book is one in a series "about the European tribes and peoples from their origins in prehistory until their present day." Should it come as a surprise when a series that includes volumes on the Gypsies and the Illyrians omits the history of the Jews in Europe?

100.   For a partisan acccount of the foundation of the society, see Lucien Wolf, "Origins of the Jewish Historical Society of England," *TJHSE* 7 (1915), pp. 206–21.

101.   J. B. Blank, *The Reign of Elizabeth, 1558–1603*, 2d ed. (Oxford: Clarendon Press, 1959).

102.   Smith, *A History of England*, p. 97.

103.   Gavin I. Langmuir, *Toward a Definition of Antisemitism* (Berkeley and Los Angeles: University of California Press, 1990), pp. 21–41.

104.   Langmuir, *Definition*, pp. 39–41.

105.   Wolf, "A Plea," pp. 1–7.

106.   Cesarani, "Dual Heritage," p. 36. Cromwell, Disraeli, and Gladstone were each in their own day perceived of as "Jewish."

107.   *Jewish Chronicle*, May 20, 1887, p. 5. For a recent study of the role of this newspaper in Anglo-Jewish affairs, see David Cesarani, *The "Jewish Chronicle" and Anglo-Jewry, 1841–1991* (Cambridge: Cambridge University Press, 1994).

108.   "Communal Self-Knowledge," *Jewish Chronicle*, May 20, 1887, pp. 8–9.

109.   *Calender of State Papers, Spanish* (1485–1509), p. 164. See, too, A. Schosche, "Spanish Jews in London in 1494," *TJHSE* 24 (1975), pp. 214–15.

110.   My account of Raphael's role in the divorce is based on the research of Katz, *Jews in the History of England, 1485–1850*, pp. 40–48.

111.   Michael Adler, "History of the 'Domus Conversorum' from 1290 to 1891," *TJHSE* 4 (1903), pp. 39–40. See *Letters and Papers, Foreign and Domestic, of Henry VIII*, eds. J. S. Brewer, J. Gairdner, and R. S. Brodie, 21 vols. (1862–1932), vol. 5, p. 1649, for an allusion to a Portuguese woman who renounced her Judaism.

112.   The only exception was the period between 1554 and 1578. For a comprehensive account of this institution, see Adler, "Domus Conversorum," pp. 16–75.

113.   See Wolf, "Jews in Tudor England," p. 3.

114.   Wolf, "Jews in Tudor England," pp. 79ff.

115.   Wolf, "Jews in Tudor England," p. 81.

116.   As cited by Susan Bridgen, *London and the Reformation* (Oxford: Clarendon Press, 1989), pp. 136–37, who gives as her source *PRO*, KB 9/547/45–6.

117.   *Acts of the Privy Council* (1540–1542), p. 304.

118.   Roger Prior, "A Second Jewish Community in Tudor London," *TJHSE* 31 (1990), p. 140. One of the most interesting of the Bassanos was Aemilia Lanyer, daughter of Giovanni Baptista Bassano and Margaret Johnson, who was christened on January 27, 1569, and raised in the Protestant household of the Dowager Countess of Kent. Aemilia Bassano went on to write a remarkable volume of religious verse with the surprising title *Salve Deus Rex Judaeorum* (1611). Bassano herself explains the title to "the doubtful reader" as follows: "if thou

desire to be resolved, why I give this title . . . know for certain that it was delivered unto me in sleep many years before I had any intent to write in this manner, and was quite out of memory, until I had written the Passion of Christ, when immediately it came into my remembrance, what I had dreamed long before" (Susanne Woods, ed., *The Poems of Aemilia Lanyer* [New York: Oxford University Press, 1993], p. 139). It is tempting to speculate that the dream that inspired this title was somehow related to Bassano's own Jewish roots. For more biographical details, see Lorna Hutson's entry on Bassano in *The Dictionary of Literary Biography: Missing Persons*, ed. C. S. Nicholls (Oxford: Oxford University Press, 1993), pp. 388–89.

119. Wolf, "Jews in Tudor England," pp. 84–89.

120. Wolf, "Jews in Tudor England," pp. 87–89.

121. Lucien Wolf, "Jews in Elizabethan England," *TJHSE* 11 (1928), pp. 4–5.

122. As cited in Paul Slack, *Poverty and Policy in Tudor and Stuart England* (London: Longman, 1988), p. 70. There are also ambiguous cases such as "Nathaniel Carnet, buried at St. Ann Blackfriars" in 1590. Carnet is described as a "Ieish" or "Jeish" boy (*GHL*, MS. 4510/1). It could also be a mangled version of "Irish." I am grateful to Roslyn Knutson for bringing this example to my attention.

123. *Acts of the Privy Council* (1547–1550), p. 28.

124. As cited in Katz, *Philo-Semitism*, p. 40.

125. Wolf, "Jews in Elizabethan England," p. 7. He adds that the "Portuguese Jews . . . then living in London . . . were all in favour of England" and he names, among others, Hector Nuñez, William Ames, and a dozen or so more. See too *Calender of State Papers, Spanish* (1587–1603), p. 326.

126. Thomas Coryate, *Coryate's Crudities; Reprinted from the Edition of 1611*, 3 vols. (London, 1776), vol. 3, sigs. U8r and U8v.

127. Edgar Samuel, "Passover in Shakespeare's London," *TJHSE* 26 (1979), pp. 117–18.

128. Wolf, "Jews in Elizabethan England," p. 19. See Wolf's appendix for a list of their names.

129. Wolf, "Jews in Elizabethan England," p. 21, and for a transcript, p. 68.

130. Roth, *History*, pp. 141–42; and C. J. Sisson, "A Colony of Jews in Shakespeare's London," *Essays and Studies* 23 (1938), pp. 41–51.

131. Charles Wriothesley, *A Chronicle of England During the Reign of the Tudors*, ed. William Douglas Hamilton (London: Camden Society, 1877), vol. 2, pp. 36–37.

132. See Frank Marcham, ed., *Lopez the Jew: An Opinion, by Gabriel Harvey* (London: Waterlow and Sons, 1927).

133. Lopez is also noted for his skill in the "art of destroying children in women's bellies," in *Leicester's Commonwealth* (1584), ed. D. C. Peck (Athens, Ohio: Ohio State University Press, 1985), p. 116.

134. As quoted in Edgar Samuel, "Dr Roderigo Lopes' Last Speech from the Scaffold at Tyburn," *TJHSE* 30 (1989), pp. 51–52.

135. Francis Bacon, *Works*, ed. James Spedding, Robert L. Ellis, and Douglas D. Heath, 15 vols. (London: Longman, 1862), vol. 8, p. 278. For this statement Spedding also cites Harl. MSS. 871, p. 59.

136. The illustration, which first appeared in *Popish Plots and Treasons from the Beginning of the Reign of Queen Elizabeth* (London, 1606), was popular enough to be reprinted in George Carleton, *A Thankfull Remembrance of Gods Mercy* (London, 1627).

137. Sidney Lee, "The Original of Shylock," *The Gentleman's Magazine* 248 (1880), p. 200.

138. Arthur Dymock, "The Conspiracy of Dr. Lopez," *English Historical Review* 9 (1894), p. 472.

139. Katz, *Jews in the History of England*, p. 105. Katz's meticulous account of the Lopez affair conclusively demonstrates that Lopez was involved in a conspiracy to poison the Queen. As

the first major Jewish historian to make this claim, Katz is well aware of what is at stake in his position: the "entire question of Jewish involvement in the numerous plots against Queen Elizabeth I has been one of extreme sensitivity for Anglo-Jewry, to the extent that suggesting any guilt by individual Jews was tantamount to a declaration of anti-Semitism" (p. 49).

140. For more on Lopez, see John Gwyer, "The Case of Dr Lopez," *TJHSE* 16 (1952), pp. 163–84; and M. Hume, "The So-Called Conspiracy of R. Lopez," *TJHSE* 6 (1912), pp. 32–55.

141. The following account is based on Lewis S. Feuer, "Francis Bacon and the Jews: Who Was the Jew in the *New Atlantis?*" *TJHSE* 29 (1988), pp. 1–25; and Israel Abrahams, "Joachim Gaunse: A Mining Incident in the Reign of Queen Elizabeth," *TJHSE* 4 (1903), pp. 83–101.

142. The surviving documents are reprinted in Abrahams, "Joachim Gaunse," pp. 99–101.

143. Abrahams, "Joachim Gaunse," pp. 99–101.

144. Hugh Broughton, *Two Epistles Unto Great Men of Britanie, in the Yeare 1599*, 2d ed. (Basil, 1606), sig. B1r.

145. Sir William Foster, ed., *The Voyages of Sir James Lancaster to Brazil and the East Indies, 1591–1603*, Hakluyt Society, series 2, vol. 85 (London, Hakluyt Society, 1940), pp. 96–97. Cf. B. L. Abrahams, "A Jew in the Service of the East India Company in 1601," *Jewish Quarterly Review* 9 (1897), pp. 173–75.

146. Cecil Roth, "Jews in Oxford after 1290," *Oxoniensia* 15 (1950), p. 64. Biblical scholars, too, had recourse to Jews, though again, most remain nameless. For example, we learn from a casual remark of Ralph Skynner in a letter to James Ussher in 1624, that he talked with "three Jews . . . and asked them the reason why they omitted these gutterals, *Cheth, He, Ayin*, in words, by reason of which their pronunciation was difficult to be understood by us which pronounced them" (*Miscellanies of the JHSE* 3 [1937], p. 63).

147. See Lionel Abrahams, "Two Jews before the Privy Council and an English Law Court in 1614–15," *Jewish Quarterly Review* 14 (1902), pp. 354–58.

148. E. R. Samuel, "Portuguese Jews in Jacobean London," *TJHSE* 18 (1958), pp. 179–80. Lopez's name appear in "Return of Aliens," vol. 3, Huguenot Society (Aberdeen, 1908), pp. 53, 55, 124, 125, 282. Waad's comment appears in *HMC Salisbury*, vol. 2, p. 253. Cf. Wolf, "Jews in Elizabethan England," p. 22.

149. Hugh Broughton, *Our Lordes Familie* [London, 1608], cited in Roth, *History*, p. 144n1.

150. Richard H. Popkin, "A Jewish Merchant of Venice," *Shakespeare Quarterly* 40 (1989), pp. 329–31.

151. Adler, "Domus Conversorum," pp. 46–47.

152. Philip Ferdinand, *Haec Sunt Verba Dei* (Cambridge, 1597). See Roth, "Jews in Oxford After 1290," p. 64; Roth, "The Jews in the English Universities," *MJHSE* 4 (1942), pp. 102–15; and Siegfried Stein, "Phillipus Ferdinandus Polonus, A Sixteenth-Century Hebraist in England," in I. Epstein, E. Levine, and C. Roth, eds., *Essays in Honour of the Very Reverend Dr. J. H. Hertz* (London: Edward Goldston, 1943), pp. 397–412.

153. E. R. Samuel, "Portuguese Jews in Jacobean London," p. 183. See Roth, *History*, pp. 283–84, for the Italian originals.

154. To cite two examples: the Elizabethan collection, *The Schoolemaster*, includes a story in the section on the "merry jests of the Jews," in which a "good fellow in Merseborough in an evening stole away a poor widow's cow, and brought her in the night unto a Jew to whom he pawned her for five shillings, and the same night he stole her away again from that Jew, and pawned her unto another Jew for so much money, and again the same night he stole her from him and and pawned her unto the third Jew for the like sum. Then devising with himself how the widow might come by her cow again, he stole her likewise from the third Jew, and brought her home in the morning betimes by the horns. And meeting with the widow's

maid that was going to the brook to wash clothes, he chid her, saying, that if he had not been, the cow had been lost forever. Thus the knave served his own necessity for money, deceived the greedy Jews and restored the widow her cow" ([Thomas Twyne?], *The Schoolemaster, or Teacher of Table Philosophie* [London, 1576], sig. N4r). The second example appears in the journal of Roberk Kirk, a Scottish minister visiting London in 1689, who records a story he was told of a "rich citizen who first built the Royal Exchange in Cornhill, hearing from abroad that his reputation and credit among merchants were lessened as being nigh broke by those vast buildings, and hearing of a Jew to whom Queen Elizabeth refused £6000 stg. for a jewel he had, sent for him, took the jewel, caused bray it, put it in a drink, and quaffed it off. Then paying for it the full price to repair his credit, he bid the Jew tell in all nations where he travelled that Queen Elizabeth had a subject that drank £6000 stg. at his morning draught" (in Donald Maclean, ed., "London in 1689–90," *Transactions of the London and Middlesex Archeological Society* n.s. 6 ([1929–1933], p. 657).

155. G. K. Hunter, "The Theology of Marlowe's *The Jew of Malta*," *The Journal of the Warburg and Courtauld Institutes* 27 (1964), p. 215.

156. Marlis, *Jewess*, p. 93. The only copy of Marlis's book that I have come across is in the collection of the Jewish Theological Seminary in New York City.

157. Baker, *Bardolotry*, p. 27.

158. This reconstruction of the English past has also been quietly framed in reaction against late nineteenth- and early twentieth-century continental writers such as Richard Wagner and Otto Weininger, who derided England's claims to cultural greatness and suggested that the absence of genius in England was best explained by the pervasive Jewishness of its people. Thus, for Weininger, it "cannot be doubted that of the Germanic races the English are in closest relationship to the Jews. Their orthodoxy and their devotion to the Sabbath afford a direct indication." Moreover, like the religion of the Jews, the "religion of the Englishman is always tinged with hypocrisy, and his asceticism is largely prudery." Weininger goes so far as to conclude that "Shakespeare and Shelley, the two greatest Englishmen, stand far from the pinnacle of humanity," and that the "English, like women, have been most unproductive in religion and in music" (Weininger, *Sex and Character* [translation of *Geschlecht und Charakter*] [London: Heinemann, 1906], p. 317).

159. Michael Dobson, *The Making of the National Poet: Shakespeare, Adaptation, and Authorship, 1660–1769* (Oxford: Clarendon Press, 1992); Jonathan Bate, *Shakespearean Constitutions: Politics, Theatre, Criticism, 1730–1830* (Oxford: Clarendon Press, 1989); and Margreta de Grazia, *Shakespeare Verbatim: The Reproduction of Authenticity and the 1790 Apparatus* (Oxford: Clarendon Press, 1991).

160. Austen, *Mansfield Park*, p. 338.

161. Dobson, *Making of the National Poet*, p. 134.

162. *Gray's Inn Journal*, December 15, 1753. As cited in Dobson, *Making of the National Poet*, p. 7. Dobson makes the cogent point here that Murphy "links Bardolotry with Anglicanism and Little-Englandism."

163. See Dobson, *Making of the National Poet*, pp. 220–21; also Garrick, *The Jubilee* (1769), in Harry W. Pedicord and Frederick L. Bergmann, eds., *The Plays of David Garrick*, 7 vols. (Carbondale: Southern Illinois University Press, 1980), vol. 2, pp. 125, 104, 122.

164. Sidney Lee, *William Shakespeare* (London, 1925), p. 601.

165. Dobson, *Making of the National Poet*, p. 185.

166. Gollancz, son of an English rabbi, brother of Hermann Gollancz (who was a professor of Hebrew at University College, London), was appointed Lecturer in English Literature at Cambridge in 1896, having previously served a Lecturer in English at University College, London.

167. Israel Gollancz, *Shakespeare Tercentenary Observance in the Schools and Other Institutions*

(London: Saint Bride Foundation Printing School, 1916); and Israel Gollancz, ed., *A Book of Homage to Shakespeare* (Oxford: Oxford University Press, 1916).

168. I have addded the italics. Gollancz, *Schools*, p. 13.

169. Shakespeare, *The Merchant of Venice*, 5.1.63–65.

170. Gollancz, *Schools*, p. 12.

171. As quoted in John Gross, *Shylock: A Legend and Its Legacy* (New York: Simon and Schuster, 1992), pp. 269–70 (first published as *Shylock: Four Hundred Years in the Life of a Legend* (London: Chatto and Windus, 1992).

172. Gollancz, *Schools*, p. 21.

173. Hermann Gollancz, "Hebrew Ode," in *A Book of Homage to Shakespeare*, pp. 307–8.

174. Gross, *Shylock*, pp. 268–69. More work needs to be done on this connection. See Israel Gollancz's posthumously published lectures on *The Merchant of Venice* in his *Allegory and Mysticism in Shakespeare* (London: G. W. Jones, 1931), printed for private circulation. See too Jonathan Bate, "Shakespeare Nationalised, Shakespeare Privatised," *English* 42 (1993), pp. 1–18, on Israel Gollancz and the creation of a national Shakespeare.

175. Hermann Gollancz, *Shakespeare and Rabbinic Thought* (London: Wertheimer, Lea, 1916), pp. 4–5, 13.

176. Baker, *Bardolotry*, pp. 29–30.

177. Baker, *Bardolotry*, pp. 30–33.

178. Hirschson, "The Jewish Key," pp. 38–40.

179. Basch, *The Hidden Shakespeare*, p. 1.

180. Baker, *Bardolotry*, pp. 37, 47–49.

181. Baker, *Bardolotry*, p. 35.

182. Marlis, *Jewess*, p. 1.

183. Marlis, *Jewess*, pp. 93, 74, 101, 125.

184. "G. K. Hunter, "Elizabethans and Foreigners," pp. 37–52; and "The Theology of Marlowe's *The Jew of Malta*," pp. 211–40.

185. Hunter, "Theology," pp. 214–15.

186. Cardozo, *The Contemporary Jew*, pp. 328–29.

187. James Parkes, *The Conflict of the Church and the Synagogue* (London, 1934), pp. 166 and 374; Jacob Cardozo, *The Contemporary Jew in the Elizabethan Drama*; and Hijman Michelson, *The Jew in Early English Literature*.

188. See also Guido Kisch, *The Jews in Medieval Germany: A Study of Their Legal and Social Status* (Chicago: University of Chicago Press, 1949).

189. Hunter, "Theology," pp. 215–16.

190. Hunter, "Elizabethans," p. 49.

191. Guido Kisch, "The Jews in Medieval Law," in *Essays in Antisemitism*, ed. Koppel S. Pinson, 2d rev. ed. (New York: Conference on Jewish Relations, 1946), p. 107.

192. For scholarship influenced by this view, see, for example, Michael Ferber's Marxist "The Ideology of *The Merchant of Venice*," in which he cites Hunter's "strong case" that "Jewishness was a moral or theological problem, not a racial one." In a reading also influenced by Marx's conception of the "spirit" of Judaism (which owes an unacknowledged debt to Paul's Romans), Ferber argues that the " 'Jew,' we might say, occupied an ideological space that might be taken by real Jews but not only by them; it could be taken by those who are Jews inwardly" (*ELR* 20 [1990], p. 441). See, too, Gillian E. Brennan's recent assertion that "sixteenth-century anti-Semitism was religious rather than racial," in "The Cheese and the Welsh: Foreigners in Elizabethan Literature," *Renaissance Studies* 8 (1994), p. 51.

193. Kisch, *Jews in Medieval Germany*, p. ix.

194. Hunter, "Theology," p. 215.

195. For a recent and important exception, see Margo Hendricks and Patricia Parker, eds.,

Women, "Race," and Writing in the Early Modern Period (New York: Routledge, 1994).

196. For examples of this criticism, see Carol Leventon, "Patrimony and Patriarchy in *The Merchant of Venice*," in *The Matter of Difference: Materialist Feminist Criticism of Shakespeare*, ed. Valerie Wayne (Ithaca: Cornell University Press, 1991), pp. 59–79; and Karen Newman, "Portia's Ring: Unruly Women and Structures of Exchange in *The Merchant of Venice*," *Shakespeare Quarterly* 38 (1987), pp. 19–33.

197. For an important exception, see the recent work of Debora K. Shuger: *Habits of Thought in the English Renaissance: Religion, Politics, and the Dominant Culture* (Berkeley: University of California Press, 1990); and *The Renaissance Bible: Scholarship, Sacrifice, and Subjectivity* (Berkeley: University of California Press, 1994).

198. Stephen Greenblatt, "Marlowe, Marx, and Anti-Semitism," *Critical Inquiry* 5 (1978), p. 291, rpt. in *Learning to Curse: Essays in Early Modern Culture* (New York, Routledge, 1990). Greenblatt clearly has the Marxist "Jewish Question" in mind when he makes this claim.

199. Stephen Greenblatt, *Marvelous Possessions* (Chicago: University of Chicago Press, 1991), p. ix.

200. Stephen Greenblatt, *Renaissance Self-Fashioning* (Chicago: University of Chicago Press, 1980), p. 79.

201. Greenblatt, *Learning to Curse*, p. 13.

3. The Jewish Crime

Epigraph sources are as follows: Purchas, drawing on the research of John Selden, in *Pilgrimage*, p. 152; and John Hooper Harvey, *The Plantagenets, 1154–1485* (London: B. T. Batsford, 1948), p. 72.

1. As cited in Furness, ed., *The Merchant of Venice, A New Variorum Edition*, p. 322.

2. Edgeworth, *Harrington* (1817), in *Tales and Novels*, 18 vols. (London, 1833), vol. 17, p. 85. Subsequent citations are quoted from this volume. Like Lichtenberg, Edgeworth specifies that it is Macklin's first appearance after winning his celebrated lawsuit against the theater manager.

3. Edgeworth, *Harrington*, pp. 2–4.

4. Edgeworth, *Harrington*, p. 14.

5. Edgeworth, *Harrington*, pp. 19–20.

6. Edgeworth, *Harrington*, p. 19.

7. Purchas, *Pilgrimage*, entry in "an alphabetical table of the principal things contained in this work," sig. Bbbbb4r.

8. Marlowe, *The Jew of Malta*, 2.3.176–200.

9. John Webster, *The Devil's Law Case* (1617), in F. L. Lucas, ed., *The Complete Works of John Webster*, 4 vols. (London: Chatto and Windus, 1927), vol. 2; 3.2.1 SD, 3.2.1–16, 3.2.69.

10. Many of the charges were dredged up in the course of the 1650s. A typical instance is James Howell's claim in his 1650 "Epistle Dedicatory" to Joseph ben Gurion, *The Wonderful and Most Deplorable History* (not printed until 1678), that Edward I had expelled the Jews not "for their religion but for their notorious crimes, as poisoning of wells, counterfeiting of coins, falsifying of seals, and crucifying of Christian children, and other villainies" (sig. B2r).

11. Calvert, "Diatriba of the Jews' Estate," in *The Blessed Jew of Marocco*, p. 17.

12. Miri Rubin, "Desecration of the Host: The Birth of an Accusation," in Diana Wood, ed., *Christianity and Judaism*, Studies in Church History 29 (Oxford: Blackwell, 1992), p. 169.

13. Rubin, "Desecration of the Host," pp. 176–85.

14. Sarah Beckwith, "Ritual, Church and Theatre: Medieval Dramas of the Sacramental Body," in David Aers, ed., *Culture and History, 1350–1600: Essays in English Communities, Identities, and Writings* (Detroit: Wayne State University Press, 1992), pp. 65–89.

15. For a helpful account of the changing attitutes toward the Eucharist in early modern Eng-

land, see Richard F. Buxton, *Eucharist and Institution Narrative: A Study in the Roman and Anglican Traditions of the Consecration of the Eucharist from the Eighth to the Twentieth Centuries*, Alcuin Club Collections, No. 58 (Essex: Mayhew-McCrimmon, 1976), pp. 52–109.

16. Reginaldus Gonsalvius Montanus, "The Preface," *A Discoverie and Playne Declaration of Sundry Subtill Practices of the Holy Inquisition of Spayne*, trans. V. Skinner (London, 1568), sigs. B3r, B3v.

17. On the circumcision of Christ, see Leo Steinberg, *The Sexuality of Christ in Renaissance Art and in Modern Oblivion* (New York: Pantheon/October, 1983).

18. Isaiah, *A Vindication of the Christian Messiah*, pp. 32–34.

19. John Meirs, *A Short Treatise Compos'd and Published by John Meirs, Formerly a Jew, Now by the Signal Mercy of God in Christ Converted to the Christian Faith* (rpt., London 1717), p. 15. Meirs's text is not elsewhere indebted to Paul Isaiah's account; the likelihood is that they drew independently on a common tradition.

20. Sir John Mandeville, *The Voyages and Travailes of Sir John Mandevile Knight, Wherein Is Set Downe the Way to the Holy Land and to Hierusalem* (London, 1625), sigs. R2r, R2v. Traces of Jews as military threat are also found in Barabas's boast of slaying both friend and enemy "in the wars 'twixt France and Germany" and Romelio's claim, also quoted above, that he would betray "a town to th' Turk, or make a bonfire" of the "Christian navy."

21. Nicolas de Nicolay, *The Navigations Into Turkie*, trans. T. Washington the Younger (London, 1585), pp. 130–31.

22. For more on this subject, see Nabil I. Matar's essays: "The Idea of the Restoration of the Jews in English Protestant Thought: Between the Reformation and 1660," *Durham University Journal* 78 (1985), pp. 23–35; and "The Idea of the Restoration of the Jews in English Protestant Thought, 1661–1701," *Harvard Theological Review* 78 (1985), pp. 115–48.

23. *News from Rome. . . . Also Certaine Prophecies of a Jew . . . Called Caleb Shilock*, trans. by W. W. (London, 1606), sig. A4v.

24. R. R., *A New Letter from Aberdeen in Scotland, Sent to a Person of Quality* (London, 1665), pp. 2–3. There follows a "Letter from Antwerp, October 10/20, 1665," with more of the same.

25. Monarchs, it seems, were particularly vulnerable to the threat posed by the Jews and their mysterious powers. Virtually all of the Tudor historians describe how Richard I "commanded that no Jews nor women should be at his coronation, for fear of enchantments which were wont to be practiced," and "for breaking of which commandment, many Jews were slain the same day" (see, for example, John Stow, *The Annales of England* [London, 1592], p. 226). The identification here of Jews with witches was unusual and is rare in the sixteenth century, despite all these two groups had in common: "enchantments," sabbaths, secret rites, interest in magic, and involvement in local and unsolved crimes. However, there may well be a relation between the banishment of the Jews from England at the close of the thirteenth century and the emergence of witch prosecutions shortly thereafter. R. Hsia notes that in Germany there was a "greater emphasis [on] ritual child murders in witchcraft discourses of the late sixteenth century, as witches seemed to have replaced Jews as the most dangerous enemies within Christian society" (R. Po-chia Hsia, *The Myth of Ritual Murder: Jews and Magic in Reformation Germany* [New Haven: Yale University Press, 1988], p. 228). See, too, Venetia Newell, "The Jew as Witch Figure," in Venetia Newall, ed., *The Witch Figure* (London: Routledge and Kegan Paul, 1973), pp. 95–124.

26. John Marston, *The Malcontent* (1604), in H. Harvey Wood, ed., *The Plays of John Marston*, 3 vols. (London: Oliver and Boyd, 1934), p. 207 (act 5, scene 3).

27. Stow, *Annales*, p. 332.

28. Pierre Boaistuau, *Certaine Secrete Wonders of Nature, Containing a Description of Sundry Strange Things, Seeming Monstrous in Our Eyes and Judgement*, trans. Edward Fenton (Lon-

don, 1569), pp. 27–28.

29. Robert Fludd, *Philosophia Moysaica* (Gouda, 1638), translated into English as *Mosaicall Philosophy: Grounded Upon the Essentiall Truth, or Eternal Sapience* (London, 1659), pp. 236–37.

30. William Biddulph, *The Travels of Certaine Englishmen* (London, 1609), p. 74.

31. As cited in Furness, ed., *The Merchant of Venice, A New Variorum Edition*, p. 322.

32. *HMC Report on the Manuscripts of the Most Honourable the Marquesse of Downshire*, Vol. 5, Papers of William Trumbull, September 1614–August 1616, ed. G. Dyfnallt Owen (London: HMSO, 1988), p. 101.

33. Purchas, *Pilgrimage* (1617), p. 171.

34. Norman Jones, *God and the Moneylenders: Usury and Law in Early Modern England* (Oxford: Basil Blackwell, 1989), pp. 173–74. My discussion draws upon Jones's excellent chapter on "The Evolution of the Concept of Usury, 1571–1624," pp. 145–74.

35. John Shakespeare was twice accused of violating usury laws, charging twenty pounds interest on loans of eighty and one hundred pounds, respectively. In one case he was fined forty shillings. For details, see David Thomas, ed., *Shakespeare in the Public Record* (London: HMSO, 1985), pp. 2–3.

36. Anon., *The Death of Usury, or the Disgrace of Usurers* (Cambridge, 1594), p. 10.

37. William Rastall, *A Collection in English, of the Statutes Now in Force* (London, 1594), p. 239.

38. Purchas, *Pilgrimage* (1617), p. 165. Purchas is probably drawing here on the early pirated edition of Edwin Sandys's diary of his foreign travels, in which Sandys explains that "the beastly trade" of "courtesans" and the "cruel trade" of Jews are tolerated by the Pope and other "princes of Italy" out of greed; Jews and prostitutes are positioned in the middle of the complex social and economic exchange in which they "suck from the mean," only "to be sucked by the great" ([Edwin Sandys], *A Relation of the State of Religion* [London, 1605], sig. X2v).

39. Sir William Brereton, *Travels in Holland, The United Provinces, England, Scotland, and Ireland, 1634–1635*, ed. Edward Hawkins (London: Chetham Society, 1844), p. 61.

40. Stow, *Annales*, p. 299. Not until the eighteenth century is a connection drawn between clipping coins and clipping foreskins.

41. Holinshed, *Chronicles*, p. 279.

42. See Colin Holmes, *Anti-Semitism in British Society, 1876–1939* (New York: Holmes and Meier, 1979), pp. 164–65. Holmes cites Arnold Leese's article in the *Fascist*, no. 86, July 1936, as well as Leese, *My Irrelevant Defence* (London, 1938), p. 7. See, too, Holmes's "The Ritual Murder Accusation on Britain," *Ethnic and Racial Studies* 4 (1981), pp. 265–88.

43. Burton, *The Jew, the Gypsy, and El Islam*, p. x. See Holmes, *Anti-Semitism*, pp. 51–54, for a valuable account of the legal battles up through 1911 that succeeded in suppressing the publication of Burton's appendix.

44. Summers's claim is reinforced by the trappings of scholarly references, along with a footnote that cites a recent case of this crime: "In 1913 Mendil Beiliss was tried upon the charge of ritually murdering a Russian lad, Yushinsky" (Summers, *The History of Witchcraft and Demonology* [London: Kegan Paul, 1926], pp. 195–97).

45. Harvey, *The Plantagenets*, pp. 72–73.

46. Kushner, "Heritage and Ethnicity: An Introduction," in *Jewish Heritage*, pp. 16–17.

47. Marlowe, *The Jew of Malta*, 3.6.48–49.

48. Holinshed notes that the "Jew that was owner of the house, was apprehended, and . . . upon promise of pardon, confessed the whole matter" (*Chronicles*, pp. 56, 253).

49. Foxe, *Actes and Monuments*, p. 213.

50. Langmuir, *Definition*, p. 212. Posidinius relates how Antiochus IV Epiphanes "invaded and desecrated the Temple in 168 B.C.E.," where he found "a Greek captive in the Temple who told him that every seven years the Jews captured a Greek, fattened him up, killed him, ate

parts of him, and took an oath of undying enmity against Greeks." Posidinius's account was passed around in literary circles and was repeated in the first century by the rhetorician Appolonius Molon and subsequently by Damocritus. It circulated as far as Alexandria, where it was slightly modified by Appion, whose account was challenged by Flavius Josephus.

51. It was Theobold, a Jewish convert to Christianity, who told Thomas that Jews annually gathered to determine in which country a Christian would be sacrificed; and in 1144 the lot fell to England, and specifically to Norwich (Langmuir, *Definition*, pp. 225–26).

52. See in particular the outstanding study of the accusations in early modern Germany: Hsia, *The Myth of Ritual Murder*. The classic account remains Hermann L. Strack, *The Jew and Human Sacrifice*, trans. Henry Blanchap (1892; New York, 1909).

53. The painting is reproduced as the frontispiece to Augustus Jessopp and Montague Rhodes James, *The Life and Miracles of St. William of Norwich by Thomas of Monmouth* (Cambridge: Cambridge University Press, 1896). Jessopp and James describe about a dozen extant portraits of William, none as explicit as this in depicting the act of mutilation. The authors also note that while "there were no doubt a good many pictures and images of the boy saint in Norwich itself, some in the Cathedral, others in parish churches," as well as a "guild of St William," there are few surviving traces (p. lxxxv). See, too, M. D. Anderson, *A Saint at Stake: The Strange Death of William of Norwich 1144* (London: Faber and Faber, 1964), which also discusses the painting.

54. Hsia, *The Myth of Ritual Murder*, p. 65.

55. The volume was produced in an unusually large press run of 1,500 Latin and 1,000 German copies in the first edition alone—of which over 1,200 survive today in public collections and libraries. See Adrian Wilson and Joyce Lancaster Wilson, *The Making of the Nuremberg Chronicle* (Amsterdam: Nico Israel, 1976), "Appendix 1." In offering a dramatic reenactment of these secret rituals, Schedel's woodcut forms part of the evidence substantiating blood libel, taking its place alongside the other important evidence in circulation: records of interrogations, copies of the Jews' confessions, contemporary chronicles, ballads, even plays (such as the *Judenspiel* of Endingen, recounting a ritual murder and the discovery and punishment of the offending Jews there in 1470). See Hsia, *The Myth of Ritual Murder*, pp. 36–41.

56. G. Brennan, ed., *The Travel Diary (1611–1612) of an English Catholic, Sir Charles Somerset* (Leeds: Leeds Philosophical and Literary Society, 1993), p. 258.

57. Meredith Hanmer, trans., *The Auncient Ecclesiasticall Histories of the First Six Hundred Yeares After Christ Wrytten in the Greeke Tongue by Three Learned Historiographers, Eusebius, Socrates, and Evagrius* (London, 1577), p. 385.

58. Thomas Lodge, trans., *The Famous and Memorable Workes of Josephus* (London, 1632), p. 788.

59. Calvert, "Diatriba of the Jews' Estate," in *The Blessed Jew of Marocco*, p. 19. And in one of the more interesting misreadings of the period, Thomas Scales described in his unpublished essay cobbled together out of various English chronicles, on the "Estate, Profession, Practice and Condition of the Nation of the Jewes," how "for crucifying a Christian child at Norwich" the Jews were "banished out of this kingdom." No chronicle ever makes such a claim, and it is worth thinking about how chronicle material was distorted or misunderstood by ordinary readers like Scales ("Condition of the Nation of the Jewes," fol. 21).

60. Prynne, *Short Demurrer*, part 1, sigs. A3r, A3v, and pp. 32–33.

61. Prynne, *Short Demurrer*, part 2, p. 132.

62. Menasseh ben Israel, *Vindiciae Judaeorum*, in Wolf, *Menasseh ben Israel's Mission*, pp. 112–13.

63. Menasseh ben Israel, *Vindiciae Judaeorum*, in Wolf, *Menasseh ben Israel's Mission*, pp. 113,

108, 110, and 117.

64. Richard Mayo, *A Conference Betwixt a Protestant and a Jew* (London, 1678), pp. 30–31.

65. Donne, *Sermons*, vol. 6, pp. 333–34.

66. For more on this topic, see, for example, Paster, *The Body Embarrassed*; and Peter Stally-brass, "Patriarchal Territories: The Body Enclosed," in *Rewriting the Renaissance: The Discourses of Sexual Difference in Early Modern Europe*, ed. Margaret W. Ferguson, Maureen Quilligan, and Nancy J. Vickers (Chicago: University of Chicago Press, 1986), pp. 123–42.

67. John Boswell, *The Kindness of Strangers: The Abandonment of Children in Western Europe from Late Antiquity to the Renaissance* (1988; New York: Vintage, 1990), p. 352.

68. Anthony Wood, *The History and Antiquities of the University of Oxford*, 2 vols., ed. J. Gutch (Oxford, 1792–96), vol. 1, p. 220.

69. Tovey, *Anglia Judaica*, p. 149.

70. Marlowe, *The Jew of Malta*, 1.2.357, 305.

71. Shakespeare, *The Merchant of Venice*, 4.1.381, 2.6.39, 2.3.20, 2.5.41–42. An additional detail in Shakespeare's play linking it to the narrative of ritual murder is the reference to Easter-time, the only allusion in the play to a specific time of the year. It occurs when Lancelot observes that it "was not for nothing that my nose fell a-bleeding on Black Monday last at six a'clock i' th' morning" (2.5.24–26). Black Monday was Easter Monday, so called in commemoration of the freezing cold Easter of 1360. Lancelot's superstitious remark may have called to mind the set of popular beliefs about Jews and bleeding Christians that were associated with Easter.

72. I have no doubt, though cannot prove, that there were serial killers and child molesters in early modern society. In the twentieth century we have various names for such individuals: criminal sociopaths, serial killers, psychopaths, etc. We also have theories that go some distance toward explaining why certain individuals steal small children, then mutilate and kill them. Psychologists offer profiles of such individuals, including in their descriptions the fact that most of these individuals were themselves subject to abuse in childhood, come from unstable homes, perhaps have some biochemical or chromosomal imbalance, etc. In early modern Europe the most satisfying theory, and one that best accounted for the child's mutilated body found by the side of the road, was that the Jews had done it. After all, the Jews had first circumcised and later killed Christ, mocking and scourging him. Their inveterate hatred of Christianity was motive enough, or alternatively, they needed the blood for any number of ritual purposes. Moreover, the Jews engaged in ritual circumcision as well as ritual slaughter, were known from the Bible to have engaged in elaborate sacrifices, and had other rites and superstitions that were either secretive or unknown.

73. Thomas Vincent, *Paria* ([1627]; London, 1648), ed. Steven Berkowitz, in *Renaissance Latin Drama in England*, ed. Marvin Spevack, J. W. Binns, Hans-Jurgen Weckermann (Hildensheim: Georg Olms Verlag, 1990), p. 10.

74. Vincent, *Paria*, pp. 391, 398.

75. Shakespeare, *The Merchant of Venice*, 1.3.44 and 2.5.14–15. Leslie A. Fiedler, who discusses this emphasis on Shylock's cannibalism, adds to these examples Shylock's comment upon Antonio's entrance: "Your worship was the last man in our mouths" (1.3.57), in "The Jew as Stranger: Or, 'These Be the Christian Husbands,'" in *The Stranger in Shakespeare* (New York: Stein and Day, 1972), p. 110.

76. Shakespeare, *The Merchant of Venice*, 3.1.50–51, 4.1.137, 4.1.133.

77. As quoted in Cardozo, *The Contemporary Jew in the Elizabethan Drama*, p. 155. Trace elements of Jewish cannibalism can also be found in Barabas's death at the end of Marlowe's *The Jew of Malta* when he is boiled in the "cauldron" he had prepared for Calymath. Fittingly, the Jew who would sup on Christians is cooked instead.

78. Prynne, *Short Demurrer*, part 1, p. 49.

79. For psychological interpretations of Shakespeare's play that make much of this, see Dennis R. Klink, "Shylock and 'Neschech,'" *English Language Notes* 17 (1979), pp. 18–22; and Paula Brody, "Shylock's Omophagia: A Ritual Approach to *The Merchant of Venice*," *Literature and Psychology* 17 (1967), pp. 229–34.

80. Reginald Scot, *The Discoverie of Witchcraft* (1584), ed. Montague Summers (New York: Dover, 1972), p. 109.

81. Purchas describes at considerable length the story of how "James the Jew had taken" a Christian boy named Edward "as he was playing in the street, and carrying him to his house, circumcised him, and there detained him one day and night, till by force" the boy's father "recovered" him, though "his circumcised member" was found to be "swollen." After the child was examined, he "confessed" that the Jews had "carried him to the house of James aforesaid, where, while one held him and covered his eyes, another circumcised him with a knife." The boy then provided an insider's view of the secret rites accompanying this ritual circumcision: the Jews would take "the piece cut of" and "put in a basin of sand." Then, "with small puffs of wind out of their mouths" the Jews "sought it." The Jew who found it" was named "Jurnepin," and the Jews renamed the child after him. Purchas goes on to relate how the "Archdeacon's official came to testify [about] this with a great company of priests," who all confirmed "that they saw [the boy's] member swollen." The tale does not end here, however, for the Jews, in their defense, "procured the boy to be seen, and his member was found covered," that is to say, his foreskin was still in place. This was insufficient to exonerate the Jews; as Purchas puts it, "this is not repugnant to the former testimony seeing by surgery the skin may be drawn forth to an uncircumcision" (Purchas, *Pilgrimage*, p. 152). I return to the topic of uncircumcision in the following chapter.

82. Holinshed, *Chronicles*, p. 219; and Foxe, *Actes and Monuments*, p. 296.

83. Wood, *History and Antiquities of Oxford*, vol. 1, p. 329.

4. "The Pound of Flesh"

Epigraph sources are as follows: Geoffrey Bullough, *Narrative and Dramatic Sources of Shakespeare*, 8 vols. (New York: Columbia University Press, 1957–75), vol. 1, p. 483; and Leon Poliakov, *A History of Anti-Semitism*, 3 vols. (New York: Vanguard Press, 1974), vol. 1, p. 223. Poliakov does not provide the source of this quotation.

1. Sigmund Freud, *The Standard Edition of the Complete Works*, trans. James Strachey et al., 24 vols. (London: Hogarth Press, 1953–1974), vol. 10, p. 36. See, too, his *Leonardo da Vinci* (1910), where Freud notes that "here we may also trace one of the roots of the anti-semitism which appears with such elemental force and finds such irrational explanation among the nations of the West." For Freud, "circumcision is unconsciously equated with castration. If we venture to carry our conjectures back to the primaeval days of the human race we can surmise that originally circumcision must have been a milder substitute, designed to take the place of castration" (vol. 11, p. 95). He added this footnote in 1919. In his *Introductory Lectures on Psychoanalysis* he similarly writes that there "seems to me no doubt that the circumcision practiced by so many peoples is an equivalent and substitute for castration" (vol. 15, p. 165). Sander Gilman's penetrating studies—*The Case of Sigmund Freud*, and *Freud, Race, and Gender* (Princeton: Princeton University Press, 1993)—discuss in great detail the historical and medical issues that informed Freud's ideas about circumcision; see especially the chapter on "The Construction of the Male Jew" in *Freud, Race, and Gender*, pp. 49–92.

2. In Freud's own analysis of Shakespeare's play he avoids Jewish questions, focusing not on the pound of flesh plot but on the tale of the three caskets. Marjorie Garber, turning Freud's psychoanalytic approach against him, brilliantly argues that by "turning *The Merchant of Venice* into *King Lear*, Freud occludes Portia and her own scene of choice, when, dressed

259

4. "The
Pound
of Flesh"

like a man, she chooses between two men, two symbolic castrates, Antonio the 'tainted wether of the flock' (4.1.114) and Shylock 'the circumcised Jew.'" Garber wonders whether Freud, by focusing on this issue, is able to avoid confronting his own patriarchy and misogyny by failing to address the more disturbing "problem of the two things he does not want to think of, the two last things that remain on the periphery of the essay on 'The Three Caskets,' discreetly offstage and off-page, the two figures central to *The Merchant of Venice*: the cross-dressed woman and the Jew?" (Marjorie Garber, *Shakespeare's Ghost Writers: Literature as Uncanny Causality* [New York: Methuen, 1987], p. 187, n. 63).

3. Tovey, *Anglia Judaica*, p. 65. Bonefand, we learn, "pleaded not guilty, and was very honourably acquitted," raising the interesting question of how, given the medical evidence, the case could ever have been successfully prosecuted.

4. Gabriel Harvey, *Works*, ed. Alexander Grosart, 3 vols. (London, 1884–1885), vol. 1, p. 203.

5. Andrew Willet, *Hexapla: That Is, a Six-fold Commentarie Upon the Most Divine Epistle of the Holy Apostle S. Paul to the Romanes* (Cambridge, 1611), p. 203.

6. As Purchas puts it in his *Pilgrimage* (1613), p. 158.

7. While this woodcut no doubt relates to his reputed escape from a crowd of hostile Venetian Jews whom he sought to convert, there is no evidence anywhere in Coryate's book that these Jews bore weapons against him. Coryate himself explains that "that some forty or fifty Jews more flocked about me, and some of them began very insolently to swagger with me, because I durst reprehend their religion. Whereupon fearing least they should have offered me some violence, I withdrew myself by little and little towards the bridge at the entrance into the ghetto" (Coryate, *Coryats Crudities* [London, 1611], pp. 236–37).

8. Coryate is subsequently imagined as facing the danger of circumcision in his travels through Islamic nations. A poem written in 1615 to Coryate by John Brown, an English merchant residing at the time in India, warns Coryate to "have a care (at Mecca is some danger) / Lest you incur the pain of circumcision." Coryate published the poem in his *Thomas Coryate, Travailer . . . Greeting . . . from the Court of the Great Mogul* (London, 1616), p. 34.

9. Coryate, *Coryats Crudities*, sigs. D7v, E1r, and A2r.

10. Coryate adds: "All his privities (before he came into the room) were besprinkled with a kind of powder, which after the circumcisor had done his business was blowed away by him, and another powder cast on immediately. After he had dispatched his work . . . he took a little strong wine that was held in a goblet by a fellow that stood near him, and poured it into the child's mouth to comfort him in the midst of his pains, who cried out very bitterly; the pain being for the time very bitter indeed, though it will be (as they told me) cured in the space of four and twenty hours. Those of any riper years that are circumcised (as it too often commeth to pass, that Christians that turn Turks) as at forty or fifty years of age, do suffer great pain for the space of a month" (Coryate, *Coryate's Crudities; Reprinted from the Edition of 1611. To Which Are Now Added, His Letters from India*, vol. 3, sig. U7r–U8v).

11. See Daniel Boyarin's essay in which he notes that "at a traditional circumcision ceremony the newly circumcised boy is addressed: 'And I say to you [feminine pronoun!]: in your [feminine] blood, you [feminine] shall live,'" and offers as a possible interpretation that "circumcision was understood somehow as rendering the male somewhat feminine," or alternatively, "that there is here an arrogation of a female symbol that makes it male, and that circumcision is a male erasure of the female role in procreation as well" (Boyarin, "'This We Know to Be the Carnal Israel': Circumcision and the Erotic Life of God and Israel," *Critical Inquiry* 19 [1992], p. 496, and n. 64).

12. Charles Hughes, ed., *Shakespeare's Europe: Unpublished Chapters of Fynes Moryson's Itinerary*, 2 vols. (London: Sherrat and Hughes, 1903), vol. 2, pp. 494–95.

13. Cf. John Evelyn, who reports in his diary entry for January 15, 1645, in Rome, that when "the circumcision was done the priest sucked the child's penis with his mouth" (as cited in

A. Cohen, *An Anglo-Jewish Scrapbook, 1600–1840* [London: M. L. Cailingold, 1943], p. 292).
Charles Weiss notes that *metzitzah* "was probably introduced during the talmudic period,"
and that "its practice never became universal" ("A Worldwide Survey of the Current Practice of *Milah* [Ritual Circumcision]," *Jewish Social Studies* 24 [1962], p. 31). See too Bernard
Homa, *Metzitzah* (2d ed., London, n.p., 1966), where the relevant Midrashic texts that are
the source of the authority for this practice are cited. Michel de Montaigne also found an
opportunity to observe and describe "the most ancient religious ceremony there is among
men," which he "watched . . . very attentively and with great profit." He too was struck by
the practice of *metzitzah*: "As soon as this glans is thus uncovered, they hastily offer some
wine to the minister, who puts a little in his mouth and then goes and sucks the glans of this
child, all bloody, and spits out the blood he has drawn from it, and immediately takes as
much wine again, up to three times." After bandaging the child, the "minister" is given "a
glass full of wine. . . . He takes a swallow of it, and then dipping his finger in it he three times
takes a drop of it with his finger to the boy's mouth to be sucked. . . . He meanwhile still hath
his mouth all bloody" (Michel de Montaigne, *Montaigne's Travel Journal*, trans. Donald M.
Frame [San Francisco: North Point Press, 1983], pp. 81–82. The event was recorded by one
of Montaigne's servants, assigned to compile the journal).

14. The Bible also failed to prepare English travelers for what they would witness in Africa:
female "circumcision." Samuel Purchas, anticipating the skepticism of his readers, writes of
one of the voyages into Ethiopia: "Let no man marvel which heareth this, for they circumcise women as well as men, which thing was not used in the old Law." He also notes that
both in Cairo and "Abassine" they "circumcise not only males, but with a peculiar rite
females also" (Purchas, *Pilgrimage*, pp. 1040, 841, and 1134). The Islamic practice of delay-
ing circumcision until sexual maturity struck Elizabethan writers, versed in a scriptural tradition of circumcision occurring on the eighth day, as unusual. Richard Jobson's description
of his trip to "Gambra" in 1620, provided readers in England with considerable details of
the practice—locally known as the "cutting of pricks"—experienced by brave adolescent
boys in Africa: "Hither we came in season for that solemnity, hearing before we came,
shouts, drums and country music. The boy knew the meaning, and told us it was for cutting
of pricks, a world of people being gather[ed] for that purpose, like an English fair. . . . We
saw our black boy circumcised, not by a marybuck [that is, a priest], but an ordinary fellow
hackling off with a knife at three cuts his praepuce, holding his member in his hand, the boy
neither holden nor bound the while" (As cited in Purchas, p. 925). See, too, a later narrative
where Richard Jobson speaks of the local African custom concerning circumcision: "It is
done without religious ceremony, and hath no name but the cutting of pricks, the party
stripped naked and sitting on the ground, and the butcher pulling the skin over very far, and
cutting it, not without terror to the beholder" (As cited in Purchas, p. 1573).

15. Purchas, *Pilgrimage*, p. 121.

16. Willet, *Hexapla*, p. 204.

17. Thorowgood, *Jews in America*, pp. 13, 15. Similarly, when Queen Elizabeth's ambassador to
Russia, Giles Fletcher, declared that the Tartars were the ten lost tribes of Israel, he too
found confirmation in the fact that they "are circumcised, as were the Israelish and Jewish
people" (Giles Fletcher, "The Tartars or, Ten Tribes," first published sixty-six years after
his death in 1611, in Samuel Lee, *Israel Redux: Or the Restauration of Israel* [London, 1677],
p. 22).

18. *List and Analysis of State Papers: Foreign Series, Elizabeth I*, vol. 6 (January to December
1595), ed. R. B. Wernham (London: HMSO, 1993), p. 269. For a facsimile and transcript of
Don Solomon's letter, see H. G. Rosedale, *Queen Elizabeth and the Levant Company* (London: Henry Fraude, 1904), pp. 19–33.

19. See Acts 16.3. Unless otherwise noted, scriptural passages are quoted from the 1589 edition

261

4. "The Pound of Flesh"

of the Geneva Bible, published in London (I have modernized spelling and orthography here as well).

20. Philippe de Mornay, _A Woorke Concerning the Trewnesse of the Christian Religion, Written in French, Against Atheists, Epicures, Paynims, Jewes, Mahumetists, and Other Infidels_, trans. Sir Philip Sidney and Arthur Golding (London, 1587), pp. 581–82.

21. William Perkins, _A Commentarie or Exposition, Upon the First Five Chapters of the Epistles to the Galatians_ (Cambridge, 1604), p. 380.

22. Jean Calvin, _Sermons of M. John Calvine Upon the Epistle of Saincte Paule to the Galatians_, trans. Arthur Golding (London, 1574), fol. 325r.

23. John Calvin, _A Commentarie upon S. Paules Epistles to the Corinthians_, trans. Thomas Timme (London, 1577), fol. 82v. Others offered an evolutionary model that would explain the different attitudes the earliest Christians held toward circumcision. For example, the Scottish preacher John Weemse writes that in the "first period," Christians "might only circumcise; in the second period, circumcise and baptize; (for they had yet more regard to circumcision than to baptism); in the third period they baptized and circumcised (now they had more regard to baptism than circumcision); in the fourth period, they only baptized" (Weemse, _The Christian Synagogue_, 4 vols. [London, 1633], vol. 1, p. 129).

24. Romans 2.25.

25. _The New Testament of Our Lord Jesus Christ Translated Out of the Greek. By Theod. Beʒa_, trans. Laurence Tomson (London, 1596). Different editions offer slightly different wording. The first edition of Tomson's revision of the Geneva New Testament (based on Beza's 1565 Latin text) appeared in 1576. It was subsequently published both independently and as part of the larger Geneva Bibles. This was the final and popular form of the Geneva Bible.

26. Romans 2.28–29.

27. For this aspect of Paul's thought, see Daniel Boyarin, who astutely observes that Paul's problem with circumcision was that it "symbolized the genetic, the genealogical moment of Judaism as the religion of a particular tribe of people. This is so both in the very fact of the physicality of the rite, of its grounding in the practice of the tribe, and in the way it marks the male members of that tribe (in both sense), but even more so, by being a marker on the organ of generation it represents the genealogical claim for concrete historical memory as constitutive of Israel." Thus, by "substituting a spiritual interpretation for a physical ritual, Paul was saying that the genealogical Israel 'according to the Flesh,' is not the ultimate Israel; there is an 'Israel in the Spirit'" (Boyarin, "This We Know to Be the Carnal Israel," p. 502).

28. See Joseph Hall, _A Plaine and Familiar Exposition by Way of Paraphrase of All the Hard Texts of the Whole Divine Scripture of the Old and New Testament_ (London, 1633), p. 160.

29. Willet, _Hexapla_, p. 142. Origen's own position may have been qualified by the possibility (according to Eusebius) that he had castrated himself in his youth in order to work unconstrained with female catechumens.

30. It should also be noted that there is a Jewish tradition that values circumcision because it curtails male desire. Daniel Boyarin cites the observation of Maimonides that circumcision was instituted "to bring about a decrease in sexual intercourse and a weakening of the organ in question, so that this activity be diminished and the organ be in as quiet a state as possible" (in Moses Maimonides, _The Guide of the Perplexed_, trans. and ed. Shlomo Pines (Chicago: University of Chicago Press, 1963), p. 609, cited in Boyarin, "'This We Know to Be the Carnal Israel," p. 486, note 37. Boyarin also notes the Platonic, allegorizing view of circumcision in Philo as well. Some of the complex ways in which circumcision was understood symbolically in Jewish exegetical traditions are explored by Elliot R. Wolfson in "Circumcision, Vision of God, and Textual Interpretation: From Midrashic Trope to Mystical Symbol," _History of Religions_ 27 (1987), pp. 189–215, and "Circumcision and the Divine Name: A Study in the Transmission of Esoteric Doctrine," _The Jewish Quarterly Review_ 78

(1987), pp. 77–112.

31. Donne concludes, "God would have them carry this memorial about them, in their flesh," in "A Sermon Preached at Saint Dunstan's Upon New-Years-Day, 1624," *Sermons*, vol. 6, pp. 190–92.

32. The gendering of the act had long been a problem for Christian interpreters of the Bible, some condemning the Jews for leaving women out of the Convenant, others answering the objection "that circumcision was an imperfect sign, because it was appointed only for the males, the females were not circumcised," by saying that "the priviledge and benefit of circumcision was extended also unto the females, which were counted with the men, the unmarried with their fathers, the married with their husbands" (Willet, *Hexapla*, p. 205).

263

4. "The Pound of Flesh"

33. Diane Owen Hughes, "Distinguishing Signs: Ear-Rings, Jews, and Franciscan Rhetoric in the Italian City State," *Past and Present* 112 (1986), p. 24.

34. Shakespeare, *The Merchant of Venice*, 3.1.82–84.

35. This problem is usually due to excessive electrocautery used in some hospitals, which burns off too much of the infant's penis to warrant reconstructing the organ. The surgeons perform a "feminizing genitoplasty," that is, reconstructing female rather than male genitalia (and at the age of puberty performing a second operation, a vaginoplasty, supplemented by estrogens). See John P. Gearhart and John A. Rock, "Total Ablation of the Penis After Circumcision with Electrocauter: A Method of Management and Long-Term Follow-up," *Journal of Urology* 142 (1989), pp. 799–801. The authors note that the "successful adaption and normal sex life of our 2 older patients are a tribute to early gender reassignment, the involvement of a complete team of specialists, including a medical sexology expert, and extensive familial counseling from the time of injury" (p. 801). I am indebted to Dr. Franklin Lowe of Columbia Physicians and Surgeons for making this scholarship available to me. I am also grateful to Patricia E. Gallagher, of Beth Israel Medical Center, for providing me with material on circumcision procedures.

36. Shakespeare, *The Merchant of Venice*, 1.3.146–48, and 4.1.249. The first hint appears in act 3, when Shylock says to Tubal "I will have the heart of him if he forfeit" (3.1.119–20).

37. "Whosoever hath an issue from his flesh is unclean because of his issue," Leviticus 15.2. Biblical anthropologists have traced the practice of using the euphemism *basar* (flesh) when referring to the penis to the priestly redactors (rather than the Jahwist, who did not use this euphemism). See Howard Eilberg-Schwartz, *The Savage in Judaism: An Anthropology of Israelite Religion and Ancient Judaism* (Bloomington: Indiana University Press, 1990), pp. 170–71.

38. Shakespeare, *Romeo and Juliet*, 1.1.29–30, and 2.4.37.

39. Shakespeare, *The Merchant of Venice*, 4.1.113. Antonio's next lines—"the weakest kind of fruit / Drops earliest to the ground, and so let me" (4.1.114–15)—may connect back to the recurrent biblical identification of fruit trees with circumcision. In his chapter on "Uncircumcised Fruit Trees," Howard Eilberg-Schwartz notes the frequent comparison in biblical literature between "fruit trees and male organs" (p. 149; see, for example, Leviticus 19.23–25), and concludes that "the symbolic equation of an uncircumcised male and a young fruit tree rests on two, and possibly three, associations. The fruit of a juvenile tree is proscribed like the foreskin of the male organ. Furthermore, a male who is uncircumcised and not part of the covenantal community is infertile like an immature fruit tree. Finally, this symbolic equation may draw part of its plausibility from an analogy between circumcision and pruning," Eilberg-Schwartz, *The Savage in Judaism*, p. 152. See, too, his "People of the Body: The Problem of the Body for the People of the Book," *Journal of the History of Sexuality* 2 (1991), pp. 1–24.

40. Shakespeare, *The Merchant of Venice*, 2.8.22, 5.1.237.

41. As cited in J. H. Baker, "Criminal Courts and Procedure at Common Law, 1550–1800," in

Crimes in England, 1550–1800, ed. J. S. Cockburn (Princeton: Princeton University Press, 1977), p. 42.

42. Before he had to leave in 1683—having run afoul of the Duke of York and England's Catholic community—Leti had even been elected to the Royal Society and asked by Charles II to write a history of England from its origins to the Restoration. See the introduction to Nati Krivatsy, *Bibliography of the Works of Gregorio Leti* (Newcastle, Delaware: Oak Knoll Books, 1982).

43. Gregorio Leti, *Vita di Sisto V*, 3 vols. (Amsterdam, 1693), vol. 3, pp. 134ff. Since the first English translation of Leti's biography—*The Life of Pope Sixtus the Vth* (London, 1704)—was based on the 1669 text, it does not contain the pound of flesh story.

44. Gregorio Leti, *The Life of Pope Sixtus the Fifth*, trans. Ellis Farneworth (London, 1754). A subsequent edition of this translation was published in Dublin in 1766.

45. Leti, *Vita di Sisto V* (1693), vol. 3, p. 136.

46. And, conveniently, to pay for a hospital that he had recently founded. See Leti, *Sixtus the Fifth*, trans. Farneworth, pp. 293–95.

47. Leti, *Sixtus the Fifth*, trans. Farneworth, p. 293, n. 19.

48. Leti writes of their "gesti ridicolosissimi." For his remarks about London's Jews, see Leti, *Del Teatro Brittanico o Vero Historia dello Stato, Antico e Presente . . . della Grande Brettagna*, 2 vols. (London, 1683), esp. vol. 1, pp. 251–52, 549–50, as cited in Jonathan I. Israel, "Gregorio Leti (1631–1701) and the Dutch Sephardi Elite at the Close of the Seventeenth Century," in *Jewish History: Essays in Honour of Chimen Abramsky*, ed. Ada Rapoport-Albert and Steven J. Zipperstein (London: Peter Halban, 1988], p. 269).

49. Edmond Malone, *The Plays and Poems of William Shakspeare* (London, 1790), vol. 3, pp. 111–13.

50. David Erskine Baker, *Biographia Dramatica or a Companion to the Playhouse Containing Historical and Critical Memoirs*, 3 vols. (London, 1812), vol. 3, p. 34. First published in 1782.

51. Edgeworth, *Harrington*, p. 96.

52. Furness, ed., *The Merchant of Venice, A New Variorum Edition*, pp. 295ff.

53. For one of the few twentieth-century citations of Leti's story in relationship to Shakespeare's play, see Berta Viktoria Wenger, "Shylocks Pfund Fleish," *Shakespeare Jahrbuch* 65 (1929), esp. pp. 148–50.

54. Bullough, *Sources*, vol. 1, p. 483.

55. Bullough, *Sources*, vol. 1, p. 484. In other sources the cutting is to be done to the eyes (as in Anthony Munday's *Zeluto*), or is left ambiguous or unspecified, in the words of Fiorentino's *Il Pecorone* (1558), "wheresoever he pleases."

56. Malone, ed., *Plays and Poems of Shakspeare*, vol. 3, p. 114.

57. Furness, ed., *The Merchant of Venice, A New Variorum Edition*, pp. 311–12.

58. Bullough, *Sources*, vol. 1, p. 484.

59. Furness, ed., *The Merchant of Venice, A New Variorum Edition*, p. 312.

60. Sprague, ed., *The Merchant of Venice* (New York: Silver, Burdett, 1889).

61. See Willet's gloss on this passage in *Hexapla*. Elizabethan editions of the Bible constantly read Pauline doctrine back into the Old Testament passages. Thus, for example, the Bishops' Bible gloss explains: "That is, let all your affections be cut off. He showeth in these words the end of circumcision"; and "Cut off all your evil affections."

62. Mornay, *Trewnesse of the Christian Religion*, pp. 581–82.

63. Peter Martyr [Vermigli], *Most Learned and Fruitfull Commentaries of D. Peter Martir Vermilius, Florentine . . . Upon the Epistle of S. Paul to the Romanes* (London, 1568), p. 49v. Andrew Willet also cites the prophet Jeremiah, who proclaims that "all the nations are uncircumcised, and all the house of Israel are uncircumcised in the heart" (9.26).

64. Hugo Grotius, *True Religion Explained and Defended* (London, 1632), p. 274.

65. Donne, *Sermons*, vol. 6, p. 193.

66. Henry Hammond, *A Paraphrase and Annotations Upon All the Books of the New Testament* (London, 1653), p. 475.

67. For this psychoanalyst (who had first witnessed Shakespeare's play as a young boy at the turn of the century in antisemitic Vienna), only "one step is needed to reach the concept that to the Gentile of medieval times the Jew unconsciously typified the castrator because he circumcised male children." The "Jew thus appeared to Gentiles as a dangerous figure with whom the threat of castration originated." Theodore Reik, "Psychoanalytic Experiences in Life, Literature, and Music," in *The Search Within* (New York: Farrar, Strauss and Cudahy, 1956), pp. 358–59; first printed as "Jessica, My Child," *American Imago* 8 (1951), pp. 3–27.

68. Willet, *Hexapla*, pp. 130–31.

69. Weemse, *The Christian Synagogue*, vol. 1, p. 127. There is considerable medical evidence for uncircumcision or reverse circumcision as far back as classical antiquity. See, for example, J. P. Rubin, "Celsus' decircumcision operation: medical and historical implications," *Urology* 16 (1980), p. 121; and B. O. Rogers, "History of External Genital Surgery," in *Plastic and Reconstruction Surgery of the Genital Area*, ed. C. E. Horton (Boston: Little, Brown, & Co., 1973), pp. 3–47. Willard E. Goodwin's "Circumcision: A Technique for Plastic Reconstruction of a Prepuce After Circumcision," *Journal of Urology* 144 (1990), pp. 1203–1205, offers a helpful overview of both the history of and the procedures for reversing circumcision.

70. Romans, 2.26–27.

71. Galatians, 5.6. He would return to this idea again shortly, when he states that in Christ Jesus neither circumcision availeth any thing, nor uncircumcision, but a new creature" (Galatians, 6.15).

72. Corinthians, 7.18–19.

73. Thomas Godwyn, *Moses and Aaron: Civil and Ecclesiastical Rites Used by the Ancient Hebrewes*, 4th ed. (London, 1631), p. 242.

74. The same information was also made available in the margin of the Geneva Bible, where Elizabethans, who had no need of this procedure themselves, were nonetheless informed that "the surgeon by art draweth out the skin to cover the part circumcised." The Geneva Bible also cross-references 1 Maccabees 1.16, which describes how the Jews followed the "fashions of the heathen" and "made themselves uncircumcised, and forsook the holy Covenant." The table of contents to the 1589 Geneva Bible (which usefully cites all biblical passages that mention circumcision) cites this passage as one in which the "Jews did uncircumcise themselves, and became apostates," indicating that the act carried with it associations of abandoning one religion for another.

   Those curious enough to follow up the medical reference would have read in the Latin text of A. Cornelius Celsus (the first English translation, from which I quote, was not published until 1756) that this procedure requires that "under the circle of the glans, the skin" is "to be separated by a knife from the inner part of the penis." Celsus explains that this "is not very painful, because the extremity being loosened, it may be drawn backwards by the hand, as far as the pubes; and no hemorrhage follows upon it." Next, the "skin being disengaged, is extended again over the glans; then it is bathed with plenty of cold water, and a plaister put round it of efficacy in repelling an inflammation." Celsus offers as postoperative advice that "the patient is to fast, till he almost be overcome with hunger, lest a full diet should perhaps cause an erection of that part." Finally, when "the inflammation is gone, it ought to be bound up from the pubes to the circle of the glans; and a plaister being first laid on the glans, the skin ought to be brought over it" (A. Cornelius Celsus, *Of Medicine. In Eight Books*, trans. James Greive [London, 1756], pp. 438–39).

75. Hammond, *A Paraphrase*, p. 565. Hammond also describes the "practice of some Jews, who

under the Egyptian tyranny first, then under Antiochus, and lastly under the Romans, being oppressed for being Jews, of which their circumcision was an evidence, used means by some medicinal applications to get a new praeputium. And these were called by the Talmudists *mishuchim*" (I transliterate the Hebrew here). Following the Geneva Bible gloss, Hammond cites as a medical authority "the famous Physician" Celsus, and, unusually, also invokes Talmudic antecedents, citing Rabbi "Aleai of Achan," who "made himself a praeputium."

4. *"The Pound of Flesh"*

76. Shakespeare, *The Merchant of Venice*, 4.1.383, 4.1.394. Cf. Reik, who argues that if "Shylock insists upon cutting out a pound of flesh from Antonio's breast, it is as if he demanded that the Gentile be made a Jew if he cannot pay back the three thousand ducats at the fixed time. Otherwise put: Antonio should submit to the religious ritual of circumcision." In addition, at "the end of the 'comedy' Antonio demands that Shylock should 'presently become a Christian.' If this is the justified amends the Jew has to make for his earlier condition, it would be according to poetic justice that the Jew be forced to become a Christian after he had insisted that his opponent should become a Jew" (*The Search Within*, pp. 358–59).

77. Martyr, *Most Learned and Fruitfull Commentaries*, p. 48r.

78. See the fascinating discussion of the philosophical implications of Shylock's circumcising cut in Stanley Cavell, *The Claims of Reason: Wittgenstein, Skepticism, Morality, and Tragedy* [(New York: Oxford University Press, 1979], pp. 479–81). Marjorie Garber notes that both "Reik and Cavell predicate their insights upon an assumption of doubling or twinship, a moment of perceptual equipoise that enforces the disconcerting confusion of identities. . . . Cavell, with 'skepticism with respect to other minds' and the epistemological uncertainty of identity. Each reader appropriates Shylock's scene, persuasively, to his own theoretical project, and finds the twinship of Shylock and Antonio in the courtroom a theatrical hypostasis, an onstage crux that reifies his own perceptions" (Garber, p. 187, n. 63). See also Marc Shell, *Money, Language, and Thought* (Berkeley: University of California Press, 1982), pp. 47–83.

5. The Hebrew Will Turn Christian

Epigraph source is as follows: Calvert, *The Blessed Jew of Marocco*, p. 216.

1. Shakespeare, *The Merchant of Venice*, 1.3.175 (after the 1623 folio). The 1600 quarto reads, "This Hebrew."

2. Even the three unnamed Jewish merchants in Marlowe's *The Jew of Malta*, when tribute money for the Turks is demanded of them, rush to offer half their estates rather than accept the alternative, which is to "become a Christian" (1.2.68–75).

3. Shakespeare, *The Merchant of Venice*, 4.1.383.

4. Shakespeare, *The Merchant of Venice*, 3.5.17–22, 28–33.

5. Shakespeare, *The Merchant of Venice*, 2.3.21.

6. Marlowe, *The Jew of Malta*, 1.2.369–71.

7. Brereton, *Travels in Holland*, p. 61.

8. Edward Coke, *The Third Part of the Institutes of the Laws of England* (London 1644), p. 89. Coke's source is Fleta, who writes that those "who have connection with Jews and Jewesses or are guilty of bestiality or sodomy shall be buried alive in the ground, provided they be taken in the act and convicted by lawful and open testimony" (in *Fleta*, ed. and trans. H. G. Richardson and G. O. Sayles, 4 vols. [London: Selden Society, 1942–1984], vol. 1, p. 90).

9. Shakespeare, *The Merchant of Venice*, 4.1.220, 329, 336.

10. Christopher Hill, "'Till the Conversion of the Jews,'" in *Millenarianism and Messianism in English Literature and Thought, 1650–1982*, Clark Library Lectures 1981–1982, ed. Richard H. Popkin (Leiden: E. J. Brill, 1988), pp. 20, 28.

11. J. E., *The Great Deliverance of the Whole House of Israel . . . in Answer to a Book Called, "The Hope of Israel," Written by a Learned Jew of Amsterdam Named Menasseh ben Israel*; and

Arise Evans, *Light for the Jews, or, the Means to Convert Them* (London, 1664). For other representative works, see Samuel Brett, *A Narrative of the Proceedings of a Great Council of Jews Assembled in the Plain of Ageda in Hungaria . . . on the 12th of October 1650* (London, 1655); J. P., *Discoveries of the Day-Dawning to the Jews* (London, 1661); and [Henry Jessey? John Dury?] *An Information Concerning the Present State of the Jewish Nation in Europe and Judea* (London, 1658).

12. Katz, *Philo-Semitism*, pp. 158–231.

13. In the paragraphs that follow I draw on the recent work of Eamon Duffy, *The Stripping of the Altars: Traditional Religion in England c. 1400–c. 1580* (New Haven: Yale University Press, 1992); Norman Jones, *The Birth of Elizabethan England: England in the 1560s* (London: Blackwell, 1993); and Christopher Haigh, *English Reformations: Religion, Politics, and Society Under the Tudors* (Oxford: Clarendon Press, 1993).

14. Resistance to these Henrician reformations remained strong in certain parts of England. To cite but one example, the popular shrine of St. Hugh in Lincoln Cathedral, commemorating his martyrdom at the hands of the Jews, would not be destroyed until 1540 (Duffy, *Stripping of the Altars*, pp. 431 and 448).

15. Duffy, *Stripping of the Altars*, pp. 466, 500–3.

16. Duffy, *Stripping of the Altars*, pp. 526, 534–43; cf. Haigh, *English Reformations*, pp. 203–34.

17. Jones, *Birth of Elizabethan England*, p. 78; cf. Haigh, *English Reformations*, pp. 235–50. For example, Corpus Christi procession at Canterbury in 1558 would draw a crowd of three thousand individuals; in other places, like Kendall, Corpus Christi plays were performed as late as 1586.

18. Duffy, *Stripping of the Altars*, pp. 565–66, 582.

19. It was not just printed texts but preachers who made the difference, and it would take a full generation after Mary's reign to train and put in place a clergy capable of promoting reformist doctrines. It would also take that long to see in place magistrates "who backed Protestant preaching and demanded Protestant social discipline" (Haigh, *English Reformations*, p. 279).

20. Duffy, *The Stripping of the Altars*, p. 593.

21. Romans 11.26.

22. The commentary also makes clear the duty of the Christian in hastening the Jews' conversion: "We may rejoice in the Lord, but so that we despise not the Jews, whom we ought rather to provoke to that good striving with us" (Geneva gloss to Romans, 11.11, 11.18).

23. Geneva gloss to Romans 11.25, 11.28.

24. This "last beast had ten horns . . . and a little horn which destroyed several of the ten. After the destruction of the last beast, the kingdom was given to the saints for ever—the 'Fifth Monarchy'" (B. S. Capp, *The Fifth Monarchy Men: A Study in Seventeenth-Century Millenarianism* [London: Faber and Faber, 1972], p. 23).

25. Katherine Firth, *The Apocalyptic Tradition in Reformation Britain, 1530–1645* (Oxford: Oxford University Press, 1979), pp. 17, 3. The details get quite complicated: "Two beasts persecute the saints, one from the earth with two horns, the other from the sea, with seven heads and ten horns. Two witnesses who testify against them are killed, lie dead for 3 1/2 days and then rise again. During this persecution, God encourages the saints by punishing His enemies—the opening of the seven seals, the blowing of the seven trumpets and the pouring out of the seven vials of wrath. After this, Satan is bound for a thousand years; Christ and the saints reign for a thousand years, and then, at the end of the world, follows the battle of Armageddon, in which Satan is slain, and then Last Judgment begins" (Capp, *The Fifth Monarchy Men*, p. 24).

26. Luther also rejected Augustine's interpretation of the passage in Revelation which saw the apocalyptic resurrection from the dead as signifying "only the change from sin to purity."

See Capp, *The Fifth Monarchy Men*, p. 23, who cites E. L. Tuveson, *Millennium and Utopia* (Berkeley: University of California Press, 1949), pp. 1–17.

27.   Capp, *The Fifth Monarchy Men*, pp. 24–25.

28.   For Andrew Willet, the "prophesy of Daniel's seventy weeks" was the most difficult and obscure crux in the Bible, one that had by the late sixteenth century already produced a "great variety of interpretations." Having "waded through this bottomless depth of Daniel's seventy weeks," Willet offers a neat summary of where others have gone wrong in their historical chronologies: "1. Some begin the account too soon and end too soon. 2. Some begin too late and end too late. 3. Some begin too soon and end too late. 4. Some begin too late and end too soon. 5. Some begin well and end not right, and they either end too soon or too late. 6. Some end well their account but begin not right, and that either too soon or too late" (Willet, *Hexapla in Danielem: That Is, a Six-Fold Commentarie Upon the Most Divine Prophesie of Daniel* [London, 1610], pp. 294, 321).

29.   Edward Lively, *A True Chronology of the Times of the Persian Monarchie* (London, 1597), pp. 36, 22–23.

30.   For a representative sample, see George Joye, *The Exposicion of Daniel the Prophet* (Geneva, 1545); John Foxe, *Eicasmi Seu Meditationes in Sacram Apocalysin* (London, 1587); and Hugh Broughton's controversial *Concent of Scripture* (London, 1589?). It would be remiss not to offer what may well be the clearest exposition of Daniel's prophesy available to English readers, Andrew Willet's, who counts "first from Cyrus I to the end of the Persian monarchy a-hundred-and-thirty years, and then three-hundred years for the government of the Grecians. There remain sixty years from the end of Cleopatra her reign in the fourth year of Herod, in whose thirty Christ was born, unto the passion of Christ in the thirty-fourth of his age, but thirty-three complete, which make up the sixty years. And so riseth the just sum of four-hundred-and-ninety years, contained in Daniel's seventy weeks" (Willet, *Hexapla in Danielem*, pp. 360, 321).

31.   James VI, *Ane Fruitfull Mediatioun Contening ane Plane and Facill Expositioun of . . . the Revelatioun* (Edinburgh, 1588), sig. Aiiir.

32.   Willet, *Hexapla in Danielem*, pp. 468–69.

33.   Ben Jonson, *The Alchemist* (1610), 4.5.4, in *Works*, vol. 5, p. 375–76.

34.   Matthew Sutcliffe, *The Subversion of Robert Parsons His Confused and Worthlesse Worke, Entituled, A Treatise of Three Conversions of England from Paganism to Christian Religion* (London, 1606), sig. A2v.

35.   William Rainolds, completed by William Gifford, *Calvino-Turcismus. Id Est, Calvinisticae Perfidiae, cum Mahumetana Collatio* (Antwerp, 1597; Cologne, 1603).

36.   Matthew Suttcliffe, *De Turco-Papismo: Hoc Est De Turcarum et Papistrarum Adversus Christi Ecclesiam & Fidem Coniuratione* (London, 1599 and 1604). This particular controversy attracted others as well. The Catholic priest Thomas Wright, drawing on Reynolds and Gifford, published *Certaine Articles and Forcible Reasons, Discovering the Palpable Absurdities and Most Notorious and Intricate Errors of the Protestants Religion* in two editions in 1600 and a third in 1605, which elicited a trio of predictable Protestant rejoinders: William Barlow, *A Defence of the Articles of the Protestants Religion* (London, 1601); Edward Bulkeley, *An Apologie for Religion; Or an Answer to an Unlearned and Slanderous Pamphlet* (London, 1602 and 1608); and Anthony Wotton, *An Answere to a Popish Pamphlet* (London, 1605).

37.   Ochinus declares, "I do renounce my former Christian faith and will embrace the ancient law of Moses and as intending to be serviceable to that religion, I will teach the doctrine of circumcision and will instantly write a book of the lawfulness of polygamy or plurality of wives." For his part, Neuserus promises to "labour with all diligence to spread the Turkish religion in Germany; and finally will go to Constantinople and there I will be circumcised." The reason that the two convert is fairly simple: they believe that "the prophesies of the Old

Testament . . . do show that the Church of God . . . must ever be visible, known, and conspicuous." But they are equally firm in their conviction that "the accomplishments of the said prophesies hath not been effected in . . . the Protestant Church." Since they refuse to accept that the "Papists' Church" is "the sole Church of God," they are left with only one possible alternative: conversion (Clare, *The Converted Jew*, pt. 2, pp. 102, 106–7, 109).

38. For a bibliography of these controversies, see Peter Milward, *Religious Controversies of the Jacobean Age: A Survey of Printed Sources* (Lincoln: University of Nebraska Press, 1978).

39. Humphrey Leech, *A Triumph of Truth. . . . Also the Peculiar Motives . . . Which Perswaded Him to Renounce the Faction of Hereticall Congregations and to Embrace the Unity of the Catholique Church* (Douai, 1609). The Anglican divine Daniel Price countered with *The Defence of Truth* (Oxford, 1610).

40. Francis Walsingham, *A Search Made Into Matters of Religion* (St. Omer, English College Press, 1609); and Benjamin Carier, *A Treatise . . . Wherein He Layeth Downe Sundry Learned and Pithy Considerations, by Which He Was Moved, to Forsake the Protestant Congregation* (Brussels, 1614); which in turn provoked George Hakewill, *An Answere to a Treatise Written by Dr. Carier* (London, 1616).

41. Theophilus Higgons, *The First Motive of T. H. . . . to Suspect the Integrity of His Religion* (Douai, 1609). This work triggered a set of responses, including one written at the behest of Higgons's own father, Sir Edward Hoby's *A Letter to Mr. T. H. Late Minister* (London, 1609). This in turn provoked *The Apology of Theophilus Higgons* (Roan, 1609), a refutatio 1 of Hoby's tract. Then, shockingly, Higgons's suprising recantation and reversion to the Church of England the following year was publicly celebrated in Higgons, *A Sermon Preached at Pauls Crosse the Third of March, 1610 . . . in Testimony of His Heartie Reunion with the Church of England* (London, 1611).

42. Richard Shelton, *The First Sermon of R. Sheldon Priest, After His Conversion from the Romish Church* (London, 1612), as well as a second volume, *The Motives of Richard Sheldon Pr. for His Just, Voluntary, and Free Renouncing of Communion with the Bishop of Rome* (London, 1612).

43. Christopher Musgrave, *Musgraves Motives, and Reasons, for His Secession and Dissevering from the Church of Rome and Her Doctrine* (London, 1621).

44. John de Nicholas, *The Reformed Spaniard* (London, 1621).

45. Ferdinand Texeda, *Texeda Retextus: Or the Spanish Monke His Bill of Divorce Against the Church of Rome* (London, 1623).

46. Marco Antonio de Dominis, *A Manifestation of the Motives* (London, 1616). His apostasy was immediately attacked by the English Jesuit John Sweet in *A Discovery of the Dalmatian Apostata* (St. Omer, English College Press, 1617). To complicate matters, Marco Antonio de Dominis apostatized and returned to Rome, and his second recantation was translated into English by the Jesuit Edward Coffin, *M. Antonius de Dominis . . . Declares the Cause of His Returne* (St. Omer, English College Press, 1623), as well as by G. K., in *The Second Manifesto of Marcus Antonius De Dominis* (Liege, 1623). Not surprisingly, this latest apostasy produced a spate of hostile Anglican reponses.

47. Burton, *Anatomy of Melancholy*, p. 606.

48. Gregory Martin, "Roma Sancta," (1581). The manuscript was first published in George Bruner Parks, *Roma Sancta*, ed. Gregory Martin (Rome: Edizioni di Storia e Letteratura, 1969).

49. Those who are baptized take off their Jewish badges, enter a converts' house, and there learn "the principles of Christian religion." After baptism they "are confirmed . . . and immediately at the Bishop's Mass receive the Blessed Sacrament." Martin specifies that the "solemn christening and confirming" take place "upon two solemn days of the year, Easter

Eve, and Whitson Eve, to signify that by baptism we are buried and rise again with Christ." Martin also notes a recent exception: on the first Sunday of August in 1577 the Cardinal of St. Severine "himself baptized certain more famous then the rest, and other Cardinals were their Godfathers" (Martin, "Roma Sancta," pp. 75–83).

50. Blount, *Levant*, p. 122.

51. Foxe, *A Sermon Preached at the Christening of a Certain Jew, at London* (London, 1578), sig. A1v.

52. Foxe, *Sermon*, sigs. L7r, P1r, H2v, H3r.

53. Foxe, *Sermon*, sigs. I4r, N1r, and E3r–E3v. The marginal note here reads, "Christian men's children here in England crucified by the Jews, Anno 1189 and Anno 1141 at Norwich, etc." (sig. E3r).

54. Foxe, *Sermon*, sigs. ❡5v, ❡6v.

55. Nathaniel Menda, *Confession of Faith, Which Nathaneal a Jewe Borne, Made Before the Congregation in the Parish Church of Alhallowes in Lombard Street at London* (London, 1578), sig. B7v.

56. Menda, *Confession of Faith*, sigs. B3v and B6v.

57. John Foxe, *De Oliva Evangelica* (London, 1578).

58. Edwards's first book had been an ill-fated manuscript submitted to Queen Elizabeth in 1568: a "Discourse on the State of England in Different Reigns," British Library, Lansdowne MS. 95. Edwards explains in a letter to John Dee that his book first met with Elizabeth's approval, but then "went abroad" by means of "other men's hands." Edwards was imprisoned in the Tower of London for fifteen months and fined the huge sum of five hundred pounds (British Library, MS. Cotton Vitellius C.7, sig. 325v). I am grateful to William Sherman for making this discovery available to me.

59. Roger Edwards, "The Conversion and Restitution of Israel" (1581), British Library MS. Lansdowne 353. So convinced was Edwards that these apocalyptic events were imminent that he scrawled in the margin of his manuscript next to a reference to earthquakes in the Psalms, "If these two points be now both past within these sixteen last months, where be we then?" (Edwards, "Conversion," fol. 219r, margin).

60. Edwards, "Conversion," fols. 312v, 313r.

61. Edwards, "Conversion," fols. 314v, 315r, and 320v.

62. Capp, *The Fifth Monarchy Men*, p. 29.

63. In claiming that England "is the land and place from which the Jews [by which he means Puritans] must be delivered," Durden points to the prophesies of both Daniel and Revelation, both of which "agree that the Jews must win victory against the beast with ten horns; which is without all doubt the government of Rome. But that little horn which Daniel speaks of . . . must needs betoken this kingdom, England." For a copy of the letter, see John Strype, *Annals of the Reformation*, 3 vols. (Oxford, 1824), vol. 3, pt. 2, pp. 480–83.

64. Strype, *Annals of the Reformation*, vol. 3, pt. 1, p. 693.

65. See Franz Kobler, in "Sir Henry Finch (1558–1625) and the First English Advocates of the Restoration of the Jews to Palestine," *TJHSE* 16 (1952), pp. 105–6. Kett was the grandson of Robert Kett, the leader of the agrarian revolt of 1549, and an associate of Christopher Marlowe. William Burton, who witnessed Kett's execution, vividly describes how Kett went to his death "leaping and dancing, being in the fire, about twenty times together clapping his hands, he cried nothing, but 'Blessed be God, blessed be God,' and so continued until the fire had consumed his nether parts, and until he was stifled with the smoke that he could speak no longer" (William Burton, *Of Davids Evidence* (London, 1592), rpt. in *Works* [London, 1602], pp. 345–46).

66. Andrew Willet, *De Universali et Nouissima Judaeorum Vocatione* (Cambridge, 1590).

67. "Kettus ille nostrus Anglus iustissma sententia nuper ignis & flammis adiudicatus est,

Norvvici crematus, in consimili haeresi deprehensus, obstinare persistens" (Willet, *De Universali*, sigs. B3v, B4r).

68. The 1609 edition of *A Fruitfull Dialogue Concerning the Ende of the World* is reprinted in William Perkins, *Works*, vol. 3 (London, 1631).

69. Perkins, *Works*, vol. 3, pp. 467, 470.

70. Meredith Hanmer, *The Auncient Ecclesiasticall Histories of the First Six Hundred Yeares After Christ Wrytten in the Greeke Tongue by Three Learned Historiographers, Eusebius, Socrates, and Euagrius* (1577).

71. Hanmer, *Auncient Ecclesiasticall Histories*, pp. 398–99.

72. Mede even wondered, "May not the Jews likewise reprove (if not more) the Church of Rome?" (Joseph Mede, "The Mystery of S. Paul's Conversion; Or, The Type of the Calling of the Jews," in *Works*, ed. John Worthington, 4th ed. [London, 1677], p. 891). Mede was best known for his influential *Clavis Apocalyptica* (Cambridge, 1627) and his *Daniels Weekes. An Interpretation of Part of the Prophesy of Daniel* (London, 1643).

73. Mede, *Works*, pp. 761, 766, 768.

74. Peter Martyr [Vermigli], *The Common Places of . . . Peter Martyr*, trans. Anthony Marten (London, 1583), p. 329.

75. Grotius, *The Truth of Christian Religion*, sigs. B2r, B2v (first published as *De Veritate Religionis Christianae* in 1629). See, too, Thomas Cooper, *The Blessing of Japheth, Proving the Gathering in of the Gentiles and Finall Conversion of the Jewes* (London, 1615).

76. Foxe, *Actes and Monuments* (1570), vol. 2, p. 1107. The work was first published (in Latin) in 1559; the earliest English edition was published in 1563. The woodcut representing the martyrdom of "a Christian Jew" was reproduced in subsequent sixteenth-century editions (see illustration 4, from the 1576 edition).

77. See Samuel C. Chew, *The Crescent and the Rose: Islam and England During the Renaissance* (New York: Oxford University Press, 1937), pp. 50–53. See, too, Sir William Foster, *England's Quest of Eastern Trade* (1933; London: Adam and Charles Black, 1966), p. 74.

78. For more on Barton and the Jews, see H. G. Rosedale, *Queen Elizabeth and the Levant Company*. The recent volumes of the *List and Analysis of State Papers, Foreign Series, Elizabeth I*, ed. R. B. Wernham (1964–), reveal just how extensive dealings were between English merchants and Jews in Constantinople.

79. Broughton, *Works*, vol. 4, p. 697.

80. Strype, *Life of Whitgift*, vol. 2, p. 407.

81. Firth, *The Apocalyptic Tradition*, p. 161.

82. Jonson, *The Alchemist*, 2.3.238, in *Works*, vol. 5, p. 329.

83. Jonson, *The Alchemist*, 4.5.25–32, in *Works*, vol. 5, pp. 376–77.

84. Jonson, *Volpone*, in *Works*, vol. 5, p. 53.

85. Broughton, *Works*, "Preface," sig. B2v. How Abraham Reuben first heard of Broughton is unclear. According to one early version suggested by Broughton himself, news of his debates with Rabbi Elias in Frankfort had circulated widely among continental Jewish communities and their "conference was reported by Jews to Constantinople" (*Works*, vol. 3, p. 617). An alternative though less likely possibility, suggested by the church historian John Strype, is that Broughton's success in Geneva arguing against the teachings of Calvin and Beza might have stimulated the interest of the Turkish Jews. The Genevans, "knowing that a learned Jew of Constantinople, called Abraham Reuben, having heard the fame of him in rabbinical learning, had sent him an Hebrew epistle, to instruct him in the religion of Jesus Christ, desired him to inform them what that Jew's epistle contained; and how he would answer him" (Strype, *Life of Whitgift*, vol. 2, p. 324). The leading scholar on Reuben's work and culture is Professor Joseph Hacker of Hebrew University.

86. I here quote from a subsequent translation that appears in British Library Add. MSS 5943,

fol. 10v.

87. Broughton, *Works*, vol. 4, p. 925.

88. Broughton, *Works*, vol. 4, p. 715.

89. Anon., *Master Broughtons Letters, Especially His Last Pamphlet to and Against the Lord Archbishop of Canterbury* (London, 1599), p. 10. A note in the margin reads at this point: "An epistle coined by Broughton with a Jew's stamp."

90. *Master Broughtons Letters*, pp. 10–12, 49, 47.

91. Hugh Broughton, *Two Epistles Unto Great Men of Britanie, in the Yeare 1599* (Basel, 1606), sig. A2v.

92. Hugh Broughton, *A Revelation of the Holy Apocalypse* (Amsterdam, 1610), p. 139.

93. Broughton, *Two Epistles*, sig. A2v.

94. Broughton, *Works*, vol. 4, pp. 691–92.

95. Hugh Broughton, preface to *Sundry Workes* (n.p., 1594?).

96. Broughton, *Works*, vol. 3, p. 614. Katherine Firth notes several earlier attempts to collect Broughton's work, alluded to by Puritan writers (*Apocalyptic Tradition*, p. 224). There was another unsuccessful attempt to bring together his scattered work, this time in the late 1640s, by George Thomason, the printer, who circulated *A Schedule of the Late Reverend and Learned Mr. Hugh Broughton as They Were Preparing for the Presse* (n.d., n.p., but Thomason died in 1666, and the Bodleian, where this document can be found, lists the date for this sheet as 1649 [Wood 658 (797)], though without explanation).

97. Hugh Broughton, *A Declaration Unto the Lordes, of the Jewes Desire These Fiftene Yeres for Ebrew Explication of Our Greke Gospell* (London, 1611), pp. 1–3.

98. Broughton, *Works*, vol. 4, p. 713.

99. John Harrison, *The Messiah Already Come* (1610; 2d ed., Amsterdam, Giles Thorp, 1619). The work was also reprinted in 1656.

100. The version Harrison carried with him was probably one of the many pocket-sized editions anonymously adopted in 1590 for the use of Protestants from the original *First Booke of the Christian Exercise Pertaining to Resolution*, first published by the Jesuit Robert Parsons in 1582 in Rouen. The volume was thought to be quite useful for converting Jews, since many of its "proofs of Christianity" were drawn from Jewish authorities. The text describes how "no man can deny but that throughout the whole body and course of Scriptures, that is, from the very beginning to the last end of their Old Testament, they had promised unto them a Messiah, which the very same that we call Christ" ([Robert Parsons], *The Second Parte of the Booke of Christian Exercise, Appertayning to Resolution, or a Christian Directorie* [London, 1601], sig. H2r).

101. Harrison, *The Messiah Already Come*, sigs. I1r, I1v.

102. Harrison, *The Messiah Already Come*, dedication to the 1619 edition.

103. John Meirs, *A Short Treatise Compos'd and Published by John Meirs, Formerly a Jew, Now by the Signal Mercy of God in Christ Converted to the Christian Faith* (rpt. London 1717), Dedicatory Epistle, n.p.

104. Moses Marcus, *The Principal Motives and Circumstances That Induced Moses Marcus to Leave the Jewish, and Embrace the Christian Faith* (London, 1724), p. xv.

105. Of course, there were conversions that did not lead to published confessions of faith, including that of Paul Jacob in the early 1620s, who wrote to King James asking for support: "Petition of Paul Jacob, a converted Jew, to the King. Considers that as the sceptre has departed from Judah, his Majesty is the true King of the Jews; is therefore his child and subject, and prays for a small allowance. Was converted by George, Bishop of Londonderry" (*Calendar of State Papers, Domestic* [1623–25], p. 517).

106. Daniel ben Alexander, *Daniel ben Alexander the Converted Jew of Prague*, trans. T. Drewe (n.p., 1621), sig. D1v.

107. Calvert, *The Blessed Jew of Marocco*, p. 227. Calvert also cites here the authority of "Andra-

dius," who knew of African Jews "'that were induced by the reading of the fifty-third chapter of Isaiah only, to leave house, country, friends, fair estates, parents, and with inflamed desires of soul to consecrate themselves to Christ'" (p. 228). See, too, Calvert's *Medulla Evangelli; Or the Prophet Isaiah's Crucifix* (London, 1657).

108. Richard Mayo, *A Conference Betwixt a Protestant and a Jew: Or, a Second Letter from a Merchant in London, to His Correspondent in Amsterdam* (London, 1678), pp. 29–31.

109. Daniel ben Alexander, *The Converted Jew of Prague*, sigs. B2r, C4r, and D3v.

110. "Fourteen or sixteen of which years remained at that time to be fulfilled," meaning that the messiah was expected no later than 1650 (Brereton, *Travels in Holland*, p. 11).

111. Calvert, *The Blessed Jew of Marocco*, pp. 197, 201, 206, 211–12.

112. The most popular version first appeared in a book by the diarist John Evelyn: *The History of the Three Late Famous Imposters, viz. Padro Ottomano, Mahamed Bei, and Sabatai Sevi* (London, 1669), which a number of subsequent versions drew upon, including R. B. [Nathaniel Crouch], "The Counterfeit Messiah or False Christ of the Jews at Smyrna in the Year 1666. Written by an English Person of Quality There Resident," in *Admirable Curiosities, Rarities, and Wonders*, 2d ed. (London, 1684). Paul Rycaut had provided Evelyn with his material, but as English consul at Smyrna, he was reluctant at the time to publish under his own name. He retold the story in greater detail in *The History of the Turkish Empire from the Year 1623 to the Year 1677* (London 1680). Yet another version, this one anonymous, appeared in a book on "notorious imposters," called *The Devil of Delphos, or the Prophets of Baal* (London, 1708).

113. Richard H. Popkin, "Three English Tellings of the Sabbatai Zevi Story," *Jewish History* 8 (1994), pp. 43–54; see, too, Michael McKeon, "Sabbatai Sevi in England," *Association of Jewish Studies Review* 3 (1977), pp. 131–69.

114. Purchas, *Pilgrimage*, p. 213.

115. See James Howell's comments in his edition of *The Wonderful and Most Deplorable History*, p. 371.

116. Moses Scialitti, *A Letter Written to the Jewes* (London, 1663).

117. Tovey, *Anglia Judaica*, pp. 280, 284.

118. Solomon Franco, *Truth Springing Out of the Earth* (London, 1668).

119. Franco, *Truth Springing*, sig. A4v, pp. 35–36, 38.

120. Monsieur de Bréval (François Durant), *La Juif Baptise* (London, 1671).

121. John Jacob, *The Jew Turned Christian* (London, 1678).

122. John Alexander, *God's Covenant Displayed, by John Alexander a Converted Jew* (London, 1689).

123. Theodore John, *An Account of the Conversion of Theodore John, a Late Teacher Among the Jews Together with His Confession of the Christian Faith* (London, 1693).

124. Thomas Humphrey, *A True Narrative of God's Gracious Dealings with the Soul of Shalome ben Shalomoh a Jew. With an Account of His Conversion*, 2d ed. (London, 1700).

125. Humphrey, *A True Narrative*, pp. i–ii, v, 2, 4, 6–7.

126. Hanmer, *Auncient Ecclesiasticall Histories*, p. 385.

127. Abrahams, "A Jew in the Service of the East India Company," pp. 173–75.

128. Foster, ed., *Voyages of Sir James Lancaster*, p. 124.

129. Albert Gray, ed., *The Voyage of François Pyrard of Laval to the East Indies, the Maldives, the Moluccas and Brazil*, 2 vols., no. 76 (London: Hakluyt Society, 1887–90), vol. 1, pp. 283–85.

130. Scales, "Condition of the Nation of the Jewes," fol. 21.

131. Another example of apostasy is offered by "B. B.," who writes of "Mr. Dupass," who "was born of Jewish parents in Holland" before he came to England "about twenty years since, and became a Christian [and] was in the protection of King Charles II." The Jews were "irritated . . . most of all . . . to see Mr. Dupass marry an English lady," and won him back

to the fold "by sending him to the Indies" (B. B., *A Historical and Law Treatise Against the Jewes and Judaism* [London, 1721], pp. 29–30).

132. Marlowe, *The Jew of Malta*, 1.2.82–83.

133. Marlowe, *The Jew of Malta*, 1.2.290–93.

134. Marlowe, *The Jew of Malta*, 1.2.323–25.

135. Marlowe, *The Jew of Malta*, 1.2.337–38, 44–45, 57–58.

136. Marlowe, *The Jew of Malta*, 2.3.311–15.

137. Marlowe, *The Jew of Malta*, 3.3.58–68, 73–74.

138. Marlowe, *The Jew of Malta*, 3.6.40.

139. Shakespeare, *The Merchant of Venice*, 5.1.12–16.

140. John Studley, trans., *Medea*, in *Seneca His Tenne Tragedies*, ed. Thomas Newton, intro. by T. S. Eliot, 2 vols. (London: Constable and Co., 1927). vol. 2, pp. 59, 64.

141. Gilbert Burnet, *The Conversion and Persecutions of Eve Cohan* (London, 1680). There was only one other narrative of a female Jewish convert published in seventeenth-century England: the anonymous and fictional *The Amorous Convert. Being a True Relation of What Happened in Holland* (London, 1679).

142. Burnet, *The Conversion and Persecutions of Eve Cohan*, pp. 3, 5, 23.

143. Eliza Fowler Haywood, *The Fair Hebrew: Or, a True, but Secret History of Two Jewish Ladies, Who Lately Resided in London* (London, 1729). While published anonymously, the work was publicly advertised under Haywood's name in the year of its publication.

144. Heywood, *The Fair Hebrew*, p. 8.

145. Haywood, *The Fair Hebrew*, pp. 48, 52–53.

146. Calvert, *The Blessed Jew of Marocco*, p. 186.

147. Andrew Willet, in a section on the apostasy of the Jews ("De Judaeis Apostatis & Relapsis") also relates an incident in which a Jewish woman was married twice—"Mulier Judaica bis nupta": "Meminerunt etiam scriptores historici mulieris cuiusdam Hebreae, qua baptismo accepto Christiano marito elocata fuit, eadem a professione resiliens iturum viro Judaeo nupserat" (Willet, *De Universali*, sig. G1v [Historians also mention a certain Jewish woman who, although she had been baptized and had been contracted to a Christian man, withdrew from her vow and married a second time, to a Jewish man]).

148. For an excellent discussion of *Harrington* in terms of its exploration of English and Jewish identity, see Michael Ragussis, "Representation, Conversion, and Literary Form: *Harrington* and the Novel of Jewish Identity," *Critical Inquiry* 16 (1989), 113–43. See, too, his recent book, *Figures of Conversion: "The Jewish Question" and English National Identity* (Durham: Duke University Press, 1995).

149. Edgeworth, *Harrington*, p. 294.

150. Shakespeare, *The Merchant of Venice*, 3.5.9–11.

151. Maria Edgeworth, *Castle Rackrent* (1800), in *Tales and Novels*, vol. 1, pp. 19–32.

152. Wood, *History and Antiquities*, vol. 2, p. 316.

153. *Acts of the Privy Council* (1613–1614), p. 257.

154. *Acts of the Privy Council* (1613–1614), pp. 272–73.

155. The ending of the story called to Smith's mind the account, quoted above, that "Socrates [Scholasticus] relateth of one of this nation, that coming to be christened, the water miraculously vanished, and the font filled again, was suddenly dried up. So on the other side, the water was here ready and remaining, but our Jew vanished, and was run away; nor did he ever return to give thanks for all the courtesies received from our reverend Doctor" (Willet, *Synopsis Papismi* [1634], sigs. B4v, C1r, C1v).

156. It is possible to date the St. Mary sermons sometime after the summer of 1614, since we know that accounts of the recent expulsion of the Jews from Frankfurt were circulating at this time, an event that Lake mentions in his sermons: "even this year God hath made us see

the truth hereof [that the Jews are vagabonds and slaves]: Germany hath yielded a spectacle of their slavery. In the city of Frankfurt which was inhabited with many thousands of
them, when they were preparing themselves to solemnize that day wherein they bewail the
destruction of Hierusalem, the inhabitants otherwise exasperated against them, wreak their
displeasure upon them, and hazarding many of their lives, rifled most of their goods, and
forced them out of their city" (p. 483). This occurred in late summer of 1614, as we know
from letters from the continent circulating in England a month or so later, such as Arthur
Ayscombe's letter to William Trumbull of September 13, 1614, which notes that "the commons of Frankfurt have mutinied and sacked the Jews that dwelt there" (HMC *Report on the
Manuscripts of the Most Honourable the Marquesse of Downshire*, vol. 5, Papers of William
Trumbull, September 1614–August 1616, ed. G. Dyfnallt Owen, p. 17).

157.　Arthur Lake, "Five Sermons Preached in Saint Maries in Oxford," in Arthur Lake, *Sermons
with Some Religious and Divine Meditations* (London, 1629), pp. 479, 507, 486–87.

158.　Calvert, *The Blessed Jew of Marocco*, p. 216.

6. Race, Nation, or Alien?

The epigraph is a translation of, "Judaei non inseruntur in gentum stirpem," in Willet, *Judaeorum
Vocatione* (Cambridge, 1590), p. 25v.

1.　"Anglia nostra, a Brittanis primo culta est, Saxones deinde eam depopulati, ipsi postea vere
Britanni (mutato tantum nomine) facti sunt" (Willet, *Judeorum Vocatione*, p. 25v).

2.　"Galli postremo in Angliam celeberriman hanc patriam nostram, vi & armis irrumpentes
ipis etiam in Anglos transierunt" (Willet, *Judaeorum Vocatione*, p. 25v).

3.　"Idem etiam aliis regnis saepius contigisse palam loquentur historiae, quorum incolae
saepius mutati & extirpati sunt" (Willet, *Judaeorum Vocatione*, p. 25v).

4.　"Si Anglus Hispaniam petierit, eius haerades Hispanorum loco censebuntur, licet ipse cog-
nationem non amittat: Si Scotus res suas deportat & transvehat in Galliam, eius posteritas
Gallicos mores redolebit, Scoticis non amplius assueta" (Willet, *Judaeorum Vocatione*, p.
25v).

5.　"Judaeus tamen sive Hispaniam, sive Galliam itinere petierit, sive in quamcumque aliam
regionem profiscatur, non Hispanum aut Gallum, sed Judaeum se profitetur" (Willet,
Judaeorum Vocatione, p. 25v).

6.　"Judaei non inseruntur in gentum stirpem" (Willet, *Judaeorum Vocatione*, p. 25v).

7.　If the Gentile who "wast cut out of the olive tree, was wild by nature, and wast grafted contrary to nature in a right olive tree, how much more," Paul asks, "shall they that are by
nature, be grafted in their own olive tree?" (Romans 11.17, 23–24).

8.　Geneva commentary to Romans 11.26. My emphasis.

9.　For a helpful discussion of this topic, see Shell, "From Coexistence to Toleration," pp.
309–12.

10.　Increase Mather, *The Mystery of Israel's Salvation* (London, 1669), p. 130.

11.　Mather, *Israel's Salvation*, p. 130. For more on this Puritan's views on the literal interpretation of the millennium, see: Mason I. Lowance, Jr., and David Watters, "Increase Mather's
'New Jerusalem': Millennialism in Late Seventeenth-Century New England," *Proceedings
of the American Antiquarian Society* n.s. 87 (1977), pp. 343–408.

12.　E. A. Freeman, "The Jews in Europe," *Historical Essays*, 3rd series, vol. 1 (London, 1879),
p. 230, as cited in Feldman, *Englishmen and Jews*, p. 92.

13.　Lucien Wolf, "What Is Judaism? A Question of Today," *Fortnightly Review* (August 1884),
pp. 240–41, as cited in Feldman, *Englishmen and Jews*, p. 126.

14.　Isaiah, *The Messiah of the Christians*, sig. B3v, p. 2. This is a direct translation of Sebastian
Munster, *Messias Christianorum et Judeaeorum* (Basel, 1539), sig. A5v.

15.　Verena Stolcke, "Invaded Women: Gender, Race, and Class in the Formation of Colonial

Society," in Margo Hendricks and Patricia Parker, eds., *Women, "Race," and Writing*, p. 276.

16. Richard Baxter, *The Glorious Kingdom of Christ* (London, 1691), p. 62.

17. Blount, *Levant*, p. 121.

18. Brereton, *Travels in Holland*, p. 61.

19. In Donald Maclean, ed., "London in 1689–90," *Transactions of the London and Middlesex Archeological Society* n.s. 7 (1937), p. 151.

20. As cited in Patai and Patai, *The Myth of the Jewish Race*, p. 32, from Francois-Maximilien Misson, *A New Voyage to Italy*, 4th ed. (1691; London, 1714), vol. 2, p. 139.

21. Menasseh ben Israel, *Humble Address*, rpt. in Wolf, ed., *Menasseh ben Israel's Mission*, p. 85.

22. Shakespeare, *The Merchant of Venice*, 3.2.283.

23. Convinced that the Jews, having "thus lived in several countries, and always in subjection ... must needs have suffered many commixtures," Browne offers as additional evidence that "fornications [are not] unfrequent" between Christians and Jews. Introducing sexual myths in order to repudiate racial and national ones, Browne claims that these "fornications" occur because Jewish "women desire copulation with" Christians, "rather than [with] their own nation, and affect Christian carnality above circumcised venery." His conclusions return to the theological issue that set this racial theory in motion: what to do with those who are to be saved but are of mixed racial stock, since it is "acknowledged, that some are lost, evident that others are mixed, and not assured that any are distinct, it will be hard to establish this quality upon the Jews, unless we also transfer the same unto those whose generations are mixed, whose genealogies are Jewish, and naturally derived from them" (Browne, *Pseudodoxia*, p. 202).

24. Shakespeare, *The Merchant of Venice*, 2.7.79, 2.1.1–2, 11–12.

25. Shakespeare, *The Merchant of Venice*, 3.5.31–36.

26. For a valuable account of race in Shakespeare, see Linda Boose, "'The Getting of a Lawful Race': Racial Discourse in Early Modern England and the Unrepresentable Black Woman," in Hendricks and Parker, eds., *Women, "Race," and Writing*, pp. 35–54.

27. Purchas, for example, saw a natural connection between Britain and Israel and between King James and his biblical namesake when he write about how "God hath showed his word unto our Jacob" and "his statutes and his judgments unto this Israel of Great Britain" (Purchas, "To the Reader," *Pilgrimage* [1617, n.p. or sig.]).

28. See Lucien Wolf, "'Jossipon' in England," *TJHSE* 6 (1912), p. 278.

29. Joseph ben Gurion, pseud., *A Compendious and Most Mervailous Historie of the Latter Times of the Jewes Common Weale*, trans. Peter Morwyng (London, 1593), sig. A3r.

30. Copies of *Jossipon* survive from editions printed in 1561, 1567, 1575, 1579, 1596, 1602, 1608, 1615, 1652, 1653, 1662, 1669, 1673, 1678, 1682, 1684, 1689, and 1699. See Wolf, "Jossipon," pp. 277–88, for a list of editions (though there are a number of extant editions of which Wolf was unaware).

31. Purchas, *Pilgrimage*, p. 140.

32. Complicating the question of the Jews' national identity still further was that early modern Sephardic Jews in Antwerp and Amsterdam referred to themselves as members of the "Portugese Jewish Nation," while in Spain and Portugal Conversos were often called "Gente de la Nacion" (people of the nation). See E. R. Samuel, "Portuguese Jews in Jacobean London," p. 172, n. 2.

33. While Stephen Nettles, in his response to Selden on tithes, agreed that things "spoken to the Jews" pertain to the English as well ("for God is no changeling"), the same does not hold true for arguments taken from the Talmud. Even less acceptable are examples drawn from Anglo-Jewish history, and he gets exasperated with Selden for shifting between the precedents provided by ancient Israelites and medieval English Jews: "Hitherto following this

historian we have been travailing in the land of Canaan, and are now upon the sudden brought into England, for multitude and variety of blessings, a second Canaan" (Stephen Nettles, *An Answer to the Jewish Part of Mr Selden's History of Tithes* [Oxford, 1625], pp. 175, 63, 162–63).

34. Among the more influential of these studies were Bonaventure Corneille Bertram, *De Politia Judaica* (Geneva, 1574); Carlo Sigonio, *De Republica Hebraorum* (Bologna, 1582; Frankfurt, 1583); Petrus Cunaeus, *Republica Hebraeorum* (1632), subsequently translated into English by Clement Barkesdale, *Of the Common-Wealth of the Hebrews* (London, 1653); and J. S. Marochius, *De Republica Hebraeorum* (Paris, 1648). For more of this tradition, see S. B. Liljegren, *Harrington and the Jews* (Lund: C. W. K. Gleerups Forlag, 1932).

35. Thomas Morton, *Salomon, or a Treatise Declaring the State of the Kingdom of Israel* (London, 1596), sig. B2v.

36. Such as the 1656 pamphlet concerning *Four Grand Inquiries: Whether This Whole Nation Must Be a Church as the Jewish Nation Was*. Royalists, too, invoked Jewish models. The extremist Arise Evans went so far as to suggest that Charles II was the messiah the Jews had long awaited. Through an interpreter, Evans even tried to persuade Menasseh ben Israel, then in London, that the son "of the late King Charles of England is he whom you call your Messiah, Captain and Deliverer." Moreover, "Jews who would come into England without his command . . . shall in a short time be spoiled and destroyed" Evans records that Menasseh's response was silence (Evans, *Light for the Jews*, p. 20).

37. The best account of this remains Katz, *Philo-Semitism*, pp. 89–126.

38. Fletcher, "The Tartars or, Ten Tribes," in Lee, *Israel Redux*, pp. 3–5.

39. Martin Luther, *A Commentarie Upon the Fiftene Psalmes*, trans. Henry Bull, preface "To the Christian Reader" by John Foxe (London, 1577), pp. 267–68.

40. Lake, *Sermons*, pp. 483, 527.

41. See A. L. Beier, *Masterless Men: The Vagrancy Problem in England, 1560–1640* (London: Methuen, 1985).

42. [Anne Dennis?] *An Answer to the Book Against the Jews: Written by B. B.* (London, 1703), p. 4.

43. Thomas Becon, *Prayers and Other Pieces*, ed. John Ayre, for the Parker Society (Cambridge: Cambridge University Press, 1844), p. 9. Edward Brerewood arrived at much the same conclusion: the "Jews have not for their mansion, any peculiar country, but are dispersed abroad among foreign nations for their ancient idolatries and their later unthankfulness in rejecting their Saviour" (*Enquiries Touching the Diversity of Languages*, p. 92).

44. Donne, *Sermons*, vol. 7, p. 427.

45. Purchas, *Pilgrimes*, vol. 1, p. 67.

46. Greenblatt, *Marvelous Possessions*, p. 51.

47. Blount, *Levant*, p. 123.

48. Purchas, *Pilgrimage*, p. 1441.

49. Prynne, *A Short Demurrer*, part 1, pp. 103–4.

50. Calvert, "Diatriba of the Jews' Estate," *The Blessed Jew of Marocco*, p. 23.

51. Roger of Wendover (d. 1236), *Flores Historiarum* (see *Rogeri de Wendover Liber qui Dicitur Flores Historiarum*, ed. H. G. Hewlett, vol. 84 of *Rolls Series* [London, 1886–1889], vol. 2, pp. 352ff.). Roger got his account from an unnamed Armenian archbishop who was visiting at St. Albans (and told the same story elsewhere on the continent, where it is similarly recorded).

52. Matthew Paris, *Chronica Majora* (London, 1571). Paris follows his predecessor's account almost verbatim, adding some additional authorities that confirm the account.

53. George K. Anderson, "Popular Survivals of the Wandering Jew in England," *JEGP* 46 (1948), pp. 372–73.

54. George K. Anderson, *The Legend of the Wandering Jew* (Providence: Brown University

Press, 1965), p. 61.

55. See Anderson, *Legend*, p. 91, for these and other contemporary allusions.

56. As cited in Anderson, *Legend*, pp. 63–65.

57. See J. Q. Adams, "Hill's List of Early Plays in Manuscript," *Library*, n.s. 20 (1939), pp. 71–99. Aside from Abraham Hill's transcription of the play's title, no other information about *The Wandering Jew* has survived.

58. Donne, "Sermon Preached at the Churching of the Countesse of Bridgewater," 1621, in *Sermons*, vol. 5, pp. 185–86. See N. I. Matar, "The Date of John Donne's Sermon 'Preached at the Churching of the Countesse of Bridgewater,'" *Notes and Queries* (December, 1992), pp. 447–48.

59. Patrick Forbes, *An Exquisite Commentarie Upon the Revelations of Saint John* (London, 1613), p. 168.

60. Finch, *The Worlds Great Restauration*, sig. A2v. Finch sees the Jews not only as a political nation here but as one that constitutes a race as well, for he writes to the Jews that only "unto those out of whose loins thou doest come, was the promise of that seed in whom all the families of the earth should be blessed." He also invokes the familiar metaphor first used by Paul in assuring the Jews that God "will graft thee by faith into that natural olive tree, from the which through infidelity thou art hitherto broken off."

61. Finch, *The Worlds Great Restauration*, sigs. A1v, A3v, and pp. 2, 6–7.

62. Finch, *The Worlds Great Restauration*, sig. A3r. See also, Franz Kobler, "Sir Henry Finch (1558–1625) and the first English Advocates of the Restoration of the Jews to Palestine," pp. 101–20.

63. Well into the late nineteenth century those sympathetic to the Jews, such as the novelist George Eliot, nonetheless assumed that "it is a calamity to the English, as to any other great historic people, to undergo a premature fusion with immigrants of alien blood." For George Eliot—who wonders whether the Jews are "destined to complete fusion with the peoples among whom they are dispersed, losing every remnant of a distinctive consciousness as Jews"—the only practical solution to preserving the two peoples from mutual contamination is the restoration of the Jews to their own homeland (Eliot, "The Modern Hep! Hep! Hep!," *The Impressions of Theophrastus Such* [London, 1879]). Cf. the conclusion to Eliot's *Daniel Deronda* (London, 1876).

64. See Edgar R. Samuel, "Sir Thomas Shirley's 'Project for Jewes'—the Earliest Known Proposal for the Resettlement," *TJHSE* 24 (1974), pp. 195–97.

65. J. G. A. Pocock, ed., *The Political Works of James Harrington* (Cambridge: Cambridge University Press, 1977), p. 159.

66. Ian W. Archer, *The Pursuit of Stability: Social Relations in Elizabethan London* (Cambridge: Cambridge University Press, 1991), p. 132. See, too, Irene Scouloudi, *Returns of Strangers in the Metropolis: 1593, 1627, 1635, 1639*, Huguenot Society of London, Quarto Series (London, 1985) vol. 57, p. 76, and her "The Stranger Community in the Metropolis, 1558–1640," in Scouloudi, ed., *Huguenots in Britain and Their French Background, 1550–1800* (London: MacMillan, 1987), pp. 42–55. For more on alien communities, see Bernard Cottret, *The Huguenots in England: Immigration and Settlement, c. 1550–1700*, trans. Peregrine and Adriana Stevenson (first published as *Terre d'exil*, Paris:, Aubier, 1985; Cambridge: Cambridge University Press, 1991); and Andrew Pettegree, *Foreign Protestant Communities in Sixteenth-Century London*, (Oxford: Clarendon Press, 1986).

67. Scouloudi, *Returns*, p. 1.

68. In medieval England the monarchy had been primarily responsible for protecting the rights of aliens, and had succeeded in abolishing the law of "hostage" ("the right by chartered towns and boroughs to lodge the alien and supervise his business transactions"), in extending the length of stay permitted by the town, in mitigating "the monopolistic claims of the

native guilds, which were afterwards reinforced by Acts of Parliament," and, following the Reformation, in helping Protestant refugees by granting them charters (E. F. Churchill, "The Crown and the Alien: A Review of the Crown Protection of the Alien, from the Norman Conquest Down to 1689," *Law Quarterly Review* 36 [1920], p. 403). But England's kings and queens had to negotiate these powers in relationship to the authority claimed not only by Parliament but also by towns and boroughs. In addition, there was also a division between alien "friends" and alien "enemies." The "friends," in exchange for their local and temporary allegiance, had in the course of the late fifteenth and sixteenth centuries gradually won the right to lodge, trade, obtain restitution in English courts, take leases, and bring personal actions. In terms of new liabilities, they could also be punished for crimes committed in England (Scouloudi, *Returns*, p. 1).

69. J. M. Ross, "Naturalisation of Jews in England," *TJHSE* 24 (1975), p. 60. According to the *Oxford English Dictionary*, the first recorded use of "naturalization" appears in the writing of John Knox in 1559. By 1593 it was being employed in a figurative sense by George Peele, who conflates naturalization and denization when he said that "Harrington . . . hath so purely naturalized strange words, and made them all free denizens." Shakespeare also uses the term; he writes in *All's Well That Ends Well*, for example, that "my instruction shall serve to naturalize thee" (1.1.207).

70. The best-known example of this problem in early modern England was the 1609 case of Calvin, a young boy born in Scotland whose right to benefit from freehold tenements in London was contested on the grounds that he was an alien. Luckily for Calvin, legal experts decided that he was born after King James had come to the English throne and thus was technically English and therefore eligible to hold property in England. His case gives some inkling of how disputed the legal status of aliens was at this time (Scouloudi, *Returns*, p. 1).

71. Pettegree, *Foreign Protestant Communities*, pp. 83, 279.

72. See Pettegree, *Foreign Protestant Communities*, p. 16, n. 22.

73. For comparison's sake, the 1568 return listed 6,684 strangers; the one in 1571 only 4,755; and two early seventeenth-century returns, in 1618 and 1635, counted 1,281 and 3,622 respectively (see Scouloudi, p. 5). The disparity undoubtedly reflects the effectiveness of the census rather than wild fluctuations in the number of strangers in London. Even in the "successful" 1593 return that totalled 7,113 stangers, Lopez, the Queen's physician who had been included in an early census, was not recorded, and we need to interpret these numbers cautiously in making claims about the percentage of aliens in the city.

74. Archer, *Stability*, pp. 4–5. In addition to Queen Mary's proclamation in 1554 (following Wyatt's rebellion and the rising in Kent against her foreign marriage) ordering that all non-denizen aliens should leave England, there was also "intermittent and faltering regulation" against aliens under Queen Elizabeth in 1563, 1566, 1567, 1571, and 1572, as well as restrictive legislation in the early 1580s—which failed to pass into law in part because the aliens lobbied effectively and because there was Privy Council sympathy for aliens and support for their potential benefit to the English economy (Pettegree, *Foreign Protestant Communities*, p. 117; and Archer, *Stability*, p. 137–39).

75. Edward Dymock sued "for a view of aliens and strangers throughout the realm and to keep a roll and a book of the names and numbers of them." And Sir Thomas Mildmay petitioned for "the erecting of an office to keep a register yearly of the names, ages, abilities of body, countries, calling, arts, sciences, places of habitation, causes of repair hither, and times of departure hence, of all foreigners and strangers, now being and inhabiting within the realm; and of all others that should from time to time come into the realm to inhabit, or pass out of the same" (John Strype, *A Survey of the Cities of London and Westminster . . . Written by John Stow . . . Corrected, Improved, and Very Much Enlarged by John Strype*, 2 vols. [London,

1720], vol. 2, p. 302).

76.   Scouloudi, *Returns*, p. 58.

77.   Scouloudi, *Returns*, p. 63.

78.   Strype, *Survey*, vol. 2, pp. 302–3.

79.   Sir Simon D'Ewes, *A Compleat Journal of the Votes, Speeches, and Debates, Both of the House of Lords and House of Commons Throughout the Whole Reign of Queen Elizabeth*, 2d ed. (London, 1693), p. 506.

80.   D'Ewes, *A Compleat Journal*, p. 506.

81.   Marlowe, *The Jew of Malta*, 1.1.102–3, 2.3.202.

82.   Marlowe, *The Jew of Malta*, 1.2.59–61, 5.1.72.

83.   I have drawn here on the summary of Arthur Freeman, "Marlowe, Kyd, and the Dutch Church Libel," *English Literary Renaissance* 3 (1973), p. 45. See, too, *Acts of the Privy Council* (1592–93), pp. 187, 200–1.

84.   As cited in Freeman, "Marlowe, Kyd, and the Dutch Church Libel," p. 50.

85.   As cited in Vittorio Gabrieli and Giorgio Melchiori, eds., *Sir Thomas More*, by Anthony Munday and others, revised by Henry Chettle, Thomas Dekker, Thomas Heywood, and William Shakespeare (Manchester: Manchester University Press, 1990), p. 17.

86.   Scott McMillin, "*The Book of Sir Thomas More*: Dates and Acting Companies," in T. H. Howard-Hill, ed., *Shakespeare and "Sir Thomas More": Essays on the Play* (Cambridge: Cambridge University Press, 1989), p. 58.

87.   *Sir Thomas More*, 2.3.141–51.

88.   See Scott McMillin, *The Elizabethan Theatre and "The Book of Sir Thomas More"* (Ithaca: Cornell University Press, 1987); Janet Clare, *"Art Made Tongue-Tied by Authority": Elizabethan and Jacobean Censorship* (Manchester: Manchester University Press, 1990), p. 37; Alfred W. Pollard, *Shakespeare's Hand in the Play of Sir Thomas More* (Cambridge: Cambridge University Press, 1923; rpt. 1967); and the various essays in T. H. Howard-Hill, ed., *Shakespeare and "Sir Thomas More"*.

89.   *Sir Thomas More*, 2.3.76–78.

90.   Strype, *Survey*, vol. 2, p. 303.

91.   Archer, *Stability*, pp. 1–9.

92.   Archer, *Stability*, p. 131.

93.   Archer, *Stability*, p. 131.

94.   Shakespeare, *The Merchant of Venice*, 1.3.33–35.

95.   Shakespeare, *The Merchant of Venice*, 4.1.322–28.

96.   Shakespeare, *The Merchant of Venice*, 4.1.339–42.

97.   Shakespeare, *The Merchant of Venice*, 4.1.342–52.

98.   M. M. Mahood, ed., *The Merchant of Venice* (Cambridge: Cambridge University Press), p. 136.

99.   Ross, "Naturalisation," p. 61.

100.   Ross, "Naturalisation," p. 62.

101.   Roth, *History*, pp. 164–65.

102.   The document appears in an appendix to Lucien Wolf, "Status of the Jews in England After the Re-Settlement," *TJHSE* 4 (1903), pp. 187–88.

103.   Wolf, "Status of the Jews in England," p. 182. Violet also invokes the familiar litany of Jewish crimes, reminding the king that the Jews had already been expelled once from England because of their "infidelity, blaphemies, apostasies, enmity to Christ and Christianity, circumcising and crucifying Christian children, clipping and coining of money, falsifying of charters, extortion, brokage, usury, frauds, rapes, murders, forgeries, violence, plunder, and unconscionable cut-throat dealing" (Wolf, "Status of the Jews in England," p. 190).

104.   Lucien Wolf engages in a little wishful thinking when, after reporting this history, he con-

cludes that the "anomolous condition of being neither aliens, denizens, nor natives gradually disappeared" ("Status of the Jews in England," pp. 178–82). His sentiments would be echoed a half-century later by Cecil Roth, who writes of these events that while the "Jews had not been recalled to England . . . their presence there was henceforth considered legitimate" (Roth, *History*, p. 166). It would be more accurate to say that the Jews' position was never quite so vulnerable again, though no one at the time could possibly have known this.

105.   Samuel Hayne, *An Abstract of All the Statutes Made Concerning Aliens Trading in England . . . Proving That Jews . . . Break Them All* (London, 1685).

106.   David S. Katz, "The Jews of England and 1688," in Ole Peter Grell, Jonathan I. Israel, and Nicholas Tyacke, eds., *From Persecution to Toleration: The Glorious Revolution and Religion in England* (Oxford: Clarendon Press, 1991), pp. 218–23.

107.   As cited in Katz, "The Jews of England and 1688," p. 223.

108.   As cited in Katz, "The Jews of England and 1688," p. 238, from *The Case of the Jews Stated* (n.p. [London], n.d. [November 11, 1689]), rpt. *TJHSE* 9 (1922), pp. 44–46.

109.   As cited from Gray's *Parlimentary Debates*, vol. 9, pp 437–38, in H. S. Q. Henriques, "Proposal for Special Taxation of the Jews After the Revolution," *TJHSE* 9 (1922), p. 51.

110.   Katz, "The Jews of England and 1688," pp. 242–43, 246.

111.   Katz, "The Jews of England and 1688," pp. 230. 258.

112.   Katz, "The Jews of England and 1688," p. 249.

113.   B. B., *A Historical and Law Treatise Against the Jewes and Judaism*, pp. 3, 5, 21.

114.   Roth, *History*, p. 256.

115.   See, for example, J. E. Blunt, *A History of the Establishment and Residence of the Jews in England with an Inquiry Into Their Civil Disabilities* (London, 1830), and H. S. Q. Henriques's *The Jews and The English Law* (London, 1908).

7. Shakespeare and the Jew Bill of 1753

Epigraph sources are as follows: John Cunningham, *Poems, Chiefly Pastoral* (London, 1766), pp. 165–66; Anon., *The Exclusion of the English; An Invitation to Foreigners* (London, 1748), p. 10; Arthur Murphy [under the pseudonym Charles Ranger], *The Gray's-Inn Journal*, 2 vols. (London, 1756), vol. 1, pp. 222, 224 [June 16, 1753].

1.   Geoffrey Alderman, *The Jewish Community in British Politics* (Oxford: Clarendon Press, 1983), p. 7.

2.   Robert Liberles, "The Jews and Their Bill: Jewish Motivations in the Controversy of 1753," *Jewish History* 2 (1987), p. 29.

3.   Anon., *A True State of the Case Concerning the Good or Evil Which the Bill for the Naturalization of the Jews May Bring Unto Great Britain* (London, 1753), p. 7.

4.   See Thomas W. Perry, *Public Opinion, Propaganda, and Politics in Eighteenth-Century England: A Study of the Jew Bill of 1753* (Cambridge: Harvard University Press, 1962); Todd Endelman, *The Jews of Georgian England, 1714–1830: Tradition and Change in a Liberal Society* (Philadephia: Jewish Publication Society of America, 1979), esp. pp. 50–117; and Katz, *The Jews in the History of England*, pp. 240–53.

5.   Perry, *Public Opinion*, p. 19. Perry notes that a Jewish Naturalization Bill had just missed passing in the Irish Parliament and that the Jewish community in England had attempted (unsuccessfully) to add a clause in their behalf to the 1751 general Naturalization Bill. Clearly, there was grounds for optimism on the part of the Jewish community that the 1753 Bill would not produce a violent response (pp. 17–18). It is also worth noting that some Irish writers expressed considerable anger at the idea of Jewish naturalization at this time, believing that "the real object of the Bill was to induce Jews to settle there that they might take the place of the Catholics who were leaving the country on account of Protestant domination" (Leon Huhner, "The Jews of Ireland," *TJHSE* 5 [1908], p. 237). See, for example, John

Curry, *An Historical and Critical Review of the Civil Wars in Ireland from the Reign of Queen Elizabeth to the Settlement of King William* (London, 1786), vol. 2, p. 262.

282

~~~

7. Shake-
   speare
   and the
   Jew Bill
   of 1753

6. For a detailed history of its passage, see Perry, *Public Opinion*, pp. 46–71.

7. Alderman, in *The Jewish Community in British Politics*, notes that the "object of the ill-fated 1753 Act was achieved, quite incidentally, in 1826, when Parliament reformed the naturalization laws without so much as mentioning the Jews" (p. 80).

8. For a helpful overview of how the debate has been interpreted, see Robert Liberles, "The Jews and Their Bill," pp. 29–36.

9. J. E., *Some Considerations on the Naturalization of the Jews* (London, 1753), p. 4.

10. Anon., *The Rejection and Restoration of the Jews, According to Scripture, Declar'd* (London, 1753), pp. 34–35.

11. "Britannia," *An Appeal to the Throne Against the Naturalization of the Jewish Nation* (London, 1753), pp. 16–17.

12. *London Evening Post*, November 13–15, 1753, p. 4.

13. *Read's Weekly Journal*, September 1, 1753, p. 1.

14. Endelman, *The Jews of Georgian England*, esp. pp. 86–117. See, too, Frank Felsenstein, *Anti-Semitic Stereotypes: A Paradigm of Otherness in English Popular Culture, 1660–1830* (Baltimore: Johns Hopkins University Press, 1995), published as this book was going to press.

15. G. A. Cranfield, "*The London Evening-Post* and the Jew Bill of 1753," *The Historical Journal* 8 (1965), pp. 16–30, has argued for the vital role of the press in this election, and suggests that the Tory paper's "campaign against the 'Jew Bill' was undoubtedly one of the most remarkable propaganda campaigns in English history." The *Post*'s "amazing mixture of political opportunism, religious fervour, and Rabelasian humour were largely responsible in forcing the ministry to repeal the Bill," in large measure because provincial papers—even loyalist, nonoppositional papers like the Whig *Norwich Mercury* or the neutral *Cambridge Journal* "soon found themselves obliged to report the more outstanding of the *Post*'s attacks" (pp. 27–30).

16. Perry, *Public Opinion*, pp. 194–95.

17. Nicholas Rogers, *Whigs and Cities: Popular Politics in the Age of Walpole and Pitt* (Oxford: Clarendon, 1989), pp. 89–90, 93.

18. Paul Langford, *A Polite and Commercial People: England, 1727–1783* (Oxford: Clarendon, 1989), pp. 224–25.

19. In advocating this approach, I build upon the suggestion of Todd Endelman, who argues that Perry "errs . . . in subsuming every tract, sermon, editorial, and speech" under the rubric of party politics. Endelman urges that a "host of nonpolitical emotions and issues were released by this controversy that deserve to be treated on their own terms. Evidence for this may be found in the fact that propagandists on both sides rarely debated the merits either of this particular bill or of the naturalization policy in general" (Endelman, *The Jews of Georgian England*, p. 60).

20. Anon., *The Exclusion of the English*, p. 10.

21. *Gentleman's Magazine*, July 1753, p. 346.

22. I draw here on the account of Daniel Statt, "The City of London and the Controversy Over Immigration, 1660–1722," *The Historical Journal* 33 (1991), pp. 45–61. See, too, Statt's unpublished Ph.D. thesis: "The Controversy Over the Naturalization of Foreigners in England, 1660–1760," Cambridge University, 1987.

23. As cited in Daniel Statt, "Daniel Defoe and Immigration," *Eighteenth Century Studies* 24 (1991), p. 297, from *The Grand Concern of England* (London, 1673).

24. John Toland, *Reasons for Naturalizing the Jews in Great Britain*, pp. 6–17. Toland's work was immediately challenged by the anonymous *A Confutation of the Reasons for Naturalizing the Jews* (London, 1715).

25. Daniel Defoe, *Lex Taliones* (London, 1698), as cited in Statt, "Daniel Defoe and Immigra-

tion," p. 298.

26. Daniel Defoe, *The True-Born Englishman. A Satyr* ([London], 1700), p. 15.

27. Anon., *The Exclusion of the English*, p. 12.

28. Samuel Johnson, *Dictionary of the English Language*, 2 vols., 4th ed., rev. (London, 1773).

29. Edward Bagshaw, *The Great Question Concerning Things Indifferent in Religious Worship* (London, 1660), as cited in Nabil I. Matar, "John Locke and the Jews," *Journal of Ecclesiastical History* 44 (1993), p. 46.

30. Gordon J. Schochet, "From Persecution to 'Toleration,'" in J. R. Jones, ed., *Liberty Secured? Britain Before and After 1688* (Stanford: Stanford University Press, 1992), p. 127.

31. Mark Goldie, "The Theory of Religious Intolerance in Restoration England," in Grell, Israel, and Tyacke, *From Persecution to Toleration*, p. 331.

32. Schochet, "From Persecution to 'Toleration,'" p. 152.

33. As cited in Nicholas Tyacke, "The 'Rise of Puritanism' and the Legalization of Dissent, 1571–1719," in *From Persecution to Toleration*, p. 41.

34. As cited in Nabil I. Matar, "John Locke and the Jews," p. 48, from Bodleian Library MS. Locke c. 28, "An Essay Concerning Toleracion 1667," printed in Carlo Augusto Viano, *Scritti Editi e Inedititi Sullo Tolleranƶa* (Turin, 1961), pp. 81–107. The text usually cited is the first version of the "Essay," located in the Public Record Office; it does not contain these additional lines.

35. Matar, "John Locke and the Jews," p. 49.

36. John Locke, *A Letter Concerning Toleration, Being a Translation of the Epistola de Tolerantia*, in *Works*, 10 vols. (London, 1823), vol. 6, p. 52.

37. Locke, *A Letter Concerning Toleration*, p. 40.

38. Jonas Proast, *The Argument of the Letter Concerning Toleration*, as cited in Matar, "Locke and the Jews," p. 53.

39. Matar, "John Locke and the Jews," p. 55.

40. John Locke, *A Paraphrase and Notes on St. Paul's Epistle to the Romans*, in *Works*, vol. 8, p. 356. The *Paraphrase* was written in 1702 and postumously published in 1707.

41. Matar, "John Locke and the Jews," pp. 61–62.

42. Matar, "John Locke and the Jews," pp. 61–62.

43. [George Coningesby], *The Jewish Naturaliƶation Considered* (London [?], 1753), p. 15.

44. Anon., *The Crisis, or an Alarm to Britannia's True Protestant Sons* (London, 1754), p. 31.

45. Anon., *An Apology for the Naturaliƶation of the Jews* (London, 1753), pp. 2–3.

46. William Romaine, *An Answer to a Pamphlet*, 2d ed. (London, 1753), p. 40.

47. Defoe, *True-Born Englishman*, p. 22.

48. Romaine, *Answer to a Pamphlet*, pp. 18 and 23.

49. Romaine, *An Answer to a Pamphlet*, p. 42. In his *Modest Apology for the Citiƶens and Merchants of London* (London, 1753), Romaine restates the entire case against the Jews in terms that recall late sixteenth-century polemic: "Their crime consisted in opposing the decrees of the Almighty, in trying to defeat them, in standing out against Jehovah and his Christ, in blaspheming them, and in persevering in their blasphemy, until having filled up the measure of their iniquity God destroyed their civil polity, and scattered them as fugitives and vagabonds over the face of the earth. Our laws have stigmatized them with this odious character, and shall the same laws honour them with the greatest privileges and immunities that free-born Englishmen can enjoy?" (pp. 10–11).

50. Linda Colley, *Britons: Forging the Nation, 1707–1837* (New Haven: Yale University Press, 1992), p. 1.

51. Colley, *Britons: Forging the Nation*, p. 5.

52. Colley, *Britons: Forging the Nation*, p. 5.

53. As quoted in Perry, *Public Opinion*, p. 108, from *The Protester*.

284

7. Shake-
speare
and the
Jew Bill
of 1753

54. As cited in Perry, *Public Opinion*. p. 108, from *The Protester*.

55. As cited in Perry, *Public Opinion*, p. 96, from the *London Evening Post*.

56. Anon., *The Jews Triumph: A Ballad* (London, [1753]), p. 4.

57. *London Evening Post*, June 1753, pp. 272–73.

58. *Parliamentary History of England*, vol. 15 (1753–1765), pp. 92, 104.

59. *Parliamentary History of England*, vol. 15 (1753–1765), p. 106.

60. Anon., *A Letter to the Publick* (London, 1753), pp. 9–10.

61. Anon., *Seasonable Remarks on the Act Lately Pass'd in Favour of the Jews* (London, 1753), p. 19.

62. Anon., *Circumcision Not Murder, but Jews No Christians* (n.p. [Oxford?], n.d. [1753?]). For a discussion of circumcision in this controversy, see Roy S. Wolper, "Circumcision as Polemic in the Jew Bill of 1753: The Cutter Cut?" in *Eighteenth Century Life* 7 (1982), pp. 28–36.

63. Anon., *The Christian's New Warning Piece: Or, A Full and True Account of the Circumcision of Sir E. T. Bart.* (London, 1753), pp. 11–12. *The Christian's New Warning Piece* and the two parts of *News for One Hundred Years Hence* have been reprinted in Roy S. Wolper, ed., "Pieces on the 'Jew Bill' (1753)," The Augustan Reprint Society, Publication Number 217 (Los Angeles: William Andrews Clark Memorial Library, 1983).

64. Romaine, *An Answer to a Pamphlet*, pp. 6–7.

65. *London Magazine*, November 1753, pp. 515, 517.

66. *A Collection of the Best Pieces and Verse Against the Naturalization of the Jews*, p. 77.

67. As quoted in [Joseph Grove], *A Reply to the Famous Jew Question . . . That the Jews Born Here Before the Late Act Were Never Intitled to Purchase and Hold Lands to Them and Their Heirs, but Were Considered Only as Aliens, or Vassals of the Crown* (London, 1754), p. 94.

68. Perry, *Public Opinion*, p. 15

69. [Grove], *A Reply to the Famous Jew Question*, pp. 78–79.

70. Richard Dorment, *New York Review of Books*, May 27, 1993, p. 20.

71. Ronald Paulson, *Hogarth*, 3 vols. (Cambridge: Lutterworth Press, 1993), vol. 3, p. 167.

72. Paulson, *Hogarth*, vol. 3, p. 168–69.

73. Paulson, *Hogarth*, vol. 3, p. 170.

74. A helpful (if somewhat apologetic) account of Hogarth and the Jew Bill, which I have drawn on here, can be found in Ronald Paulson, *Hogarth: His Life, Art, and Times*, 3 vols. (New Haven: Yale University Press, 1971), vol. 2, pp. 199–200; and Paulson, ed., *Hogarth's Graphic Works*, 3rd ed., rev. (London: Print Room, 1989). See, too, John Smith, *A Poetical Description of Mr. Hogarth's Election Prints, in Four Cantos* (London, 1759).

75. Smith, *Mr. Hogarth's Election Prints*, p. 9. "Cole" is contemporary slang for money.

76. Dobson, *The Making of the National Poet*, p. 7.

77. Bate, *Shakespearean Constitutions*, p. 1.

78. George Granville, *The Jew of Venice* (1701), rpt. in Christopher Spenser, ed., *Five Restoration Adaptations of Shakespeare* (Urbana: University of Illinois Press, 1965). Granville's overhaul of Shakespeare's text is substantial. He cut the play from twenty scenes to nine, although retaining Shylock's appearance in five of them. Morocco, Arragon, the two Gobbos, Salario, Salanio, and Tubal were all banished, while Bassanio's and Portia's parts were enlarged.

79. William S. E. Coleman, "Post-Restoration Shylocks from Prior to Macklin," *Theater Survey* 8 (1967), p. 17.

80. George Granville, *The Jew of Venice*, Prologue, lines 26–31, pp. 348–49. As editors have noted, the allusion no doubt refers to the recent decision by the Corporation of London, mentioned above, to admit a dozen Jewish brokers (though not jobbers) to the Exchange. The play itself, however, contains little in the way of topical concern with English Jewry.

For a recent discussion of the play that emphasizes 'Jewish questions' (quite loosely defined), see Richard Braverman, "Politics in Jewish Disguise: Jacobitism and Dissent on the Post-Revolutionary Stage," *Studies in Philology* 90 (1993), pp. 347–70.

81. William W. Appleton, *Charles Macklin: An Actor's Life* (Cambridge: Harvard University Press, 1960), p. 54, and note 37.

82. Reported in *Connoisseur*, January 31, 1754, as cited in Toby Lelyveld, *Shylock on the Stage* (London: Routledge and Kegan Paul, 1961), p. 26.

83. Cooke, *Memoirs of Charles Macklin*, as cited in Lelyveld, *Shylock on the Stage*, p. 25.

84. For the record of performances, see George Winchester Stone, Jr., ed., *The London Stage, 1660–1800. Part 4: 1747–1776* (Carbondale: Southern Illinois University Press, 1962).

85. *The Cambridge Journal*, August 25, 1753, p. 1.

86. Stone, *The London Stage*, part 4, vol. 1, p. 377.

87. L. W. Conolly, "*The Merchant of Venice* and the Jew Bill of 1753," *Shakespeare Quarterly* 25 (1974), p. 125.

88. As cited in *The London Magazine, or Gentleman's Monthly Intelligencer*, July 1753, p. 302, which reprinted the piece from the *Craftsman*, July 14, 1753, of which no copies survive.

89. *London Evening Post*, September 11, 1753, p. 1.

90. *London Magazine*, July 1753, p. 303.

91. *London Magazine*, pp. 302–3.

92. *London Magazine*, p. 303.

93. Conolly, "*The Merchant of Venice* and the Jew Bill of 1753," p. 127.

94. J. E., *Some Considerations on the Naturalization of the Jews*, pp. 17–21.

95. Anon., *The Repository: For the Use of the Christian Electors of Great-Britain; In Opposition to All Jews, Turks, and Infidels*, no. 2 (London, 1753), p. 33.

96. *The Repository*, p. 51.

97. See Perry, *Public Opinion*, p. 166; from *Gray's Inn Journal*, April 27, 1754.

98. See Isaiah Shachar, "The Emergence of the Modern Pictoral Stereotype of 'the Jews' in England," in Dov Noy and Issachar Ben-Ami, eds., *Studies in the Cultural Life of the Jews in England*, Folklore Research Center Studies 5 (Jerusalem: Magnes Press, Hebrew University, 1975), p. 346. Shachar's essay, not widely known, is one of the best on the Jew Bill. For additional pictorial evidence concerning Jewish stereotypes during the Jew Bill debate of 1753, see Israel Salomons, "Satirical and Political Prints on the Jews' Naturalization Bill, 1753," *TJHSE* 7 (1912), pp. 205–33.

99. *Read's Weekly Journal, or British Gazateer*, July 28, 1753, p. 2.

100. *London Evening Post*, October 18–20, 1753; *Cambridge Journal*, October 27, 1753.

101. *London Evening Post*, October 16–18, 1753.

102. Two more are worth recording. The first, a poem by "John Christian," appears in the *London Evening Post*, October 25–27, 1753, and includes the following couplet: "Oh no! Let G[ideon]'s fold and old sly Shylock's purse / Instead of blessing, prove to them a curse." The second, which appears in the same journal a month later (*London Evening Post*, November 22–24, 1753), concerns "A New Prologue to the *Jew of Venice*," to be spoken by Miss N–r, offered by "R. S.": "Through Shylock's glass the great Messiah sees; / Speaks, writes, and votes, for infidels—and fees."

103. Anon., *Seasonable Remarks on the Act Lately Pass'd*, pp. 27–28.

104. *London Evening Post*, August 11–14, 1753, p. 1.

105. *Gray's Inn Journal*, October 6, 1753, p. 12.

106. *Gray's Inn Journal*, October 6, 1753, p. 12.

107. *The Jew Apologist, or Considerations on the Revival of the Jew-Bill* (London, 1765), sig. A2r.

108. R. Shylock, *The Rabbi's Lamentation Upon the Repeal of the Jew Act* (London, 1768).

109. Perry, *Public Opinion*, p. 75.

286

7. Shake-
speare
and the
Jew Bill
of 1753

110. For more on attacks against itinerant Jewish peddlers during the Jew Bill controversy, see Endelman, *The Jews of Georgian England*, pp. 114–15.

111. Perry, *Public Opinion*, pp. 75–76; cited from the *London Evening Post*.

112. As cited in *Gentleman's Magazine* (London, 1753), p. 484, from *Gray's Inn Journal*, October 27, 1753.

113. The note in *The London Stage* for October 24, 1753 reads: "'Tis said, Miss Bellamy, who engaged recently with Mr. Rich is off again. Mr. Colthorp, who kept her, swears to kick Rich, etc. Great noise about it in the Bedford Coffee House" (cited from the diary of Richard Cross), vol. 4, pt. 1, p. 386.

114. Cunningham, *Poems*, pp. 165–66.

115. See the entry for *naturalization* in the *Oxford English Dictionary*.

116. Moses Margoliouth, *The History of the Jews in Great Britain*, 3 vols. (London: Richard Bentley, 1851), vol. 1, p. 321.

Conclusion

1. See for example, the organizing structure of Cecil Roth's *History of the Jews in England*. The recent rewriting of the place of the Jews in modern British society by David Cesarani, Eugene C. Black, Tony Kushner, Bryan Cheyette, David Feldman, Lara Marks, Geoffrey Alderman, and others offers an important corrective to earlier celebratory narratives, and has begun to alter the ways in which modern British culture—especially its attitutes toward liberalism, racism, labor, and immigration—has been understood.

2. A typical recent example is J. G. A. Pocock, ed., *The Varieties of British Political Thought, 1500–1800* (Cambridge: Cambridge University Press, 1993); the "varieties" of political thought in this recent and wide-ranging exploration of political traditions in early modern Britain never extend far enough to encompass any of the Jewish questions or political models that informed a good deal of contemporary writing.

3. For the best general treatment of this topic, see H. S. Q. Henriques, *Jewish Marriages and the English Law* (Oxford: Oxford University Press, 1909). Also see, for example, Elizabeth Cary, *The Tragedy of Mariam*, ed. Barry Waller and Margaret W. Ferguson (Berkeley: University of California Press, 1994); Dympna Callaghan, "Re-reading Elizabeth Cary's *The Tragedie of Mariam, Faire Queene of Jewry*," in Hendricks and Parker, eds., *Women, "Race," and Writing*, pp. 163–77; and Jonathan R. Ziskind, trans. and intro., *John Selden on Jewish Marriage Law: The "Uxor Hebraica"* (Leiden: E. J. Brill, 1991).

4. *Calendar of State Papers, Domestic* (1619–23), pp. 319–20.

5. Menasseh ben Israel, *Vindiciae Judaeorum*, in Wolf, ed., *Menasseh ben Israel's Mission*, p. 120.

6. Richard Hole, "An Apology for the Character and Conduct of Shylock," in *Essays by a Society of Gentlemen, at Exeter*, 2 vols. (Exeter: Trewman, 1796), vol. 2, pp. 559–64, 566–73.

7. For a brief sketch of productions in Nazi Germany (including the practice of omitting the intermarriage of Jessica and Lorenzo), see Werner Habicht, "Shakespeare and Theatre Politics in the Third Reich," in Hanna Scolnovic and Peter Holland, eds., *The Play Out of Context: Transferring Plays from Culture to Culture* (Cambridge: Cambridge University Press, 1989), esp. pp. 113–17. For details about the production Barry Kyle directed in Israel, see Avi Oz, "Transformations of Authenticity: *The Merchant of Venice* in Israel, 1936–1980," *Jarbuch der Deutchen Shakespeare-Gesellschaft West* (1983), p. 176.

8. See, for example, Maria Verch, "*The Merchant of Venice* on the German Stage Since 1945," *Theatre History Studies* 5 (1985), pp. 84–94; Hermann Sinsheimer, *Shylock, The History of a Character, or The Myth of the Jew* (London: Victor Gollancz, 1947), subsequently published in the original German as *Shylock, Die Geschichte einer Figur* (München: Ner-Tamid-Verlag, 1960); and Dietrich Schwanitz, *Shylock* (Hamburg: Verlag Dr. R. Krämer, 1989).

9. See, for example, Avi Oz, "Transformations of Authenticity," pp. 166–77; Arye Ibn-Zahav,

"Dmuto shel Shylock" (Portrait of Shylock), *Tarbiẓ* 13 (1942), pp. 178–90 [Hebrew]; and Immanuel Levi, *Habima—Israel's National Theater, 1917–1977* (New York: Columbia University Press, 1979), pp. 126ff., on the "trial of Shakespeare, the Habima, and the director" by Jewish intellectuals and artists in Palestine in the late 1930s, who were debating the merits of Leopold Jessner's production of *The Merchant of Venice*.

10. The literature on this subject is vast, and a few representative examples must suffice. For an example of the appropriation of Shylock for antisemitic propaganda in the United States, see Gordon Clark, *Shylock as Banker, Bondholder, Corruptionist, Conspirator* (Washington, D.C., 1894). For the debate over the teaching of *The Merchant of Venice* in the United States in the decade after the Holocaust, see, for example, Alan Shapiro, "Should *The Merchant of Venice* Offend Jewish Students?" *English Journal* 41 (1952), pp. 432–33; and Jerome Carlin, "The Case Against *The Merchant of Venice*," *English Journal* 42 (1953), pp. 388–90. For the impact of *The Merchant of Venice* on contemporary literary culture, see, for example, Philip Roth, *Operation Shylock* (New York: Simon and Schuster, 1993).

11. See, for example, David G. Goodman and Masanori Miyazawa, *Jews in the Japanese Mind: The History and Uses of a Cultural Stereotype* (New York: Free Press, 1995), pp. 29–36. The authors note that *The Merchant of Venice* was "the first work by Shakespeare to be performed in Japan, and it remained the most frequently produced Shakespearean drama into the 1970s" (p. 29).

⟶ Select Bibliography

This select bibliography primarily lists early modern English books concerned with Jewish questions as well as scholarship on the place of the Jews in early modern English society. I have retained the original spelling of early modern titles, though I have regularized capitalization. For fairly comprehensive bibliographies on the subject of Jews in England, see Joseph Jacobs and Lucien Wolf, *Bibliotheca Anglo-Judaica* (1888), updated by Cecil Roth in *Magna Bibliotheca Anglo-Judaica* (1927), and subsequently updated by Ruth P. Lehmann in *Nova Bibliotheca Anglo-Judaica* (1961), *Anglo-Jewish Bibliography 1937–1970* (1973), and Ruth P. Goldschmidt-Lehmann, *Anglo-Jewish Bibliography, 1971–1990*, augmented by Stephen W. Massil and Peter Shmuel Salinger (1992). For scholarship on *The Merchant of Venice*, see Thomas Wheeler, *The Merchant of Venice: An Annotated Bibliography* (New York, 1985). The abbreviation *TJHSE* stands for *The Transactions of the Jewish Historical Society of England*. Unless otherwise noted, the place of publication is London.

Abraham, Philip, *Curiosities of Judaism* (1879).
Abrahams, Barnett Lionel, "The Condition of the Jews of England at the Time of Their Expulsion in 1290," *TJHSE* 2 (1895), 76–105.
——— *The Expulsion of the Jews from England in 1290* (Oxford, 1895).
——— "A Jew in the Service of the East India Company in 1601," *Jewish Quarterly Review* 9 (1897), 173–75.
——— "Two Jews Before the Privy Council and an English Law Court in 1614–15," *Jewish Quarterly Review* 14 (1902), 354–58.
Abrahams, Israel, "Joachim Gaunse: A Mining Incident in the Reign of Queen Elizabeth," *TJHSE* 4 (1901), 83–101.
Addison, Lancelot, *The Present State of the Jews* (1675).
Adler, Elkan Nathan, *History of Jews in London* (Philadelphia, 1930).
Adler, Michael, "History of the 'Domus Conversorum': From 1290 to 1891," *TJHSE* 4 (1903),

74–75.

Aitken, James M., ed., *The Trial of George Buchanan Before the Lisbon Inquisition* (Edinburgh, 1939).

Alderman, Geoffrey, *The Jewish Community in British Politics* (Oxford, 1983).

Alexander, John, *God's Covenant Displayed, by John Alexander, a Converted Jew* (1689).

The Amorous Convert (1679).

Anderson, George K., *The Legend of the Wandering Jew* (Providence, 1965).

—— "Popular Survivals of the Wandering Jew in England," *Journal of English and German Philology* 46 (1948), 367–82.

—— "The Wandering Jew Returns to England," *Journal of English and German Philology* 45 (1946), 237–50.

An Apology for the Naturalization of the Jews (1753).

[Arnall, William], pseud., Solomon Abrabanel, *The Complaint of the Children of Israel*, 7th ed. (1736).

B., B., *A Historical and Law Treatise Against the Jewes and Judaism: Shewing That by the Ancient Establish'd Laws of the Land, No Jew Hath Any Right to Live in England* (1703, 1721, 1732, 1753).

B., D., [John Falconer], *A Briefe Refutation of John Traskes Judaical and Novel Fancyes* (n.p., 1618).

Bacon, Francis, "A True Report of the Detestable Treason, Intended by Dr. Roderigo Lopez," *Works*, ed. James Spedding et al., 15 vols. (1857–1874), vol. 8, 271–87.

Baer, Yitzhak, *A History of the Jews in Christian Spain*, 2 vols. (Philadelphia, 1961).

Baker, Elliott, *Bardolotry* (1992).

Baron, Salo Wittmayer, *A Social and Religious History of the Jews*, 2d ed., 18 vols. (New York, 1952–1983).

Basch, David, *The Hidden Shakespeare: A Rosetta Stone* (West Hartford, Conn., 1994).

Beckwith, Sarah, "Ritual, Church, and Theater: Medieval Dramas of the Sacramental Body," *Culture and History, 1350–1660: Essays in English Communities, Identities, and Writings*, ed. David Aers (Detroit, 1992).

Becon, Thomas, *Prayers and Other Pieces*, ed. John Ayre (Cambridge, 1844).

Bible [Geneva] (1589).

Bible [Geneva], *The Newe Testament of Our Lord Jesus Christ, Translated Out of the Greeke, by Thomas Beza*, trans. L. Tomson (1596).

Biddulph, William, *The Travels of Certaine Englishmen* (1609).

Black, Eugene C., *The Social Politics of Anglo-Jewry, 1880–1920* (1988).

Blount, Henry, *A Voyage Into the Levant* (1636).

Blunt, J. E., *A History of the Establishment and Residence of the Jews in England With an Inquiry Into Their Civil Disabilities* (1830).

Boaistuau, Pierre, *Certaine Secrete Wonders of Nature, Containing a Description of Sundry Strange Things, Seeming Monstrous in Our Eyes and Judgement*, trans. Edward Fenton (1569).

Borde, Andrew, *The Fyrst Boke of the Introduction of Knowledge* (1555? 1562?).

Boyarin, Daniel, "'This We Know to Be the Carnal Israel': Circumcision and the Erotic Life of God and Israel," *Critical Inquiry* 19 (1992), 474–505.

Brabourne, Theophilus, *A Discourse Upon the Sabbath Day* (1628).

Brennan, Michael G., ed., *The Travel Diary (1611–1612) of an English Catholic, Sir Charles Somerset* (Leeds, 1993).

Brereton, Sir William, *Travels in Holland, The United Provinces, England, Scotland, and Ireland, 1634–1635*, ed. Edward Hawkins (1844).

Brerewood, Edward, *Enquiries Touching the Diversity of Languages, and Religions* (1614).

Brett, Samuel, *A Narrative of the Proceedings of a Great Councel of Jews, Assembled in the Plain of Ageda in Hungaria* (1655).

Bréval, Monsieur de (François Durant), *La Juif Baptise* (1671).

Britannia, pseud., *An Appeal to the Throne Against the Naturalization of the Jewish Nation* (1753).

Broughton, Hugh, *An Answeare Unto the Right Honorable the Lordes, of the Quene of Englandes Most Honorable Privy Councell: Concerning an Ebrew Epistle of a Rarely Lerned Jewe* (Basel, 1597).

———— *A Concent of Scripture* (1589?).

———— *Daniel His Chaldie Visions and His Ebrew* (1596).

———— *A Declaration Unto the Lordes, of the Jewes Desire These Fiftene Yeres for Ebrew Explication of Our Greke Gospell* (1611).

———— *An Epistle of an Ebrew Willinge to Learne Christianity: Sent by Him to London* (Basel, 1598).

———— *Our Lordes Familie and Many Other Poinctes Depending Upon It: Opened Against a Jew, Rabbi David Farar* (Amsterdam, 1608).

———— *A Petition to the King. For Authority and Allowance to Expound the Apocalyps in Hebrew and Greek, to Shew Jewes and Gentiles* (Middleburg, 1611).

———— *Works*, ed. John Lightfoot (1662).

Browne, Thomas, *Pseudodoxia Epidemica* (1646).

Bunny, Edmund, *The Scepter of Judah: Or, What Maner of Government It Was, That Unto the Common-Wealth or Church of Israel Was by the Law of God Appointed* (1584).

Burnet, Gilbert, *The Conversion and Persecutions of Eve Cohan* (1680).

B[urton], R[ichard], [Nathaniel Crouch], *Two Journeys to Jerusalem* (1685).

Burton, Sir Richard, *The Jew, the Gypsy, and El Islam*, ed. W. H. Wilkins (1898).

Burton, Robert, *The Anatomy of Melancholy* (Oxford, 1628).

Burton, William, *Of Davids Evidence* (1592).

———— *Works* (1602).

Calvert, Thomas, "Diatriba of the Jews' Estate," preface to [Samuel, Marochitanus], *The Blessed Jew of Marocco; Or a Blackmoor Made White, by Rabbi Samuel, a Jew Turned Christian* (York, 1648).

———— *Medulla Evangelli; Or the Prophet Isaiah's Crucifix* (1657).

Calvin, Jean, *A Commentarie Upon S. Paules Epistles to the Corinthians*, trans. Thomas Timme (1577).

———— *Sermons of M. John Calvin Upon the Epistle of Saincte Paule to the Galatians*, trans. Arthur Golding (1574).

Capp, B. S., *The Fifth Monarchy Men: A Study in Seventeenth-Century Millenarianism* (1972).

Cardozo, Jacob Lopes, *The Contemporary Jew in the Elizabethan Drama* (Amsterdam, 1925).

Carleton, George, *A Thankfull Remembrance of Gods Mercy* (1627).

Cartwright, Thomas, *Help for Discovery of the Truth in Point of Toleration* (1648).

The Case of Anthony Gomezsera and Several Other Jews (1685).

The Case of the Jewes Stated: Or the Jewes Synagogue Opened (1656).

The Case of the Jews Stated (n.p. [London], n.d. [1689]).

Cesarani, David, "Dual Heritage or Duel of Heritages? Englishness and Jewishness in the Heritage Industry," *The Jewish Heritage in British History: Englishness and Jewishness*, ed. Tony Kushner (1992).

Chamberlain, John, *Letters*, ed. Norman E. McClure, 2 vols. (Philadelphia, 1939).

Chamberlen, Peter, *The Sons of the East: Being an Epistle to the Synagogue of the Jews in London* (1682).

Chazan, Robert, *Daggers of Faith: Thirteenth-Century Christian Missionizing and Jewish Response* (Berkeley, 1989).

Cheyette, Bryan, *Constructions of "the Jew" in English Literature and Society: Racial Representations, 1875–1945* (Cambridge, 1993).

The Christian's New Warning Piece: Or, a Full and True Account of the Circumcision of Sir E. T. Bart. (1753).

Churchill, E. F., "The Crown and the Alien: A Review of the Crown's Protection of the Alien, From the Norman Conquest Down to 1689," *Law Quarterly Review* 144 (1920), 402–28.

291

Select
Bibliography

Circumcision not Murder, but Jews No Christians [ballad] (Oxford? 1753?).

Clare, John, [Roger Anderton], *The Converted Jew* (n.p., 1630).

Cohen, Abraham, ed., *An Anglo-Jewish Scrapbook, 1600–1840: The Jew Through English Eyes* (1943).

Coke, Edward, *The Second Part of the Institutes of the Lawes of England* (1642).

—— *The Third Part of the Institutes of the Laws of England* (1644).

A Collection of the Best Pieces in Prose and Verse, Against the Naturalization of the Jews (1753).

Collier, Thomas, *A Brief Answer to Some of the Objections and Demurs Made Against the Coming in and Inhabiting of the Jews in This Common-wealth* (1656).

Collinson, Patrick, "The Beginnings of English Sabbatarianism," *Studies in Church History* 1 (1964), 207–21.

—— *The English Puritan Movement* (Berkeley, 1967).

A Confutation of the Reasons for Naturalizing the Jews (1715).

[Coningesby, George], *The Jewish Naturalization Considered* (1753).

Conolly, L. W., "*The Merchant of Venice* and the Jew Bill of 1753," *Shakespeare Quarterly* 25 (1974), 125–27.

Cooper, Thomas, *The Blessing of Japheth, Proving the Gathering in of the Gentiles and Finall Conversion of the Jewes* (1615).

Copley, Joseph, *The Case of the Jews Is Altered* (1656).

Coryate, Thomas, *Coryats Crudities* (1611).

—— *Coryate's Crudities: Reprinted from the Edition of 1611. To Which Are Now Added His Letters from India*, 3 vols. (1776).

—— *The Counterfeit Jew* (n.p., 1653).

—— *Thomas Coryate, Travailer . . . Greeting . . . From the Court of the Great Mogul* (1616).

Coxe, Nehemiah, *A Discourse of the Covenants That God Made With Men Before the Law* (1681).

Cranfield, G. A., "*The London Evening-Post* and the Jew Bill of 1753," *The Historical Journal* 8 (1965), 16–30.

The Crisis: Or, an Alarm to Brittania's True Protestant Sons (1754).

Cunaeus, Petrus, *Of the Common-wealth of the Hebrews*, trans. C. B. (1653).

Cunningham, John, *Poems, Chiefly Pastoral* (1766).

Daborne, Robert, *A Christian Turn'd Turk, or the Tragicall Lives and Deaths of the Two Famous Pyates, Ward and Dansiker* (1612).

[Da Costa, Uriel], *The Remarkable Life of Uriel Acosta* (1740).

Daniel ben Alexander, *Daniel ben Alexander the Converted Jew of Prague*, trans. T. Drewe (n.p., 1621).

Daniel, Samuel, *The Collection of the History of England* (1618; 4th ed., 1650).

The Death of Usury, or the Disgrace of Usurers (Cambridge, 1594).

D'Ewes, Simon, *A Compleat Journal of the Votes, Speeches, and Debates, Both of the House of Lords and House of Commons Throughout the Whole Reign of Queen Elizabeth*, 2d ed. (1693).

Defoe, Daniel, *The True-Born Englishman, A Satyr* (1700).

Dekker, Thomas, *The Whore of Babylon* (1607).

[Dennis, Anne], *Answer to the Book Against the Jews: Written by B. B.* (1703).

Diamond, A. S., "The Community of the Resettlement, 1656–1684: A Social Survey," *TJHSE* 24 (1975), 134–50.

Dimick, Arthur, "The Conspiracy of Dr. Lopez," *English Historical Review* 9 (1894), 440–72.

A Discoverie and Playne Declaration of Sundry Subtill Practices of the Holy Inquisition of Spayne, trans. [V. Skinner], 2d ed., (1569).

Dodsley, Robert, *A Fragment of the Chronicles of Zimri* (Edinburgh, 1753).

Donne, John, *Sermons*, ed. George R. Potter and Evelyn M. Simpson, 10 vols. (Berkeley, 1953–62).

Draxe, Thomas, *The Worldes Resurrection, or the Generall Calling of the Jewes* (1608).

Drelincourt, Charles, *The Roote of Romish Rites and Ceremonies: Shewing That the Church of Rome Hath Borrowed Most Part of Her Ceremonies of the Jewes and Ancient Pagans*, trans. M. T. (1630).

Duffy, Eamon, *The Stripping of the Altars: Traditional Religion in England c. 1400–c. 1580* (New Haven, 1992).

Dymock, Arthur, "The Conspiracy of Dr. Lopez," *English Historical Review* 9 (1894), pp. 440–72.

E., J., *The Great Deliverance of the Whole House of Israel . . . in Answer to a Book Called, "The Hope of Israel," Written by a Learned Jew of Amsterdam Named Menasseh ben Israel* (1652).

E., J., *Some Considerations on the Naturalization of the Jews* (1753).

Edgeworth, Maria, *Castle Rackrent*, in *Tales and Novels*, 18 vols. (1832–33), vol. 1.

————— *Harrington*, in *Tales and Novels*, 18 vols. (1832–33), vol. 17.

Edwards, Roger, "The Conversion and Restitution of Israel" (1581), British Library MS. Lansdowne 353.

Egan, Charles, *The Status of the Jews in England, From the Time of the Norman Conquest to the Reign of her Majesty Queen Victoria, Impartially Considered* (1848).

Eilberg-Schwartz, Howard, ed., *People of the Body: Jews and Judaism from an Embodied Perspective* (Albany, 1992).

————— *The Savage in Judaism: An Anthropology of Israelite Religion and Ancient Judaism* (Bloomington, 1990).

Endelman, Todd M., ed., *Jewish Apostasy in the Modern World* (New York, 1987).

————— *The Jews of Georgian England, 1714–1830* (Philadelphia, 1979).

————— *Radical Assimilation in English Jewish History, 1656–1945* (Bloomington, 1990).

Esther's Suit to King Ahasueros on Behalf of the Jews (1753).

Evans, Arise, *Light for the Jews, or, the Means to Convert Them* (1664).

Evelyn, John, *The History of the Three Late Famous Imposters, viz. Padro Ottomano, Mahamed Bei, and Sabatai Sevi* (1669).

The Exclusion of the English: An Invitation to Foreigners (1748).

Feldman, David, *Englishmen and Jews: Social Relations and Political Culture, 1840–1914* (New Haven, 1994).

Fell, Margaret, *For Menasseh ben Israel. The Call of the Jewes Out of Babylon* (1656).

————— *Loving Salutation to the Seed of Abraham Among the Jewes* (1657).

Felsenstein, Frank, *Anti-Semitic Stereotypes: A Paradigm of Otherness in English Popular Culture, 1660–1830* (Baltimore, 1995).

Ferdinand, Philip, *Haec Sunt Verba Dei* (Cambridge, 1597).

Feuer, Lewis S., "Francis Bacon and the Jews: Who Was the Jew in the *New Atlantis?*" *TJHSE* 29 (1988), 1–25.

Finch, Henry, *The Worlds Great Restauration. Or the Calling of the Jews* (1621).

Fines, John, "'Judaising' in the Period of the English Reformation—the Case of Richard Bruern," *TJHSE* 21 (1968), 323–26.

Firth, Katherine, *The Apocalyptic Tradition in Reformation Britain, 1530–1645* (Oxford, 1979).

Fisch, Harold, *The Dual Image: The Figure of the Jew in English and American Literature* (New York, 1971).

————— *Jerusalem and Albion: The Hebraic Factor in Seventeenth-Century Literature* (1964).

Fletcher, Giles, "The Tartars or, Ten Tribes" (1611) in Samuel Lee, *Israel Redux* (1677).

Florio, John, *Queen Anne's New World of Words* (1611).

Fludd, Robert, *Philosophia Moysaica* (Gouda, 1638).

————— *Mosaicall Philosophy: Grounded Upon the Essentiall Truth, or Eternal Sapience* (1659).

Forbes, Patrick, *An Exquisite Commentarie Upon the Revelations of Saint John* (1613).

Foster, Sir William, ed., *The Travels of John Sanderson in the Levant, 1584–1602*, Hakluyt Society (1931).

————— *The Voyages of Sir James Lancaster to Brazil and the East Indies, 1591–1603*, Hakluyt Society (1940).

Foxe, John, *Actes and Monuments* (1570).

———— *De Oliva Evangelica* (1578).

———— *Eicasmi Seu Meditationes in Sacram Apocalysin* (1587).

———— *A Sermon Preached at the Christening of a Certain Jew, at London* (1578).

Franco, Solomon, *Truth Springing Out of the Earth* (1668).

Friedman, Jerome, "Jewish Conversion, the Spanish Pure Blood Laws, and Reformation: A Revisionist View of Racial and Religious Antisemitism," *The Sixteenth Century Journal* 18 (1987), 3–30.

———— *The Most Ancient Testimony: Sixteenth-Century Christian-Hebraica in the Age of Renaissance Nostalgia* (Athens, Ohio, 1983).

Furness, H. H., ed., William Shakespeare, *The Merchant of Venice, A New Variorum Edition* (Philadephia: J. P. Lippincott, 1888).

G[ace], W[illiam], trans., *Special and Chosen Sermons of D. Martin Luther, Collected Out of His Writings* (1581).

Gad ben Arad, pseud., *The Wandering-Jew, Telling Fortunes to English-men* (1640).

Gartner, Lloyd P., *The Jewish Immigrant in England, 1870–1914* (1960).

———— "A Quarter Century of Anglo-Jewish Historiography," *Jewish Social Studies* 48 (1986), 105–26.

Gilman, Sander L. *The Case of Sigmund Freud* (Baltimore, 1993).

———— *Freud, Race, and Gender* (Princeton, 1993).

———— *The Jew's Body* (New York, 1991).

Gilman, Sander L., and Steven T. Katz, eds., *Anti-Semitism in Times of Crisis* (New York, 1991).

Glassman, Bernard, *Anti-Semitic Stereotypes Without Jews: Images of the Jews in England, 1290–1700* (Detroit, 1975).

Godwyn, Thomas, *Moses and Aaron: Civil and Ecclesiastical Rites Used by the Ancient Hebrewes*, 4th ed. (1631).

Goldberg, David Theo, and Michael Krausz, eds., *Jewish Identity* (Philadelphia, 1993).

Gollancz, Hermann, *Shakespeare and Rabbinic Thought* (1916).

Gollancz, Israel, *Allegory and Mysticism in Shakespeare* (1931).

Gollancz, Israel, ed., *A Book of Homage to Shakespeare* (Oxford, 1916).

———— *Shakespeare Tercentenary Observance in the Schools and Other Institutions* (1916).

Gonsalvius Montanus, Reginaldus, *A Discoverie and Playne Declaration of Sundry Subtill Practices of the Holy Inquisition of Spayne*, trans. [V. Skinner] (1568).

Granville, George (Baron Lansdowne), *The Jew of Venice* (1701).

Grebanier, Bernard, *The Truth About Shylock* (New York, 1962).

Greenblatt, Stephen Jay, "Marlowe, Marx, and Anti-Semitism," *Critical Inquiry* 5 (1978), 291–307.

———— *Marvelous Possessions* (Chicago, 1991).

Gross, John, *Shylock: A Legend and Its Legacy* (New York, 1992).

Grotius, Hugo, *True Religion Explained and Defended* (1632).

[Grove, Joseph], *A Reply to the Famous Jew Question* (1754).

Gwyer, John, "The Case of Dr Lopez," *TJHSE* 16 (1952), 163–84.

Habicht, Werner, "Shakespeare and Theatre Politics in the Third Reich," *The Play Out of Context: Transferring Plays From Culture to Culture*, ed. Hanna Scolnovic and Peter Holland (Cambridge, 1989), 110–20.

Haigh, Christopher, *English Reformations: Religion, Politics, and Society Under the Tudors* (Oxford, 1993).

Hall, Joseph, *A Plaine and Familiar Exposition by Way of Paraphrase of All the Hard Texts of the Whole Divine Scripture of the Old and New Testament* (1633).

Hammond, Henry, *A Paraphrase and Annotations Upon All the Books of the New Testament* (1653).

Hanmer, Meredith, *The Auncient Ecclesiasticall Histories of the First Six Hundred Yeares After Christ*

Wrytten in the Greeke Tongue by Three Learned Historiographers, Eusebius, Socrates, and Evagrius (1577).

Harrington, James, *The Common-Wealth of Oceana* (1656).

———— *The Political Works of James Harrington*, ed. J. G. A. Pocock (Cambridge, 1977).

Harrison, John, *The Messiah Already Come. Or Profes of Christianitie, Both Our of the Scriptures, and A*uncient *Rabbins, to Convince the Jews, of Their Palpable, and More Then Miserable Blindnesse* (Amsterdam, 1619).

Hasan-Rokem, Galit, and Alan Dundes, eds., *The Wandering Jew: Essays in the Interpretation of a Christian Legend* (Bloomington, 1986).

Hayne, Samuel, *An Abstract of All the Statutes Made Concerning Aliens Trading in England . . . Proving that the Jews . . . Break Them All* (1685).

Haywood, Eliza Fowler, *The Fair Hebrew, or, a True but Secret History of Two Jewish Ladies Who Lately Resided in London* (1729).

Hendricks, Margo, and Patricia Parker, eds., *Women, "Race," and Writing in the Early Modern Period* (New York, 1994).

Henriques, H. S. Q., *Jewish Marriages and the English Law* (1909).

———— *The Jews and the English Law* (Oxford, 1908).

———— *The Return of the Jews to England* (1905).

Hertz, Gerard Berkeley [afterward, Sir. G. B. Hurst], "No Jews; No Wooden Shoes. A Frenzy of 1753," *British Imperialism in the Eighteenth Century* (1908), 60–109.

Heylyn, Peter, *The History of the Sabbath* (1636).

Hicks, George, *Peculiam Dei, a Discourse About the Jews as the Peculiar People of God* (1681).

Hill, Christopher, *The English Bible and the Seventeenth-Century Revolution* (1993).

———— "Till the Conversion of the Jews," *Millenarianism and Messianism in English Literature and Thought, 1650–1982*, ed. Richard H. Popkin (Leiden, 1988), 12–36.

Hirschson, Neil, "The Jewish Key to Shakespeare's Most Enigmatic Creation," *Midstream* (February/March 1989), 38–40.

Hole, Richard, "An Apology for the Character and Conduct of Shylock," *Essays by a Society of Gentlemen, at Exeter*, 2 vols. (Exeter, 1796).

Holinshed, Raphael, *The Chronicles of England, Scotlande, and Ireland* (1587).

Holmes, Colin, *Anti-Semitism in British Society, 1876–1939* (New York, 1979).

———— "The Ritual Murder Accusation in Britain," *Ethnic and Racial Studies* 4 (1981), 265–88.

Hooker, Richard, *Of the Lawes of Ecclesiasticall Politie* ([1594]–1597).

Howell, James, "Epistle Dedicatory" to Joseph ben Gurion, *The Wonderful and Most Deplorable History of the Latter Times of the Jews* (1678).

Hsia, R. Po-chia, *The Myth of Ritual Murder* (New Haven, 1988).

Hughes, Charles, ed., *Shakespeare's Europe: Unpublished Chapters of Fynes Moryson's Itinerary*, 2 vols. (1903).

Hughes, Diane Owen, "Distinguishing Signs: Ear-Rings, Jews and Franciscan Rhetoric in the Italian City State," *Past and Present* 112 (1986), 3–59.

H[ughes], W[illiam], *Anglo-Judaeus, or the History of the Jews, Whilst Here in England* (1656).

Hume, M., "The So-Called Conspiracy of R. Lopez," *TJHSE* 6 (1912), 32–55.

Humphrey, Thomas, *A True Narrative of God's Gracious Dealings With the Soul of Shalome ben Shalomoh a Jew. With an Account of His Conversion*, 2d ed. (1700).

Hunter, G. K., "Elizabethans and Foreigners," *Shakespeare Survey* 17 (1964), 37–52.

———— "The Theology of Marlowe's *The Jew of Malta*," *The Journal of the Warburg and Courtauld Institutes* 27 (1964), 211–40.

Hyamson, Albert, "The Jew Bill of 1753," *TJHSE* 6 (1912), 156–88.

An Information Concerning the Present State of the Jewish Nation in Europe and Judea (1658).

Ingmethorpe, Thomas, *A Short Cathechisme, by Law Authorized in the Church of England, for Young*

Children to Learne: Translated into Hebrew (n.p., 1633).

[Isaiah, Paul], Eleazar Bargishai, pseud., *A Brief Compendium of the Vain Hopes of the Jews Messias* (1652).

———— Eleazar bar Isaiah, pseud., *The Messiah of the Christians, and the Jewes* (1655).

———— *A Vindication of the Christian Messiah* (1653).

Israel, Jonathan I., *European Jewry in the Age of Mercantilism, 1550–1750* (Oxford, 1985, 2d ed., 1989).

Jacob, John, *The Jew Turned Christian* (1678).

Jacobs, Joseph, and Lucien Wolf, eds., *Catalogue of Anglo-Jewish Historical Exhibition, Royal Albert Hall* (1888).

James VI, *Ane Fruitfull Meditatioun* (Edinburgh, 1588).

[Jessey, Henry], *A Narrative of the Late Proceeds at White-Hall, Concerning the Jews* (1656).

The Jew Apologist, or Considerations on the Revival of the Jew-Bill (1765).

The Jews Triumph: A Ballad (1753).

The Jews Advocate (1753).

John, Theodore, *An Account of the Conversion of Theodore John, a Late Teacher Among the Jews* (1693).

Jones, G. Lloyd, *The Discovery of Hebrew in Tudor England: A Third Language* (Manchester, 1983).

Jones, Norman, *The Birth of Elizabethan England: England in the 1560s* (1993).

———— *God and the Moneylenders: Usury and Law in Early Modern England* (Oxford, 1989).

Jonson, Ben, *Works*, ed. C. H. Herford, Percy Simpson, and Evelyn Simpson, 11 vols. (Oxford, 1925–1952).

John, Theodore, *An Account of the Conversion of Theodore John, a Late Teacher Among the Jews Together with His Confession of the Christian Faith* (1693).

Joseph ben Gurion, psued., *A Compendious and Most Mervailous Historie of the Latter Times of the Jewes Common Weale*, trans. Peter Morwyng (1558, 1593, 1652, 1662).

Joseph ben Israel, [Thomas Ramsey], *The Converted Jew* (Newcastle, 1653).

Josselin, Ralph, *Diary*, ed. Alan Macfarlane (1976).

Joye, George, *The Exposicion of Daniel the Prophet* (Geneva, 1545).

Kamen, Henry, "The Mediterranean and the Expulsion of Spanish Jews in 1492," *Past and Present* 119 (1988), 30–55.

Kaplan, Yosef, "The Jewish Profile of the Spanish Portuguese Community of London During the Seventeenth Century," *Judaism* 41 (1992), 229–40.

———— "Wayward New Christians and Stubborn New Jews: The Shaping of a Jewish Identity," *Jewish History* 8 (1994), 27–41.

Kaplan, Yosef, Henry Méchoulan, and Richard H. Popkin, eds., *Menasseh ben Israel and His World* (Leiden, 1989).

Katz, David S., "Edmund Gayton's Anti-Jewish Poem Addressed to Menasseh ben Israel, 1656," *The Jewish Quarterly Review* 71 (1981), 239–50.

———— "English Charity and Jewish Qualms: The Rescue of the Ashkenazi Community of Seventeenth-Century Jerusalem," *Jewish History: Essays in Honour of Chimen Abramsky*, ed. Ada Rapoport-Albert and Steven J. Zipperstein (1988), 245–66.

———— "English Redemption and Jewish Readmission in 1656," *Journal of Jewish Studies* 34 (1983), 73–91.

———— *The Jews in the History of England* (Oxford, 1994).

———— "The Jews of England in 1688," *From Persecution to Toleration: The Glorious Revolution and Religion in England*, ed. Peter Grell, Jonathan Israel, and Nicholas Tyackne (Oxford, 1991), 217–49.

———— "The Marginalization of Early Modern Anglo-Jewish History," *The Jewish Heritage in British History: Englishness and Jewishness*, ed. Tony Kushner (1992), 60–77.

———— *Philo-Semitism and the Readmission of the Jews to England 1603–1655* (Oxford, 1982).

———— "The Return of the Jews to England and the Establishment of Their Community" [Hebrew], *Exile and Return: Anglo-Jewry Through the Ages*, ed. David Katz and Yosef Kaplan (Jerusalem, 1993), 105–22.

———— *Sabbath and Sectarianism in Seventeenth-Century England* (Leiden, 1988).

Katz, David S., and Jonathan I. Israel, eds., *Sceptics, Millenarians, and Jews* (Leiden, 1990).

Katz, David S., and Yosef Kaplan, eds., *Exile and Return: Anglo-Jewry Through the Ages* [Hebrew] (Jerusalem, 1993).

Katz, Jacob, *Tradition and Crisis: Jewish Society at the End of the Middle Ages*, trans. and afterward Bernard Dov Cooperman (1961; New York, 1993).

Kett, Francis, *Glorious and Beautiful Garlands of Mans Glorification* (1585).

The Kingdom of England Restored by Christ (1753).

Kobler, Franz, "Sir Henry Finch (1558–1625) and the First English Advocates of the Restoration of the Jews to Palestine," *TJHSE* 16 (1952), 101–20.

Krausz, Michael, "On Being Jewish," *Jewish Identity*, ed. David Theo Goldberg and Michael Krausz (Philadelphia, 1993).

Kushner, Tony, ed., *The Jewish Heritage in British History: Englishness and Jewishness* (1992).

L., D., *Israels Condition and Cause Pleaded* (1656).

Lake, Arthur, *Sermons With Some Religious and Divine Meditations* (1629).

Langmuir, Gavin I., *History, Religion, and Antisemitism* (Berkeley, 1990).

———— *Toward a Definition of Antisemitism* (Berkeley, 1990).

Lee, Samuel, *Israel Redux* (1677).

Lee, Sidney, "Elizabethan England and the Jews," *Transactions of the New Shakspere Society* (1887–1892), series 1, part 2, 143–66.

———— "The Original of Shylock," *The Gentleman's Magazine* 248 (1880), 185–200.

———— "Shakespeare and the Spanish Inquisition," *The Living Age* 313 (1922), 460–66.

Lelyveld, Toby, *Shylock on the Stage* (1961).

Leti, Gregorio, *The Life of Pope Sixtus the Fifth*, trans. Ellis Farneworth (1754, Dublin, 1766).

———— *Vita di Sisto V*, 3 vols (Amsterdam, 1693).

A Letter to the Publick, on the Act for Naturalizing the Jews (1753).

Liberles, Robert, "The Jews and Their Bill: Jewish Motivations in the Controversy of 1753," *Jewish History* 2 (1987), 29–36.

Liljegren, S. B., *Harrington and the Jews* (Lund, 1932).

Lipman, Vivian D., "The Anatomy of Medieval Ango-Jewry," *TJHSE* 21 (1968), 65–77.

———— *A History of the Jews in Britain Since 1858* (1990).

Lipman, Vivian D., ed., *Three Centuries of Anglo-Jewish History* (1961).

A List of Some of the Grand Blasphemers (1654).

Lithgow, William, *The Total Discourse of the Rare Adventures and Painefill Peregrinations of Long Nineteene Yeares Travayles from Scotland* (1632).

Lively, Edward, *A True Chronology of the Times of the Persian Monarchie* (1597).

Locke, John, *A Letter Concerning Toleration, Being a Translation of the Epistola de Tolerantia* in *Works*, 10 vols. (1823), vol. 6.

———— *A Paraphrase and Notes on St. Paul's Epistle to the Romans* in *Works*, 10 vols. (1823), vol. 8.

Lodge, Thomas, trans., *The Famous and Memorable Workes of Josephus* (1602, 1632).

Luther, Martin, *A Commentarie of M. Doctor Martin Luther Upon the Epistle of St. Paul to the Galatians* (1575).

———— *A Commentarie Upon the Fiftene Psalmes*, trans. Henry Bull, with preface "To the Christian Reader" by John Foxe (1577).

MacDougall, Hugh A., *Racial Myth in English History: Trojans, Teutons, and Anglo-Saxons* (Hanover, N.H., 1982).

Mandeville, Sir John, *The Voyages and Travailes of Sir John Mandevile Knight* (1625).

Manuel, Frank E., *The Broken Staff: Judaism Through Christian Eyes* (Cambridge, Mass., 1992).

Marcus, Moses, *The Principal Motives & Circumstances That Induced Moses Marcus to Leave the Jewish, and Embrace the Christian Faith* (1724).

Margoliouth, Moses, *The Anglo-Hebrews: Their Past Wrongs, and Present Grievances: Two Epistles* (1856).

———— *The History of Jews in Great Britain*, 3 vols. (1851).

———— *Vestiges of the Historic Anglo-Hebrews in East Anglia* (1870).

Marlis, Alan, *Queen Elizabeth Tudor, a Secret Jewess* (n.p., 1978).

Marlowe, Christopher, *The Famous Tragedy of the Rich Jew of Malta* (1633).

Martin, Gregory, "Roma Sancta" (1581), ed. George Bruner Parks (Rome, 1969).

Martyr, Peter [Vermigli], *The Common Places of the Most Famous and Renowned Divine Doctor Peter Martyr*, trans. Anthony Marten (1583).

———— *Most Learned and Fruitfull Commentaries of D. Peter Martir Vermilius, Florentine . . . Upon the Epistle of S. Paul to the Romanes* (1568).

Master Broughtons Letters, Especially His Last Pamphlet to and Against the Lord Archbishop of Canterbury (1599).

Matar, Nabil I., "The Controversy Over the Restoration of the Jews in English Protestant Thought: 1703–1753," *Durham University Journal* 80 (1988), 241–56.

———— "The Date of John Donne's Sermon 'Preached at the Churching of the Countesse of Bridgewater,' " *Notes and Queries* (Dec., 1992), 447–48.

———— "George Herbert, Henry Vaughan, and the Conversion of the Jews," *Studies in English Literature* 30 (1990), 79–92.

———— "The Idea of the Restoration of the Jews in English Protestant Thought: Between the Reformation and 1660," *Durham University Journal* 78 (1985), 23–35.

——, "The Idea of the Restoration of the Jews in English Protestant Thought, 1661–1701," *Harvard Theological Review* 78 (1985), 115–48.

———— "John Locke and the Jews," *Journal of Ecclesiastical History* 44 (1993), 45–62.

———— "Milton and the Idea of the Restoration of the Jews," *Studies in English Literature* 27 (1987), 109–24.

———— "The Renegade in English Seventeenth-Century Imagination," *Studies in English Literature* 33 (1993), 489–505.

Mather, Increase, *The Mystery of Israel's Salvation* (1669).

Mayerne Turquet, Louis de, *The Generall Historie of Spaine* (1583), trans. Edward Grimeston (1612).

Maynard, John, *A Judicious Answer to Six Queries Concerning the Jews and Their Conversion* (1666).

Mayo, Richard, *A Conference Betwixt a Papist and a Jew* (1678).

———— *A Conference Betwixt a Protestant and a Jew* (1678).

Mede, Joseph, *Clavis Apocalyptica* (Cambridge, 1627).

———— *Daniels Weekes. An Interpretation of Part of the Prophesy of Daniel* (1643).

———— "The Mystery of S. Paul's Conversion; Or, The Type of the Calling of the Jews," *Works*, ed. John Worthington, 4th ed. (1677).

Meirs, John, *A Short Treatise Compos'd and Published by John Meirs, Formerly a Jew, Now by the Signal Mercy of God in Christ, Converted to the Christian Faith* (1709, 1717).

Menasseh ben Israel, *The Hope of Israel*, trans. Moses Wall (1650).

———— *To His Highnesse the Lord Protector of the Common-wealth of England, Scotland, and Ireland, the Humble Addresses of Menasseh ben Israel* (1655?).

———— *Vindiciae Judaeorum, or a Letter in Answer to Certain Questions Propounded by a Noble and Learned Gentleman, Touching the Reproaches Cast on the Nation of the Jewes* (1656).

Menda, Nathaniel, *Confession of Faith, Which Nathaneal a Jewe Borne, Made Before the Congregation in the Parish Church of Alhallowes in Lombard Street at London* (1578) [bound with Foxe, *Sermon* (1578)].

Michelson, Hijman, *The Jew in Early English Literature* (Amsterdam, 1926).

Modena, Leone, *The History of the Rites, Customes, and Manner of the Life, of the Present Jews throughout the World*, trans. Edmund Chilmead (1650).

A Modest Apology for the Citizens and Merchants of London (1753).

Moore, R. I., *The Formation of a Persecuting Society: Power and Deviance in Western Europe 950–1250* (Oxford, 1987).

Mornay, Philippe de, *A Woorke Concerning the Trewnesse of the Christian Religion, Written in French, Against Atheists, Epicures, Paynims, Jewes, Mahumetists, and Other Infidels*, trans. Sir Philip Sidney and Arthur Golding (1587).

Morton, Thomas, *Salomon, or a Treatise Declaring the State of the Kingdom of Israel* (1596).

Mosse, Miles, *The Arraignment and Conviction of Usurie* (1595).

Nash, Thomas, *The Unfortunate Traveller* (1594).

Nettles, Stephen, *An Answer to the Jewish Part of Mr Selden's History of Tithes* (Oxford, 1625).

Nicolay, Nicolas de, *The Navigations Into Turkie*, trans. T. Washington the Younger (1585).

Osterman, Nathan, "The Controversy Over the Proposed Readmission of the Jews to England (1655)," *Jewish Social Studies* 3 (1941), 301–328.

Oz, Avi, "Transformations of Authenticity: *The Merchant of Venice* in Israel, 1936–1980," *Jahrbuch der Deutchen Shakespeare-Gesellschaft West* (1983), 166–77.

Palliser, David M., "Martin Soza—A Tudor Jewish Convert," *Clifford's Tower Commemoration, A Programme and Handbook* (York, 1990), 56.

Papers Read at the Anglo-Jewish Historical Exhibition, Royal Albert Hall, 1887 (1888).

Paris, Matthew, *Chronica Majora* (1571).

The Parliamentary History of England, vol. 15, 1753–1765 (1813).

Parsons, Robert, *The First Booke of the Christian Exercise, Appertayning to the Resolution* (Rouen, 1582).

——— *The Second Parte of the Booke of Christian Exercise, Appertayning to Resolution. Or a Christian Directorie* (1601).

Patai, Raphael, and Jennifer Patai, *The Myth of the Jewish Race*, rev. ed. (Detroit, 1989).

Pater, Erra, *A Prognostication for Ever, Made by Erra Pater, a Jewe, Borne in Jury, Doctor in Astronomie and Phisicke* (1582? 1607).

Patinkin, Don, "Mercantilism and the Readmission of the Jews to England," *Jewish Social Studies* 8 (1946), 161–78.

Patrick, Simon, *Jewish Hypocrisie, a Caveat to the Present Generation*, 2d ed. (1670).

——— *The Truth of the Christian Religion* (1680).

Perkins, William, *A Commentarie or Exposition, Upon the First Five Chapters of the Epistles to the Galatians* (Cambridge, 1604).

——— *A Fruitfull Dialogue Concerning the Ende of the World* (1587) rpt. in *Works* (1609).

P[errot], J[ohn], *Discoveries of the Day-Dawning to the Jews* (1661).

Perry, Thomas W., *Public Opinion, Propaganda, and Politics in Eighteenth-Century England: A Study of the Jew Bill of 1753* (Cambridge, Mass., 1962).

Phillips, Henry E. I., "An Early Stuart Judaising Sect," *TJHSE* 15 (1946), 63–72.

Pollins, Harold, *The Economic History of the Jews in England* (1982).

Popish Plots and Treasons From the Beginning of the Reign of Queen Elizabeth. Illustrated With Emblems, and Explain'd in Verse (1606).

Popkin, Richard H., "The Fictional Jewish Council of 1650: A Great English Pipedream," *Jewish History* 5 (1991), 7–22.

——— "The First College for Jewish Studies," *Revue des Études Juives* 143 (1984), 351–64.

——— "Jewish-Christian Relations in the Sixteenth and Seventeenth Centuries: The Conception of the Messiah," *Jewish History* 6 (1992), 163–77.

——— "A Jewish Merchant of Venice," *Shakespeare Quarterly* 40 (1989), 329–31.

——— "The Lost Tribes, the Caraites and the English Millenarians," *The Journal of Jewish Studies* 37 (1986), 213–27.

——— "Three English Tellings of the Sabbatai Zevi Story," *Jewish History* 8 (1994), 43–54.

Popkin, Richard H., ed., *Millenarianism and Messianism in English Literature and Thought, 1650–1800* (Berkeley, 1988).

Popkin, Richard H., and Gordon M. Weiner, eds. *Jewish Christians and Christian Jews From the Renaissance to the Enlightenment* (Dordrecht, 1994).

Prior, Roger, "Jewish Musicians at the Tudor Court," *The Musical Quarterly* 59 (1983), 253–65.

——— "A Second Jewish Community in Tudor London," *TJHSE* 31 (1990), 137–52.

Prynne, William, *A Short Demurrer to the Jewes*, 2 pts. (1656).

Purchas, Samuel, *Hakluytus Posthumus or Purchas His Pilgrimes* (1625).

——— *Purchas His Pilgrimage* (1613, 1614, 1617, 1626).

R., R., *A New Letter from Aberdeen in Scotland Sent to a Person of Quality; Wherein Is a More Full Acount of the Proceedings of the Jews Than Hath Been Hitherto Published* (1665).

Rabb, Theodore K. "The Stirrings of the 1590s and the Return of the Jews to England," *TJHSE* 26 (1979), 26–33.

Ragussis, Michael, *Figures of Conversion: "The Jewish Question" and English National Identity* (Durham, N.C., 1995).

——— "Representation, Conversion, and Literary Form: *Harrington* and the Novel of Jewish Identity," *Critical Inquiry* 16 (1989), 113–43.

Rainolds, William, completed by William Gifford, *Calvino-Turcismus* (Antwerp, 1597).

Reflections on the Past and Present State of the Jews (1753).

Reik, Theodore, "Jessica, My Child," *American Imago* 8 (1951), 3–27.

The Rejection and Restoration of the Jews, According to Scripture, Declar'd (1753).

The Repository: For the Use of the Christian Electors of Great-Britian; In Opposition to All Jews, Turks, and Infidels (1753).

Richmond, Colin, "Englishness and Medieval Anglo-Jewry," *The Jewish Heritage in British History: Englishness and Jewishness*, ed. Tony Kushner (1992).

Rogers, Thomas, trans., *Of the Ende of This Worlde* (1577).

Rokeah, Zephira Entrin, "The Expulsion of the Jews from England in 1290 A.D.: Some Aspects of Its Background," Diss., Columbia University (1986).

Romaine, William, *An Answer to a Pamphlet, Entitled, Considerations on the Bill to Permit Persons Professing the Jewish Religion to Be Naturalized*, 2d ed. (1753).

——— *Modest Apology for the Citizens and Merchants of London* (1753).

Rosedale, H. G., *Queen Elizabeth and the Levant Company: A Diplomatic and Literary Episode of the Establishment of Our Trade with Turkey* (1904).

Ross, Alexander, *A View of All Religions in the World* (1672).

Ross, J. M., "Naturalisation of Jews in England," *TJHSE* 24 (1975), 59–72.

Roth, Cecil, "The Background of Shylock," *Review of English Studies* 9 (1933).

——— *A History of the Jews in England*, 3rd ed. (Oxford, 1964).

——— "The Jews in the English Universities," *MJHSE* 4 (1942), 102–115.

——— "Jews in Oxford after 1290," *Oxoniensia* 15 (1950), 63–80.

——— "The Middle Period of Anglo-Jewish History (1290–1655) Reconsidered," *TJHSE* 19 (1960), 1–12.

——— "The Resettlement of the Jews in England," *Three Centuries of Anglo-Jewish History*, ed. V. D. Lipman (1961), 1–26.

Rubens, Alfred, "Jews and the English Stage, 1667–1850," *TJHSE* 24 (1975), 151–170.

Rubin, Miri, "Desecration of the Host: The Birth of an Accusation," *Christianity and Judaism*, Studies in Church History 29, ed. Diana Wood (Oxford, 1992), 169–85.

Sadler, John, *Rights of the Kingdom* (1649).

Samuel, Edgar R., "Dr Roderigo Lopes' Last Speech from the Scaffold at Tyburn," *TJHSE* 30 (1989), 51–53.

—— "The First Fifty Years," *Three Centuries of Anglo-Jewish History*, ed. V. D. Lipman (1961), 27–44.

—— "Passover in Shakespeare's London," *TJHSE* 26 (1979), 117–18.

—— "Portuguese Jews in Jacobean London," *TJHSE* 18 (1958), 171–87.

—— "The Readmission of the Jews to England in 1656, in the Context of English Economic Policy," *TJHSE* 31 (1990), 153–69.

—— "'Sir Thomas Shirley's Project for Jewes'—the Earliest Known Proposal for the Resettlement," *TJHSE* 24 (1974), 195–97.

Samuel, Wilfred S., "The Strayings of Paul Isaiah in England, 1651–1656," *TJHSE* 16 (1952), 77–87.

Sanderson, John, "Diary, 1560–1610," British Library Lansdowne MS. 241.

Sandys, Edwin, *A Relation of the State of Religion* (1605).

Scialitti, Moses, *A Letter Written to the Jewes* (1663).

Scales, Thomas, "The Original, or Moderne Estate, Profession, Practise, and Condition of the Nation of the Jewes" (c. 1630), Huntington Library MS. 205.

Schochet, Gordon J., "From Persecution to 'Toleration,'" *Liberty Secured? Britain Before and After 1688*, ed. J. R. Jones (Stanford, 1992).

Schosche, A., "Spanish Jews in London in 1494," *TJHSE* 24 (1975), 214–15.

Schwanitz, Dietrich, *Shylock* (Hamburg, 1989).

Scot, Reginald, *The Discoverie of Witchcraft* (1584), ed. Montague Summers (New York, 1972).

Scouloudi, Irene, *Returns of Strangers in the Metropolis 1593, 1627, 1635, 1639: A Study of an Active Minority*, Quarto Series of the Huguenot Society of London, vol. 57 (1985).

Scult, Mel, *Millennial Expectations and Jewish Liberties: A Study of the Efforts to Convert the Jews in Britain, up to the Mid-Nineteenth Century* (Leiden, 1978).

Seasonable Remarks on the Act Lately Pass'd in Favour of the Jews (1753).

Selden, John, *The History of Tithes* (1618).

—— *Uxor Ebraica* (1646).

—— *Works*, ed. David Wilkins, 3 vols. (1726).

Shachar, Isaiah, "The Emergence of the Modern Pictoral Stereotype of 'the Jews' in England," *Studies in the Cultural Life of the Jews in England*, Folklore Research Center Studies 5, ed. Dov Noy and Issachar Ben-Ami (Jerusalem, 1975), 331–65.

Shakespeare, William, *The Most Excellent Historie of the Merchant of Venice* (1600).

Shell, Marc, "Marranos (Pigs), or From Coexistence to Toleration," *Critical Inquiry* 17 (1991), 309–12.

Shillocke, Calebbe, *His Prophesie, or the Jewes Prediction* [ballad] (1607).

Shuger, Debora K., *The Renaissance Bible: Scholarship, Sacrifice, and Subjectivity* (Berkeley, 1994).

Shylock, R., *The Rabbi's Lamentation Upon the Repeal of the Jew Act* (1768).

Simonsohn, Shlomo, "Some Well-Known Jewish Converts During the Renaissance," *Revue des Études Juives* 148 (1989), 17–52.

Sinsheimer, Hermann, *Shylock: The History of a Character*, foreword by John Middleton Murry (1947).

Sisson, C. J., "A Colony of Jews in Shakespeare's London," *Essays and Studies* 23 (1938), 41–51.

Smith, John, *A Poetical Description of Mr. Hogarth's Election Prints, in Four Cantos* (1759).

Solomons, Israel, "Satirical and Political Prints on the Jews' Naturalization Bill, 1753," *TJHSE* 7 (1912), 205–33.

Stacey, Robert C., "1240–1260: A Watershed in Anglo-Jewish Relations?" *Historical Research* 61 (1988), 135–50.

—— "The Conversion of Jews to Christianity in Thirteenth-Century England," *Speculum* 67 (1992), 263–83.

———— "Recent Work on Medieval English Jewish History," *Jewish History* 2 (1987), 61–72.

———— "Thirteenth-Century Anglo-Jewry and the Problem of the Expulsion" [Hebrew], *Exile and Return: Anglo-Jewry Through the Ages*, ed. David Katz and Yosef Kaplan (Jerusalem, 1993), 9–25.

Statt, Daniel, "The City of London and the Controversy Over Immigration, 1660–1722," *The Historical Journal* 33 (1991), 45–61.

———— "The Controversy Over the Naturalization of Foreigners in England, 1660–1760," Diss., Cambridge University (1987).

Stein, Siegfried, "Phillipus Ferdinandus Polonus, A Sixteenth-Century Hebraist in England," *Essays in Honour of the Very Reverend Dr. J. H. Hertz*, ed. I. Epstein, E. Levine, and C. Roth (1943), 397–412.

Stow, John, *The Annales of England* (1592).

———— *A Survay of London* (1603).

Stow, Kenneth R., *Alienated Minority: The Jews of Medieval Latin Europe* (Cambridge, Mass., 1992).

Strype, John, *Annals of the Reformation*, 3 vols. (Oxford, 1824).

———— *The Life and Acts of John Whitgift*, 3 vols. (Oxford, 1822).

———— *A Survey of the Cities of London and Westminster . . . Written by John Stow . . . Corrected, Improved, and Very Much Enlarged by John Strype*, 2 vols. (1720).

Sturtevant, Simon, *Dibre Adam, or Adam's Hebrew Dictionarie: A Rare and New Invention* (1602).

Sutcliffe, Matthew, *De Turco-Papismo* (1599, 1604).

Tany, Thomas, *Theauraujohn His Theousori Apokolipikal* (1651).

Tayler, Francis, *A Godly Zealous, and Learned Sermon Upon the 18, 19, 20, 21 Verses of the 10th Chapter to Romaines* (1583).

Thorowgood, Thomas, *Jews in America, or, Probabilities, That Americans Are of That Race* (1650, 1660).

Three Hundred Years: A Volume to Commemorate the Tercentenary of the Re-Settlement of the Jews in Great Britain, 1656–1956 (1957).

Tillam, Thomas, *Banners of Love* (Newcastle, 1653).

Tishbi, Isaiah, "New Information on the 'Converso' Community in London According to the Letters of Sasportas from 1664–1665" [Hebrew], *Exile and Diaspora: Studies in the History of the Jewish People, Presented to Professor Haim Beinart*, ed. A Mirsky et al. (Jerusalem, 1988), 470–96.

Toland, John, *Reasons for Naturalizing the Jews in Great Britain and Ireland, on the Same Foot With All Other Nations* (1714).

Tomlinson, W., *A Bosome Opened to the Jewes* (1656).

Tovey, D'Blossiers, *Anglia Judaica: Or, the History and Antiquities of the Jews in England* (Oxford, 1738).

Trachtenberg, Joshua, *The Devil and the Jews: The Medieval Conception of the Jew and Its Relation to Modern Antisemitism* (New Haven, 1943).

"Trask in the Star-Chamber, 1619," *Transactions of the Baptist Historical Society* 5 (1916–1917), 8–14.

Traske, John, *A Treatise of Libertie from Judaisme* (1620).

A True Report of Sundrie Conspiracies Complotted Against the Queenes Most Excellent Majestie by Many English Traiterous Rebels, and Forraine Puissant Enemies (1594).

The True State of the Case Concerning the Good or Evil Which the Bill for Naturalization of the Jews May Bring Unto Great Britain (1753).

[Twyne, Thomas?], *The Schoolemaster, or Teacher of Table Philosophie* (1576).

Udall, John, trans., *The Key of the Holy Tongue* (Leiden, 1593).

Usque, Samuel, *Consolation for the Tribulation of Israel*, trans. Martin A. Cohen (Philadelphia, 1965).

Vincent, Thomas, *Paria* ([1627] 1648), *Renaissance Latin Drama in England*, ed. Steven Berkowitz (Hildensheim, 1990).

Wakefield, Robert, *On the Three Languages* (1524), ed. G. Lloyd Jones (Binghamton, New York, 1989).

Warner, John, *The Devilish Conspiracy, Hellish Treason, Heathenish Condemnation, and Damnable Murder Committed and Executed by the Jewes, Against the Anointed of the Lord* (1648).

Webb, Philip Carteret, *The Bill Permitting the Jews to Be Naturalized by Parliament* (1753).

———— *The Question, Whether a Jew, Born Within the British Dominions, Was, Before the Making the Late Act of Parliament, a Person Capable, by Law, to Purchase and Hold Lands to Him, and His Heirs* (1753).

Webbe, Edward, *The Rare and Most Wonderful Things Which Edw. Webbe an Englishman Borne, Hath Seene and Passed in His Troublesome Travailes* (1590).

Weemse, John, *The Christian Synagogue* (1623, 1633).

Weld, Thomas, Samuel Hammond, William Durant et al., *A False Jew: Or, a Wonderfull Discovery of a Scot* (Newcastle, 1653).

White, Francis, *A Treatise of the Sabbath Day* (1635).

Wilensky, Mordechai, "The Literary Controversy in 1656 Concerning the Return of the Jews to England," *American Academy for Jewish Research* 20 (1951), 357–93.

Willet, Andrew, *De Universali et Nouissima Judaeorum Vocatione* (Cambridge, 1590).

———— *Hexapla in Danielem: That is, a Six-Fold Commentarie Upon the Most Divine Prophesie of Daniel* (Cambridge, 1610).

———— *Hexapla: That Is, a Six-fold Commentarie Upon the Most Divine Epistle of the Holy Apostle S. Paul to the Romanes* (Cambridge, 1611).

———— *Synopsis Papismi, That Is, a General View of Papistrie* (1592; 11th ed., 1634).

Williams, A. Lukyn, *Adversus Judaeos: A Bird's-Eye View of Christian 'Apologiae' Until the Renaissance* (Cambridge, 1935).

Williamson, Arthur H., "British Israel and Roman Britain: The Jews and Scottish Models of Polity from George Buchanan to Samuel Rutherford," *Jewish Christians and Christian Jews From the Renaissance to the Enlightenment*, ed. Richard H. Popkin and Gordon M. Weiner (Dordrecht, 1994).

———— "The Jewish Dimension of the Scottish Apocalypse: Climate, Covenant, and World Renewal," *Menasseh ben Israel and His World*, ed. Y. Kaplan, H. Méchoulan, and R. H. Popkin (Leiden, 1989), 7–30.

———— "Latter-day Judah, Latter-day Israel: The Millennium, the Jews, and the British Future," *Chiliasmus in Deutschland und England im 17. Jahrhundert*, ed. Klaus Deppermann et al. (Göttingen, 1988), 119–49.

———— "'A Pil for Pork-Eaters': Ethnic Identity, Apocalyptic Promises, and the Strange Creation of the Judeo-Scots," *The Expulsion of the Jews: 1492 and After*, ed. Raymond B. Waddington and Arthur H. Williamson (New York, 1994), 237–58.

Wolf, Lucien, "Crypto-Jews Under the Commonwealth," *TJHSE* 1 (1894), 55–88.

———— "Jews in Elizabethan England," *TJHSE* 11 (1928), 1–91.

———— "Jews in Tudor England," *Essays in Jewish History*, ed. Cecil Roth (1934), 71–90.

———— "'Jossipon' in England," *TJHSE* 6 (1912), 277–81.

———— "The Middle Age of Anglo-Jewish History, 1290–1656," *Papers Read at the Anglo-Jewish Historical Exhibition, Royal Albert Hall, 1887* (1888), 53–79.

———— "Origins of the Jewish Historical Society in England," *TJSHE* 7 (1915), 206–221.

———— "A Plea for Anglo-Jewish History," *TJHSE* 1 (1894), 1–7.

———— "Status of the Jews in England After the Re-Settlement," *TJHSE* 4 (1903), 177–93.

Wolf, Lucien, ed., *Menasseh ben Israel's Mission to Oliver Cromwell* (1901).

Wolper, Roy S., "Circumcision as Polemic in the Jew Bill of 1753: The Cutter Cut?" *Eighteenth Century Life* 7 (1982), 28–36.

Woolf, Maurice, "Foreign Trade of London Jews in the Seventeenth Century," *TJHSE* 24 (1975), 38–58.

Wright, Charles H., "The Jews and the Malicious Charge of Human Sacrifice," *The Nineteenth Century* 14 (1883), 753–78.

Yardeni, Myriam, *Anti-Jewish Mentalities in Early Modern Europe* (Lanham, Md., 1990).

Yerushalmi, Yosef, *From Spanish Court to Italian Ghetto* (New York, 1971).

Yovel, Yirmiyahu, *Spinoza and Other Heretics*, 2 vols. (Princeton, 1989).

Zafran, Eric Myles, "The Iconography of Antisemitism: A Study of the Representation of the Jews in the Visual Arts of Europe, 1400–1600," Diss., New York University (1973).

Zagorin, Perez, *Ways of Lying: Dissimulation, Persecution, and Conformity in Early Modern Europe* (Cambridge, Mass., 1990).

Zapthet, Scaptheth, *Prophecies of Scaptheth Zapthet, the Wandering Jew* (Edinburgh, 1718).

313

Index

Designer:	Teresa Bonner
Text:	Fournier
Compositor:	Columbia University Press
Printer:	Maple Vail
Binder:	Maple Vail